Florian Sallmann

# Knowledge-Based Risk Management

Florian Sallmann

# Knowledge-Based Risk Management

## A strategic systems approach for industrial corporations

VDM Verlag Dr. Müller

Bibliografische Information der Deutschen Nationalbibliothek:
Die Deutsche Nationalbibliothek verzeichnet diese Publikation in der Deutschen Nationalbibliografie; detaillierte bibliografische Daten sind im Internet über http://dnb.d-nb.de abrufbar.


Kontakt: VDM Verlag Dr. Müller e.K., Dudweiler Landstr. 125 a,
D-66123 Saarbrücken, Telefon 0681/9100-698, Telefax 0180 5060 3388 4322,
Email: info@vdm-verlag.de
Coverbild: www.purestockx.com
Covererstellung: Nina Michaltzik

Herstellung:
Schaltungsdienst Lange o.H.G., Zehrensdorfer Str. 11, D-12277 Berlin
Books on Demand GmbH, Gutenbergring 53, D-22848 Norderstedt

**ISBN: 978-3-8364-1031-1**

# Foreword

Originating from academic and business concepts in the United States, risk management has received widespread recognition over the past decades. It is perhaps the most perfect showpiece that scientific results do have practical implications. The list of academic publications, ranging from conceptual work to application guidelines, has become very long. In a parallel development, risk management has become an integral part of decision making in large as well as in smaller enterprises.

Later, knowledge management has been developed in an attempt to better organise und utilise an organisation's know-how. These two areas, risk management and knowledge management, have long been discussed separately. However, since much in the risk management process is about gathering, organising and using information, it appears straightforward to implement techniques of knowledge management into the risk management concept.

It is due to Dr. Sallmann that risk management is now a richer and more modern concept. But, not only is this present work adding to the academic line of research, at the same time, it remains clear to the reader interested in applicability and managerial value.

Vienna, March 2007 ao. Univ.-Prof. Dr. Michael Theil

## Acknowledgements

This book is decicated to my wife Karen. Without her loving commitment and endless patience, this book would not have been written. And to my daughters Selina and Sydney, who are the most beautiful blessings on earth.

Thanks goes to my parents for paving the way for this achievement.

I am appreciative and thankful for the great assistance of ao. Univ.-Prof. Mag. Dr. Michael Theil and ao. Univ.-Prof. Mag. Dr. Dietmar Rößl. Their support, input and leadership during the whole course of writing this book made it a great and successful learning experience.

A special thanks goes to Dkfm. Dr. Martin Beste for giving me the chance to discover Austria and Central Eastern Europe.

Mag. Andreas Krebs earns special credit for advising me with his language skills in the process of the empirical analysis.

I also would like to thank my parents-in-law, Andy J. Czuchry, Ph.D. for encouraging me in good and in bad times in pursuing this book, Sandra Czuchry for the time and effort to eliminate the unavoidable Germanisms.

Last, but not least, I would like to thank Michael L. Czuchry, Ph.D. and Tiffiny Sia, Ph.D. for helping me understand and appreciate the psychology of industry insurance.

Vienna, March 2007 Dr. Florian Sallmann

# Table of Contents – Overview

# Table of Contents – Detailed

# List of Tables

# List of Figures

# Glossary

| | |
|---|---|
| ALM | Asset - Liability - Management |
| Captive | Corporate in-house insurance company |
| CUP | Clean Up Policy |
| E.g. | for example |
| EIL | Environmental Impairment Liability |
| GMO | Genetically modified organism |
| I.e. | that is |
| IAIS | International Association of Insurance Supervisors |
| IP | International industry insurance programme |
| IT | Information technology |
| KM | Knowledge Management |
| KonTraG | German Corporate Sector Supervision and Transparency Act |
| M & A | Mergers & Acquisitions |
| MBO | Management buy out |
| P & C | Property & Casualty |
| R & D | Research and Development |
| RM | Risk Management |
| SIC | Standard Industrial Classification |
| UmweltHG | German environmental protection law |

## Executive summary

"Knowledge-based risk management - A strategic systems approach for industrial corporations", examines the potential connection between knowledge management and risk management in industrial corporations. Key elements of this book include: identifying three main risk trends and their five primary characteristics, linking knowledge management with risk management scientifically and practically, developing a knowledge-based risk management process and conducting a risk management-knowledge management survey. Methodology for this book is conducted in six phases and consists of a combination of qualitative and quantitative analysis.

Three main risk trends threatening industrial corporations seem to materialise from the current literature on industrial insurance and risk management. These trends are (1) the emergence of increasingly complex and bigger corporate structures, (2) the development of risk potential in positive and negative direction and (3) the problems of the Property and Casualty insurance market. Five primary characteristics to describe each trend are derived from the literature. Each trend/characteristic pair is detailed in the state of field analysis.

Knowledge management is one way to supply industrial corporations with the tools to avoid, compensate or mitigate risk threats. Knowledge management for this book means providing lessons learned and best practices to corporate risk managers in order to deal with the above mentioned three risk trends.

A knowledge-based risk management process is developed to incorporate the necessary knowledge management concepts into the existing risk management processes. This new process is a synthesis of Theil's model for "Risk management for IT systems" and Tah and Carr's "Risk management process model". Its strengths lie in: reusability, adaptability, promoting knowledge transfer, and providing visible, measurable plus controllable results.

A risk management-knowledge management survey is conducted to test whether or not the link between the use of knowledge management and risk management exists. This survey is targeted at the risk managers of the leading Austrian industrial corporations. Results of the survey show that globalisation and networked economy are key risk trend drivers for industrial corporations.

Finally, application of the survey results and comparison with the theoretic part demonstrates the applicability of the proposed knowledge-based risk management process.

# 1 Introduction

Introduction chapter provides the basic foundation for the research conducted for "Knowledge-based risk management - A strategic systems approach for industrial corporations". This chapter consists of four sections: (1) problem statement, (2) theoretic-conceptual approach, (3) structure of the book and (4) research limitations. Problem statement section brings to light the necessity for a specific study on risk and knowledge management in industrial corporations. Theoretic-conceptual approach section provides a brief explanation of the risk theoretic-conceptual approach used to carry out the research. Structure of the book section describes a six part guideline on how the study was performed and what results and conclusions can be expected. Finally, the research boundaries section outlines the limitations for this book.

## 1.1 Problem statement

Industrial corporations are shaping the future development of the global, networked economy. Positive development of these corporations thus plays a vital role in the development of the world society. However, industrial corporations are increasingly threatened by changes in the corporate risk environment. This risk environment, if not managed, could endanger the productivity and existence of a corporation.

Many existing and new risks seem to threaten the future development of industrial corporations. Out of the numerous risk threats producing potential vulnerability to the corporation, three major risk trends seem to emerge at the moment. These three risk trends are: (1) the emergence of increasingly complex and bigger corporate structures, (2) the development of risk potential in positive and negative direction and (3) the problems of the Property and Casualty insurance market.

Each of the three corporate risk trends has been examined in depth by numerous experts on risk and insurance management. A selection of authors who have investigated each risk trend is provided below.

Risk trend one, emergence of increasingly complex and bigger corporate structures, authors include:

Aarsteinsen (2002), Achleitner et al. (2002), Anderson (2002), Angwin (2001), Apfelthaler et al. (2002), Baker (2002), Bate (1997), Bloomer (2004), de Castries (2004), de la Martinière (2003), Dickinson (2001), Dorfman (2002), Eickstädt (2001), Farny (2000), Forstmann (1998), Gleason (2000), Gouillart and Kelly (1995), Haller (1995a, 1995b), Hallikas et al. (2002), Happel and Liebwein (2000), Harland et al. (2003), Harrington and Niehaus (2003), Heidenhain (2001), Hoffmann (1985), Hörmann (1999), Kaen (2000), Karten (1998), Kloman (1992), Koslowski (2000), Kunreuther (2002), Manghetti (2002), Marsh (2003), Martin (2001), Mathmann (2002), OECD (2002), Pausenberger and Nassauer (2000), Raffler (1988), Sandner (1992), Schinzler (2003), Schließer (1996), Shleifer and Vishny (1997), Sigma (2002), Sigma (2003a), Smith and Quella (1995), Steward et al. (1999), Ullberg et al. (2002), Weber (2000), Witt (2000), Zech (2001).

Risk trend two, development of risk potential in positive and negative direction, authors include:

Aarsteinsen (2002), Achleitner et al. (2002), Adams (2000), Anderson (2002), Angwin (2001), Batabyal and Beladi (2001), Blondeau (2001), Brealey and Myers (1996), Brühwiler (1994), Conrad (1988), Coster and Hankin (2003), Covello and Merkhofer (1993), Daniel (2003), de Castries (2004), De Mey (2003), Doherty et al. (2003), Marsh (2003), Farny (2000), Flanigan (2004), Grace et al. (2003), Haller (1996, 1995a, 1991), Harrington and Niehaus (2003), Heidenhain (2001), Hoffmann (1985), Jaiswal et al. (2002), Karten (1998, 1991), Kirchsteiger (1999), Kirckpatrick et al. (2002), Kloman (1992), Kramer (2003), Kunreuther (2002), Levene (2004), Minor (2003), O'Rourke (2003), OECD (2002), Pfeiffer (1999), Pressman (2003), Property-Casualty (2001), Raffler (1988), Reactions (2003), Renn (2004), Marsh (2003), Schettler et al. (2002), Schließer (1996), Sigma (2002), Sigma (2003a), Stahel (2002), Stam et al. (1998), Ullberg et al. (2002), USDOJ (2000), Wagner (2000), White and Etkin (1997), Wiedenlübbert (2001), Wopperer (2002), Zech (2001).

Risk trend three, Property and Casualty market problems, numerous authors include:

Achleitner et al. (2002), Alff (2004, 2002), Anderson (2002), Aon (2002), Baker (2002), Blondeau (2001), Brühwiler (1994), de Castries (2004), De Mey (2003), Doherty et al. (2003), Dorfman (2002), Eickstädt (2001), Farny (2000, 1999, 1996), Fields et al. (1998), Garven (2002), Geipel-Kern (2004), Geratewohl (1988), Haller (1996, 1995a, 1991), Harrington and Niehaus (2003), Hoffmann (1985), Hohlfeld (2004, 2002), Hommel (2000), Hörmann (1999), Jablonowski (2002), Karten (1998), Kielholz and Murray (2004),

Kloman (1992), Kunreuther and Pauly (2004), Kunreuther (2002), Levene (2004), Lohse (2001), Manghetti (2002), Mathmann (2002), Mikosch (1991), OECD (2002), Pottier and Sommer (1999), Pressman (2003), Property-Casualty (2001), Raphael (1994), Rejda (1992), Risk Perception (2004), Schinzler (2003), Schließer (1996), Sigma (2002), Sigma (2003a), Sigma (2003b), Steward et al. (1999), Stewart (2002), Strejcek and Theil (2002), Theil (2003, 1996), Ullberg et al. (2002), Van den Berghe and Verweire (2001), Wagner (2000), Ward and Zurbruegg (2000), White and Etkin (1997), Wiedenlübbert (2001), Willis (2003), Wopperer (2002), Zech (2001).

As a result of this comprehensive risk management & trends research, numerous risk management processes and measures have been developed. Unfortunately, the risk management processes and measures most frequently appearing in the literature seem to remain focused around each individual risk trend. What corporate risk managers are currently lacking in order to deal with these risk trends is a standardised knowledge-based process which:

- assesses their company's risk exposure with regard to the above mentioned three trends
- classifies their company in order to find comparable benchmarks
- links their company to existing lessons learned and best practices from other companies
- monitors the results of available and applied risk management knowledge
- captures new lessons learned and best practices for future exploitation
- adapts to changes in risk trends and risk environments
- supports the strategic planning process of the corporation

Research shows while eliminating known risks, technology is at the same time creating new risks (Renn, 2004: 103; Wiedenlübbert, 2001: 195-196; Schließer, 1996: 279; Kloman, 1992: 309). While technological progress has reduced the occurrence probability of a catastrophe, it has also resulted in the increase of risk potential (Renn, 2004: 103; 2002: 77). However, the necessary improvement of risk management to help prevent this undesirable development is lacking. At the same time, the knowledge gap between the risk environment and relevant risk measures is growing rapidly. Only quick closure of this knowledge gap with reusable risk management lessons learned and best practices will allow risk management processes to fulfil today's corporate and insurance requirements. As MacMinn (2002: 298) points out, "risk management is about the creation and preservation of value rather than the elimination or reduction of risk". Risk management "systematically identifies and analyses the various loss exposures faced by a firm or organisation, and the best methods of treating the loss exposure consistent with the organisation's goals and objectives" Rejda (1992: 47). Thus industrial corporations must have a vital interest in the improvement of risk management. Yet in reality, Peter (2001: 222) and Hoffmann (1985: 3) show that most corporations do not see risk management as one of their core functions. Insurers could seize this opportunity by offering increased corporate risk management know-how to their clients (Peter, 2000: 222). As a result, insurers could gain an additional business segment by exploiting currently untapped risk knowledge and expertise.

Already in 1995, Haller (1995a: 16) had the vision of a "networked thinking approach" for risk management. Haller argues that in order for a networked thinking approach to become a reality, both the technical as well as human obstacles must be cleared. Haller's view is incorporated in Seufert et al.'s (2002: 151) theory on knowledge networks. According to Seufert et al.'s theory, access to and use of knowledge is the key success factor for sustainable competitive advantage. Martin (2001: 1460) points out that industry insurers possess knowledge on industrial risks and the available and necessary risk management measures. Heidenhain (2001: 274) advances Haller's and Martin's idea in practice and explains how knowledge-based engineering insurance takes advantage of the existing exposure and catastrophe knowledge. This information needs to be assessed, kept constantly up-to-date, feeding in relevant new risk information. Above all, the information needs to be accessible instantaneously at any time wherever it is needed. What is required today is an extension of Haller's, Seufert et al.'s, Martin's and Heidenhain's work to allow an effective assessment and analysis of all catastrophes threatening industrial corporations.

One hindrance to more effective assessment and handling of corporate risks seems to lie in today's relationship between industry insurers and industrial corporations. Figure 1: Role of industry insurers for industrial corporations contrasts the past and present role with the visionary role of industry insures for corporations. The present business model of industry insurers is displayed on the left side of Figure 1. In this model, industry insurers are seen as pure insurance capacity providers to various industrial corporations. Industrial corporations can purchase insurance capacity in the form of "immaterial insurance products" (Farny, 2000: 532). For instance, the most common industry insurance products offered in Austria include fleet, liability, legal indemnity, property, technical, business interruption, credit and transport insurance (Ennsfellner and Gassner-Möstl, 2000). However, risk management knowledge and expertise is not explicitly noted among the most common products provided by insurers. The discrepancy in insurance knowledge and expertise between industry insurer and industrial corporation is for instance acknowledged by Mikosch (1991: 40) and defined as "know how deficits". While catastrophes obtain widespread attention, underlying reasons for such catastrophes are neglected (Schüz, 2002: 54) and "trivial 'lessons learned' from past accidents have not yet been sufficiently implemented in the industrial practices" (Kirchsteiger, 1999: 13). However, valuable knowledge in order to avoid, mitigate or compensate such catastrophes in the future is collected and looked at (Schüz, 2002: 54). Risk management is missing, since it is only a side-product of insurance, with the sole purpose of industrial corporations saving premiums (Karten, 1978: 45). Industrial corporations generally take high quality risk management services from industry insurers for granted and do not have to pay for them (Brühwiler, 1994: 300; Peter, 2001: 225; Hargassner, 1990: 58; Haller, 1975: 77). Risk knowledge still does not appear to be gathered and evaluated systematically within the management process (Hoffmann, 1985: 2). As a result, the present-day relationship between insurer and company appears to be limited on pure risk transfer. As Farny (2000: 55-57) points out, the service relationship is one-way from insurer to company. Hence, hardly any knowledge-transfer, as described by Albrecht (1992: 3-5) between company and insurer and vice versa exists.

One possible new business model for industry insurers is depicted on the right side of Figure 1. In this visionary model, the industrial insurer acts as a provider of risk management knowledge and expertise, thus extending beyond its core competency as a risk transfer provider to industrial companies. The new industry insurance model could match Lohse's (2001: 7-8) three insurance service components "risk service", "handling service" and "customer service". Risk service would be the pure risk transfer, handling service the way the risk service is facilitated and customer service the risk management knowledge and expertise offered to the industrial corporation beyond the core insurance product. In addition, the new approach fits well with Kromschröder et al.'s (1994: 51) "insurance quality model", which includes "information, consulting and service" as part of the overall insurer service spectrum. The interactive relationship of the new business model could be beneficial for both industrial corporations as well as industrial insurers. Combined purchase of risk capacity and risk management services could be both beneficial for insurers and industrial corporations (Harrington and Niehaus, 2003: 450; Brealey and Myers, 1996: 708-709). The new industry insurance and industrial corporations network is "characterised by multi-directionality", where every participant can take advantage of the experiences of the other members and gain knowledge (Büchel and Raub, 2002: 589). In the new business model, the risk manager acts as knowledge manager, "translating the knowledge of the organization's goals and resources into a complete risk map" (Louisot, 2004). Hence, the new approach goes beyond Müller's (1994: 364) and Albrecht's (1992: 35) existing pure risk information transfer. Müller (1994: 364) points out that risk information is incorporated in insurance products, whose possession help to reduce decision risks. Albrecht (1992: 35) argues that the risk information transfer facilitates "diagnosis and prognosis" of insurance claims probabilities. Corporations could benefit from the risk management knowledge by reducing their exposure to major risk threats. This reduction in risk exposure could lead to fewer damages over time and potentially lowering their insurance premiums (Brealey and Myers, 1996: 709). By adopting this visionary model, industry insurers would receive valuable risk management knowledge from numerous corporate clients. Knowledge gathered could be used for improving underwriting, claims management and risk management with both existing and new corporate customers. Brühwiler (1994: 300) stresses that only visible achievement of these goals through effective risk management can possibly result in a competitive advantage for industry insurers. One way to achieve the new approach could be by strengthening independent risk management consulting spin-offs, owned by and operating closely with industry insurers. Two successful practical examples for risk management consulting spin-offs at industry insurer Gerling are Gerling Consulting Group and Gerling-Cert, which both provide risk management knowledge and expertise to industrial corporations in addition to Gerling's classical industry insurance products (Wiedenlübbert, 2001: 110-111; Hargassner, 1990: 57-60). In summary, the visionary insurance – corporation model would satisfy Karten's (1988: 218) requirements of an optimal use of insurers' "technical and organisational know-how". In addition, this visionary model would meet Harrington and Niehaus's (2003: 591) call for a "unified framework" towards managing risks within industrial corporations.

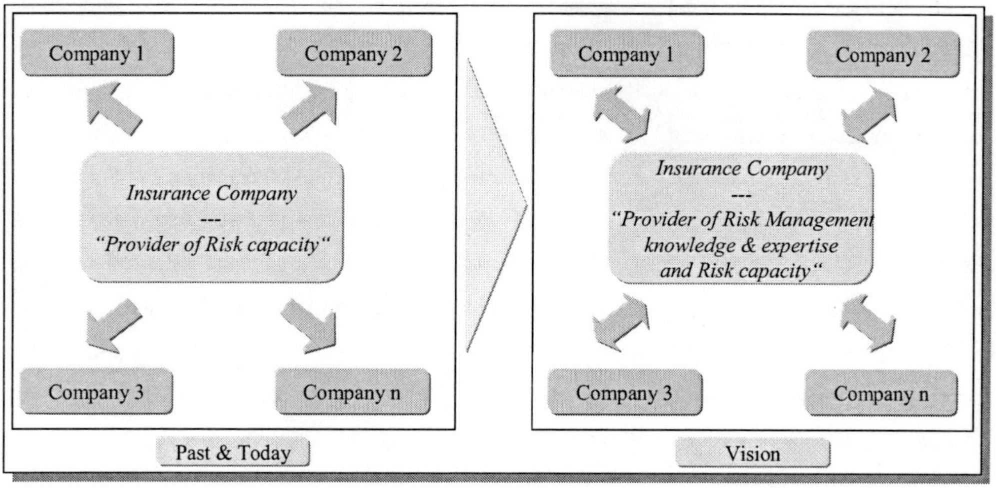


**Figure 1: Role of industry insurers for industrial corporations**

One result of achieving the vision depicted in Figure 1 might be a mutually beneficial relationship between corporations and insurers. The advantage of such a desirable relationship between corporations and insurers is that the primary needs of both partners are fully met. Primary needs of both corporations and insurers are listed in Figure 2: Industrial corporations' vs. industry insurers' needs.

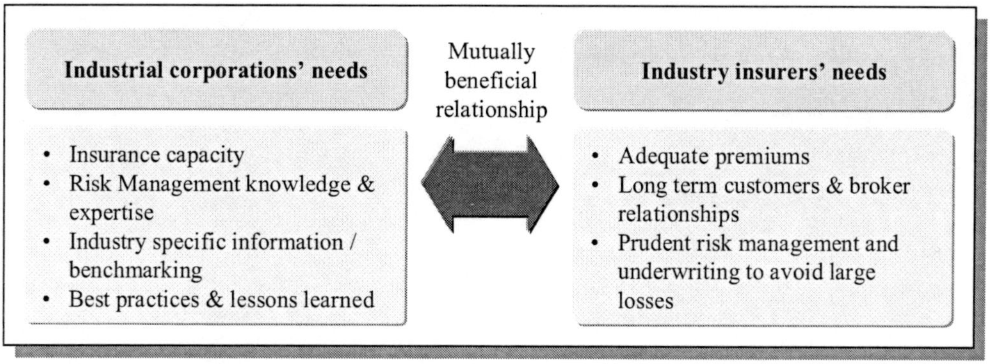


**Figure 2: Industrial corporations' vs. industry insurers' needs**

The previously outlined corporate and insurer risk situation demonstrates an increasingly difficult and more complex risk environment for industrial corporations and insurance companies. Consequently, the vulnerability of industry and insurance companies is escalating. Risk management processes and measures aimed at addressing the risk threats exist; however, they do not exploit the benefits of knowledge management. Thus, the research subject to be examined is how the existing risk management processes applied by corporate and insurance risk managers need to be improved through the concepts of knowledge management in order to help industrial companies deal with growing complexity, increasing risk potential and insurance market problems. The risk management process improvement should show a measurable increase in efficiency, transparency and reusability of risk management lessons learned and best practices. How the risk management processes can be improved is addressed in chapter 4.

## 1.2 Theoretic-conceptual approach

A risk-theoretic approach as applied by Dickinson (2001), Heidenhain (2001), Zech (2001), Haller (1996, 1995a, 1991, 1975), Theil (1996), Schradin (1994), Albrecht (1992), Kloman (1992) and other risk management experts was selected for this book. Risk-theoretic approach aims at the determination, evaluation and handling of risk trends in order to improve the risk exposure of the industrial corporation. Alternative approaches, in particular a decision-theoretic approach by Kromschröder (1994: 69-94), Kleindorfer et al. (1993: 289-343), Müller (1993: 3813-3824), Ritchie and Marshall (1993: 48-79), Karten (1972: 5-9) and others, were evaluated. A risk-theoretic approach was selected for the following reasons:

- its focus on a corporation's risk situation,
- the focal point of this book is risk management,
- it is the most useful in determining the appropriate risk management measures dealing with the three selected risk trends,
- it is the fitting technique for examination and usage of the risk management process approach,
- the necessity for increased research undertaken in the proposed area due to the constant change in risk environment

Risk-theoretic in the context of the book means selected threats potentially posing a risk to the corporation are reviewed, evaluated and handled. Three of the most threatening risk trends derived from the current literature on risk and insurance management are studied and their influence on corporations and insurers assessed. Reasons for selecting these three particular risk trends are:

- their current importance for industrial corporations and industry insurers
- their applicability to a systematic risk management approach
- their usability within the empirical analysis of this research

Each risk trend is described through five primary characteristics. These characteristics are a collection of the major risk threats to corporations today and are derived from the literature published by risk management scientists. It is assumed this assessment demonstrates that the existing risk-management processes are no longer sufficient under increasing corporate complexity, the increasing risk potential in both positive and negative direction and the problems of the property and casualty insurance market. Changes in the risk environment seem to lie in the fast changing economic, legal, technological, societal, environmental and political landscape. These changes appear to have a negative impact on the existing risk management capability of corporations today. A strategic systems approach to knowledge-based risk management in industrial corporations is one possible solution to better manage this new risk environment. The approach introduces the concepts of knowledge management in the form of lessons learned and best practices to the existing risk-theory and risk management processes.

## 1.3 Structure of the book

A strategic systems approach to knowledge-based risk management in industrial corporations is developed using a combination of qualitative and quantitative analysis. The analysis is performed in six parts, graphically displayed in Figure 3: Structure of this book.

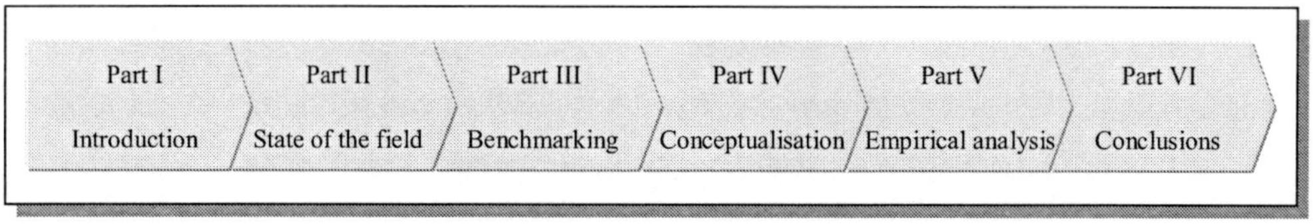


**Figure 3: Structure of this book**

Part one is the introduction and part six presents the conclusion of the book. The theoretic part is conducted in parts II through IV and the empirical part is conducted in part V.

Part one provides the general foundation of the research to be conducted. This part introduces the changing risk environment threatening industrial corporations and points out that existing risk management measures for the risk trends are no longer sufficient. Knowledge management is proposed as an enhancement to available state of the art risk management processes. A risk-theoretic approach is presented as the research framework. Finally, the structure of the book is displayed and the boundaries of the research drawn.

Part two defines the detail scope and refines the area of research. First, the methodical approach of the state of the field analysis is explained. Next, the existing literature on risk management is examined. A general overview of the literature sheds light on three main risk trends threatening industrial corporations today, namely: (1) the emergence of increasingly complex and bigger corporate structures, (2) the development of risk potential in positive and negative direction and (3) the problems of the Property and Casualty insurance market. Thus, these three risk trends are the primary focus of the state of the field analysis. In addition, the existing "Risk management measures" dealing with these three risk trends are examined. The three risk trends together with the risk management measures constitute the structure in which the risk management literature review is conducted. The matrix depicted in Table 1: State of the field research matrix in 2.1 Methodical approach is used to summarise the literature review.

Upon completion of the general risk trend overview, five main characteristics for each trend mentioned above are identified. Characteristics are a compilation of the major risk threats to corporations today as pointed out by risk management experts. A total of 15 trend/characteristic combinations are defined. Each trend/characteristic combination is extracted from Appendix 3: State of the field research matrix for corporate risk trends, and therefore derived from the current literature on risk management. Extracted combinations are presented using Figure 4: Trend and characteristics matrix. A detailed description of each trend/characteristic combination is provided in the state of the field analysis. The three identified risk trends and their associated characteristics are essential in assessing the individual risk situation of industrial corporations. An exemplary risk assessment is performed in the empirical analysis in phase five.

The next step of part two demonstrates the linkage between knowledge-management and risk management. The literature suggests (Patton, 2002: 329-336; Bhatt 2001: 65-68) that knowledge management can be applied through lessons learned and best practices. Hence, collecting risk management lessons learned and best practices is one way to show the linkage between knowledge management and risk management measures. Analogous to the introduction of the three risk trends, an overview of the literature sheds light on current states of corporate knowledge management. Literature overview is performed using Appendix 4: State of the field research matrix for corporate knowledge management. Exemplary risk management measures for each trend/characteristic set, presented as lessons learned and best practices, are extracted from Appendix 3: State of the field research matrix for corporate risk trends. Examples are displayed in Table 2: Lessons learned and best practices matrix.

Research question & knowledge advancement and summary conclude the state of the field analysis. Why and how traditional risk management needs to be improved in industrial corporations through the capabilities of knowledge management is summarised.

Part three provides practical benchmarking to support the theoretic findings of the state of the field analysis. Two benchmarks of Austrian industrial corporations are presented. One benchmark points out the lessons learned of RHI and the second one shows the best practices of Glanzstoff Austria. For each of the two companies, a company overview, description of the crisis, reason for selection and possible learnings for other industrial corporations are provided in the context of risk and knowledge management.

Part four conceptually establishes and describes a knowledge-based risk management process. The new knowledge-based risk management process is synthesised from two existing and proven risk management processes. This new process consists of five steps. Each of the five process steps are described and visualised. Roles of corporate and insurance risk managers in the course of the knowledge-based risk management process are outlined and the results of the phase four summarised.

Benefits of an enhanced risk management process are:

- it provides a reusable scientific approach,
- it makes the procedure reusable and adaptable in corporations,
- it allows knowledge transfer between corporations and
- it makes changes in the corporate risk situation visible, measurable and controllable over time.

Part five empirically tests whether or not a link between the use of knowledge management and risk management exists. Establishment of this link indicates a positive relationship between lessons learned and best practices to help corporations move from being highly affected to hardly affected by complexity and large size, development of risk potential and problems of the P&C market. The survey in Appendix 2: Risk & Knowledge management survey content is conducted utilising a statistically significant number of industrial corporations in Austria. Survey questions consist of two clusters derived from the state of the field analysis. Cluster one questions are developed from the identified risk trends and their five main characteristics. Cluster two questions contain questions targeted at knowledge management, i.e. lessons learned and best practices. Results of the survey are processed using the SPSS statistical analysis tool. Processing the survey results shows how the Risk assessment and analysis (Steps II & III) of the knowledge-based risk management process work in practice, i.e. how corporations are classified and assessed.

Part six draws conclusions from the risk and knowledge management study. First, theoretic results of phases II through IV are compared with the empirical results of phase V. Both similarities and differences between theory and practice are stated and discussed. Finally, an outlook on the possible future developments of knowledge-based risk management is provided.

## 1.4 Research limitations

Corporate risk and knowledge management is the main focus of this research study. Four main limitations are necessary to arrive at reasonable answers towards solving the tasks put forward in the problem statement as well as making a contribution to the scientific community.

Limitation one is the focus on three risk trends at the current point in time. Thus, an examination of the evolvement of the risk trends over time – as mentioned for example by Karten (2000: 91) and Haller (1990: 250; 1975: 48-49) – is not a focus of this book. Potential changes of the risk environment are not neglected but incorporated in the adaptability of the proposed knowledge-based risk management process.

Limitation two is the description of each risk trend with five main characteristics. Five characteristics are sufficient to describe each risk trend and result in a feasible survey length. A subsequent research area for future development could be the refinement of the identified trends with new or different characteristics. In addition, each characteristic could even be described with a number of attributes. However, this book concentrates on the five main present-day characteristics for each trend.

Limitation three is the focus on only Risk assessment and Risk analysis (Steps II and III) in the practical application of the knowledge-based risk management process. The Risk identification, Risk handling and Risk monitoring (Steps I, IV & V) are dependent on good project management within each individual corporation. Due to the lack of influence on this capability, their strategic importance is described but not actually pursued in this book.

Limitation four is the concentration on explicit risk management knowledge only, i.e. structured, codifiable corporate information which in general can be stored in a database (Bollinger and Smith, 2001: 8-18; Lang, 2001: 43-57; Davies, 2000: 62; Krebs, 2000: 128-129). Knowledge conversion from tacit to explicit risk management knowledge is not addressed in this book.

# 2 State of the Field

The aim of the state of the field analysis is to provide a current theoretical as well as practical view on the risk trends threatening industrial corporations today and the available risk management measures against those risk threats. State of the field chapter contains five sub-sections. Section one explains the methodical approach of the state of the field analysis. Section two provides definition and development of three major risk trends and their underlying five main characteristics. Section three presents knowledge-management in the form of applied lessons learned and best practices as a possible enhancement to existing risk management measures in dealing with the three identified risk trends. Section four defines the research question and attempted knowledge advancement. Lastly, section five summarises the results of the state of the field analysis.

## 2.1 Methodical approach

The state of the field analysis on risk and knowledge management is performed by using a morphological approach. Articles and publications are selected based on their title and abstracts which demonstrate they address the area of research to be examined. A mixture of theoretic and practical sources is used for the literature review. Theoretic sources provide solid, proven foundations for the developed concepts and models. Theoretic sources have successfully completed the required academic quality assurance processes. A downside to this quality assurance processes could be, however, that theoretic sources are sometimes not as current as practical contributions. In contrast, practical sources might not have passed through the academic quality assurance processes. Therefore, conclusions derived from practical sources in the literature review need to be viewed critically, due to their lack of scientific confirmation. Advantages of practical sources are the actuality and the proximity to the examined topic, which complement and support the quality of the theoretic sources.

Selected articles and publications are analysed with regard to four research matrices. Structure, content and significance of each research matrix are detailed in the following paragraphs. Findings and conclusions from the four completed research matrices are tested in Chapter 5: Empirical analysis using a survey shown in Appendix 2: Risk & Knowledge management survey content.

The first research matrix displayed in Table 1: State of the field research matrix contains pertinent information regarding each risk trend. Risk trend information is categorised around the four major fields: (1) emergence of increasingly complex and bigger corporate structures, (2) development of risk potential in positive and negative direction, (3) problems of Property & Casualty Insurance market and (4) Risk management measures. State of the field research matrix consists of ten attributes. Each attribute is named and briefly explained in Table 1 below. Important points, existing overlaps and gaps in each matrix field are easily identified by displaying the examined articles in this matrix and evaluating each individual contribution.

| MATRIX ATTRIBUTE | ATTRIBUTE EXPLANATION |
|---|---|
| **Article** | Title of the examined article |
| **Author** | Name of the article's author(s) |
| **Journal / Publication** | Name of the journal / publication in which the article is published |
| **Publication date** | Date the article was published |
| **Examined questions** | Questions investigated in the article |
| **Emergence of increasingly complex and bigger corporate structures** | Problems and issues arising for conventional risk management due to the development of larger, intransparent, and globally networked company structure |
| **Development of risk potential in positive and negative direction** | Causes and effects which influence the risk potential of corporations and insurers |
| **Problems of Property & Casualty Insurance market** | Reasons and possible solutions for the current difficulties faced by Property & Casualty insurers |
| **Risk management measures** | Suggested measures, i.e. lessons learned and best practices which should be used to handle the risks addressed in the article |
| **Open scientific questions** | Questions which are unanswered in the article and which could lead to further research projects |

**Table 1: State of the field research matrix for corporate risk trends**

The second matrix in Figure 4 supports the extraction and structuring of the characteristics for each risk trend. Characteristics are derived from the completed Appendix 3: State of the field research matrix for corporate risk trends. The risk trend and characteristics matrix is necessary to determine and to monitor the risk situation of industrial companies. Each characteristic has an equal weight and is rated on a scale from 1 (very low risk exposure) to 10 (very high risk exposure). Therefore, the total score for each risk trend varies between 5 and 50 and the sum of all three risk trends varies between 15 and 150. Structure of the risk trend and characteristics matrix is illustrated below:

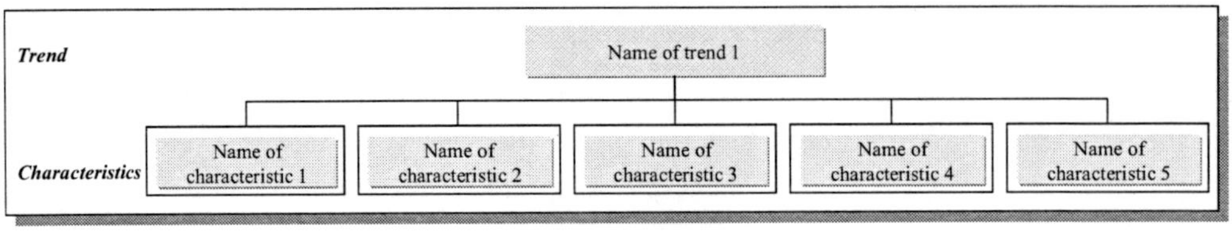


**Figure 4: Trend and characteristics matrix**

The third matrix in Table 2: Lessons learned and best practices matrix gathers lessons learned and best practices for each trend/characteristic set to demonstrate the linkage between knowledge management and risk management. Examples are extracted from "Risk management measures" in the completed state of the field research matrix for corporate risk trends shown in Appendix 3. Results are summarised for both lessons learned and best practices in section 2.3 Linking knowledge management with risk management. Attributes and structure of the lessons learned and best practices matrix are depicted below:

| **Trends and Characteristics** | **Lessons learned (Root cause analysis)** | **Best practices** |
|---|---|---|
| **Complex and bigger corporate structures** | | |
| Networked economy | | |
| Shareholder Value | | |
| Multiple Economic systems | | |
| Globalisation | | |
| Mergers & Acquisitions | | |
| **Development of risk potential** | | |
| Natural catastrophes | | |
| Industrial pollution | | |
| Terrorism | | |
| Technological advancement and failure | | |
| Societal, political, cultural change | | |
| **Problems of the P & C Insurance market** | | |
| Price & capacity cycles | | |
| Competitive disadvantages of the industry sector | | |
| Legal changes | | |
| Larger catastrophes | | |
| New risks | | |

**Table 2: Lessons learned and best practices matrix**

The fourth matrix in Table 3: State of the field research matrix for knowledge management aids in the collections of relevant knowledge management information from the current literature. State of field research matrix for knowledge management is categorised around the four major fields: (1) Corporate knowledge management, (2) Knowledge-based risk management for complex corporations, (3) Suggestions for practical implementation of knowledge-based risk management and (4) Knowledge management for insurance companies. The structured examination of the current literature on knowledge management supports the linking of knowledge management with risk management in section 2.3 Linking knowledge management with risk management. The knowledge management research matrix consists of nine attributes. Each attribute is named and briefly explained below:

| MATRIX ATTRIBUTE | ATTRIBUTE EXPLANATION |
|---|---|
| **Article** | Title of the examined article |
| **Author** | Name of the article's author(s) |
| **Journal / Publication** | Name of the journal / publication in which the article is published |
| **Publication date** | Date the article was published |
| **Examined questions** | Questions investigated in the article |
| **Corporate Knowledge Management – State of the field** | Latest views and scientific results on the implementation and use of knowledge management within a corporate environment |
| **Knowledge-based risk management for complex corporations** | Role description of knowledge management within existing or desired corporate risk management processes |
| **Suggestions for practical implementation of knowledge-based risk management** | Proposed measures for a successful application of knowledge management within risk management processes |
| **Knowledge Management for Insurance companies** | Description on how insurance corporations might benefit from applying knowledge management during their external risk management consulting services or within their own operations |

**Table 3: State of the field research matrix for knowledge management**

Subsequent section of this chapter uses the methodical approach explained above to expose three risk trends and their underlying characteristics from the current risk management literature.

## 2.2 Definition and development of the three risk trends and their characteristics

The following sections define and develop three major risk trends presently threatening the continuity of industrial corporations. First, a general introduction to the overall corporate risk environment is provided. Secondly, a detailed description of the three risk trends and each of their underlying five main characteristics are presented.

### *2.2.1 General introduction to the existing corporate risk environment*

Over the last ten years, the number as well as severity of extreme catastrophes has shown a dramatic increase (Grace et al., 2003: 1; Aarsteinsen, 2002: 10; Sigma, 2002: 3; Schließer, 1996: 280-281; Kloman, 1992: 309; Conrad, 1988: 144-145; Hoffmann, 1985: 7-8). This development already has had and in the future will have a big impact on the risk management of industrial corporations and industry insurers. Risk management has been developed as a scientific discipline, helping companies to address situations which could endanger their existence. For instance, Fatemi and Luft (2002: 37) point out that "the strongest motive for risk management behaviour is the avoidance of financial distress". Successful risk management in turn can help to increase value of the company (Fatemi and Luft, 2002: 37), resulting in securer jobs and supply of innovative products (Hoffmann, 1985: 9). Insurance companies, apart from providing financial risk transfer mechanisms, have been trying to supply companies with risk management expertise to help them with assessing and mitigating existing risks (Dickinson, 2001: 363; Albrecht, 2000: 3-5). However, industry insurance companies have traditionally been in the past an unintentional hindrance to, not a driver for the further development of risk management (Theil, 1996: 217; Kloman, 1992: 311).

The shift towards a global, networked economy has led to the growth and increasing complexity of corporations. The scientific progress, continued industrialisation and the enormous socio-political changes have increased the up- and downscale risk potential for all economic actors, especially for industrial corporations. Furthermore, the insurance industry, an enabler for the industrial revolution in the 20th century, is undergoing a difficult transition phase, impacting the worldwide economic system.

Given this macroeconomic situation, three major trends seem to materialise from the current literature on industrial insurance and risk management: (1) the emergence of increasingly complex and bigger corporate structures, (2) the development of risk potential in positive and negative direction and (3) the problems of the Property and Casualty insurance market. Grouped around these three trends are Risk management measures, i.e. tools used to avoid, compensate or mitigate corporate threats.

A thorough examination of this changing environment is required by both industrial and insurance corporations. A better understanding of the existing and future environmental challenges seem to be missing and are necessary for maintaining sustainable competitive advantage and protection against the new risk situations which endanger their existence. For this purpose, a strategic systems approach, helping to provide the required risk management knowledge for industrial corporations, is developed and explained. A practical way to portray this approach is through a reusable process and a simple methodology which can be used in versatile business environments. Result of a methodical risk management process can be an "increase in security of the risk carrier" (Jirsa and Oppl, 1988: 24). Risk carriers in the context of this book are industrial corporations. For application of the new process, the three above mentioned emerging trends are selected, but can be adapted if needed. Each trend is described through a set of five characteristics. This set of characteristics is not exhaustive but represents the primary characteristics for each trend as depicted by the recognised risk management researchers in the current literature. Risk management measures are tools used by risk managers to avoid, mitigate or transfer risk. The risk management measures consist of explicit risk management knowledge in the form of lessons learned and best practices which are suggested by risk management experts in the current literature.

The definition and development of the three risk trends consists of four sections. The first section provides a brief introduction to the existing corporate risk environment. The next three sections name and describe in detail the five main characteristics of each risk trend.

Chapter 4: Knowledge-based risk management process describes a new and enhanced risk management process. This process can be applied for handling any potential risk trend which threatens an industrial corporation. For this book, the process uses the selected and described risk trends and risk management measures to assess and to improve the risk situation of industrial corporations. While the risk management process is reusable, it needs to be noted that the selection of the risk trends and their describing characteristics are currently applicable and can be adjusted to meet changes over time as needed.

### *2.2.2 Risk trend 1: Emergence of increasingly complex and bigger corporate structures*

Authors like Farny (2000), Haller (1995a, 1995b), Karten (1998), Kloman (1992), Kunreuther (2002) and others have examined and confirmed that the size and complexity of corporations is rapidly increasing. This risk trend is described in the current literature with the following five main characteristics: (1) networked economy, (2) shareholder value, (3) multiple economic systems, (4) globalisation and (5) mergers & acquisitions. Figure 5 depicts the trend, emergence of increasingly complex and bigger corporate structures, and its associated characteristics. Each characteristic noted above is defined sequentially below.

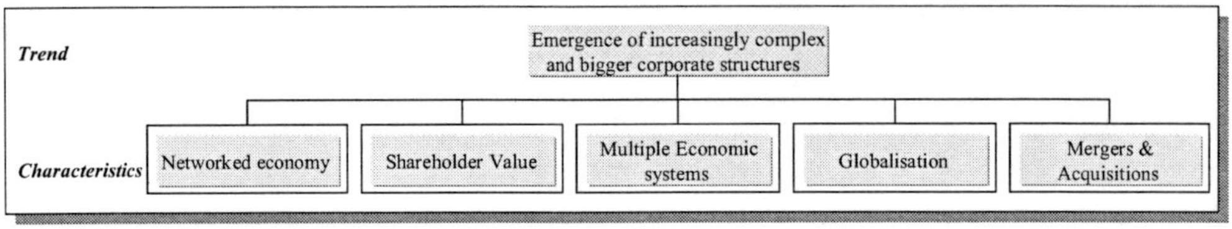


**Figure 5: Characteristics for emergence of increasingly complex and bigger corporate structures**

### *2.2.2.1 Risk trend 1 - Characteristic 1: Networked economy*

***Networked economy*** is noted as a major characteristic for emergence of increasingly complex and bigger corporate structures by Hallikas et al. (2002: 45-55), Harland et al. (2003: 51-62), Marsh (2003: 19), Aarsteinsen (2002: 10, 12), Achleitner et al. (2002: 279), Gleason (2000: 97-100; 261), Witt (2000: 5-6), Steward et al. (1999: 124-132), Bate (1997: 222-228), Schließer (1996: 280), Gouillart and Kelly (1995: 215), Haller (1995b: 10), Sandner (1992: 148), Raffler (1988: 362) and Hoffmann (1985: 7).

A networked economy as defined by Aarsteinsen (2002: 10) and Witt (2000: 5-6) is an economy's continued tendency towards digitisation of industries, introduction of new business processes and models and reduction of transaction costs. Networked economy affects the vulnerability of industrial corporations both externally and internally.

Industrialised economies are highly dependent on each other due to "interconnected production networks and supply chains" (Hallikas et al., 2002: 45-55; Achleitner et al., 2002: 279; Steward et al., 1999: 125; Schließer, 1996: 280). Complexity of supply networks for industrial corporations stems from the interacting factors "increasing product/service complexity, e-business, outsourcing, and globalisation" (Harland et al., 2003: 51). These factors cause "high value accumulations" and growing national and international reliance, resulting in higher vulnerability of corporations and whole economic sectors (Raffler, 1988: 362). Investment or product introduction risk is growing within the increasingly networked economy (Hoffmann, 1985: 7). For instance, nearly 25% of goods produced in the EU are exported to the US, where they are subject to the problematical local liability and consumer protection laws (Marsh, 2003: 19).

In addition to industrial production networks, financial markets are highly dependent on each other on a global scale. One example of unforeseen negative networking effects around the world was experienced following the uncoupling of the British Pound from other European currencies in 1992, forced by the intervention of money speculator George Soros. Other examples of financial market interconnection include the devaluation of the Mexican Peso in 1994 and the Thai Baht in 1997 (Gleason, 2000: 97-100; 261). The devaluations resulted in nearby breakdowns of large portions of the world financial markets, with negative impact on the global economy.

In addition to the externally networked economy, internal corporate networks exist (Sandner, 1992: 148). Corporate networks consist of "interests" and "resources" (Sandner, 1992: 148). Specific strengths and features of the corporate network determine the "freedom of action" of their members, the employees (Sandner, 1992: 148). Bate (1997: 222-228) makes a further distinction between formal and informal business networks. Informal networks are used to achieve specific goals (Bate, 1997: 223). On the other hand, formal networks are only there to legitimise decisions that have been already made elsewhere (Bate, 1997: 223). The underlying driver for corporate networks can be seen in information technology, which develops "connectors across corporate boundaries into the lives of other organisations, giving birth to new corporate communities" (Gouillart and Kelly, 1995: 215). In the networked economy, "production and distribution" is reduced in importance while knowledge becomes the key success factor (Gouillart and Kelly, 1995: 215).

Hallikas et al. (2002: 52) point out that networking can result both in benefits and threats for industrial corporations and provide a conceptual framework for "assessment and auditing of networks risk" in production networks. Industrial corporations have to come to terms with the fact that they are not isolated, protected units but "individual identities within the network" Haller (1995b: 10). As such, industrial corporations are dependent on the success or the failure of the overall business network. Improving their own networking capability therefore might help industrial corporations to gain sustainable competitive advantage (Hallikas et al., 2002: 46).

#### *2.2.2.2 Risk trend 1 - Characteristic 2: Shareholder Value*

***Shareholder value*** is described as a major characteristic for emergence of increasingly complex and bigger corporate structures by Harrington and Niehaus (2003: 441-462), Schinzler (2003: 2),

Marsh (2003: 1), Heidenhain (2001: 273), Zech (2001: 81), Koslowski (2000: 137-148), Karten (1998: 227) and Kloman (1992: 304).

This characteristic results from the growing competition between corporations. The "focus on shareholder value" seems to be partly responsible for increased competition (Schinzler, 2003: 2; Zech, 2001: 81). Shareholder value according to Koslowski (2000: 140) is becoming the sole purpose for a corporation. Karten (1998: 227) defines shareholder value as the "probability distribution of the corporations' value". Koslowski (2000: 137) even draws a connection between shareholder value and the characteristic "globalisation" mentioned below.

One effect of the shareholder value approach is the transformation of formerly state-owned industries into privately held companies, aiming at profit maximisation and risk minimisation (Heidenhain, 2001: 273). Shareholder value also affects the strategic focus of industrial corporations. The focus has shifted from existing, long-term core products and services to capital investments and short-term stock market rises (Koslowski, 2000: 141, 143). Subsequently, Koslowski (2000: 141, 143) stresses the importance of monitoring this focus shift by industrial risk managers. This focus shift could lead to a negative effect, especially when capital markets fall and losses results in the operating business need to be offset. In order to hedge corporations' balance sheets, appropriate insurance coverage needs to be chosen (Marsh, 2003: 1), which can be supported by the effective use of risk management measures.

#### *2.2.2.3 Risk trend 1 - Characteristic 3: Multiple economic systems*

***Multiple economic systems*** is pointed out as a major characteristic for emergence of increasingly complex and bigger corporate structures by Bloomer (2004: 56-62), de la Martinière (2003: 92), Schinzler (2003: 3), Baker (2002: 356), Manghetti (2002: 310, 312), Mathmann (2002: 1930), Sigma (2002: 5, 9, 13), Dickinson (2001: 360), Martin (2001: 1460), Zech (2001: 71), Gleason (2000: 39-40), Happel and Liebwein (2000, 228), Kaen (2000: 247-262), Pausenberger and Nassauer (2000: 264), Shleifer and Vishny (1997: 2), Haller (1995a: 8) and Kloman (1992: 304).

A corporation's vulnerability increases with every additional economy in which it conducts business (Haller, 1995a: 8). One threat which has already led to the bankruptcy of large, international corporations is the differing level of corporate governance across different economies (Sigma, 2002: 5; Dickinson, 2001: 360). Shleifer and Vishny (1997: 2) list three major aims of corporate governance. First of all, corporate governance is about how investors can assure that the management team returns a payoff from their investments. Secondly, it is about ensuring that managers "do not steal" or waste investors' money in unprofitable projects. Thirdly, it deals with investors' control of managers. Successful introduction and use of corporate governance could be facilitated by the use of risk management processes (Mathmann, 2002: 1930; Martin, 2001: 1460; Happel and Liebwein, 2000: 228; Kaen, 2000: 247-262).

One example of integrating corporate governance into the economic system is Germany. Following the failure of several large firms, the German government instituted the corporate governance law "Gesetz zur Kontrolle und Transparenz im Unternehmensbereich" (KonTraG) in 1998 (Martin, 2001: 1460; Happel and Liebwein, 2000: 228; Pausenberger and Nassauer, 2000: 264). The primary objective of the KonTraG is the early detection of critical corporate risk before a major damage has occurred (Happel and Liebwein, 2000: 228). The German corporate governance integration could be utilised in other countries and across industries in order to increase risk management standards.

Another issue surfacing from multiple economic systems is the lack of harmonised accounting standards (Bloomer, 2004: 56; de la Martinière, 2003: 92; Schinzler, 2003: 3; Sigma, 2002: 5, 13) and the subsequently missing corporate transparency (Manghetti, 2002: 312; Sigma, 2002: 9). Corporations have to spend time and money, dealing with several supervisory bodies (de la Martinière, 2003: 92; Schinzler, 2003: 3; Manghetti, 2002: 310).

Finally, industrial corporations operating in several different countries have to come to terms with the significant divergence of industry regulations (Baker, 2002: 356; Kloman, 1992: 304; Sigma, 2002: 9; Zech, 2001: 71). Unfortunately, regulatory authorities are often not capable of coping with the increased demands on speed and flexibility of the economy (Gleason, 2000: 39). Due to the lack of swift and harmonised reactions through financial authorities in the various world economies, global financial markets nearly collapsed in 1998 (Gleason, 2000: 39-40).

#### *2.2.2.4 Risk trend 1 - Characteristic 4: Globalisation*

***Globalisation*** is examined as a major characteristic for emergence of increasingly complex and bigger corporate structures by Harland et al. (2003: 51-62), de la Martinière (2003: 87), Achleitner et al. (2002: 279), Anderson (2002: 173), Apfelthaler et al. (2002: 108-118), Dorfman (2002: 341), Kunreuther (2002: 663), Ullberg et al. (2002: 468), Heidenhain (2001: 271), Zech

(2001: 81), Farny (2000: 403), Gleason (2000: 261-263), Steward et al. (1999: 130) and Haller (1995a: 8).

The scientific community concurs on the continuing and inevitability of globalisation. Globalisation is seen as "a common economic, societal and political principal" (Farny, 2000: 403). Steward et al. (1999: 130) postulated that "Internet and eCommerce ... are global phenomena". Four years later, Harland et al. (2003: 52) notice growing "transnational mobility of capital, information, people, products and services" as globalisation drivers.

As a result of the global economy, "corporations face increasingly competitive, complex and uncertain environments" (Apfelthaler et al., 2002: 108). While corporations are a main driver of the decentralisation development, they also have to deal with its advantages and disadvantages. Gleason (2000: 261) points out that both markets, as well as risks have become global. Corporate risk managers of global corporations therefore have to "develop comprehensive, coordinated risk management programs applied on a worldwide basis" (Dorfman, 2002: 341).

One way to enable a long-term healthy decentralisation process is by establishing "centralised organisational control or third-party inspections" (Kunreuther, 2002: 663-664). For instance in the field of financial transactions, Gleason (2000: 262-263) calls for the collection of global business data storage, which might limit the risk potential in upcoming financial crises. Therefore, business and risk management strategies must incorporate a world-wide, rather than a regional or even national view.

#### *2.2.2.5 Risk trend 1 - Characteristic 5: Mergers & Acquisitions*

***Mergers & Acquisitions*** are described as a major characteristic for emergence of increasingly complex and bigger corporate structures by de Castries (2004: 38), Sigma (2003a: 13), Sigma (2002: 5, 9, 12), Anderson (2002: 173), OECD (2002: 26), Ullberg et al. (2002: 468), Weber (2000), Angwin (2001: 32-57), Dickinson (2001: 360), Eickstädt (2001: 41-42), Heidenhain (2001: 274), Zech (2001: 79), Gleason (2000: 145-222), Hörmann (1999: 83), Forstmann (1998), Smith and Quella (1995) and Raffler (1988: 362).

There is widespread recognition of the continued consolidation process through Mergers & Acquisitions (M & A). According to Angwin (2001: 34), M & A are mainly targeted at "improved performance and increased shareholder value". Angwin (2001: 34) also identifies several other goals of M & A. These goals include "establishing a presence in a new geographic area, gaining critical size to improve bargaining power along the value chain, economies of scale, acquiring technology and know-how" as well as "building market share and strengthening business".

Insurers act as "enablers" of the economic development (de Castries, 2004: 38). The resulting larger structures possess increased market power and financial strength (Eickstädt, 2001: 41) in their relationship with industry insurers. The increasingly larger company combinations lead to an increase in (re-) insured values (Sigma, 2003a: 13; Hörmann, 1999: 83; Raffler, 1988: 362) and an accumulation in unprotected, endangered areas (Sigma, 2003a: 13).

Merging with another company can be riskier than conducting normal business. Precaution should be taken in respect to the threats of "company failure" (Dickinson, 2001: 360), "credit risk" (Sigma, 2002: 12; Dickinson, 2001: 360; Gleason, 2000: 145-222), "leveraged balance sheets" and "impaired profitability" (OECD, 2002: 26). For example, Gleason's extensive study on credit risk management comprises a best practice benchmarking of Enron. Enron is portrayed as one of the leading companies dealing with raw materials shortages. The possibility of Enron collapsing in a credit risk disaster only a year later was unthinkable in 2000, when Gleason wrote his book.

Due diligence is determined by Angwin (2001: 33) as one of the key prerequisites for successful M & A activities. In a qualified due diligence, "issues which might de-rail negotiations or may lead to the failure of the acquisition" are revealed (Angwin, 2001: 35). Due diligence helps to limit the lack of transparency in major financial dealings thereby avoiding devastating effects, as exposed in the examples of Enron and WorldCom (Sigma, 2002: 5, 9). Another important factor in M & A activities is swift and proficient "post-merger integration", to enable "realising synergies and establishing momentum" (Weber, 2000; Forstmann, 1998 and Smith and Quella, 1995 in Apfelthaler et al., 2002: 116).

### *2.2.3 Risk trend 2: Development of risk potential in positive and negative direction*

Numerous authors address the development of risk potential, such as Brühwiler (1994), Doherty et al. (2003), Harrington and Niehaus (2003), Karten (1998, 1991) and Schließer (1996). The present literature for this trend reveals the subsequent five characteristics: (1) natural catastrophes, (2) industrial pollution, (3) terrorism, (4) technological advancement and failure and (5) societal, political and cultural change. Figure 6 depicts this trend, development of risk potential in positive and negative direction, and its associated characteristics. Each characteristic noted above is defined below.

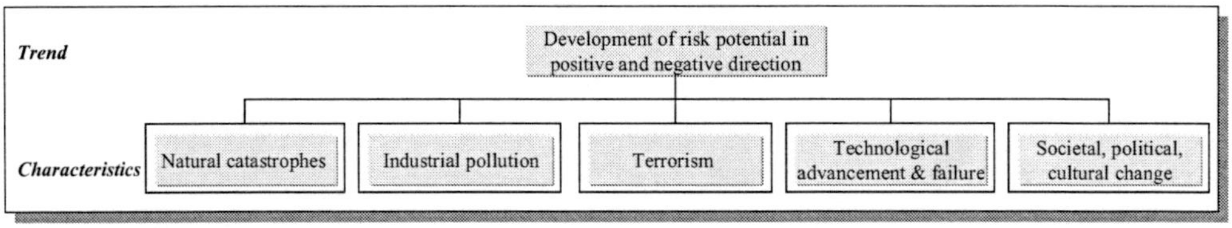


**Figure 6: Characteristics for development of risk potential in positive and negative direction**

### 2.2.3.1 *Risk trend 2 - Characteristic 1: Natural catastrophes*

***Natural catastrophes*** are mentioned as a major characteristic of development of risk potential in positive and negative direction by Grace et al. (2003: 1), Sigma (2003a: 12, 34), Achleitner et al. (2002: 279), Anderson (2002: 173), Jaiswal et al. (2002: 1-10), Kunreuther (2002: 655-664), Ullberg et al. (2002: 472), Batabyal and Beladi (2001: 875-876), Wiedenlübbert (2001: 110-111), Zech (2001: 72), Farny (2000: 92), Wagner (2000: 126-129), Kirchsteiger (1999: 10), White and Etkin (1997: 136), Haller (1996: 336), Schließer (1996: 280), Kloman (1992: 309), Conrad (1988: 133-164) and Karten (1988: 208).

Among the many natural catastrophes which not only threaten society but also the continuity of industrial corporations are climate change, hurricanes & tornados, earthquakes, floods and fires. Geophysical prediction is one attempt to reduce the extent of natural catastrophes. Geophysical prediction is already being scientifically tested with earthquakes in Japan and hurricanes in the US (Conrad, 1988: 149-150). "Risk zone mapping" and "satellite remote sensing" are being employed in India in order to identify, analyse and observe forest fires (Jaiswal et al., 2002: 2).

Unfortunately, possibilities of predicting natural catastrophes have not resulted in a reduction of risk (Karten, 1988: 208). Instead, Grace et al. (2003: 1), Wiedenlübbert (2001: 110-111), Schließer (1996: 281) and Karten (1988: 208) observe a growing risk potential, caused by our civilisation, which needs to be acknowledged and dealt with. Furthermore, Wagner (2000: 129) and Kirchsteiger (1999: 10) argue that the dangerous impact of natural catastrophes is not the catastrophic event itself, but rather the effects it has on areas which are settled and cultivated by humans and the assumed countermeasures. Regrettably, the world population is still growing and this growth is concentrated on predestined natural catastrophe areas (Wiedenlübbert, 2001: 111).

Corporate risk managers have to take into account that insurance capacity is limited and not always raised to sufficient levels following large natural catastrophes. For instance, even though Hurricane Andrew devastated Florida in 1992, hurricane coverage is still not fully available in Florida in 2003. (Grace et al., 2003: 6; Sigma, 2003: 34). In addition to hurricanes, large areas of the US are threatened by earthquakes (Batabyal and Beladi, 2001: 875). However, risk managers are confronted with insurers providing only a limited, insufficient amount of insurance capacity against earthquake risk (Batabyal and Beladi, 2001: 876). Risk management is also required to address the aforementioned insurance capacity restrictions.

#### *2.2.3.2 Risk trend 2 - Characteristic 2: Industrial pollution*

***Industrial pollution*** is identified as a major characteristic of development of risk potential in positive and negative direction by Flanigan (2004: 28-31), Coster and Hankin (2003: 545-550), Harrington and Niehaus (2003: 613-618), Anderson (2002: 158, 170), Kirckpatrick et al. (2002: 111-117), Blondeau (2001: 151), Wiedenlübbert (2001: 120-122, 128-132, 155-156, 160), Kirchsteiger (1999: 8-10), Karten (1998: 227-278), Stam et al. (1998: 371-374), Haller (1996: 333-334), Covello and Merkhofer (1993: 34-49), Conrad (1988: 133-163) and Hoffmann (1985: 7-8).

Although corporations are not directly responsible for natural catastrophes, they can cause severe environmental pollution which endangers not only their ongoing business operations but also "populations and ecosystems" (Kirchsteiger, 1999: 8). Safety of industrial compounds seems to have generally increased however accidents cannot be completely avoided (Stam et al., 1999: 371). The likelihood of an industrial site releasing hazardous material is determined by "operational factors (maintenance, working procedures, level of education), management factors and the technical design" Stam et al. (1998: 372).

Contamination of the environment can have many different origins. Two possible origins are the regular business process and accidents. Examples of environmental contamination through regular business process include the effects of $CO_2$ and Chlorofluorocarbons (Anderson, 2002:

158, 170; Conrad, 1988: 161-162), toxic metals, solvents and pesticides (Covello and Merkhofer, 1993: 36-45). Examples of environmental contamination through accidents consist of the failure of a nuclear power plant as experienced in Harrisburg 1979 and Tschernobyl 1986 (Harrington and Niehaus, 2003: 614; Wiedenlübbert, 2001: 122-128; Kirchsteiger, 1999: 9; Haller, 1996: 333-334; Covello and Merkhofer, 1993: 36, 47-49), fires of a chemical plant, such as in Sandoz in Basel in 1986 (Wiedenlübbert, 2001: 120-122) and oil tanker havarie grosses, for instance of the Amoco Cadiz 1974, Exxon Valdez 1989 and Diamond Grace 1997 (Wiedenlübbert, 2001: 128-132, Kirchsteiger, 1999: 9-10).

Lately, the characteristic "terrorism" explained below adds a new dimension to the industrial pollution problem. For example, the threat of terrorists attacking industrial sites could cause severe environmental damage. Coster and Hankin (2003: 545-550) and Kirckpatrick et al. (2002: 111-117) have extensively examined the effects of "accidental or intentional release of a toxic industrial chemical". The focus of Coster and Hankin and Kirckpatrick et al.'s research is primarily military, however their work could possibly be transferred to industrial corporations. Basis for this knowledge transfer are the direct results of industrial pollution for corporations, which can be major liability claims and image losses (Harrington and Niehaus, 2003: 613; Karten, 1998: 229; Hoffmann, 1985: 7-8).

Environmental protection laws like the "Umwelthaftungsgesetz" (UmweltHG) in Germany have been passed as a consequence of major environmental catastrophes (Wiedenlübbert, 2001: 155-156). The new environmental protection legislation soon led to an increase in legal cases against industrial corporations polluting the environment (Wiedenlübbert, 2001: 160). As a result, industry insurers have developed extended liability insurance solutions for industrial corporations to help these companies deal with this growing problem (Flanigan, 2004: 31; Wiedenlübbert, 2001: 160). Industrial pollution insurance products are currently known as "Environmental Impairment Liability (EIL) insurance" (Flanigan, 2004: 29). An example of an environmental liability product is Gerling's Clean UP Policy (CUP) (Krebs, 2003). EIL insurance solutions for instance are important for industrial corporations in the above mentioned M & A process to compensate the loss in value and clean-up costs of a purchased industrial site which turns out to be contaminated (Flanigan, 2004: 31).

#### *2.2.3.3 Risk trend 2 - Characteristic 3: Terrorism*

***Terrorism*** is recognised as a major characteristic of development of risk potential in positive and negative direction by de Castries (2004: 38), Coster and Hankin (2003: 545-550), De Mey (2003: 66, 67, 69), Doherty et al. (2003: 179-199), Marsh (2003: 4), Reactions (2003), Schettler et al. (2002: 3-31), Kunreuther (2002: 655-664), Sigma (2003a: 8), OECD (2002: 29), Sigma (2002: 14), Property-Casualty (2001: 11), USDOJ (2000: 1-47) and Wagner (2000: 122).

The terror attacks on the world trade centre on $11^{th}$ September 2001 have dramatically changed the risk situation of industrial corporations. Terrorism and related crimes such as sabotage, kidnapping and ransom were already recognised and described prior this date, for example by USDOJ (2000) and Wagner (2000: 122). Previous acts of terrorism led to the assumption that the scope and extent of threat to industrial corporations was calculable and controllable. The financial magnitude of the September 11 loss has changed this perception completely (De Mey, 2003: 67; Sigma, 2002: 14).

Coster and Hankin (2003: 547-548) and USDOJ (2000: 2) describe industrial corporations as suitable terrorist targets due to their potential for the release of harmful substances. Coster and Hankin (2003: 547-549) identify and describe nine factors which determine the vulnerability of industrial sites as terrorist targets. The nine factors are "access, security, visibility, opacity, secondary hazard, robustness, law enforcement response, victim profile, and political value". In addition to the financial impact, the people behind terrorist acts, their motives and future targets are unknown, adding further complexity to fighting the problem (Kunreuther, 2002: 662).

September 11 also revealed industrial corporations' vulnerability towards "operational risks", the importance of "crisis management" and "business continuity management" in the case of such man-made catastrophic events (Schettler et al., 2002: 3-31). As a result, industry corporations find themselves confronted with no or inappropriate terror insurance coverage (Marsh, 2003: 4; De Mey, 2003: 66; Sigma, 2002: 14; Property-Casualty, 2001: 11) and an unstable economic and political environment, nourishing the threat of terrorist acts. Legal reinforcement of terrorism insurance on a national level, for instance, through the US Terrorism Risk Insurance Act (TRIA) (Doherty et al., 2003: 189) to support industrial corporations is still in the early stages of development. Key problems such as pricing the insurance (Reactions, 2003) and defining the government role (de Castries, 2004: 38) so far remain unsolved.

#### *2.2.3.4 Risk trend 2 - Characteristic 4: Technological advancement and failure*

***Technological advancement and failure*** is examined as a major characteristic of development of risk potential in positive and negative direction by Levene (2004), Renn (2004: 103), Marsh (2003: 6), O'Rourke (2003: 8), Pressman (2003: 39), Aarsteinsen (2002, 10), Anderson (2002: 163), Sigma (2002: 14), Stahel (2002: 268-269), Ullberg et al. (2002: 472), Wopperer (2002: 384, 393), Blondeau (2001: 152), Heidenhain (2001: 268), Wiedenlübbert (2001: 196-198), Adams (2000: 313-332), Farny (2000: 92), USDOJ (2000: 1-47), Wagner (2000: 130-133), Pfeiffer (1999: 22), Karten (1998: 199, 215; 1991: 219-226), Schließer (1996: 280), Haller (1995a: 8), Brühwiler (1994: 46), Covello and Merkhofer (1993: 45-65) and Kloman (1992: 309).

Risk management experts widely acknowledge the fact that while attempting to improve our quality of life, in many cases technology fails and creates enormous problems for individuals and corporations. As a result, required "insurance sums and covers are continuously growing", while "risks are becoming more difficult and complex" (Pfeiffer, 1999: 22). At first glance, mobile telephone networks, cloned organs for medical purposes, genetically modified organisms (GMOs) offer tremendous opportunities. However, they also incorporate enormous risks which might come to light when substantial damage to people and companies has occurred (Anderson, 2002: 163; Blondeau, 2001: 152; Wiedenlübbert, 2001: 196-198; Adams 2000: 313-332; Farny, 2000: 92; Karten, 1998: 199, 215; 1991: 219-226; Schließer, 1996: 280; Haller, 1995a: 8; Covello and Merkhofer, 1993: 45-65).

Karten (1991: 220) summarises the risk of GMOs by stating that even though the risk of dangerous organisms is very limited, the consequences of them occurring are enormous. The benefits of information technology for corporations, especially the Internet, are also widely recognised. Yet, this development encompasses "systems risks" (Ullberg et al., 2002: 472), which threaten the availability and stability (Stahel, 2002: 268) of the tools and technologies corporations rely on. Also security gaps facilitate costly virus damage, hacker attacks and system breakdowns (Levene, 2004; O'Rourke, 2003: 8; Pressman, 2003: 39; Aarsteinsen, 2002: 10; Stahel, 2002: 268; Ullberg et al., 2002: 472; Wopperer, 2002: 384; USDOJ, 2000: 19, 43-45; Karten, 1998: 199; Haller, 1995a: 8; Brühwiler, 1994: 46). Promising advances in medical research and treatment are followed by a dramatic increase in maltreatment liability claims (Marsh, 2003: 6).

The provided examples for technical advancement and failure show that the role and use of technology differs amongst various industrial corporations (Wagner, 2000: 132). Bearing the possibilities of technological downfalls in mind, industrial corporations are well advised to adapt their worst case scenarios (Sigma, 2002: 14; Stahel, 2002: 269) and to upgrade existing and new technologies, such as nuclear power plants (Stahel, 2002: 269) and the Internet (Wopperer, 2002: 393). In this context, Wiedenlübbert's (2001: 198) request for an open and active debate regarding technological advancement and failure could become critical for both industrial corporations and industry insurers.

#### *2.2.3.5 Risk trend 2 - Characteristic 5: Societal, political, cultural change*

***Societal***[a]***, political***[b]***, cultural***[c] ***change*** is described as a major characteristic of development of risk potential in positive and negative direction by [c]Daniel (2003: 102-110), [a]Kramer (2003: 8), [b]Minor (2003: 18, 20), [a]Anderson (2002: 175), [b,c]Stahel (2002: 272), [b,c]Ullberg et al. (2002: 472), [a,b,c]Angwin (2001: 36, 55), [a,b]Farny (2000: 92-93), [a,b,c]Wagner (2000: 123, 134), [b]Brealey and Myers (1996: 976-977), [b]Brühwiler (1994: 47), [a]Kloman (1992: 304), [a]Haller (1991: 532), [b]Raffler (1988: 357-398), [b]Karten (1988: 207) and [b]Hoffmann (1985: 7-8).

Corporations are operating in constantly changing business environments. Corporate risk managers have to take into account these environmental differences between every state, region and continent. Attention to differences in business environments should be given not only when operating in a foreign country, but especially when attempting to enter a new market. Industrial corporations have to consider potential societal, political, cultural problems in foreign M & A activities (Angwin, 2001: 36, 55).

One problem existing in some societies is corruption and fraud (Kramer, 2003: 8; Farny, 2000: 92). Changes in consumption, expectations and risk handling within a population might cause increased liability claims, affecting industrial corporations and insurers alike (Farny, 2000: 92; Wagner, 2000: 134). Also, competition and corporate success can be negatively affected by an unforeseen change of regimes, politically-biased public invitations to tender and unfair protection of national industries (Minor, 2003: 19; Farny, 2000: 92). In addition, erupting violence (Stahel, 2002: 272; Farny, 2000: 92; Raffler, 1988: 362; Brühwiler, 1984: 47) and emergence of new diseases (Anderson, 2002: 175; Farny, 2000: 93) are constantly increasing the corporations' business risk. Abruptly imposed trade barriers might lead to severe supply shortages and or sales drops (Wagner, 2000: 123; Farny, 2000: 92; Hoffmann 1985: 7), which can be only partially offset by insurance coverage.

The dramatic results of these developments could even result in a global economic recession, impacting the vast majority of industrial corporations (Minor, 2003: 20; Karten: 1988: 207). Possibilities of insuring corporations against political change are still lacking an in-depth examination (Karten, 1988: 207). The only way corporations can deal proactively with the threat of economic downturn is by preparing themselves against it with the help of insurance and risk management. Brealey and Myers (1996: 976) state that successful global corporations are already shaping their business organisation in order to limit the effects of political risks. Unfortunately, within many companies the social component needed for the worst-case preparation is not far enough developed (Haller, 1991: 532). Reasons for this lack of preparation could lie in differing attitudes towards insurance due to religious and cultural backgrounds as explained by Daniel (2003: 102-110). Managing risk of societal, political and cultural change is therefore an important task for risk managers.

### *2.2.4 Risk trend 3: Problems of the Property and Casualty insurance market*

The difficult situation of the Property and Casualty insurance segment is studied by Dorfman (2002), Geratewohl (1988), Haller (1996, 1995a, 1991), Harrington and Niehaus (2003), Theil (2003, 1996) and others. The literature on this trend distinguishes the following five main characteristics: (1) price & capacity cycles, (2) competitive disadvantages of the industry sector, (3) legal changes, (4) larger catastrophes and (5) new risks. Figure 7 displays this trend, problems of the Property and Casualty insurance market, and its associated characteristics. Each characteristic noted above is defined below.

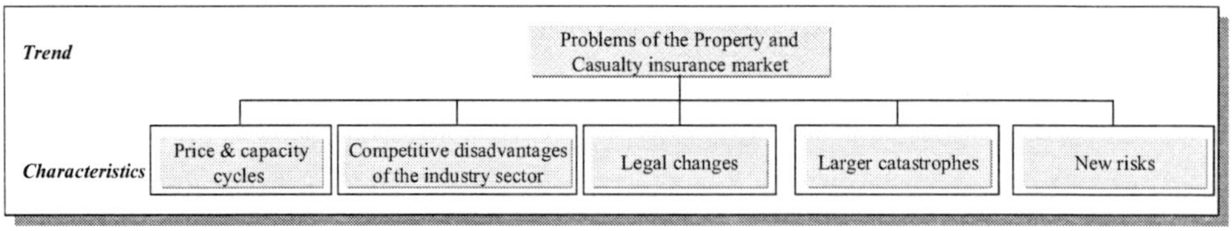


**Figure 7: Characteristics for problems of the Property and Casualty insurance market**

#### 2.2.4.1 *Risk trend 3 - Characteristic 1: Price & capacity cycles*

***Price & capacity cycles*** are explained as a major characteristic of the problems of the Property and Casualty insurance market by Alff (2004: 10, 13, 26; 2002: 2), Kielholz and Murray (2004: 3), Levene (2004), De Mey (2003: 66), Harrington and Niehaus (2003: 148-152), Achleitner et al. (2002: 277-278), Baker (2002: 356), Sigma (2002: 3), Eickstädt (2001: 24-27), Property-Casualty (2001: 5), Zech (2001: 81), Fields et al. (1998: 173), White and Etkin (1997: 158), Theil (1996: 217), Haller (1995a: 11) and Geratewohl (1988: 60).

One of the major characteristics of the P & C (re-) insurance market is the cyclical development of prices and available capacity, called "underwriting cycles" (Alff, 2004: 10; Levene, 2004; Harrington and Niehaus, 2003: 151-152; White and Etkin, 1997: 158; Geratewohl, 1988: 60). For industrial corporations, this cycle means that purchasing insurance cover is not static but varies heavily over time. In a soft phase of the cycle, (re-) insurance capacity is easily available and thus, industry corporations tend to solve their problems by simply purchasing insurance cover (Theil, 1996: 217). In a hard phase of the cycle, (re-) insurance capacity is limited, resulting in sharp price increases (Haller, 1995a: 11). Thus, P & C insurance premiums are assumed to "fluctuate in a cyclical fashion around fair premium levels" (Harrington and Niehaus, 2003: 151; Eickstädt, 2001: 25).

Currently, the P & C insurance market finds itself in a phase where (re-) insurance capacity is very limited (Alff, 2004: 13, 2002: 26; De Mey, 2003: 66; Achleitner et al., 2002: 277-278; Sigma, 2002: 3; Fields et al., 1998: 173). Unlike often proclaimed, the hard market has not exclusively been caused by but only accelerated by the 11$^{th}$ September terror attacks (De Mey, 2003: 66; Sigma, 2002: 3). One reason for the hard insurance market could be reinsurance market problems (Zech, 2001: 81; Fields et al, 1998: 173). Also, pricing for liability insurance is not precise but a vague assessment of the potential risks (Baker, 2002: 356). Unfortunately, the special nature of insurance market cycles is in some cases exploited by insurers in a negative fashion (Kielholz and Murray, 2004: 3). In hard market periods, these market participants are providing highly demanded long-term capacity to the market and generate high revenues. In the soft market period, number and size of losses explode and the company breaks down. Finally, large losses over the last decade have reduced the capital funds of P & C insurers (De Mey, 2003: 66; Sigma, 2002: 3; Property-Casualty, 2001: 5).

In conclusion, underwriting cycles are unfavourably impacting "availability and price" of insurance capacity for industrial corporations (Harrington and Niehaus, 2003: 151). Corporate risk managers have to accept and proactively deal with the negative effects from the unforeseeable movements of the P & C insurance market.

#### *2.2.4.2 Risk trend 3 - Characteristic 2: Competitive disadvantages of the industry sector*

***Competitive disadvantages of the industry sector*** are depicted as a major characteristic of the problems of the Property and Casualty insurance market by Kielholz and Murray (2004: 3), Harrington and Niehaus (2003: 81, 550-569), De Mey (2003: 68-70), Pressman (2003: 40), Schinzler (2003: 5), Achleitner et al. (2002: 275), Alff (2002: 25-26), Aon (2002: 2), Baker (2002: 356), Dorfman (2002: 331-333), Garven (2002: 105-106), Mathmann (2002: 1930), Sigma (2002: 4), Stewart (2002: 293), Ullberg et al. (2002: 472), Wopperer (2002: 392), Blondeau (2001: 152), Eickstädt (2001: 30-31, 101-111), Van den Berghe and Verweire (2001: 179), Wiedenlübbert (2001: 59-62), Hommel (2000: 39-62), Wagner (2000: 386-393), Ward and Zurbruegg (2000: 489-506), Farny (2000: 40-43; 1999: 154-155, 800-804; 1996: 272-273), Hörmann (1999: 80), Steward et al. (1999: 125-126; 130), Karten (1998: 257), Schließer (1996: 282), Kloman (1992: 311), Rejda (1992: 666-667), Mikosch (1991: 178-180), Geratewohl (1988: 61) and Hoffmann (1985: 248).

There is an apparent common belief that the P & C insurance market has structural problems. These insurance industry-specific difficulties can in turn have a negative impact on insurance clients, i.e. industry companies. Industry insurers are faced with the problem of providing and maintaining high quality insurance services and support, as required in remote countries due to the globalisation of their clients, i.e. industrial corporations (Farny, 1996: 272). Existing insurers currently experience competition by "Alternative Risk Transfer" (ART) (Harrington and Niehaus, 2003: 550-569; Sigma, 2002: 4; Farny, 2000: 40-43; Hommel, 2000: 39-40; Farny, 1999: 154-155), "captives" (Alff, 2002: 25; Eickstädt, 2001: 101-111; Hörmann, 1999: 80; Schließer, 1996: 282; Mikosch, 1991: 178-180), "banks" (Rejda, 1992: 666-667), newly founded "virtual insurers" (Garven, 2002: 105-106; Blondeau, 2001: 152; Farny, 2000: 43; Steward, 1999: 125-126) and the intrusion of "Third Party Administrators" into the insurance value chain (Blondeau; 2001: 152).

For example, captives are professional insurance companies owned by and operated exclusively on behalf of individual, large industrial corporations (Karten, 1998: 257; Mikosch, 1991: 178; Hoffmann, 1985: 248). Reason for industrial corporations to run a captive is their improved capability to bear risk themselves (Karten, 1998: 257).

The core competency of industry insurers, i.e. effective knowledge and management of hazards, is increasingly missing (Kloman, 1992: 311). Therefore, P & C insurers often do not fulfil their role as "crisis managers" (Stewart, 2002: 293) but instead "run away from losses" (Baker, 2002: 356). When it comes to major catastrophes, the insurance industry is punished with heavy "compensatory and punitive damages" (Kielholz and Murray, 2004: 3; Geratewohl, 1988: 61). In addition, these claims have to be settled "from taxed reserves" (Schinzler, 2003: 5). Scientific evidence supports the fact that the insurance industry can have a highly positive impact on an economy (Ward and Zurbruegg, 2000: 491). Insurance can reduce risk-adversity and thus enables investments, employment and innovations (Ward and Zurbruegg, 2000: 491). But the general public's attitude seems to neglect this unequal treatment, since insurers are "mean and evil" (Kielholz and Murray, 2004: 3). Wiedenlübbert (2001: 59-62) examines reasons for the negative opinion about the insurance industry. Wiedenlübbert (2001: 60) believes the public's negative attitude "is based on a "cliché". This negative attitude remains unaffected by positive examples such as the insurance industry's quick claims handling of major catastrophes, as seen for instance after the Munich hail storm in 1984. In addition to the public's negative perception of insurance, governments tend not to provide stimulating incentives for risk aware corporations. Governments' negative attitude is reflected in increased state insurance taxes. For example, the German government increased the general insurance tax level from 5% in 1988 to 16% in 2002 (Aon, 2002: 2; Eickstädt, 2001: 30).

Recently, a simultaneous occurrence of both "investment and underwriting risks" (De Mey, 2003: 68; Achleitner et al., 2002: 275) cast serious doubt on the existing models of "Asset-Liability-Management" (ALM) strategies (Wagner, 2000: 386-393; Farny, 2000: 800-804) of industry insurers. Both "underwriting and claims management skills" are essential, but have been neglected in the past (De Mey, 2003: 69). P & C insurers experience competition from related industries via financial convergence and over the Internet (Harrington and Niehaus, 2003: 81; Schinzler, 2003: 5; Dorfman, 2002: 331-333; Garven, 2002: 105-106; Ullberg et al., 2002: 472; Van den Berghe and Verweire, 2001: 179; Farny, 2000: 434; Steward et al., 1999: 130). The "outdated technology" (Pressman, 2003: 40; Mathmann, 2002: 1930) and the commitment lacking towards customer-centric e-solutions (Garven, 2002: 105-106; Wopperer, 2002: 392) result in the industry's ineffectiveness (De Mey, 2003: 70).

The structural problems described are a competitive disadvantage for the insurance industry, if not properly addressed and dealt with by an effective risk management. Those having to bear the consequences are the clients of industry insurers, i.e. industrial corporations.

### *2.2.4.3 Risk trend 3 - Characteristic 3: Legal changes*

***Legal changes*** are described as a major characteristic of the problems of the Property and Casualty insurance market by de Castries (2004: 39), Hohlfeld (2004: 78, 82, 86; 2002: 6), Kielholz and Murray (2004: 4), Harrington and Niehaus (2003: 96-114), Sigma (2003b: 3, 5-6), Theil (2003: 154), Willis (2003: 21, 23), Dorfman (2002: 135), Garven (2002: 68, 70, 114-115), Manghetti (2002: 316-317), Strejcek and Theil (2002: 305-313), Wopperer (2002: 392), Lohse (2001: 10), Van den Berghe and Verweire (2001: 180), Wiedenlübbert (2001: 51), Wagner (2000: 122-123), Ward and Zurbruegg (2000: 492, 504), Farny (1999: 151), Pottier and Sommer (1999: 623-624, 640), Schließer (1996: 289-299) and Rejda (1992: 646).

Industry insurers, like other corporations, are subject to legal risks of the foreign countries in which they operate (Wagner, 2000: 122-123). The P & C insurance industry worldwide is currently undergoing a challenging legal transition. Reasons for this transition are the missing world-wide accepted rules for minimum capital requirements and e-insurance (Garven, 2003: 68, 70; Wopperer, 2002: 392). Under these circumstances, insurance and reinsurance company ratings increase in importance and exclusions to electronic risks are introduced (Willis, 2003: 21, 23).

Importance in insurance company ratings might increase for "solving growing market intransparencies and decision problems" between "insurers, customers and brokers" (Sigma, 2003b: 5; Wiedenlübbert, 2001: 51; Pottier and Sommer, 1999: 623-624). Additional stakeholders benefiting from insurance company ratings include investors and regulators (Sigma, 2003b: 3; Pottier and Sommer, 1999: 623). The four most notable P & C insurance company rating agencies are A.M. Best, Standard & Poor's, Moody's and Fitch (Sigma, 2003b: 6; Pottier and Sommer, 1999: 625). By using insurance company ratings, insurers seem to attempt to reduce stakeholders' concerns regarding their particular "level of insolvency risk" (Pottier and Sommer, 1999: 640).

Existing regulatory standards are inconsistent within Europe and the rest of the world (Ward and Zurbruegg, 2000: 492, 504; Schließer, 1996: 292, 299). Plus, they are lacking adaptability and competitiveness (de Castries, 2004: 39). For instance in the US, the insurance industry is highly regulated on a state level and a vivid debate about harmonising the regulation on a federal level persists (Harrington and Niehaus, 2003: 104-106). Reasons for insurance regulation according to Dorfman (2002: 135) and Rejda (1992: 646) are bankruptcy countermeasures, handling of knowledge discrepancies between insurers and customers, insurance pricing issues and public reasons. Similarly, Theil (2003: 154) sees "consumer protection" as the main goal of insurance regulation in order to reduce risk judgement deficits. Contrary to the US, Hohlfeld (2002: 6) and Farny (1999: 151) point out that after 1994, deregulation has taken place in Europe. While deregulation in the EU provides insurers with increased "autonomy", it also resulted in tremendous competitive pressure and intransparency (Hohlfeld, 2002: 6; Lohse, 2001: 10; Farny, 1999: 151).

In addition to deregulation, effects of the new phenomenon "e-government" as described by Strejcek and Theil (2002: 305-313) on the insurance and financial services industry are unforeseeable. The results of the insurance legislature transition are also unpredictable. Kielholz and Murray (2004: 4) go even further and argue that insurers lack the insight of the surrounding "legal environment". Legal changes will hopefully have a positive impact on "insurance regulation" (Garven, 2003: 68, 70) and "financial market supervision" (Manghetti, 2002: 316-317; Van den Berghe and Verweire, 2001: 180). The success of insurance regulators depends on finding the right balance of "efficient, fair, safe and stable insurance markets" while at the same time not imposing too much regulation (Hohlfeld, 2004: 86). As a result of insurance internationalisation, insurance regulators are now cooperating under the International Association of Insurance Supervisors (IAIS) on a worldwide level and reinsurance supervision is increasing in importance (Hohlfeld, 2004: 78, 82; 2002: 6).

Current uncertainties about the importance of insurance ratings and the future legal framework including regulatory and deregulatory effects of the insurance industry could pose a threat to corporate P & C insurance capacity buyers, i.e. industrial corporations.

#### *2.2.4.4 Risk trend 3 - Characteristic 4: Larger catastrophes*

***Larger catastrophes*** are recognised as a major characteristic of the problems of the Property and Casualty insurance market by Kunreuther and Pauly (2004: 18), Schinzler (2003: 2), Sigma (2003a: 8-9), Sigma (2002: 6), Kunreuther (2002: 661), Eickstädt (2001: 34-35), Zech (2001: 72), Haller (1996: 333-334; 1991: 565) and Schließer (1996: 279-281).

The size of catastrophes P & C insurers have to deal with for their clients, industrial corporations, is constantly growing on a global scale (Schinzler, 2003: 2; Schließer, 1996: 280-281). The size of natural catastrophes have reached tremendous levels, for instance the floods in central Europe in 2002 (Sigma, 2003a: 8-9) or the hurricanes Martin & Lothar in 1999 (Sigma, 2002: 6). Insurance capacity limits are reached by the continuous growth of risk potential (Eickstädt, 2001: 34-35). Kunreuther (2002: 661) points out that major catastrophes such as Hurricane Andrew and the California Northridge earthquake led to the creation of government insurance pools as a result of the lacking capacity by private insurers. In addition, the size of other catastrophes such as fires, pollution, etc. appears to be increasing as well (Zech, 2001: 72). These changes cannot be neglected by any stakeholders, i.e. industry insurers, industrial corporations and the public.

Unfortunately, industrial corporations need to face the reality that there is a positive correlation between handling risks and increased new risks (Schließer, 1996: 279; Haller, 1991: 565). "State insurance commissioners, ... insurance trade associations and consumer advocacy organisations" should play an active role in this mindset change, in order to convince corporate risk managers' to have a proactive behaviour against major catastrophic events (Kunreuther and Pauly, 2004: 18).

#### *2.2.4.5 Risk trend 3 - Characteristic 5: New risks*

***New risks*** are discussed as a major characteristic of the problems of the Property and Casualty insurance market by Alff (2004: 13, 2002: 26), Geipel-Kern (2004: 73), Kielholz and Murray (2004: 1), Levene (2004), Risk Perception (2004: 11), Doherty et al. (2003: 182, 185, 198), Harrington and Niehaus (2003: 149-150), Achleitner et al. (2002: 277), Alff (2002: 26), Anderson (2002: 170), Baker (2002: 352), Jablonowski (2002: 27), OECD (2002: 126), Eickstädt (2001: 34), White and Etkin (1997: 152), Brühwiler (1994: 49) and Raphael (1994: 129-161).

Apparently over the last few years, the risk environment of industrial corporations has grown by a component of new, previously unknown risks. Anticipating, calculating and controlling these new threats, for example global warming, intellectual capital lawsuits or terrorism (Levene, 2004; Doherty et al., 2003: 182; Achleitner et al., 2002: 277; Anderson, 2002: 170; OECD, 2002: 126; White and Etkin, 1997: 152) is in many cases not possible for insurance and industry corporations. Yet, Harrington and Niehaus (2003: 150) mention that "fair premiums depend on expected future claim costs and underwriting expenses". Information on new risks such as terrorism or natural catastrophes therefore has an impact on insurance corporations' premium calculation (Harrington and Niehaus, 2003: 150).

However, new risks like the September 11 terror attacks are responsible for "massive property loss, business interruption, workers compensation and potential open-ended liability losses, all of which are extremely difficult to estimated with any accuracy" (Doherty et al., 2003: 182). Insuring new risks is difficult or even impossible, due to lacking claims experience (Eickstädt, 2001: 34).

The costs arising from unknown risks can be enormous, and therefore pose a big challenge to risk managers (Jablonowski, 2002: 27). A good illustrative example is asbestos (Baker, 2002: 352; Brühwiler, 1994: 49; Raphael, 1994; 129-161). Asbestos was initially seen as an ideal isolation material, used in a wide range of products ranging from the construction to automotive industry over many years (Raphael, 1994: 130). In the 1930s, medical reports already suggested (Brühwiler, 1994: 49; Raphael, 1994: 131-132) the deadly effects of asbestos. However, when it finally became evident that asbestos could cause asbestosis and cancer, the damage had already been done (Raphael, 1994: 130). In the first wave of liability claims, individuals whose health was negatively affected by asbestos received financial compensation from responsible corporations and their liability insurers (Kielholz and Murray, 2004: 1). Now that the primary claims of asbestos-affected individuals are increasingly settled, the new phenomenon of "liability without fault" (Kielholz and Murray, 2004: 1) arises. Liability without fault means according to Kielholz and Murray (2004: 1) that companies are being sued and punished for potentially damaging individuals' health in the future. Both industrial corporations and industry insurers need to be blamed for not reacting quickly enough on the evidence of the new liability risk of asbestos. However, knowledge about the serious health threats did not stop manufactures' from producing asbestos, nor did it end liability insurers from covering asbestos manufacturers (Raphael, 1984: 129-161). As a result of the changing legal environment and the growing number of law suits from asbestos victims, a large number of producers and liability insurers have already become or will in the near future become insolvent (Brühwiler, 1994: 52; Raphael, 1994: 161).

The effects of new, unforeseen risks for industrial corporations and industry insurers should also be kept in mind during the currently hot debate regarding nanotechnology. Nanotechnology according to Risk Perception (2004: 11) and Geipel-Kern (2004: 73) is the art of constructing and employing particles which are less then 100 nanometres of size. The particles' small size gives them unique chemical features, allowing the construction of new groundbreaking products. Possible areas for applying nanoparticles range across a wide spectrum of industries, e.g. automobile, construction, textile, medicine, energy, environment and cosmetics (Geipel-Kern,

2004: 74-78). Due to their extremely small size, nanoparticles have a previously unimagined ability to enter and influence the human body as well as the environment (Risk Perception, 2004: 15-32). However, risks of extremely small particles which can virtually enter all parts of the human body or other substances are only slowly becoming acknowledged and might only come to light when major damage has already occurred (Risk Perception, 2004: 43). As a consequence, similarities between the effects of asbestos and nanotechnology on the insurance industry and industrial corporations are already drawn (Risk Perception, 2004: 42-43).

In summary, severity of new risk catastrophes has reduced the capital reserves of industry insurers (Alff, 2004: 13, 2002: 26; Raphael, 1994: 161). Sharp reduction of capital reserves due to occurrence of new risk, as witnessed in the September 11 terror attacks ultimately has the potential to cause industry insurer insolvency (Doherty et al., 2003: 185, 198). In the case of industry insurer insolvency, increase in risk potential of new risks also affects industrial corporations which rely on the financial stability of their insurers in the case of a potential damage.

## 2.3 Linking knowledge management with risk management

The three risk trends described in detail above threaten industrial corporations and therefore need to be dealt with by applying the appropriate risk management measures. Risk management measures in this book are suggested tools to avoid, compensate or mitigate threats. As Karten (1978: 38, 41) states, "nearly any [insurance or risk management] publication provides its own catalogue of risk management measures". Haller (1975: 43, 179) further explains that the scientific roots of risk management measures date back to the 1920s. Various risk management measures are available for industrial corporations. However, the issues are locating, understanding and implementing the appropriate set of risk management measures for the risks threatening the corporation. Risk avoidance, compensation or mitigation seem to be three dominant appropriate measures for risk managers in industrial corporations and thus suitable for the ongoing discussion.

A necessity exists to "incorporate the data from risk assessment studies" in order to "reduce losses" and provide "protection against extreme events" (Kunreuther, 2002: 659). One way to provide industrial corporations with the right knowledge and expertise about the available and appropriate risk management measures is through effective knowledge management. This risk management knowledge transfer might be achievable by combining the roles of risk and knowledge managers (Louisot, 2004). Aim of this book is the examination of the possible applicability of certain knowledge management concepts, i.e. lessons learned and best practices, within the existing risk management discipline. Overlaps of the two broad scientific fields knowledge management and risk management are depicted in Figure 8: Possible overlaps of risk management & knowledge management disciplines.

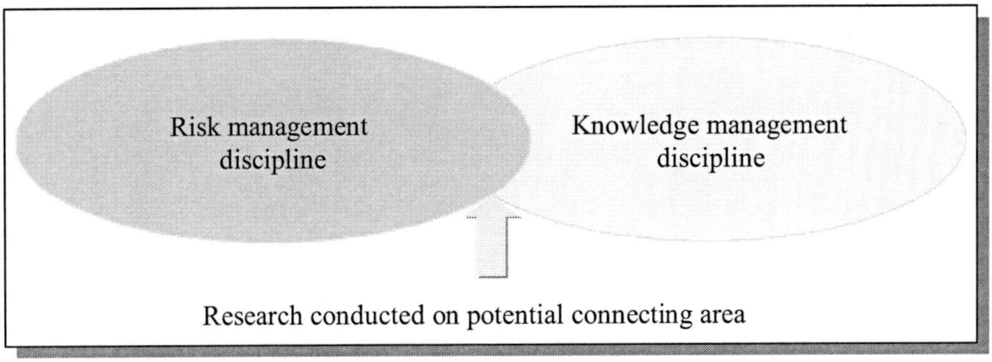


**Figure 8: Possible overlaps of risk management & knowledge management disciplines**

### *2.3.1 Introduction of knowledge management within the research framework*

It is a widespread belief that knowledge management is a key success factor and necessary for the survival of corporations (Patton, 2002: 329-336; Seufert et al., 2002: 151; Tuomi, 2002: 11-12; Bhatt, 2001: 68-75; Bollinger and Smith, 2001: 8-18; Güldenberg, 2001: 2; Lang, 2001: 43-57; Davies, 2000: 62; Carayannis and Alexander, 1999: 198; Sage and Rouse, 1999: 205; Gerling: 1986: 195, 205). As Carayannis and Alexander (1999: 198) point out, "knowledge can be transferred between firms or individuals, like other forms of currency". The key distinction of knowledge is that after the transfer has taken place, it is possessed by "both the donor and the recipient" of the knowledge (Carayannis and Alexander, 1999: 198). Thus the unique feature of knowledge is that it can increase in value by simply being shared (Carayannis and Alexander, 1999: 198-199). The value increasing aspect of knowledge sharing between insurance and industrial corporations is always considered in the remaining parts of this book. Knowledge is divided into two parts: "explicit" and "tacit / implicit" knowledge (McBriar et al., 2003: 31;

Seufert et al., 2002: 133; Bollinger and Smith, 2001: 8-18; Lang, 2001: 43-57; Hall, 2001: 19-32). Explicit knowledge represents all structured, codifiable corporate information which in general can be stored in a database (McBriar et al., 2003: 31; Seufert et al., 2002: 133; Bollinger and Smith, 2001: 8-18; Lang, 2001: 43-57; Davies, 2000: 62; Krebs, 2000: 128-129). On the other hand, tacit or implicit knowledge consists of the unarticulated experiences, know-how and expertise existing in the minds of the employees of a corporation (McBriar et al., 2003: 31; Seufert et al., 2002: 138; Bollinger and Smith, 2001: 8-18; Davies, 2000: 62). A large portion of the research on knowledge management tries to answer the question of how tacit knowledge is converted into useful explicit knowledge (Güldenberg, 2001: 234; Sage and Rouse, 1999: 213). In contrast, this book focuses on the effective capturing and usage of explicit risk management knowledge to provide insight into the effective selection and application of available and appropriate risk management measures to avoid, compensate or mitigate risks. Hence, conversion of tacit risk management knowledge to explicit risk management knowledge is not a focus of this book. Two prerequisites for the successful introduction of knowledge management within industry insurers and industrial corporations are worth mentioning. At first, the existence of an organisational environment that is committed to constant learning, as described by Apfelthaler et al. (2002: 108) and Senge (1990) is required. Secondly, the recognition of the resulting knowledge from the organisational learning process as a key success factor (Gerling, 1986: 195, 205). Numerous examples of the practical introduction of corporate knowledge management already exist in the literature but a focus on risk management appears to be lacking. An extensive case study collection on knowledge management in other corporate processes and disciplines is provided by Bellmann et al. (2002). The know-how offered in this collection could be helpful to introduce the knowledge-based risk management process explained below to industry insurers' business operations.

Patton (2002: 329-336) and Bhatt (2001: 65-68) argue that knowledge management can be applied through best practices and lessons learned. Definition of best practices and lessons learned vary in the literature. Neumann et al. (2002: 5), for instance, define lessons learned as "areas of conflict, which were exposed as barriers for the realisation of knowledge management". Lessons learned for Kirchsteiger (1999: 13) are experiences gained from industrial accidents, which might help to prevent future catastrophes if successfully "implemented in industrial practices". Best practices represent "the ability to realise organisationally specific knowledge in the form of intelligent and innovative products and/or services". Best practices and lessons learned are defined for this book as follows: Best practices are reusable examples of how an industrial corporation was able to avoid, to compensate for or to mitigate a threat arising through the three above described risk trends. Lessons learned are reusable experiences of industrial corporations, where the mechanisms of avoidance, compensation and mitigation regarding the three above described risk trends failed, leading to damage to an industrial corporation. Successful engineering insurers, for instance, require lessons learned and best practices from technological progress (Heidenhain, 2001: 271). Insurance sales organisations need information about best practices of their best sales people in order to increase customer loyalty as well as lessons learned from lost insurance contracts (Venohr, 1995: 71). Other industries, such as consumer goods producer Whirlpool, already employ lessons learned and best practices within their organisational learning and development programmes (Duarte and Snyder, 1997: 51-55). Gathering lessons learned can be achieved through root cause analysis (Venohr, 1995: 71), that is by uncovering the main reasons for accidents and their full consequences. In conclusion, industry insurers' future core competency lies in "knowledge, talent and technology", rather than previously in "assets and financial strength" (Van den Berghe, 1996: 60). In order to provide suitable as well as comparable examples for knowledge management in practice, the theoretic part of this book looks at lessons learned and best practices as equally important components of knowledge. This assumption seems justified because both avoiding negative experiences in the first place through best practices as well as learning from negative experiences and avoiding them in the future are important in the business context.

### *2.3.2 Introduction of benchmarking within the research framework*

Collecting lessons learned and best practices for the avoidance, compensation and mitigation of the three risk trends can be obtained by examining benchmark companies. Like lessons learned and best practices, various definitions for benchmarking appear in the literature. In Güldenberg's (2001: 266-268) extensive examination of knowledge management and knowledge controlling in learning organisations, benchmarking is defined as an analysis and planning tool, providing individual corporations with process comparison and learnings from best-in-class corporations. Drew (1997: 427) uses Main's (1992: 102-106) benchmarking definition, i.e. "the art of finding out, in a perfectly legal and aboveboard way, how others do something better than you do – so you can imitate – and perhaps improve upon – their technique". Lohse (2001: 82-99) describes benchmarking as a management technique used for studying and benefiting from best possible solutions. Thus, "benchmarking seeks out, internalizes and improves upon competitors' best-practice capabilities" (Drew, 1997: 427).

Current benchmarking theory is also supported by practical references. The Benchmarking Exchange (TBE, 2004), a US-based industry benchmarking platform, extends the benchmarking definition by selecting any organisation as a potential benchmark, rather than limiting it solely to competitors. The scope across multiple industries ensures that valuable knowledge can be transferred between unrelated industries while at the same time avoiding negative influences from industry-internal problems (TBE, 2004). The Public Sector Benchmarking Service (PSBS, 2004), a UK-based governmental organisation defines benchmarking as an "effective tool for bringing about collaborative approaches to resolving common problems". Finally, consulting company Best Practices LLC defines benchmarking as the "process of seeking out and studying the best internal practices that produce superior performance" (Best Practices, 2004). Benchmarking allows corporations to "compare their processes, identify gaps in performance and discover proven tactics and winning strategies for closing those gaps" (Best Practices, 2004). In addition to benchmarking best practices (TBA, 2004), benchmarking lessons learned (PSBS, 2004; Best Practices, 2004) is an important aspect of this book, since knowledge consists of both best practices and lessons learned. Another benchmarking association, with a focus on providing corporations with the most effective risk management processes, exists with the International Risk Management Benchmarking Association™ (IRMBA, 2004). In summary, all of the four benchmarking platforms presented have in common that they offer knowledge sharing of benchmarking examples across different industries, business processes and functions and that they successfully operate in practice.

Benchmark companies in the context of this book are corporations which have effectively limited the threats of the three risk trends (1) the emergence of increasingly complex and bigger corporate structures, (2) the development of risk potential in positive and negative direction and (3) the problems of the Property and Casualty insurance market.

Various forms of benchmark companies exist and each form has distinct advantages and disadvantages. Güldenberg (2001: 267) notes that benchmark companies might exist in different countries, industries and positions of the supply chain. Drew (1997: 429) suggests a suitable categorisation of the sources of benchmarks and their individual benefits and drawbacks. Drew's (1997: 429) categorisation is depicted in Table 4. The five designated partner types are potentially available to industry insurers and industrial corporations when searching for appropriate risk management benchmarks in dealing with the three risk trends. For this study, partner type focus will be on the same and or related company classes. Company class is determined by the proceeding three criteria: (1) commercial register information (company name, legal form, principal office, address and branch), (2) Number of employees, operations in Austria/Europe/Worldwide, revenues in previous business year and (3) SIC code. Therefore, company class is related to two types of partners identified by Drew: competitor and related industry.

| Type of partner | Benefits | Drawbacks |
|---|---|---|
| Internal | • Breaking down internal barriers<br>• Improved communication and information sharing<br>• Ease of access to partner, cost | • Does not identify global 'best practices'<br>• Internal politics/'turfguarding' |
| Competitor | • As part of consortium can share costs and effort<br>• Ease of identifying partners<br>• Opening up to ideas from outside | • Legal, proprietary issues |
| Related industry | • Study of 'best practices' in generic functional or business process management<br>• As with competitors (above) | • Legal, proprietary issues<br>• Harder to identify partners |
| Unrelated industry | • As for a related industry, but you may have a greater chance of discovering new ideas and breakthroughs | • Harder to identify appropriate partners |
| International | • Identifies global 'best practices'<br>• As with unrelated industry (above) | • Cost, time, effort<br>• Difficulty of identifying partners |

**Table 4: Benefits and drawbacks of different benchmarking partners (Drew, 1997: 429)**

Even though benchmarking is not a new phenomenon, its importance has recently grown due to "global competition, development of information technology, databases and networks" (Drew, 1997: 428). While these environmental changes seem to be enablers for the effective use of benchmarking, they also seem to be incorporated in risk trends one, increasing corporate complexity and risk trend two, growing risk potential, threatening industrial corporations today. Thus, these environmental changes affect the perceived risk threats of risk trends one and two. So far, insurance companies seem to lag behind in using the above mentioned opportunities and capabilities of benchmarking (Lohse, 2001: 92). With the focus on gathering suitable lessons learned and best practices benchmarks for their customers, this research framework tries to address and work on this deficit.

Finally, benchmarking can be conducted in differing ways and does not follow a structured process map (PSBS, 2004). Typical steps normally used on benchmarking projects according to PSBS (2004) include:

- Planning
- Collecting data & information
- Analysing the findings
- Recommendations - making & doing
- Monitoring & reviewing

The flexibility of the benchmarking process allows its tailoring to individual organisations' "overall approach to continuous improvement and background culture" (PSBS, 2004). Concluding, following the benchmarking methodology in the course of this book attempts to assure that results meet both academic, as well as practical standards.

### *2.3.3 Lessons learned and best practices for each risk trend and characteristic pair*

The following Figure 9: Lessons learned and best practices matrix is extracted from Appendix 3: State of the field research matrix for corporate risk trends and graphically displayed. Chosen lessons learned and best practices demonstrate how appropriate risk management measures can be extracted in a structured way from corporate risk management literature. Empty fields in the research matrix represent knowledge gaps regarding lessons learned and best practices in the literature. McBriar et al. (2003: 30) define knowledge gaps as "the difference between the knowledge that an organisation needs to fulfil its obligations and the knowledge that an organisation possesses as a result of employing staff or maintaining other forms of knowledge resource". McBriar et al.'s knowledge gap definition stems from Senge's definition of learning gaps. Senge (1990: 252-253) defines learning gaps as the difference between "what is known and what needs to be known". Knowledge gaps in the research matrix are continuously eliminated over time by examining broader literature sources and when industry corporations and insurers make regular use of the knowledge-based risk management process.

Completed fields in the research matrix in Table 2 identify lessons learned and best practices corresponding to a specific characteristic of one of the three risk trends. How transferring and applying these lessons learned and best practices can help comparable industrial corporations to deal with the characteristics of the three risk trends (complex corporate structures, development of risk potential and problems of the P & C insurance market) is explained and examined in Chapter 4: Knowledge-based risk management process.

| Trends & Characteristics | Lessons learned (Root cause analysis) | Best practices |
|---|---|---|
| **Complex and bigger corporate structures** | | |
| Networked economy | • "The following case was reported by the police in Heidelberg, Germany. Swindlers ordered from a computer company goods valued at some millions of euros. The company delivered at once and never received the payment due. The gangsters hardly left any trace. All information that they gave to the e-mail server was incorrect. Personal data mostly is not verified by the companies that offer online services. Many of them only check if the data given are plausible and could theoretically be correct. At the German police academy in Freiburg, the police are learning how they can trace the perpetrators in such cases through communication protocols of e-mail service companies and access providers.", Wopperer (2002: 388)<br>• "If consumers' data become accessible, for example, you need a rapid way of identifying what the fault is and where its origin lies. Regular testing of security systems is necessary to ensure that all systems are working properly and no violations have taken place. Encryption disguises data in a way that protects anyone from reading it without the respective key. In principle, an encrypted credit card number cannot be read without the key to unencrypted it. The most sophisticated type of encryption is Public Key Infrastructure as well as digital signatures.", Wopperer (2002: 389) | "Amongst insurers, the Cologne-based Gerling Group has taken the position of a forerunner with its "Trusted Shops" which is a joint venture with a consulting company. "Trusted Shops" was created in late 1999 in close co-operation with consumer protection agencies and with the support of the European Commission. Amongst other features like certification of online-shops and various customer services, "Trusted Shops" offers a money-back guarantee (underwritten by Gerling) to online customers. All participating shops have to meet strict demands as to data security and delivery, and to refund payment to the customer in the event of non-delivery or return of goods within due time. Moreover, it requires the supplier to provide the customer with a contact person if problems should arise, price transparency, general terms and conditions of trade that are easy to understand, as well as prompt customer service. […]. Renowned international companies are members of "Trusted Shops". By October 2001, more than 250,000 customers had already used "Trusted Shops"; 250 online shops were already certified, and another 180 were in the process of certification. More than 1,000 buyers a day with a purchase volume of €130 on average register for the money-back guarantee. "Trusted Shops" is active at international level, among others in major European markets like the U.K., France and Germany.", Wopperer (2002: 389-390) |
| Shareholder Value | "Following the Enron investigation, the SEC drastically reduced the accounting deadlines for filing quarterly and annual reports. Reporting duties which become too burdensome could have a detrimental effect on the quality of the data. I believe that there is an area of conflict, or even a conflict of interests between:<br>o the scope and complexity of reporting;<br>o the quality of the date; and<br>o the time that is available to draw up the reports.<br>The acceleration of reporting is certainly in the best interests of companies; in markets that change rapidly, the survivors will be those who know at all times how they stand and how matters may develop. Fast close is, therefore, an understandable matter of concern. Fast close, however, means not just optimised processes and systems, and having the financial resources to create them. | |

**Figure 9: Lessons learned and best practices matrix**

| Trends & Characteristics | Lessons learned (Root cause analysis) | Best practices |
|---|---|---|
| Shareholder Value (continued) | "Fast close also requires well-trained staff who knows what they are doing. Above all, it demands the right prerequisites. Specifically, this means an appropriate and co-ordinated regulatory framework established by governments, standard-setting bodies and supervisory authorities.", Schinzler (2003: 4) | |
| Multiple Economic systems | | |
| Globalisation | "The same logic applies to the incentive of divisions of firms to invest in protection against a catastrophic accident that could bankrupt the entire organization. The actions of Nick Leeson and the trader he hired at the Barings Futures Singapore office were primarily responsible for bringing down Barings Bank. Arthur Anderson was sent into bankruptcy by the actions of its Houston branch. Both these examples illustrate this type of contamination. If a division knows that other divisions in the firm are not investing in protection, it has less incentive to incur these costs than if the other units were investing in safety measures. There may thus be a need for centralized organizational controls or third-party inspections from outside the firm to deal with this situation.", Kunreuther (2002: 663-664) | |
| Mergers & Acquisitions | | |
| **Development of risk potential in positive and negative direction** | | |
| Natural catastrophes | "To mitigate against the consequences of natural disasters one can build safer structures or move out of harm's way", Kunreuther (2002: 662) | • "If the private sector feels it cannot provide insurance protection against losses from catastrophic events, then one may need some type of government pooling arrangement to cover theses losses. The Florida Hurricane Catastrophe Fund was established by Florida following Hurricane Andrew when a number of insurers claimed that they could not in the future include windstorm coverage as part of the standard homeowner coverage (Lecomte and Gahagan, 1998). After the 1994 California Northridge earthquake, insurers had similar reaction to providing |

**Figure 9: Lessons learned and best practices matrix (continued)**

| Trends & Characteristics | Lessons learned (Root cause analysis) | Best practices |
|---|---|---|
| Natural catastrophes (continued) | | earthquake coverage in California. In 1996, the state formed the California Earthquake Authority, which offers homeowners earthquake coverage as a separate polity (Roth, 1998). At the national level, a successful example of the use of an insurance pool is the one that provides coverage against losses from nuclear power plant accidents in the United States. Under the Price-Anderson Act, a group of private insurers agreed to provide coverage to utility companies for losses that can total up to $8.2 billion (U.S. Congress, 1995).", Kunreuther (2002: 661) |
| Industrial pollution | • "Chlorofluorocarbons (CFCs) and dichlorodiphenyltrichloroethane (DDT) are examples of environmentally harmful substances that have been removed from business processes and products in many countries. Their removal required direct regulation because it was so difficult to identify the specific responsible parties (manufacturers, users) with the environmental harm (ozone depletion, decreasing bird population). For those unregulated substances that are potentially harmful to the environment, loss-control expertise could be applied to assist in developing techniques for the removal or reduction of such substances from business processes.", Anderson (2002: 158)<br>• "In the case of chemical accidents, one can reduce the inventory level and/or production of specific toxins to lower the risk of another mishap occurring", Kunreuther (2002: 662) | • "...companies like International Paper and Westvaco that have eliminated elemental chlorine in their paper-bleaching mills (Hilton and Marlin, 1997). By eliminating the elemental chlorine environmental risk "upstream", it will not be present to cause environmental costs 'downstream'.", Anderson (2002: 157) |
| Terrorism | | • "There is an additional challenge associated with allocating resources for dealing with terrorism. Due to our deeply rooted fear, we may not adequately take into account the extraordinarily small likelihood that we will be impacted by a future attack. Hence the government invests huge sums of money in protection to provide reassurance. This may not be the most cost-effective way to utilize our resources. In this sense, Mayor Guiliani's constant reassurances to New Yorkers following the September 11 attacks on the World Trade Center may have done more to reduce the social amplifications of risk than millions of dollars of expenditures on pseudo-protective measures such as stationing the National Guard at airports and train stations.", Kunreuther (2002: 662) |

**Figure 9: Lessons learned and best practices matrix (continued)**

| Trends & Characteristics | Lessons learned (Root cause analysis) | Best practices |
|---|---|---|
| Technological advancement and failure | "Avoidance is a risk management control tool that often cannot be utilised for obvious practical reasons. […]. On the other hand, avoidance can be a very practical tool for developers and users of GMO technology, as firms have a choice. For instance, earlier in this article, Gerber, Heinz, McDonald's, and Frito-Lay were discussed regarding their decisions to discontinue using GM ingredients in their foods. ", Anderson (2002: 168) | "One option for the industry would be to assist in educating the public and the politicians to understand the need to reduce greenhouse gas emissions as speedily as possible. Other efforts should go into monitoring and research activities that can enable us to adapt to the climate changes to which our actions have already committed us. The first issue for all players in the industry (and its regulators) to face is that climate change will increase the level of uncertainty. Accepting this proposition will require traditional responses such as reserve accumulation, loss reduction and so on. ", White and Etkin (1997: 159) |
| Societal, political, cultural change | • "The education effort may be the most important factor of the legislation. According to study by The St. Paul Companies of St. Paul, Minnesota, U.S. companies continue to underestimate risks involved with e-commerce and do not adequately train employees to deal with them. Risk managers at many companies have insufficient knowledge of technology-related risks, generally leaving that concern to information technology managers. As a result, only about half of risk managers surveyed have reviewed their existing insurance policies to determine their level of coverage for Internet liability exposure.", O'Rourke (2003: 8)<br>• "One conclusion is therefore that the problem of culture, and promoting cultural ecology, should be given much greater attention by politicians.", Stahel (2002: 272) | "A few basic techniques to mitigate political risk include:<br>• Contractual undertakings with the host governments. Although contracts cannot prevent a government from exercising its sovereign rights to change laws and policies, they can establish a right to compensation if the government makes such changes to the detriment of investors. Enforcement may be assisted by an agreement to refer disputes to international arbitration. Governments may also waive sovereign immunity to the enforcement of such awards in national courts.<br>• Involving local private interest. Local joint venture partners can help to navigate the local political scene and may be in a position to exercise more influence over government policy making. More importantly, governments are less likely to act to the detriment of enterprises if doing so would harm significant local interests. Joint ventures with the government are less desirable. Historical analysis suggests that public/private joint ventures are more, not less, likely to be subject to expropriation and that such joint ventures may perform less efficiently than even wholly government-owned enterprises. The government's roles as owner, operator and regulator are easily blurred.<br>• Community relations. Common measures include educating the public on the benefits of foreign investment and the role of the private sector in providing previously public services. Schemes to promote social welfare (schools, hospitals, etc.) and rural development can be helpful.", Minor (2003: 20-21) |

**Figure 9: Lessons learned and best practices matrix (continued)**

| Trends & Characteristics | Lessons learned (Root cause analysis) | Best practices |
|---|---|---|
| **Problems of the P & C Insurance market** | | |
| Price & capacity cycles | "The fall of equity markets following September 11 and again during the second quarter of 2002 has done serious damage to the financial health of general insurers and reinsurers As profitability can no longer depend on continuous capital gains on their equity portfolios, insurers and reinsurers will need to focus again on their core underwriting and claims management skills while at the same time improving their efficiency.", De Mey (2003: 70) | "The overall value proposition of any investment policy for P / C companies is to optimise capital management by explicitly considering any potential correlation between investments and underwriting. General principles have already been well established by extensive work on ALM procedures for life insurance companies. Those applications can principally be transferred to P / C insurance companies. In a general structure, underwriting insurance risk represents the core competence of an insurance company and should therefore constitute the starting point for the investment portfolio construction. The structure of the insurance portfolio yields the necessary risk capital and establishes a transfer portfolio representing the maturity structure of expected cash outflows. Any deviation from the transfer portfolio represents an ALM mismatch which has to be supported by risk capital that has to be charged correspondingly. The riskiness of the deviation has to be determined based on possible correlation between the mismatch and insurance events on the liability side.", Achleitner et al. (2002: 280) |
| Competitive disadvantages of the industry sector | "ERC is also realising success with its Global Claims Induction project. A historically manual, paper-intensive process, claims processing is now completely digitised at ERC. The web-based solution leverages digital imaging technology and automated tools to convert claims documents into images and instigate workflow tasks, without human intervention. Claims are received electronically, reviewed and automatically linked to ERC's customers' system to automatically triage and dispatch claims documents to the appropriate claims adjudicators around the world. […] Global Claims Induction has enabled ERC to provide the global claims team with digital information anywhere, anytime. The project has also been beneficial for ERC customers, who have the advantage of quicker decisions, consistent and on-time payments, and greater access to ERC's global expertise.", Pressman (2003: 46) | "Crisis management played a key role after 11 September to restore confidence, safeguard the financial system and avoid a self-fulfilling depression. Decisions taken by the Federal Reserve, other central banks and governments were essential in this respect. One lesson of this crisis is that when policymakers have to take rapid decisions in an environment of deep uncertainty and imperfect information, priority ought to be given to liquidity management.", OECD (2002: 118) |
| Legal changes | • "Insufficient recognition of group structures […] The follow-up of accumulated positions at group level, or the prevention of infectious and image risks, is such that new functions have to be created at the level of central HQ (ALM, risk management, fight against money laundering, etc.). Even if these | "To tackle the risks connected with intra-group transactions in Italy there is a provision according to which undertakings must inform ISVAP of their intention to effect significant transactions with other undertakings of the same group. ISVAP has the power to prohibit the transaction if it may undermine the interests of |

**Figure 9: Lessons learned and best practices matrix (continued)**

| Trends & Characteristics | Lessons learned (Root cause analysis) | Best practices |
|---|---|---|
| Legal changes (continued) | functions are exercised in liaison with all the subsidiaries, the difficulty of assigning a specific service to each of them can make it difficult to cover the corresponding costs, whose sharing and justification must be very strict.", de la Martinière (2003: 91)<br>• "The resolution of these issues lies in the hands of all the players, be it the regulators, the rating agencies or the insurers, in order to meet the stakeholders' (client, shareholder, employee) expectations. In order to work effectively, the insurance industry requires a clear, stable and agreed definition of rules, from the regulators (solvency, distribution issues) and from the accounting bodies and rating agencies. Internally, insurers need to gain full control of the value chain: from product pricing and reserving, to distribution through adequate risks, asset liability, solvency, capital management, and human capital management. This requires an appropriate combination of profitability mindset and ethics and a constant desire to protect the stakeholders' interests.", de Castries (2004: 38-39) | policyholders. In all cases in which the counterpart in the transaction is an insurance company situated in another state or an undertaking in any way connected to it, co-operation with the authority responsible for the said company is indispensable to ISVAP's preliminary investigation.", Manghetti (2002: 318) |
| Larger catastrophes | • "Thanks to new methods and modern technology, the insurance industry's exposure to flooding can usually be assessed with a high degree of accuracy today, thereby fulfilling an essential condition for the insurability of flood risks. However, the risk analysis requires a lot of time and data. Furthermore, the necessary data for a lot of countries are available but are very often difficult to come by. For this reason, it is sometimes a good idea to finance such projects collectively, for example, in collaboration with national insurance associations.", sigma (02/03: 11)<br>• "The insurance industry can also take control of this issue – via premiums that are commensurate with risk, for example – and thus contribute to the increase in the population's awareness of danger and thereby to the reduction in the loss burden.", sigma (02/03: 13) | "When accepting new technological risks, in particular major engineering and construction risks, careful risk assessment and expert control is a precondition. Thorough evaluation of comprehensive underwriting information, site inspections, loss prevention and research as well as claims handling are part of this process of risk management. This process attempts to reduce the probability and the magnitude of hazards, whilst at the same time trying to manage residual risks. Greater emphasis is recently placed on monitoring construction progress and physically inspecting larger, complex projects. Only through that active involvement can be ensured that engineering lines of business can be further pursued successfully, particularly in times of low premiums and extensive covers.", Heidenhain (2001: 272) |
| New risks | "It will be crucial, and a matter of urgency, for the insurance industry to develop models that are at least able to estimate the severity of loss resulting from terrorism risks. This would be a decisive step towards quantifying the risk and the most important condition for making terrorism risks insurable in the private market. Innovative solutions involving pools, new forms of insurance (e.g., finite treaties) and the financial markets are required to achieve a broad risk spread.", sigma (04/02: 15) | |

**Figure 9: Lessons learned and best practices matrix (continued)**

## 2.4 Research question & Knowledge Advancement

The question arising from the problem statement along with the state of the field analysis is how industrial corporations have to introduce or improve traditional risk management, specifically the risk management processes, in order to limit the threat by the three risk trends explained above. In addition, the role and importance of industry insurers in the risk management process needs to be re-evaluated. Finding a suitable solution could enable industry insurers to make a substantial contribution to their customers' business. One possible answer is an extended risk management process, which incorporates knowledge management concepts. How this process should be designed and whether industrial corporations would benefit from it is the primary aim of this book, "Knowledge-based risk management - A strategic systems approach for industrial corporations".

Valuable risk management knowledge in the form of lessons learned and best practices remains untapped. Leveraging this knowledge can be achieved by adding the following knowledge-management strengths to existing risk management processes:

- Assessment, i.e. the clear and comprehensive evaluation of the individual corporate risk situation along the characteristics of each current risk trend
- Classification, i.e. the categorisation of the assessed company relative to companies in similar industry and risk situations
- Knowledge management, i.e. the introduction and application of lessons learned and best practices from within and/or outside the company to reduce a company's risk exposure
- Monitoring, i.e. the continuous measurement and evaluation of the applied risk management knowledge and when necessary taking the appropriate corrective action
- Knowledge capturing, i.e. the systematic collection of new lessons learned and best practices for future exploitation

Examination of the three risk trends (1) the emergence of increasingly complex and bigger corporate structures, (2) the development of risk potential in positive and negative direction and (3) the problems of the Property and Casualty insurance market and their associated five main characteristics suggests companies are lacking the right information from the right people at the right time. Even though the three risk trends have different root causes, all three risk trends affect the effectiveness of the existing risk management measures. Risk trend one and two relate to industry-internal problems, while risk trend three relates to the constant structural crisis of the insurance market. Figure 10: Risk management measures under distress graphically displays how each risk trend affects the risk management measures.

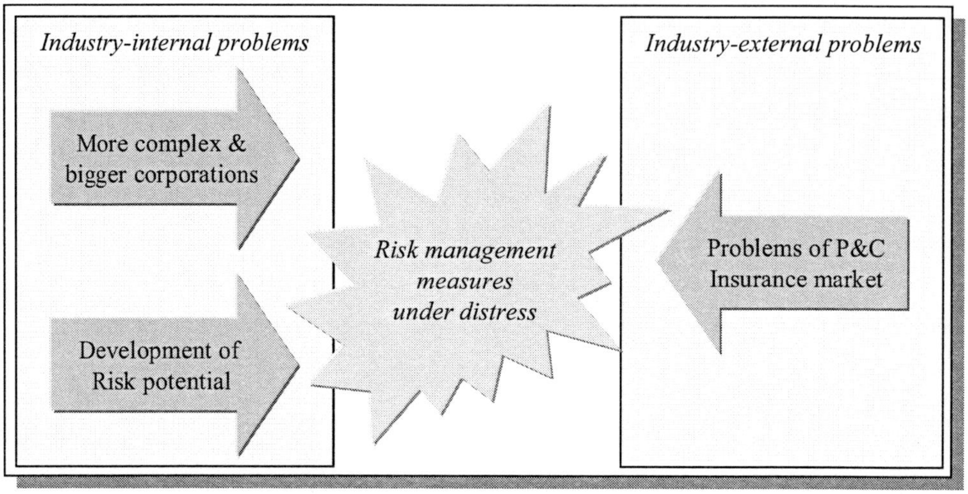


**Figure 10: Risk management measures under distress**

Main reasons for the industry-internal problems due to increasing complexity and size of corporations and the development of risk potential are summarised with "the increase in insured values, their concentration in highly exposed areas and their high susceptibility to external influences" (Sigma, 2003a: 13). On the other hand, primary causes for the industry-external problems of the Property & Casualty (P & C) insurance market are the cyclical movements of the insurance and reinsurance prices and the enormous overcapacity of capital in the last decade (Alff, 2004: 8-14; 2002: 19-20, 26; Harrington and Niehaus, 2003: 151-152; Sigma, 2002: 3-4, 6, 9). As predicted by Hörmann (1999: 83), the number of industry insurers worldwide will be reduced as a result of internationalisation and other economic influences. In Austria for example, the recent exit of prominent market participants include Basler (in 2000), Anker (in 2001), Axa (in 2002) and nearly Gerling (in 2002) (Krebs, 2003). P & C insurance market problems lead to a focus shift for encouraging new developments such as Alternative Risk Transfer (ART) (Hölscher, 2002: 16-18; Sigma, 2002: 4). Different origins and requirements to deal with these three risk trends add to the complexity of the risk management process.

Various risk management measures and processes exist. However, the research indicates they do not take into account the concepts of knowledge management and do not fully meet the requirements of today's global networked economy. Today's corporate risk management does not have a holistic, networked view but rather focuses on individual, independent risks (Hölscher, 2002: 8). Furthermore, the literature implies that many corporations have no systematic access to and use of risk management knowledge. Risk management process deficiencies result in a constant, time and money consuming process of reinventing risk management knowledge. Yet, the literature also sheds light on positive examples of companies dealing well with these risk trends by using knowledge management. Sixteen hypotheses displayed in Table 9: Hypotheses – survey questions matrix are posed in order to investigate the situation outlined above. Main premises of these hypotheses are:

- Corporations highly affected by a risk trend do not possess or use Risk management knowledge for dealing with this risk trend
- Corporations hardly affected by a risk trend, possess and use extensive Risk management knowledge for dealing with this risk trend

Testing of these sixteen hypotheses is performed using a risk & knowledge management survey targeted at Austrian industrial corporations. The risk & knowledge management survey used is found in Appendix 2: Risk & Knowledge management survey content. Survey questions are based on and evaluate the findings of the state of the field analysis. Gathered risk & knowledge management survey data is used to operationalise the Risk assessment and Risk analysis steps of the developed and described knowledge-based risk management process, step II & III in Figure 13. In addition, the proposed hypotheses are evaluated and the results presented and discussed. Thus, this book exhibits whether a link between knowledge management and risk management exists.

**Dealing with speculation**

The theory developed in this book is a logical step, following those renowned authors, who have successfully performed research in the areas of risk management and knowledge management. By using a methodology consisting of both qualitative and quantitative analysis, the outcome of this research is continually checked, verified and improved. The approach is divided in six parts and each part is based on the successful completion of the previous part. As a result, the quality of research is maintained.

## 2.5 Summary

State of the field analysis suggest three major risk trends, namely the (1) Emergence of increasingly complex and bigger corporate structures, the (2) development of risk potential in positive and negative direction and the (3) Problems of P & C Insurance market threaten the future of industrial and industry insurers today. Many risk management measures are provided by risk management experts, but appear to focus only on specific problem areas and not on the whole risk spectrum. A reusable process on how to avoid, compensate or mitigate the specific danger arising through the three risk trends is missing. Therefore, it is difficult to transfer the necessary lessons learned and best practices from one company to another. Thus extending the current information on the previously explained risk trends and risk management measures by linking them together with a new, strategic systems approach seems to be necessary from both a scientific as well as a business perspective.

# 3 Exemplary lessons learned and best practices benchmarks

Examination of the current literature on risk and knowledge management reveals three major risk trends which are threatening the existence of industrial corporations today. The three risk trends are (1) the emergence of increasingly complex and bigger corporate structures, (2) the development of risk potential in positive and negative direction and (3) the problems of the Property and Casualty insurance market. Unfortunately, existing risk management measures are no longer sufficient in dealing successfully with the changing risk environment. Lessons learned and best practices knowledge are suggested in the literature by leading risk and insurance management experts in order to deal with the risk of the three risk trends. However, the question is what are typical lessons learned and best practices benchmarks for industrial corporations. Two practical examples from Austrian industrial corporations shed light on the meaning of lessons learned and best practices. Results of the benchmarking depend on the quality of the literature sources used and interviews conducted. Since benchmarking is currently a recognised scientific and practical discipline (Güldenberg, 2001; Main, 1992; Lohse, 2001; Drew, 1997; Best Practices, 2004; IRMBA, 2004; PSBS, 2004; TBE, 2004), the quality of the results, i.e. the demonstration of lessons learned and best practices in the context of this research, are ensured. Example lessons learned benchmark company RHI, is based in Vienna, Austria. Example best practice benchmark corporation Glanzstoff Austria, is based in St. Pölten, Lower Austria, Austria. Each example is described in detail in the next two sections.

## 3.1 Lessons learned example: RHI

The following lessons learned example from RHI contains a brief company overview, a crisis description, reasons for selection as lessons learned, and possible learnings for similar companies and situations.

### *3.1.1 Company overview*

RHI is a Vienna based company. Its roots date back to 1881, when the "Veitscher Magnesitwerke Actien-Gesellschaft" was founded (Börse Express, 2003: 1). After a MBO in 1997, a company renaming in 1998 and going public, RHI became one of the largest industrial corporations in Austria (Börse Express, 2003: 1). The company's core business was traditionally refractories (Börse Express, 2003: 1), i.e. materials resistant to fire. Refractories, primarily made out of magnesite, are used in ceramic products employed in high temperature production processes such as for steel, cement, chalk and glass (Zehetner, 2003: 4). Other RHI business segments included engineering and insulating (Börse Express, 2003: 2). In 1995, RHI acquired Didier-Werke, a German competitor. In 1999, the purchase of GIT, RHI's largest competitor in the US, was announced (Börse Express, 2003: 1). As a result of the mergers, the company's revenues grew from Euro 1.7 billion in 1999 to Euro 2.2 billion in 2000 (Börse Express, 2003: 2-3; Richter, 2002: 1).

### *3.1.2 Crisis description*

Only two years after the purchase of GIT, the newly acquired company becomes a financial nightmare for RHI. Former GIT employees successfully sued RHI, the legal successor of GIT, for asbestos damages (Zehetner, 2003: 7; Börse Express, 2003: 2). Reason for the workers' law suits were the negative effects on their health due to asbestos which they had worn as isolation materials in the 60s and 70s (Börse Express, 1993: 3). At the beginning of the RHI crisis, sufficient liability insurance cover existed and the insurers quickly paid out the claims (Zehetner, 2003: 7; Börse Express, 2003: 2). However, due to the large number of liability claims and the enormous amounts of money being paid out per claim, insurers started to pay out money more slowly, leading to tremendous financial stress for RHI in the US and Europe (Zehetner, 2003: 7; Börse Express, 2003: 2).

The result of this crisis was that the US part of RHI was deconsolidated into two groups NARCO and GIT (Richter, 2003a). Both groups subsequently filed for bankruptcy under Chapter 11[1] (Richter, 2003a). The outcome of the Chapter 11 process no longer affects the rest of RHI. As a result of the deconsolidation, RHI's net equity was reduced to € -549 Mio, leading to the near bankruptcy of the overall RHI group in 2002 (Zehetner, 2003: 8). Consequently, the top management of RHI was partly exchanged and a major capital injection made by the creditors, in order to avoid a total loss of investments (Zehetner, 2003: 9-12; Börse Express, 2003: 2). At the moment, it appears RHI can even regain a compensation of USD 10 Mio from

[1] In the case of insolvency, US companies have two ways of filing for bankruptcy, namely Chapter 11 and Chapter 7 (SEC, 2004: 1). Chapter 11 allows the company to sort out its financial and organisational problems and in the long run become a successfully operating company again (SEC, 2004: 1). Chapter 7 is the full liquidation of the company, where the sale of the company's assets is used to pay as much as possible of the existing debt.

its previous owners, Honeywell and Halliburton (Richter, 2003a; "RHI erreicht wichtige Vereinbarung", 2004; "RHI: Einigung", 2004).

Following this tremendously difficult time, it seems very surprising that RHI was able to regain the second position in the refractories sector in 2002 (Zehetner, 2003: 23) and even the market leadership position in 2003 (Himmelbauer, 2004). The overall debt of the corporation was reduced from € 1.07 billion to € 295 Mio and is expected to be paid off one and a half years prior to the agreed upon date of 2007 (Himmelbauer, 2004; Fellhuber, 2004). As a result of the successful restructuring, RHI has become again a highly demanded share at the Austrian stock exchange, with over 100% growth in 2003 (Himmelbauer, 2004; Zehetner, 2003: 27).

After the crisis, RHI is again successfully producing in 26 production plants all over the world (Zehetner, 2003: 11), thus diversifying its globalisation risk while at the same time being close to the world's industrial customers. RHI's management is confident of regaining parts of the lost US market by entering it from outside countries such as Canada, Mexico, China and Europe (Zehetner, 2003: 9; Fellhuber, 2004).

### *3.1.3 Reasons for selection as lessons learned*

RHI is selected as lessons learned example due to the heavy toll the company had to pay for its strive for global leadership. Even though RHI nearly failed in this process, it was able to regain its former strength and is now again a market leader in its refractories core segment. The negative experiences over the past few years has however certainly changed RHI's overall risk perception regarding risk trend one, growing complexity and corporate size. Primarily risk trend one characteristic Mergers & Acquisitions seems to be the driver, due to the disastrous M & A activities of the company.

Within a two year time frame, the company had lost almost half of its revenues and was nearly forced to file for bankruptcy (Börse Express, 2003: 2; Richter, 2002: 1). Within a very short time frame, RHI was not only able to recover financially from this major crisis, but also regained its previous market (Börse Express, 2003: 5; Richter, 2003b). The tremendous comeback was enabled by RHI management's stout-hearted reaction to file for Chapter 11 in the United States. Only by selling the asbestos affected unit were they able to save the rest of the company. Sale of the company was made possible through the financial support of banks and other creditors, which realised that the bankruptcy of the whole group would lead to a total loss of their investments. At the same time, creditors recognised RHI's healthy core business outside the US in the refractories sector as well as the positive long-term growth aspects of the overall refractories market (Zehetner, 2003: 21; Börse Express, 2003: 2; Richter, 2003c: 55-56). With a bankruptcy of the overall RHI group, these opportunities would have been lost altogether. Within less than one year, the United States holding company of RHI was spun off, enabling them to solve their own problems, while the rest of the company could now start focussing on its core refractory business. The fast reaction time of the newly established RHI management shows that especially for industrial corporations in a crisis, time is of the essence to survive.

RHI restructuring process also demonstrates that the company's management and employees have learned their lesson and therefore are now more protected against future risks. A dedicated risk & insurance management team under the supervision of finance and investors relations is monitoring the group's risk management results (Mair, 2003: 4). The risk and insurance management team structure enables a corporate-wide introduction of insurance guidelines and standards. Furthermore the team insures all foreign insurance policies are up to a similar level meeting the requirements of the local markets (Mair, 2003: 4). AON, the world's largest industry insurance broker, supports the risk & insurance management team in their global work (Mair, 2003: 5). It is likely that RHI's asbestos troubles would have been far smaller, if the risk & insurance management team structure had been put in place before the crisis. In order to limit RHI's risk exposure, a global claims database has been established (Mair, 2003: 6). The claims database allows the uniform gathering and monitoring of the company's risk situation. In addition, continuous risk management audits are taking place at the production sites (Mair, 2003: 6). Risk management audits result in a combination of organisational, as well as physical changes which attempt to lower the overall risk threat (Mair, 2003: 8-9). RHI's aim in 2004 is to achieve a global renewal up to the current standard, a continuity of production site risk analysis and improvements and finally an extension of the risk management concepts to the areas of logistics, procurement, R & D, quality, sales and legal (Mair, 2003: 11).

### *3.1.4 Possible lessons learned for similar companies and business situations*

The story of RHI shows how a wrong M & A decision can lead to the overall failure of a successful industrial corporation with sound products and services. Therefore, growing at any price is not always the best solution for industrial corporations. Carefully weighing advantages and disadvantages of an M & A against each other is required in order to make a sensible decision. In some cases, maintaining a highly profitable and healthy business with a lower market share is a better option than growing at too fast a pace. Several lessons can be drawn from the experience of RHI. These lessons learned are certainly important for the future of RHI, but could also be relevant for other industrial corporations. The learnings include:

- Thorough due diligence is a very critical task in the M & A process. A focus on risk management and possible long term obligations of the new company might help to detect future problems. While some companies are selling parts of their business because it does not fit anymore strategically, others are selling because they want to get rid of existing problems. Detecting the true reasons for selling a corporation can be key in making the right M & A investments. Impact of unknown risks, such as liability claims, is not easily foreseeable and therefore needs special consideration in due diligence processes.

- A swift reaction to a problem limited to one region but affecting the cash flow of the overall organisation helped to save the rest of the company.

- Industrial corporations in a crisis need a believable story and a strong business case to receive further financial support by banks and creditors. Outcomes of restructuring must lead to positive results, otherwise funding will be refused.

- Determined introduction of risk and insurance management processes are more likely to be successful, if top management is involved and a dedicated team is put in place.

- Global industry insurance brokers can be a great leverage in supporting industrial corporation's risk management efforts

## 3.2 Best practices example: Glanzstoff Austria

The following best practices example of Glanzstoff Austria contains a brief company profile, a crisis description, reasons for selection as best practice and possible learnings for similar companies and situations.

### *3.2.1 Company overview*

The founding of "Vereinigte Glanzstoff AG" in Wuppertal, Germany in 1899 established the starting point for industrial chemical fibre production (Glanzstoff, 1999: 1). In 1904, Vereinigte Glanzstoff subsequently set up the "Erste Österreichische Glanzstoff-Fabrik Aktiengesellschaft" in St. Pölten, Lower Austria, Austria (Glanzstoff, 1999: 1). Artificially produced fibres revolutionised both the textile, as well as the technical durable goods industry, especially for woven fabric inlays made out of rayon (Glanzstoff, 1999: 1). Over the years, the company's history was highly influenced by economic cycles, wars and other external influences, resulting in two near bankruptcies in 1982 and 1994 (Glanzstoff, 1999: 1). Opening of the eastern borders and a recession in the car industry resulted in the virtual closure of Glanzstoff Austria AG, which at that time was owned by Lenzing AG, another Austrian industrial company (Glanzstoff, 1999: 1). In 1994, just before the company was forced to file for bankruptcy, the investor group CAG holding, owned by entrepreneur Cornelius Grupp, bought the company from Lenzing. Grupp changed Glanzstoff Austria to a limited liability company. Glanzstoff was then successfully restructured (Schinnerl, 2000) and integrated into CAG holding. Today, Glanzstoff Austria is once again the number two company in the rayon sector, producing one third of the world wide capacity and delivering to tire companies such as Goodyear, Dunlop and Pirelli (Haase, 1997; Widmayer, 1996). The outlook for Glanzstoff Austria's industry segment can be seen as positive due to new developments in the car industry such as "runflat-tires", made out of rayon (Schinnerl, 2000).

### *3.2.2 Crisis description*

Apart from the structural problems of Glanzstoff Austria's industry sectors for rayon and viscose, growing environmental concerns started to become an issue for the company. Traditionally, the nature of Glanzstoff Austria's production process for viscose fibres leads to two major problems for the surrounding environment, water and air pollution.

Viscose production requires large amounts of water, which is polluted with the chemicals used in the fabrication process. Viscose consists of 80% water. During the production process, viscose is made from cellulose (Glanzstoff, 2004). Viscose is spun to a very thin cord while being washed with chemically treated water. In order to clean the chemicals out of the water which polluted the river Traisen, a purification plant was built from 1989 to 1991 (Glanzstoff, 2004). The purification plant insures that the water leaving the factory reaches the second highest water quality level (Glanzstoff, 2004). High water quality is reached by a combination of physical separation and biological processing through micro organisms (Glanzstoff, 2004).

Viscose production process requires carbon disulfide to liquefy the cellulose, leading to 15-18% hydrogen sulphide as a side product (Glanzstoff, 2001: 1). Hydrogen sulphide is a gas with the distinct smell of rotten eggs and negative health effects. Residents of the neighbouring city of St. Pölten had been complaining about the smell of hydrogen sulphide for a very long time. In 1988, Glanzstoff Austria started to address the air pollution problem with a first scientific project in co-operation with the Vienna University of Technology and Waagner-Biro[1] (Glanzstoff, 2001: 1). The aim of the initial project was the organic purification of the air with micro organisms. However, the resulting organic purification process was unable to clean the entire amount of polluted air which was to be purified (Glanzstoff, 2001: 1-2). Realisation of the shortfalls of the first research project did not stop Glanzstoff Austria from looking for an adequate solution for its air pollution problem. As a result, a three-step air purification concept was developed in 1995 and successfully submitted to the public authorities (Glanzstoff, 2001: 2). Results of the first step of the project show a 13% reduction in carbon disulfide discharge and 70% reduction in hydrogen sulphide discharge (Glanzstoff, 2001: 3). At the end of the third step of the project, the discharge amounts will be even further limited. An 85-87% reduction in carbon disulfide discharge and a 93-94% reduction in hydrogen sulphide discharge should be reached (Glanzstoff, 2001: 6). According to Plank (2003), results of the overall project leads to a recognisable improvement of the air quality and a significant reduction of hydrogen sulphide related health problems in the city of St. Pölten.

### *3.2.3 Reasons for selection as best practice*

Glanzstoff Austria was chosen as best practice due to the company's elegant dealing with the threats of risk trend two, development of risk potential in both positive and negative direction. In particular, the two characteristics industrial pollution and societal, political and cultural change are addressed. Glanzstoff Austria could also be classified as a lessons learned, because the company nearly had to file for bankruptcy twice. Although classification is correct from the point of view of the former Glanzstoff Austria, it is not however the view of the investor CAG holding and its new owner, Cornelius Grupp. Grupp's considers the repeated purchase of a

[1] Waagner-Biro is an Austrian-based international plant engineering and construction company (Waagner-Biro, 2004)

damaged company in a healthy market environment and the successful restructuring a very positive best practice (Widmayer, 1996).

Furthermore, the financial problems of Glanzstoff are not the primary reason for selecting it as an example best practice. Rather more importantly are the aspects of introducing a water and an air purification plant in order to solve the problems with environmentalists. These solutions are perceived as a great know-how advantage over other industrial companies which have not taken the same steps. A rethinking process in Glanzstoff Austria management and workforce began as a consequence of the increasing pressure from environmentalist groups and public authorities. The result of this process is Glanzstoff Austria's acknowledgement to act with, not against nature in all of its business activities (Glanzstoff, 2004).

Overall, Glanzstoff Austria has invested € 16 Mio in the water purification plant and € 10 Mio in the air purification plant (Glanzstoff, 2004). Even though this investment seems high in relationship to the relative size of Glanzstoff Austria's revenues of €135 Mio in 2002 (Himmelbauer, 2002), the overall benefit of the company is likely to be much higher. As Plank (2003) states, Glanzstoff Austria is currently the only viscose fibres producing company with such high environmental standards. As a result of Glanzstoff Austria's environmental efforts and successful restructuring, the negative press has completely disappeared. On the contrary, renowned politicians on all levels up to the president of Austria are mentioning Glanzstoff Austria as a positive best practice example for industrial modernisation (Widmayer, 1996).

### *3.2.4 Possible best practices for similar companies and business situations*

Glanzstoff Austria was able to recover from its near failure in 1994 and is now once again a technology leader in its market segments rayon and viscose. Apart from this great restructuring success, the proactive introduction of environmental technology in order to avoid public criticism and hurdles has made Glanzstoff a know-how carrier in the field of environmental protection. Some best practices learnings for other companies include:

- Companies possessing best practices can use them not only internally, but can also transfer knowledge to other market participants through seminars and know-how transfer sessions. In the case of Glanzstoff, the knowledge regarding the air and water purification plants is being transferred to the sister production plant Glanzstoff Bohemia in the Czech Republic, leading to a reduction in time and effort (Plank, 2003). In addition, other companies from all over the world are contacting Glanzstoff Austria in order to learn from its successful environment projects. Glanzstoff Austria's benchmark leadership role is likely to lead to new business contacts which might be beneficial for the overall company success.

- Industrial corporations may find themselves in a position such as Glanzstoff Austria where textbook solutions for major problems are not yet available. In such cases, the help of research facilities such as universities and technology leaders can be a possible solution in speeding up the acquisition of best practices knowledge.

- The proactive addressing of environmental concerns saved Glanzstoff Austria from problems with the public authorities. The resulting improvements in the environment are likely to positively affect decisions necessary for Glanzstoff Austria's future development in the geographic area of St. Pölten. Other industrial companies should realise acting with and not against the surrounding community is the best way to gain support from the public community and authorities.

## 3.3 Summary

Practical demonstration of two Austrian industrial corporations, RHI and Glanzstoff Austria, further supports the findings of the state of the field analysis. These two benchmarks show the necessity of knowledge management in the form of lessons learned and best practices in order to deal with major crises. In addition, these benchmarks illustrate how knowledge management is one way to supply industrial corporations with the measures to avoid, compensate or mitigate risk threats. The examples of RHI and Glanzstoff Austria also illustrate that risk management lessons learned and best practices can in practice be closely related. In the case of RHI, the asbestos problem nearly led to the overall bankruptcy of the corporation, whereas in the case of Glanzstoff Austria, the lacking environmental measures could have potentially led to a closure of the corporation in the future. Hence, both companies examined represent benchmark examples for corporations in similar situations or industries in helping to deal with major risk trends. Risk management knowledge gathered by RHI and Glanzstoff Austria can be both beneficial within these corporations and might assist other companies in the same or similar risk situation.

How risk management lessons learned and best practices of industrial corporations are more effectively gathered, identified and reapplied is described in the following chapter four, Knowledge-based risk management process.

# 4 Knowledge-based risk management process

Chapter four consists of four main sections. Section one defines a new knowledge-based risk management process. Reasons for developing this process are the requirement of both industrial corporations as well as industry insurers for handling the increased risk threats of the three risk trends identified in the state of the field analysis. These three risk trends are (1) the emergence of increasingly complex and bigger corporate structures, (2) the development of risk potential in positive and negative direction and (3) the problems of the Property and Casualty insurance market. Section two provides a detailed description of how the knowledge-based management process, consisting of five steps could be applied in industrial corporations. Section three clarifies the role of corporate risk manager and insurance risk manager during the application of the knowledge-based risk management process. Finally, section four summarises possible benefits for industrial companies and industry insurers in using the process.

## 4.1 Definition of the knowledge-based risk management process

The knowledge-based risk management process, shown in Figure 13, is a synthesis of Theil's model for "Risk management for IT systems" (1995), see Figure 11: Illustrated Risk Management for Information Systems process according to Theil (1995), and Tah and Carr's "Risk management process model" (2001a: 841), see Figure 12: The risk management process model (Tah and Carr, 2001a: 841). Theil's and Tah and Carr's risk management models are briefly explained in sections 4.1.1 and 4.1.2 respectively. The new knowledge-based risk management process builds on the strengths of both Theil's and Tah and Carr's risk management processes. Key improvements lie mainly in the Risk assessment, Risk analysis, Risk handling and Risk monitoring steps. Reason for dividing the risk management function in process steps lies in improved transparency and gathering of information regarding the risk situation (Karten, 1978: 39-40). Application of the knowledge-based risk management process can be carried out with any potential risk trends. However, this book focuses on the three previously mentioned risk trends: (1) emergence of increasingly complex and bigger corporate structures, (2) development of risk potential in positive and negative direction and (3) problems of the Property and Casualty insurance market. An overview of the process is provided in section 4.1.3 Synthesised knowledge-based risk management process for industrial corporations. As described in section 4.1.3, the knowledge-based risk management process consists of five steps.

Each process sub-step is explained in section 4.2 Description of the knowledge-based risk management process. An explanation of the corporate and insurance risk manager and their roles in the knowledge-based risk management process is given in section 4.3 Practical application of the knowledge-based risk management process.

### *4.1.1 Process model I: Risk management for IT systems according to Theil*

Theil (1995) develops and explains a three steps process approach towards risk management for information systems. A graphical depiction of Theil's risk management process is provided in Figure 11: Illustrated Risk Management for Information Systems process according to Theil (1995). As illustrated in Figure 11, this process consists of three steps: (1) risk identification, (2) risk assessment and (3) risk handling. In step one, risk identification, risks are identified using appropriate risk recognition methods (Theil, 1995: 6). In step two, risk assessment, damage severity and occurrence likelihood are calculated and their relationship discussed (Theil, 1995: 6). Finally, in step three, risk handling, damage avoiding and damage compensating measures are proposed for dealing with the determined risk situations in steps one and two (Theil, 1995: 6).

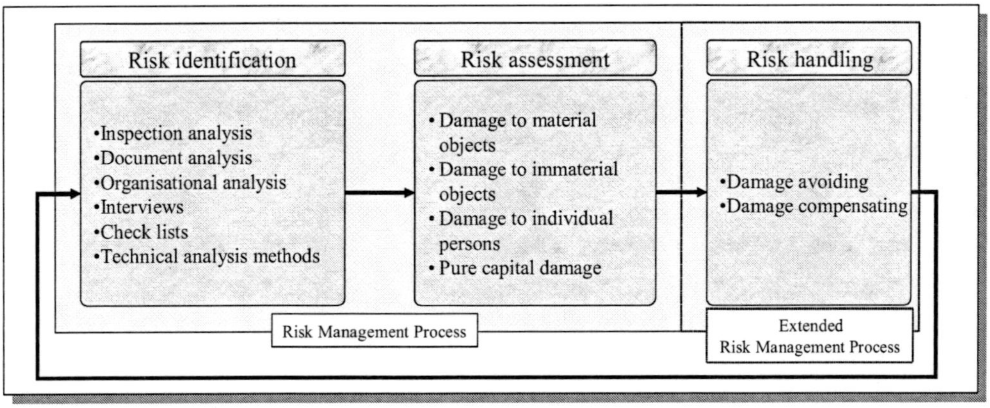


**Figure 11: Illustrated Risk Management for Information Systems process according to Theil (1995)**

Even though the primary focus of Theil's contribution lies on the risk threats from the application of information technology, Theil's approach is based on proven "practical and scientific foundations of risk management" (Theil, 1995: 5). Thus, Theil's risk management for information systems process can serve as a starting point for the development of an improved risk management process. Key enhancement could lie in the incorporation of the currently not included concept of knowledge management and the extension to other risk trends threatening industrial corporations today.

### *4.1.2 Process model II: The risk management process model according to Tah and Carr*

Tah and Carr (2001a, 2001b) lay out a five step approach toward project risk knowledge management in the construction supply chain. The risk management process is graphically displayed in Figure 12: The risk management process model (Tah and Carr, 2001a: 841). The five steps of the process are: (1) risk identification, (2) risk assessment, (3) risk analysis, (4) risk handling and (5) risk monitoring. In step one, risk identification, the entire risk threats of a project and their origins are isolated (Tah and Carr, 2001b: 854). In step two, risk assessment, each of the risk threats for the project is measured and classified (Tah and Carr, 2001b: 854). In step three, risk analysis, possible outcomes of the risk threats on and the required assignments within the project are revealed (Tah and Carr, 2001b: 855). In step four, risk handling, required and adequate means in dealing with the risk situation are put in place (Tah and Carr, 2001b: 855). Finally, in step five, risk monitoring finishes the first iteration of the risk management process. Risk monitoring is the continuous supervision of the risk prevention measures put in place (Tah and Carr, 2001b: 855). Therefore, the risk monitoring can be seen as a starting point towards further iterations of the risk management process. Only when the project has come to an end will the monitoring step finish (Tah and Carr, 2001b: 855).

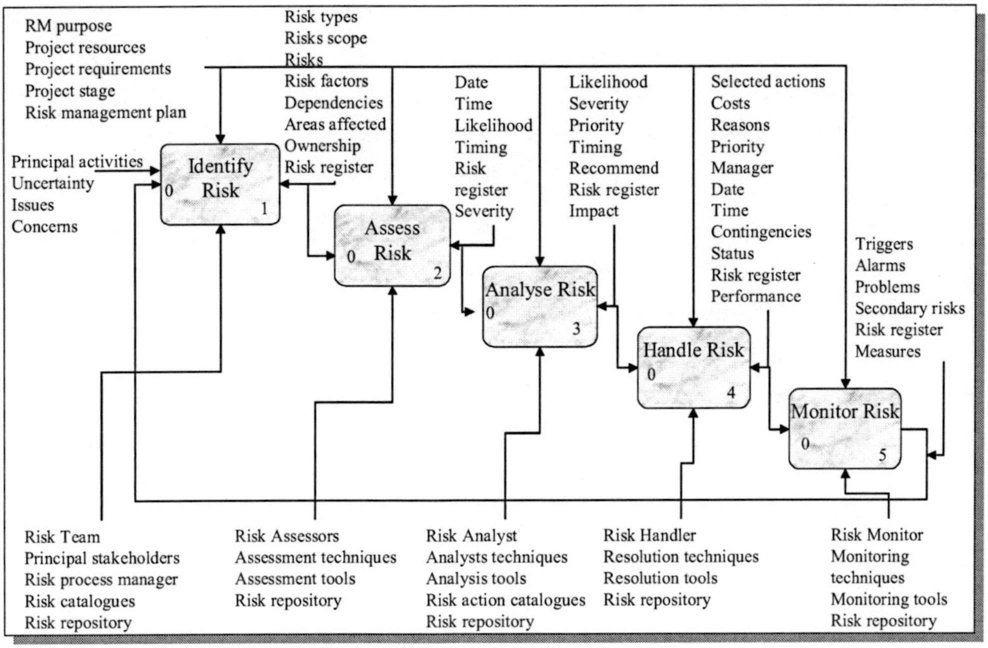


**Figure 12: The risk management process model (Tah and Carr, 2001a: 841)**

While Tah and Carr's risk management approach is tailored to the construction supply chain, it is transferable and applicable in other scientific and practical areas. Reasons for selecting Tah and Carr's approach as a starting point in developing a new risk management process dealing with major risk trends threatening industrial corporations lie in its focus on project management and knowledge management capabilities (Tah and Carr, 2001a: 835-836). First of all, project management capabilities seem to play a major role today in the successful application of risk management in industrial corporations. Secondly, knowledge management is a keystone identified as missing in the state of the field analysis in dealing with major risk trends. Even though Tah and Carr (2001a: 836) call for "tools using knowledge-based system techniques" to enable their risk management process, the actual knowledge management function is not included in their process map (2001a: 841). Tah and Carr's model therefore serves as a second starting point in addition to Theil's contribution in the subsequent synthesis towards a new knowledge-based risk management process.

### *4.1.3 Synthesised knowledge-based risk management process for industrial corporations*

Industrial corporations already have access to the risk management capabilities of industry insurers. Most insurance companies either employ risk managers or possess in-house consulting companies which are available to provide risk management consulting services to industrial corporations. However, the existing risk management services do not take advantage of knowledge management. Introduction of knowledge management concepts would provide better help against the changing risk environment. One way corporate risk managers in industrial corporations could improve their capabilities and services is by applying a new, knowledge-based approach. This new approach could be introduced with close interaction with and support by the insurance corporations' risk managers. The knowledge-based approach explained below was developed by blending the existing Theil's model for "Risk management for IT systems" (1995) and Tah and Carr's "Risk management process model" (2001). Process resulting from this synthesis was then enhanced with knowledge management principles. A graphic display of the knowledge-based risk management process is provided in Figure 13: Knowledge-based risk management process for industrial corporations. The knowledge-based risk management process consists of five steps: risk identification, risk assessment, risk analysis, risk handling and risk monitoring.

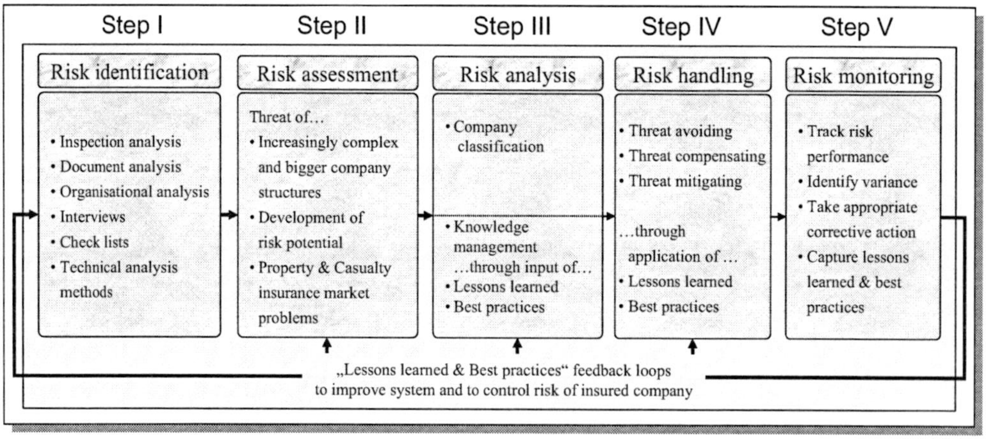


**Figure 13: Knowledge-based risk management process for industrial corporations**

Execution of this process is only one element toward successful knowledge-based risk management. Results for industrial corporations will always be just as good as the gathering, storing and reusing of experiences and data along the whole process and on all organisational levels, as noted by Gerling (1986: 94-95).

Furthermore, willingness to share knowledge within and between corporations and insurers plays an important role. By pointing out the necessary incentives leading to optimal behaviour and increasing shareholder value, the corporate risk manager can achieve top management commitment (Gleason, 2000: 273). Peter (2001: 5) and Hoffmann (1985: 2-3, 5, 27) argue that only a risk aware top management can proactively deal with the challenges of the complex and networked risk situations of corporations today. Risk management provides "decision makers with practical knowledge for solving corporate risk problems" (Peter, 2001: 245). In addition to managing the knowledge-based risk management process, the risk managers' job functions range from "loss exposure identification and measurement, arrangement of insurance handling claims, design and installation of employee benefit plans, participation in loss control measures, safety group insurance, and self-insurance administration" (Rejda, 1992: 59). Properly established, risk management plays a vital part in supporting the corporations' decision making process (Peter, 2001: 162). In order for the rest of the employees to follow, top management must support the risk management efforts through leading by example (Ritchie and Marshall, 1993: 256).

A method to achieve an efficient application across all process steps is presented in 4.2 Description of the knowledge-based risk management process. Industrial corporations, beneficiaries of the knowledge-based risk management process provided by industry insurers, generally pass through a company life cycle, as described by Schradin (1994: 114). The adaptability of the knowledge-based risk management process insures its continuous and optimal use during these different life cycle stages of industrial corporations. Necessary roles of the risk managers when applying the knowledge-based risk management process of both the industrial corporation and the insurance company are explained in 4.3 Practical application of the knowledge-based risk management process.

## 4.2 Description of the knowledge-based risk management process

Definition and explanation of the five knowledge-based risk management process steps, namely risk identification, risk assessment, risk analysis, risk handling and risk monitoring are provided in the following five sections.

### *4.2.1 Risk identification*

Step I (Risk identification) employs Theil's (1995: 23-49) extensive list of measures for gathering all relevant information relating to a corporation's risk situation. In the context of this book, a corporation's risk situation is constrained to the threats regarding the three risk trend: (1) the emergence of increasingly complex and bigger corporate structures, (2) the development of risk potential in positive and negative direction and (3) the problems of the Property and Casualty insurance market need to be identified. Risk information collected in the risk identification step is essential for the successful completion of Steps II through V. The importance of risk identification for the overall success of the risk management process is acknowledged by both Theil (1995: 27) and Tah and Carr (2001b: 854).

As Theil (1995: 27) along with Jirsa and Oppl (1988: 15) and Wagner (2000: 202) point out, a wide range of different risk identification tools exist. Only the optimal combination of the tools insures a detection of all risks (Theil, 1995: 27). Tools identified by Theil include: inspection analysis, document analysis, organisational analysis, interviews, check lists and technical analysis methods. Each of Theil's proposed risk identification measures is briefly presented in the context of the knowledge-based risk management process below. A comprehensive explanation of the available identification measures is found in "Risikomanagement für Informationssysteme" (Theil, 1995).

- **Inspection analysis**

  One of the most effective risk identification measures is inspection analysis (Theil, 1995: 28). The only negative aspects of inspection analysis are its rather time consuming and expensive nature (Theil, 1995: 28). Considering the high leverage of a successful inspection analysis, these pitfalls can be seen as rather small in major industrial corporations. In order to gain access to the required risk knowledge, not only risk managers but all employees with risk know-how need to be involved in the inspection process (Theil, 1995: 28). Involvement of key personnel is one of the major strengths of the inspection analysis. Theil (1995: 28) differentiates between the three individual types of inspection analysis, i.e. general inspection, special inspection and supplementary inspection.

- **Document analysis**

Corporate and insurance risk managers can use a large variety of documents containing information regarding risk threats (Theil, 1995: 30). Primary sources for risk information can be financial and cost accounting, annual reports and files (Theil, 1995: 30). Further sources for information on the threats regarding the three risk trends could be strategy papers and meeting minutes. Document analysis includes all necessary files with relevant risk information content, both on paper and electronically. One of the key issues for a successful document analysis is the availability and accessibility of all relevant documents for corporate and insurance risk managers. Availability and accessibility can be insured by the commitment and involvement of top management, which enforces open access to documents required in the risk identification process.

- **Organisational analysis**

Both operational and organisational structures are examined in the organisational analysis (Theil, 1995: 36). While organisational structure analysis is related to the general inspection, operational structure analysis focuses on processes rather than risk threats (Theil, 1995: 36, 38). Both methods are useful in providing an accurate view on the functioning of the corporation. Thus, organisational analysis allows risk managers to make adaptations where required in the later stages of the knowledge-based risk management process.

- **Interviews**

Risk identification measures are supported by explanatory and supplementary interviews (Theil, 1995: 39). Interviews could be conducted with employees possessing risk management knowledge regarding the three risk trends.

- **Check lists**

Use of check lists ensure that all relevant information is gathered in the course of the risk management process (Mugler, 1979: 106, quoted in Theil, 1995: 39). Structure of an optimal checklist should not be too focused on the individual risk manager's claims experience or the aims of an external third party (Theil, 1995: 40). Therefore, insurance risk managers must design general, unbiased checklists for industrial corporations in order to reach comparable and suitable risk improvement results. The risk and knowledge management survey depicted in Appendix 2: Risk & Knowledge management survey content could for instance serve as a primary example for a general check list regarding the three risk trends examined in this research. Its applicability in leading Austrian industrial corporations is successfully demonstrated in chapter 5 Empirical analysis.

- **Technical analysis methods**

Technical analysis methods subsume failure effect analysis, event flow analysis and fault tree analysis (Theil, 1995: 40-41). In the past, these analysis methods were limited to very critical industrial areas such as nuclear risks (Haller in Farny et al., 1978: 328, quoted in Theil, 1995: 40). With the new possibilities of high speed computers and internet technology, previously too expensive and stochastically unfunded technical analysis (Haller in Farny et al., 1978: 328, quoted in Theil, 1995: 40) could increase in efficiency and usability. In this case, technological progress could be highly beneficial for industrial corporations in leveraging an additional risk identification method.

A summary of Theil's (1995: 28-49) proposed risk identification measures demonstrates that corporate and insurance risk managers have numerous tools and techniques at hand for discovering risk threats. Both insurance and corporate risk managers need to decide on the suitable mix of identification methods. Carefully selected identification methods guarantee the successful completion of the following four steps of the knowledge-based risk management process.

### *4.2.2 Risk assessment*

Step II (Risk assessment) determines and graphically displays the corporation's existing risk situation and vulnerability with regard to potential risk trends. The company's potential damage for each risk trend is assessed by using the risk information gathered during Step I and rating the company against each trend/characteristic combination. Each characteristic is rated on a scale from 1 to 10. Rating denotes how the company views the characteristic's risk potential: 1-very low and 10-very high. Each trend has 5 associated characteristics, therefore, a trend can obtain a score ranging from 5 (1 point for each characteristic) to 50 (10 points for each characteristic) as shown in Figure 14. A company with the lowest trend score (5 points) has the lowest trend risk exposure. A company with highest trend score (50 points) has the highest trend risk exposure. Companies with a low risk exposure for a particular risk threat seem to possess risk management lessons learned and best practices in order to deal with that particular threat. On the contrary, companies with a high risk exposure seem to be short of risk management knowledge. Testing of the last two statements regarding risk threats and knowledge management is one of the major goals in the Empirical analysis.

Results of the corporations' risk threat rating are graphically displayed to show the company's risk positioning, see Figure 14: Step II - Risk assessment. Company risk positioning is displayed using a two dimensional matrix. Each risk trend being assessed is positioned on one axis of a matrix. Only two risk trends can be displayed per matrix. Hence, the number of matrices depends on the number of risk trends being evaluated. Each quadrant of the matrix indicates a specific risk threat rating for a company. Lower left quadrant denotes low risk exposure for risk trends on both the x- and y-axis. Upper right quadrant indicates high risk exposure for risk trends on both the x- and y-axis. Upper left quadrant specifies high risk exposure for trend on the y-axis and low risk exposure for risk trend on the x-axis. Lastly, the lower right quadrant denotes low risk exposure for the risk trend on the y-axis and high risk exposure for risk trend on the x-axis. Risk positioning of an exemplary company, company A, in regards to the three identified risk trends is demonstrated in Figure 14 and described below.

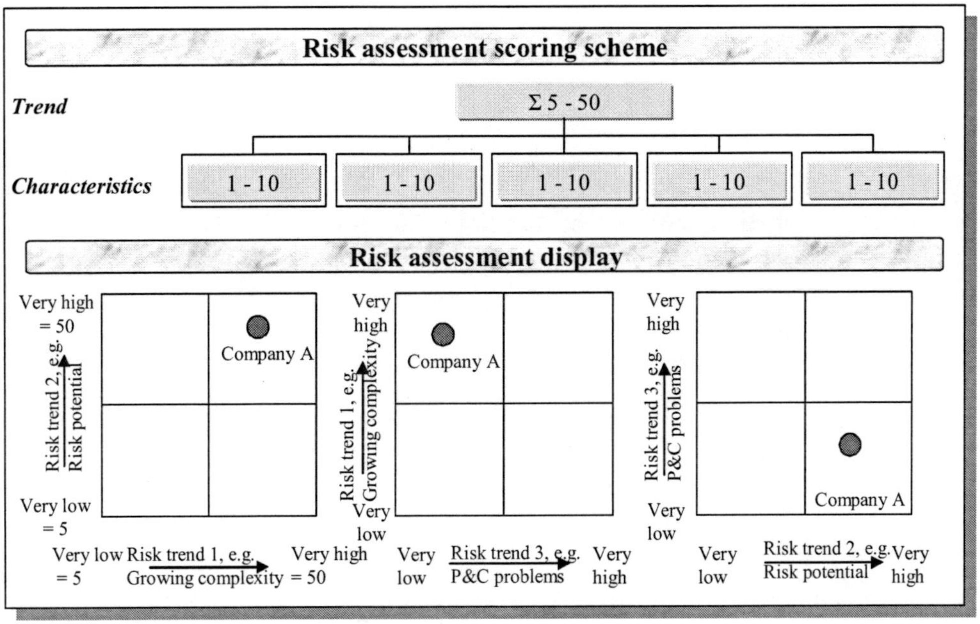


**Figure 14: Step II - Risk assessment**

Three matrices are produced for company A's risk assessment: (1) risk trend one versus risk trend two, (2) risk trend three versus risk trend one and (3) risk trend two versus risk trend three. From the risk data gathered for company A during Step I (Risk identification), company A is placed in the three matrices. Company A could for example obtain the positions depicted in Figure 14: Step II - Risk assessment. In the left matrix, company A has a high exposure for risk trend one and risk trend two. Therefore, company A finds itself in the top right quadrant. In the middle matrix, company A has a high exposure for risk trend one and a low risk exposure for risk trend three. Accordingly, company A is situated in the top left quadrant of the matrix. Finally in the right matrix, company A has a high risk exposure for risk trend two and a low risk exposure for risk trend three. In consequence, company A is situated in the lower right matrix quadrant. The graphical display of company A's risk exposure with the three risk trend matrices helps to visualise the risk positioning of the company and the relative danger of each of the three risk trends. As will be shown in the following sections, the graphical display also helps to clarify the required risk management improvements in order to limit the risk trend threat.

### *4.2.3 Risk analysis*

Step III (Risk analysis) consists of two parts: "Company classification" and "Knowledge management". The two parts are subsequently explained below.

#### *4.2.3.1 Company classification*

Company classification starts with a set of companies and categorises these companies according to pertinent general information and the Standard Industrial Classification (SIC) code[1] (EPA, 2004; OSHA, 2003; SSO, 2003). EPA (2004) defines SIC code as "a set of codes used to classify the economic activities of most of the industries or kinds of business establishments". Category fields for the general information are primarily derived from the information required by the commercial register[2] in Austria (Help, 2003a; 2003b), i.e. company name, legal form,

---

[1] The SIC code is an internationally recognised company classification code. In scientific research for instance, the SIC code was applied by Shah & Ward (2003: 129-149). In practice for example, the SIC code is used at Gerling Allgemeine Versicherungs-AG (Krebs, 2003) as a means for classifying its industrial clients. Only the 10 top level division of the SIC code are used in this book for simplification reasons. Drilling deeper is however possible to the fourth level. The 10 top level divisions are (A) Agriculture, Forestry, and Fishing, (B) Mining, (C) Construction, (D) Manufacturing, (E) Transportation, Communications, Electric, Gas, and Sanitary Services, (F) Wholesale Trade (G) Retail Trade, (H) Finance, Insurance, and Real Estate, (I) Services.

[2] Information required by law for the registration in the Austrian commercial register (Firmenbuch) for a corporation include company name, legal form, principal office, business address, branch, date of company agreement, first name, surname and

principal office, business address and branch. Additional category fields employed are: the total number of employees, operations in Austria, Europe and Worldwide and total revenues in the previous business year. Each company is positioned in the risk assessment display matrix based on the results of step II (Risk assessment). The resulting categorisation is then used to connect and position the examined company relative to comparable benchmark companies. Benchmark companies are selected if they appear in the lower left hand quadrant of the risk assessment display matrix and are in the same or a related SIC industry class as the examined company. Hence, benchmark companies are hardly affected by the three identified risk trends. It is important to note that the risk situation of benchmark companies should be generally evaluated according to the knowledge-based risk management process in order to allow a first comparison with other companies.

#### *4.2.3.2 Knowledge management*

Knowledge management involves the collection, identification and suggestion of risk management measures, i.e. lessons learned and best practices, from benchmark companies. These lessons learned and best practices should have led to genuine, sustained and successful actions in the benchmark company. In addition, the applied lessons learned and best practices should have led to a risk reduction regarding the three risk trends. Application of knowledge-management, following the company classification, is graphically displayed in Figure 15: Step III - Risk analysis.

---

date of birth of all shareholders, extent of power of representation of representing shareholders, first name, surname and date of birth of all limited partners, amount of capital contribution of limited partners (Help, 2003a; 2003b)

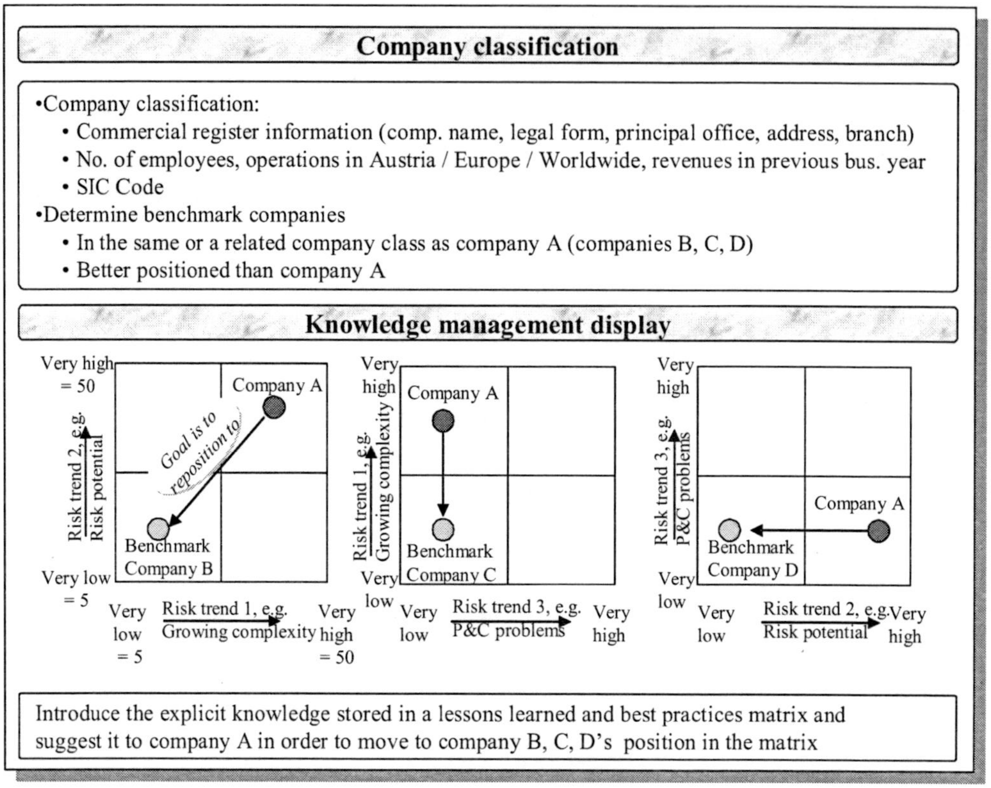


**Figure 15: Step III - Risk analysis**

In the depicted example in Figure 15, company A has a high risk exposure towards risk trends one and two (growing corporate complexity and increasing risk potential) but only limited exposure towards risk trend three (problems of the P & C insurance market). Company B has low exposure towards risk trends one and two. Company C has low exposure towards risk trends one and tree. Company D has low exposure towards risk trends two and three. As a result of this graphical display, companies B, C and D are selected as possible benchmark companies for company A. These companies serve as benchmark companies because they possess and have already effectively applied necessary lessons learned and best practices knowledge which makes them less vulnerable for the three risk trends in comparison to company A. Company A's aim is to reposition itself towards the favourable positioning of benchmark companies B, C and D. How company A can achieve this desired repositioning is explained in the following section regarding Step IV – Risk handling.

### *4.2.4 Risk handling*

Step IV (Risk handling) applies the relevant lessons learned and best practices captured in Step III, Risk analysis, in order to make the best risk management decision. This decision results in the avoidance, compensation (Theil, 1995: 150, 155) or mitigation of the risk trends threatening the organisation. If genuinely sustained and successfully implemented, the corporation is capable of repositioning itself from a higher to a lower influence from the risk trends, as shown in Figure 17: Step V - Risk monitoring. Current state of the risk environment encompasses influences from complexity and size of corporate structures, growing risk potential and problems of the P&C insurance market.

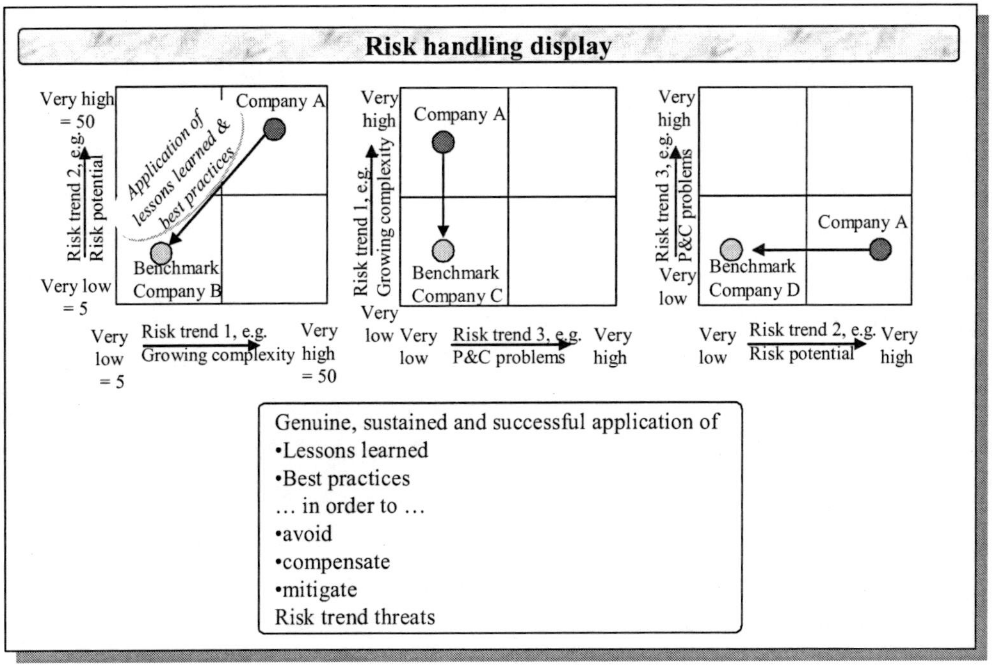


**Figure 16: Step IV - Risk handling**

In the left matrix example, lessons learned and best practices from company B are applied by company A in order to reposition from the top right to the lower left quadrant of the risk trend matrix for risk trends one and two.

In the middle matrix example, lessons learned and best practices from company C are applied by company A in order to relocate from the top left to the lower left quadrant of the risk trend matrix for risk trends one and three.

In the right matrix example, lessons learned and best practices from company D are applied by company A in order to change the position from the lower right to the lower left quadrant of the risk trend matrix for risk trends one and two.

Since the outcomes of applied lessons learned and best practices in Step IV – Risk handling are only visible after a certain time, the following Step V – Risk monitoring is crucial in determining the success of the overall risk management process.

#### *4.2.5 Risk monitoring*

Step V (Risk monitoring) continuously tracks at significant, for instance yearly, intervals the risk performance of the examined industrial company. Thus reapplying the knowledge-based risk management process insures the success of the industry insurer's and corporate risk manager's role (Ritchie and Marshall, 1993: 252). Periodic evaluation of the company is performed using the same procedure as described in steps I through IV of the knowledge-based risk management process. Variation in the examination results indicate whether the lessons learned and best practices have been successfully introduced and exploited within the corporation. If necessary, corrective action can be taken. Application of the necessary risk management measures "is not a one time event, but rather a continuous process, with the result of increased security" (Haller, 1975: 57). The knowledge-based risk management process meets Haller's criteria of continuity. In a feedback loop (Hölscher, 2002: 16; Gerling, 1986: 93), the knowledge gathered in the course of the process is collected and stored in the form of new lessons learned & best practices which can be reapplied in other companies. This step is show in Figure 17: Step V - Risk monitoring.

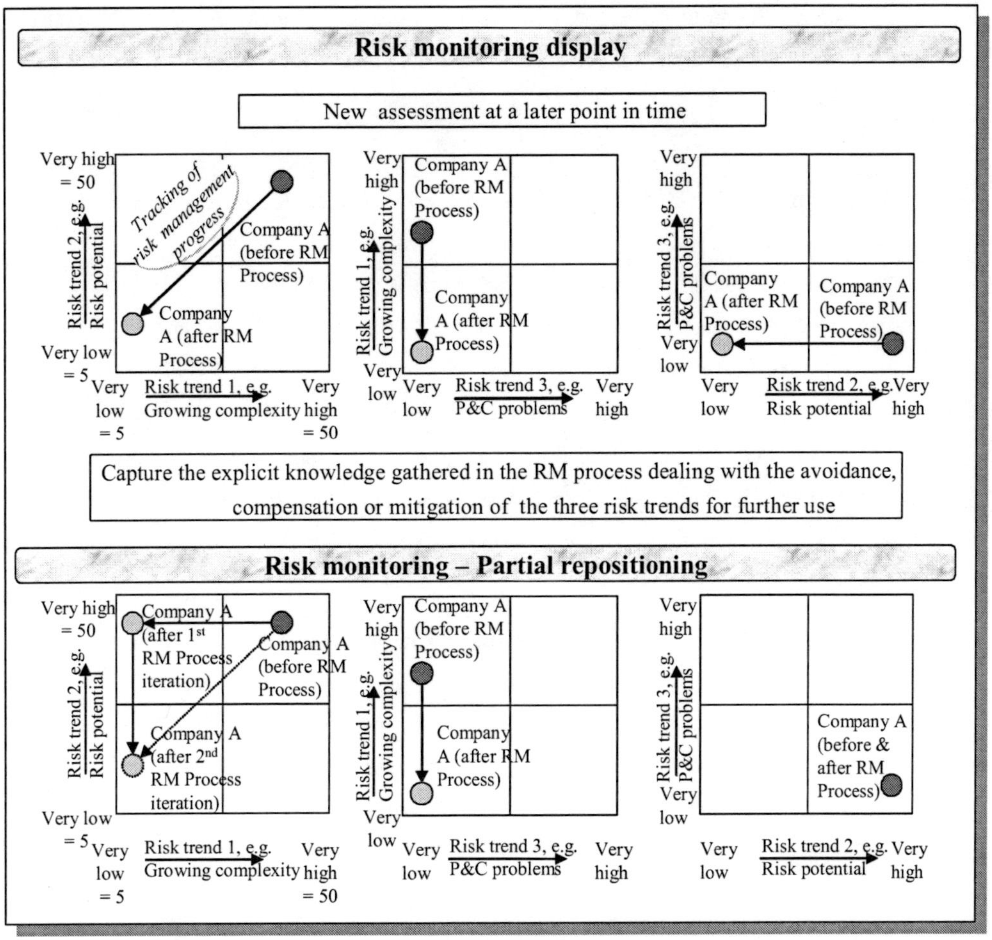


**Figure 17: Step V - Risk monitoring**

After a successful iteration of the knowledge-based risk management process, company A was able to reposition itself towards the lower left quadrant of each risk trend matrix. In some cases, only a partial repositioning might have resulted in the first knowledge-based risk management process iteration, depicted in the first risk trend matrix in Figure 17. Causes for partial repositioning along one risk trend might include a lack of complete examination, incomplete discovery of risk threats, inadequate handling and incomprehensive implementation of lessons learned and best practices for the particular risk trend threat in the first process iteration. In such a case, a repetition of the risk management process is needed. Focus of this iteration is on the missing lessons and best practices for the so far unimproved risk threat. As a result of the second iteration of the risk management process, company A could successfully reposition itself to the desired lower left matrix quadrant, with a low risk threat regarding risk trends one and two.

## 4.3 Practical application of the knowledge-based risk management process

An important aspect of the knowledge-based risk management process is the roles and tasks of the corporate and insurance risk managers involved in this process. Definition and description of these roles and tasks are provided in the next two parts of this section. Part one gives an overview on the different roles of the insurances' and the corporations' risk managers with regards to the five steps of the knowledge-based risk management process. For these role descriptions, 21 necessary tasks are identified and assigned to the insurance or the industrial corporation. Part two explains each of the 21 identified tasks in detail.

### *4.3.1 Overview of the insurances' and corporations' risk managers' roles*

The knowledge-based risk management process can be divided into activities of the insurer and of the corporation. Figure 18: Insurer's and corporation's role in knowledge-based risk management process provides an overview of these activities and helps as a process guideline for risk managers applying knowledge-based risk management.

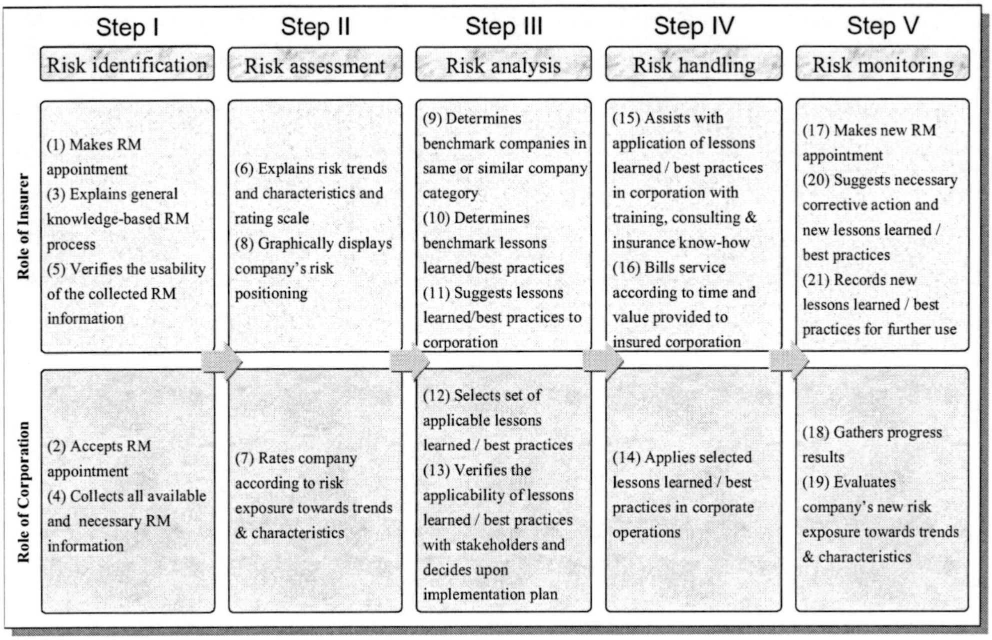


**Figure 18: Insurer's and corporation's role in knowledge-based risk management process**

Each of the five steps is explained in detail from the perspective of the insurer and the industrial corporation below.

### *4.3.2 Detailed role description of the insurances' and corporations' risk managers*

The knowledge-based risk management process normally starts with the insurer, since the insurer has a key interest in its clients' pursuing the knowledge-based risk management process. However, this is not mandatory. Both the industry insurers and the industry companies benefit from the introduction of the knowledge-based management process. Industrial corporations can avoid or reduce potential losses due to major risk threats. Industry insurers gain additional consulting and premium revenues when advising industry companies and can help their clients avoid major catastrophes. Hence, industry insurers have a possible new way to improve their combined ratio, an important target imposed by their shareholders.

In the past, the role of the insured corporation might have been too passive. Nevertheless, involvement and active role of the corporation's risk manager is a key success factor in knowledge-based risk management. While the top management should be responsible for managing the corporation, the risk manager's responsibility concentrates on its protection (Ritchie and Marshall, 1993: 248). Risk managers have to assure the long term survival of the company, instead of striving for short term financial goals (Ritchie and Marshall, 1993: 248). The suggested limited role of corporate risk managers (Karten, 1978: 47) might have led to the narrow focus on "risk analysis, avoidance and insurance". Today, talented risk managers need to be knowledge managers (Louisot, 2004). For instance, risk managers must be able to "translate the knowledge of the organization's goals and resources into a complete risk map" (Louisot, 2004). An intimate, high-level client relationship between insurance and corporate risk manager is required for the knowledge-based risk management process to work successfully. However, required intimacy clashes with the ambiguities generally existing between product buyers and suppliers (Rößl, 1999: 22). In this research, buyers are the industrial corporations and suppliers are the industry insurers. Ambiguity is particularly high in the sales process of a knowledge-based risk management consulting service, due to the highly sensible and confidential areas covered in the course of the process. Uncertainties must therefore be dealt with by reducing ambiguity and building trust. A detailed description on how these two important elements of a client relationship can be achieved is available in Rößl (1999: 22-27). Aim of a successful ambiguity reduction between insurers and corporations is a true, long-term partnership (Rößl, 1999: 28).

A long-term partnership also involves defined roles and responsibilities. Furthermore, roles and their associated tasks are essential for implementing a smooth running process. As a result, 21 tasks for the knowledge-based risk management process were defined. These 21 tasks are explained in the paragraph below. Whether the insurance or the corporate risk manager takes the lead role is highlighted with capital letters after the numbered task.

#### *4.3.2.1 Insurer's and corporation's role in step one – Risk identification*

(1) INSURANCE RISK MANAGER makes risk management (RM) appointment: Insurer's risk manager makes a risk appointment with the industrial corporation's risk manager or a comparable function. The risk management function is a must in today's industry insures, because most clients' industrial operations need to be examined on a regular, often yearly basis. A risk examination is key for the renewal of the existing insurance contract and also influences the pricing of the insurance premium. In cases where the risk examination delivers unfavourable results, necessary safety improvements are discussed with the client. A decision to cancel the insurance contract is chosen in some instances. Corporate risk managers on the insured

corporations' side attempt to guarantee on a daily basis the security of the corporations' human, tangible and intangible assets. Typically, their function is titled risk managers although risk managers could often be the head of finance, personnel or even the CEO. For process simplification, the person responsible for the risk management of the corporation will only be denoted as the corporate risk manager, even though their organisational title might actually differ. If an insurance risk manager wants to make an appointment with a corporation, they usually take advantage of the existing relationship with the industrial corporation already insured by the same insurer. However, it is also possible that the risk manager offers the insurance services as well as the risk management advice to a new, potential client of the insurance company.

(2) CORPORATE RISK MANAGER accepts RM appointment: Corporate risk manager accepts the insurance risk manager's invitation to examine the corporation using the knowledge-based risk management process. Acceptance of the invitation presumes: (a) the risk manager is aware of the need to improve his risk management capabilities and (b) the insurer does not provide this service free of charge.

(3) INSURANCE RISK MANAGER explains general knowledge-based RM process: Insurers' risk manager explains the methodology of the knowledge-based risk management process to the corporate risk manager during the risk management appointment. The corporate risk manager obtains a general idea of the necessary inputs for the risk management process. Furthermore, the corporate risk manager is given the opportunity to re-examine whether or not the process should continue.

(4) CORPORATE RISK MANAGER collects all available and necessary RM information: Corporate risk manager has the task of collecting all available and necessary risk management information. What is considered necessary risk information is pre-defined by the industry insurance risk manager. The corporate risk manager must thoroughly prepare this information. The quality of this task has a high impact on the success of the overall process, since this information is used for all subsequent process steps.

(5) INSURANCE RISK MANAGER verifies the usability of the collected RM information: Insurer's risk manager verifies the gathered risk information and filters the provided information accordingly. Wrong or unnecessary data is put aside while essential missing information is requested. This sub step is completed only when the insurance risk manager is convinced that

the information provided is sufficient to successfully finish the knowledge-based risk management process.

#### *4.3.2.2 Insurer's and corporation's role in step two – Risk assessment*

(6) INSURANCE RISK MANAGER explains risk trends and characteristics and rating scale: Insurance risk manager explains to the corporate risk manager the three risk trends (1) the emergence of increasingly complex and bigger corporate structures, (2) the development of risk potential in positive and negative direction and (3) the problems of the Property and Casualty insurance market. Each trend is described using the five main characteristics derived from the current state of the field analysis. Next, the insurance risk manager explains the risk assessment defined scoring scheme. Each characteristic is rated on a scale from 1 to 10. The rating denotes how the company views the characteristic's risk potential: 1-very low and 10-very high. Each trend has 5 associated characteristics, therefore, a trend can obtain a score ranging from 5 (1 point for each characteristic) to 50 (10 points for each characteristic). A company with the lowest trend score (5 points) has the lowest trend risk exposure. A company with highest trend score (50 points) has the highest trend risk exposure. Results are then graphically displayed to show the company's risk positioning. In addition to the scoring of the trends and characteristics vulnerability, the corporate risk manager explains the significance of the company classification in order to find suitable benchmarks in step three. The examined corporation can be classified using the top level company classification of the SIC (Standard Industrial Classification) code (OSHA, 2003; SSO, 2003).

(7) CORPORATE RISK MANAGER rates the company according to risk exposure as regards trends & characteristics: Corporate risk manager uses all available codified and tacit knowledge collected about the corporation's risk exposure to rate the company accordingly. In addition, the corporate risk manager classifies the corporation with regard to the SIC code.

(8) INSURANCE RISK MANAGER graphically displays company's risk positioning: Results of the corporate risk manager' assessment are graphically displayed by the insurance risk manager. This is necessary in order to demonstrate the gap between the examined corporation and the comparable benchmarks in step three.

#### *4.3.2.3 Insurer's and corporation's role in step three – Risk analysis*

(9) INSURANCE RISK MANAGER determines benchmark companies in same or similar company category: Using the provided company classification, the insurance risk manager determines the available benchmark companies relevant to the examined corporation. Depending on the availability of benchmark companies, the insurance risk manager may not find a benchmark company within the same company class and thus may need to search for comparable benchmarks from related classes. For example, a related class for "Services" could be "Finance, Insurance or Real Estate".

(10) INSURANCE RISK MANAGER determines benchmark lessons learned/best practices: Insurance risk manager selects the most appropriate lessons learned and best practices from the benchmark companies identified and selected in the previous step. The insurance risk manager needs to judge each lesson learned and best practice depending on its usefulness and applicability for the examined industrial corporation when making this selection. This selection demands a highly specialised and experienced insurance risk manager in order to make the most appropriate decision.

(11) INSURANCE RISK MANAGER suggests lessons learned/best practices to corporation: Insurance risk manager presents the selected lessons learned and best practices to the corporate risk manager. This includes all available information concerning the positive implementation of the lessons learned and best practices. However, the identity of the benchmark is not disclosed, thus the presentation remains neutral. Confidentiality helps to build the necessary confidence and trust with the examined industrial corporation so that it will provide its own new lessons learned and best practices in step five of the knowledge-based risk management process.

(12) CORPORATE RISK MANAGER selects set of applicable lessons learned/best practices: While the industry insurance manager presents as many suitable lessons learned and best practices as possible to the corporation, the final management decision is made within the corporation. Therefore, the corporate risk manager decides which lessons learned and best practices could be implemented by the corporation. This task relies on the quality of the options reviewed in the previous task.

(13) CORPORATE RISK MANAGER verifies the applicability of lessons learned/best practices with stakeholders and decides upon implementation plan: The selected lessons learned and best practices are presented to the major stakeholders affected by their implementation. This

is necessary for two reasons. First, in those cases where the corporate risk manager does not posses the necessary power in order to execute the selection, he or she needs the positive feedback from the key decision maker, e.g. the CEO, CFO, head of operations etc.. Secondly, the people affected by the solutions outlined in the lessons learned and best practices need to be involved in order to assess the applicability of the knowledge-based risk management and to gain their support and confidence. This task ends with the selection of those lessons learned and best practices to implement in order to improve the risk positioning of the examined industrial corporation.

#### *4.3.2.4 Insurer's and corporation's role in step four – Risk handling*

(14) CORPORATE RISK MANAGER applies selected lessons learned/best practices in corporate operations: Once the corporation decides which lessons learned and best practices are applicable and provide a potential benefit with regards to the risk exposure of the corporation, an implementation plan is developed. The corporate risk manager acts as a project manager to implement the new tools and knowledge within his organisation. Thus, success of this task highly depends on the project management skills of the corporate risk manager and the people supporting him.

(15) INSURANCE RISK MANAGER assists with application of lessons learned/best practices in corporation with training, consulting & insurance know-how: The implementation phase of the lessons learned and best practices is supported by the insurance risk manager. This support assures that the latest information relevant to the success of the knowledge-based risk management process is swiftly provided to the organisation through his corporate counterpart. Depending on the needs of the corporation, the industry insurer provides his training capabilities, consulting services and insurance know-how in order to insure the success of the overall project.

(16) INSURANCE RISK MANAGER bills service according to time and materials provided to insured corporation. Billing the knowledge-based risk management process is a critical task in the overall process. On the one hand, finding an adequate price is required to show the value of the service to the corporation and to cover the arisen costs. On the other hand, industrial corporations are accustomed to insurers providing some consulting services for free as reciprocity for the insurance premium paid. The knowledge-based risk management process, however, brings extended consulting services and additional know-how to the customer. Other consulting company's offers will be used as a baseline for pricing of these value added services and know-how transfer.

#### *4.3.2.5 Insurer's and corporation's role in step five – Risk monitoring*

(17) INSURANCE RISK MANAGER makes new RM appointment: Continuous improvement and follow-up of the knowledge-based risk process is very important. To insure the continuity and follow-up of the knowledge-based risk process, the insurance risk manager takes the initiative and arranges a meeting with the industrial corporation. The time frame for the new meeting should not be too close to the beginning of the process, so that effects of the first process round are already visible.

(18) CORPORATE RISK MANAGER gathers progress results: The corporate risk manager gathers and prepares the results and experiences of the knowledge-based risk management process.

(19) CORPORATE RISK MANAGER evaluates company's new risk exposure towards trends & characteristics: A new positioning of the corporation is determined by analysing the progress results gathered. The same rating scale described in step two is used. The corporate risk manager can now graphically display the corporation's new risk position relative to the starting point before implementation of the knowledge-based risk management process.

(20) INSURANCE RISK MANAGER suggests necessary corrective action and new lessons learned/best practices: Depending on the experiences gained and the new risk situation, the insurance risk manager suggests the necessary corrections and changes of the corporation's implementation strategy. In addition, newly found lessons learned and best practices supporting the success of the examined company are provided to the corporate risk manager, who can decide about their usage.

(21) INSURANCE RISK MANAGER records new lessons learned/best practices: The first interval of a foreseen iterative process ends with the recording of the newly established lessons learned and best practices. The time spent on this task is a key success factor for the overall process, not only within the examined company but also for the application in other, equivalent industry companies.

Either the industry insurer or the corporation can reinitiate the knowledge-based risk management process. In theory, this process has unlimited iterations. The aim of several process iterations is to guide the corporation through the changing risk environment while at the same time improving its risk exposure in order to maintain a competitive advantage.

## 4.4 Summary

Chapter four develops and explains in detail a conceptually new, knowledge-based approach towards risk management. Foundations of the new knowledge-based risk management process lie on the existing and proven risk management models by Theil and Tah and Carr. The knowledge-based risk management process can be applied by risk managers in industrial corporations with the help of industry insurers. For the execution of this process, a detailed role description for the corporate as well as insurance risk manager is given. Main advantages for industry insurers and industrial corporations of applying the new process within industrial corporations are as follows: (1) knowledge management allows reduction of risk trend exposure; (2) valuable knowledge & expertise is continually gathered, improving underwriting know-how; (3) industry insurers obtain lower internal costs due to process efficiencies and (4) knowledge-based risk management process is adaptable to changing risk environment. Each of these advantages are described in detail below.

**Knowledge management allows reduction of risk trend exposure**

Industrial corporations applying the knowledge-based risk management process successfully with the help of an industry insurance risk management team might reduce the corporation's vulnerability towards major risk trends. A systematic approach gives corporate risk managers a means to identify the corporation's risk situation and to assess its current vulnerability towards risk threats. Risk assessment is followed by risk analysis where the required lessons learned and best practices are selected. Selected lessons learned and best practices are applied in order to avoid, compensate or mitigate the risk threats. Success of the knowledge-based risk management process is sustained through continuous monitoring and making the necessary adjustments. A benefit of a successfully implemented process is that corporations are adequately prepared in dealing with major risk trends and therefore possess a competitive advantage over their rivals.

Industry insurers benefit from applying the knowledge-based risk management process by having to pay out fewer and less expensive claims to their customers, i.e. industrial corporations. Prerequisites for successful risk avoidance include:

- risk threats are discovered before damage arises
- necessary lessons learned and best practices are provided in order to avoid the risk
- suggestions are followed by the industrial corporation's management and staff

For the industry insurer, risk avoidance results in improved underwriting profitability, an important target imposed by industry insurers' shareholders. Thus both involved parties, industrial corporation and industry insurer can benefit from the decreased risk exposure.

**Valuable knowledge & expertise is continually gathered, improving underwriting know-how**

The structured and iterative knowledge-based risk management process helps both the industry insurer and the industrial corporation to capture and reuse valuable new knowledge. Constant gathering, verifying and updating of risk management knowledge is important for the industrial corporation in handling the increasing risk exposure and for the industry insurer in improving its underwriting capability and quality. Currently, no industry insurer in Austria employs such a methodical approach. Therefore, the pioneering companies in applying the knowledge-based risk management process could obtain superior risk management strengths, leading to a competitive advantage. However this strength depends on how seriously and successfully the methodical approach is pursued by all company employees.

**Industry insurers obtain lower internal costs due to process efficiencies**

Industrial corporations require risk management consulting services in order to improve their existing risk positioning. Numerous third parties could act as potential knowledge providers for industrial corporations, such as industry insurers, management consultancies, risk management experts and loss adjusters. Amongst all options, industry insurers seem to be the best choice and could lead to a mutually beneficial relationship with industrial corporations. The reason for this postulation lies in the industry insurer's focus on a large number of client relationships with industrial corporations. Therefore, managing industrial corporations' risk threats should be one of the core competencies of a top industry insurer. Application of the iterative knowledge-based risk management process helps industry insurers reuse necessary underwriting information.

Information which is normally gathered over and over again is stored in a central place and updated continuously over time. Central access to reusable risk management knowledge and expertise allows industry insurers to reduce the time and effort spent on an individual customer while at the same time improving the quality of the work. This increase in productivity creates the opportunity for serving the existing customers better and subsequently asking for a higher premium, or serving more customers at the same level. Which of the two options are chosen depends on the insurer's management. Industrial corporations benefit from the constantly updated know-how of the industry insurer and have a partner at hand during possible crises.

**Knowledge-based risk management process adaptable to changing risk environment**

Strengths of the knowledge-based risk management process lie in its adaptability toward changes in the risk environment. Benefits of the process are:

- it provides a reusable scientific approach,
- it makes the procedure reusable and adaptable in corporations,
- it allows knowledge transfer between corporations and
- it makes changes in the corporate risk situation visible, measurable and controllable over time,
- it supports the strategic planning process of the corporation.

Adaptability of the process is very important for industrial corporations which find themselves in very dynamic, fast evolving business environments. Flexibility of the knowledge-based risk management process insures that increasing control and transparency requirements (Peter, 2001: 187) are continuously met. This environment might continuously pose different or new risk trends which could be addressed with an adapted version of the knowledge-based risk management process. If a change in risk environment occurs, the process can be extended with new or modified risk trends and underlying characteristics. Due to the industry insurer's continuous monitoring of the changing risk environment in a large number of globally spread industrial corporations, each of its clients can rest assured that its risk management knowledge is always up-to-date.

Substantiation of all five steps of the knowledge-based risk management process can only be achieved in an industrial corporation's business environment. Success of the process application depends on good project management practice. Risk project management experience is particularly needed for steps I, IV & V (Risk identification, handling and monitoring). Steps I, IV & V are therefore not the main focus of the subsequent chapters. Extensive project management guidelines, e.g. by Krüger et al. (1999) exists and could support the practical application of knowledge-based risk management. Steps II & III (Risk assessment and analysis) of the process are verified through an empirical analysis in the 250 leading industrial corporations in Austria. Technique and results of the empirical analysis are presented in the following chapter.

# 5 Empirical analysis

Chapters two through four of this book present an extensive theoretical analysis of the relationship between risk management and knowledge management and the required development of a new knowledge-based risk management process. Chapter five seeks to establish and substantiate a connection between theory and practice via a risk & knowledge management survey. The aim of the survey as well as its execution is briefly explained in the first section of this chapter. Sections two though four are dedicated to the hypotheses to be tested and the qualitative and quantitative results. The final section provides a discussion of the findings.

The primary goal of this chapter is to examine the influence of knowledge management on risk management in leading Austrian industrial corporations, from the perspective of key decision makers in risk and insurance management is. This examination was conducted through an online risk & knowledge management survey focussed at the 250 leading Austrian industrial companies. Aim and description of the conducted survey are detailed below. A 30% response rate for the survey was achieved. This response rate is above the response rates of comparable management research (Yasin et al., 1997: 465). Therefore, outcomes and analysis of the survey can be viewed as significant and the survey as an overall success. In addition, this survey demonstrates the practical application of phases two (Risk assessment) and three (Risk analysis) of the knowledge-based risk management process, explained in detail in the previous theoretical part.

## 5.1 Aim and description of Risk & Knowledge management survey

The risk & knowledge management survey is designed to answer 12 fundamental questions from a defined target group. These questions are focused on gathering information relating to the target group's perception of the three identified risk trends (risk of complexity and large corporate size, development of risk potential in both positive and negative direction and P & C insurance market problems) and the target group's possession and use of knowledge management. Knowledge management for this survey is defined as lessons learned and best practices.

The risk & knowledge management survey's addresses the following 12 basic questions:

1. How do the corporations perceive the risk of complexity and large corporate size?
2. How do the corporations perceive the risk of the development of risk potential in both positive and negative direction?
3. How do the corporations perceive the risk of the P & C insurance market problems?
4. How do the corporations perceive their overall risk, i.e. complexity and large corporate size, development of risk potential in both positive and negative direction and P & C insurance market problems combined?
5. Do the corporations possess lessons learned and best practices to deal with complexity and large corporate size?
6. Do the corporations use these lessons learned and best practices in order to limit the risk of complexity and large corporate size?
7. Do the corporations possess lessons learned and best practices to deal with the development of risk potential in both positive and negative direction?
8. Do the corporations use these lessons learned and best practices in order to limit the risk of the development of risk potential in both positive and negative direction?
9. Do the corporations possess lessons learned and best practices to deal with the P & C insurance market problems?
10. Do the corporations use these lessons learned and best practices in order to limit the risk of the P & C insurance market problems?
11. Is there a correlation between possession of lessons learned and best practices and the perceived risk for each individual trend and for the overall risk perception?
12. Is there a correlation between usage of lessons learned and best practices and the perceived risk for each individual trend and for the overall risk perception?

The previously stated twelve questions pose sixteen hypotheses. The hypotheses derived are displayed in Table 9: Hypotheses – survey questions matrix.

### *5.1.1 Mailing of the survey*

**Selection of target group**

Target group for the empirical analysis is composed of the 250 leading industrial corporations in Austria. This particular group's vulnerability with regard to the risk trends, growing corporate complexity, increase in risk potential and the problems of the P & C insurance market as described in the state of the field analysis was the initial selection criteria. Moreover, the total annual revenues of the target group in 2002 were €96.9 billion[1], which is 65% of the total production revenues of Austrian corporations in 2001[2] (Statistik Austria, 2004: 329). Therefore, this group represents a significant portion of the Austrian economy and industrial production. In addition, industry "plays an important role for development of the Austrian economy" (Rößl, 1997: 7). Expected professionalism with regard to risk & insurance management as well as public relations for these corporations also contributed to the overall selection. Corporations identified in this target group were extracted from the 2003 version of "The 250 largest industrial corporations" of Industriemagazin (2003). The Industriemagazin's company ranking is renewed on a yearly basis, thus insuring alignment with the development of the corporations cited in the magazine. Detailed contact data for each corporation to be examined was extracted from the current Hoppenstedt database. Extraction process is described in detail in Appendix 1: Risk & Knowledge Management online survey design.

**Structure of the risk & knowledge management survey**

The risk & knowledge management survey developed for the empirical study contains four main sections. A copy of the online survey is provided in Appendix 2: Risk & Knowledge management survey content. Section one of the survey requests general information pertaining to the respondent and the respondent's company. Section two of the survey examines the influence of the three identified risk trends (risk of complexity and large corporate size,

[1] Figures taken from Industriemagazin (2003: 42-67). If no data was available for 2002, figures were taken from 2001. In cases where Industriemagazin did not provide any figures, revenues were taken from Hoppenstedt company database.

[2] The production revenues of Austrian corporations in Austria in 2001 was €148.878 billion according to Statistik Austria (2004: 329), industry codes C-F, figures for 2002 not yet available

development of risk potential in both positive and negative direction and P & C insurance market problems) on the corporation. Section three of the survey covers the handling of these three risk trends with regard to knowledge management. Finally, section four of the survey leaves space for feedback and comments. Since German is the business language in Austria, the survey was written in the German language. Each question was written in a self explanatory way, so respondents could answer the questions without further information.

**Process of the risk & knowledge management survey mailing and feedback**

Respondents to the risk & knowledge management survey were the key decision makers for risk and insurance management for each of the 250 Austrian industrial companies within the target group. Selection of these individuals was carried out via email and by telephone. Hence, each corporation personally identified the appropriate person to complete the survey. The survey was conducted fully online. Invitations for filling out the survey and all follow-up correspondence were done via email. The risk & knowledge management survey form was part of a newly created website for the Institute of Risk Management and Insurance, Vienna University of Economics and Business Administration. Thus, respondents logged on to the website, completed the survey form and the answers provided were saved on the website. Appendix 1: Risk & Knowledge Management online survey design provides a detailed description of the website and survey creation process.

Execution period of the risk & knowledge management survey consisted of five milestones, shown in Figure 19: Survey time frame, mailing dates and reception of replies over time. The first milestone, completed on the 28$^{th}$ August 2003, was the pre-announcement of the survey. This announcement also included the initial request for the name and email address of the corporations' key decision maker in risk and insurance management. The second milestone, completed on 4$^{th}$ September 2003, was the actual mailing of the survey invitation and the start of the survey response period. Milestones three and four were two reminder emails sent on the 15$^{th}$ September and the 7$^{th}$ October 2003. The fifth milestone was the conclusion of the survey period which occurred on the 15$^{th}$ October 2003. Figure 19 graphically displays the number of replies over the survey period.

Job functions of respondents in the target group covered a wide spectrum including CEO, assistant to the CEO, CFO, head of personnel, treasury, sales, or legal department, risk manager, insurance manager and industry insurance broker. Industry insurance broker or consultant is typically an expert in the particular risk situation for the represented corporation. Consequently, some target companies explicitly designated their insurance broker or consultant as respondent for the risk & knowledge management survey.

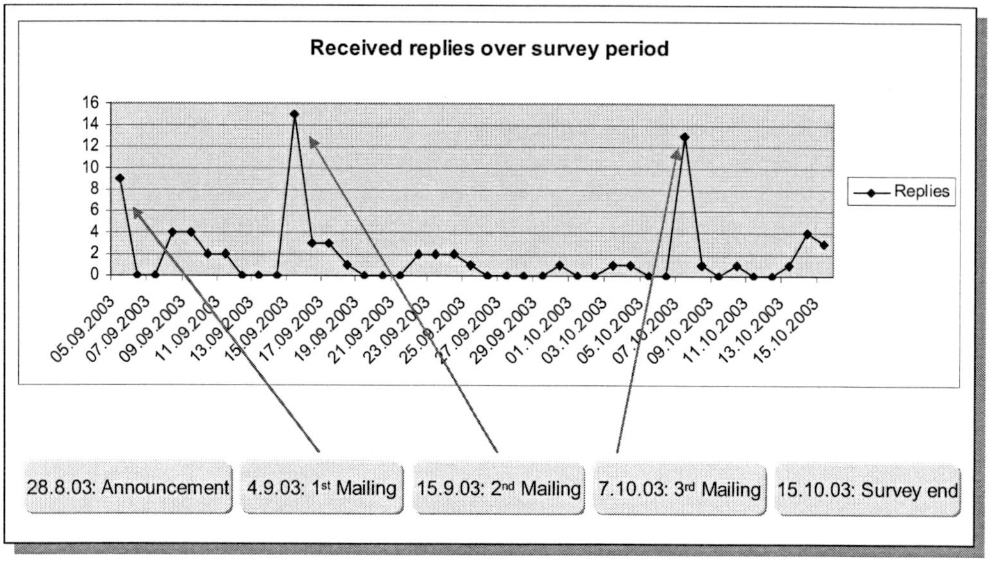


**Figure 19: Survey time frame, mailing dates and reception of replies over time**

### *5.1.2 Reception of the risk & knowledge management survey*

**An above average response rate was achieved for this study**

Survey response reception over time is depicted in Figure 19. On the first day of the survey and following the first mailing, nine replies were received. The second mailing, the first reminder email, resulted in 15 additional responses. Finally, the third mailing, the second reminder email, generated 13 further responses. Thus, the immediate responses to mailings represent 37 or 48.7% of the overall responses. This finding shows that reaction to online surveys is generally very quick and reliable, if the right target group is confronted with the appropriate questions. Furthermore, it indicates the importance of continuous dialogue with the respondents. Days following each mailing showed a sharp decline but steady response rate. Upon completion of the survey, 76 replies or 30.4% of the total 250 targeted Austrian industrial corporations were collected.

Aggregated revenues of the 76 corporations which responded are €38.9 billion, which is 27% of the total production revenues of Austrian corporations in 2001 (Statistik Austria, 2004: 329) and moreover 41% of the revenues of the Top 250 corporations in 2002. According to Yasin et al. (1997: 465), management research studies consisting of an extensive research questionnaire is significant with survey response rates of 18.7%. Therefore, the achieved return rate of 30.4% can be seen as highly satisfactory, particularly due to the far-reaching length and depth of the risk & knowledge management survey. In addition, the respondents' high qualification, the even spreading of replies across the overall target group and the representation of all industry sectors added to the quality of the results.

### Respondents' job functions

The respondents' overall job descriptions, depicted in Figure 20, demonstrate that the majority of the respondents come from top or upper management. By far the two largest groups are insurance managers (including two head of insurance) with 19 members and CFOs with 17 members. The high profile of these groups strengthens the qualitative and quantitative analysis.

| Survey respondents' job description | Sum |
|---|---|
| Insurance | 23 |
| CFO | 17 |
| Head of Personnel | 5 |
| Finance | 5 |
| Risk Management | 4 |
| Accounting | 4 |
| Head of Insurance | 3 |
| Assistant to CEO | 2 |
| CEO | 2 |
| Legal & Insurance | 2 |
| Inhouse Insurance Broker | 2 |
| Insurance Broker | 2 |
| Head of Real Estate | 1 |
| Head of Controlling | 1 |
| Procurement | 1 |
| Head of Accounting | 1 |
| Senior Consultant | 1 |
| Total | 76 |

**Figure 20: Survey respondents' job description**

**Responses spreading across industry ranking**

The ranking of the 76 corporations responding to the risk & knowledge management survey is evenly spread across the overall population of the 250 leading Austrian industrial corporations, as shown in Figure 21. For confidentiality reasons, a histogram (Kachigan, 1991: 24-27) was used for presenting the participating companies rather than listing each individual company. The 250 leading Austrian industrial corporations were divided into ten sub-groups. Number of responses for each grouping is noted in Figure 19. Figure 19 shows that every sub-group had a representative number of responses. The top tier sub-group, companies from one to 26, had the highest number of responses with 14 responses. The lowest number of responses was four, occurring within the sub-groups 51 to 76 and 225 to 250. The even spread of the survey respondents across the top 250 Austrian industrial corporations sample suggests that the interest in the topic of risk and knowledge management is independent of company size.

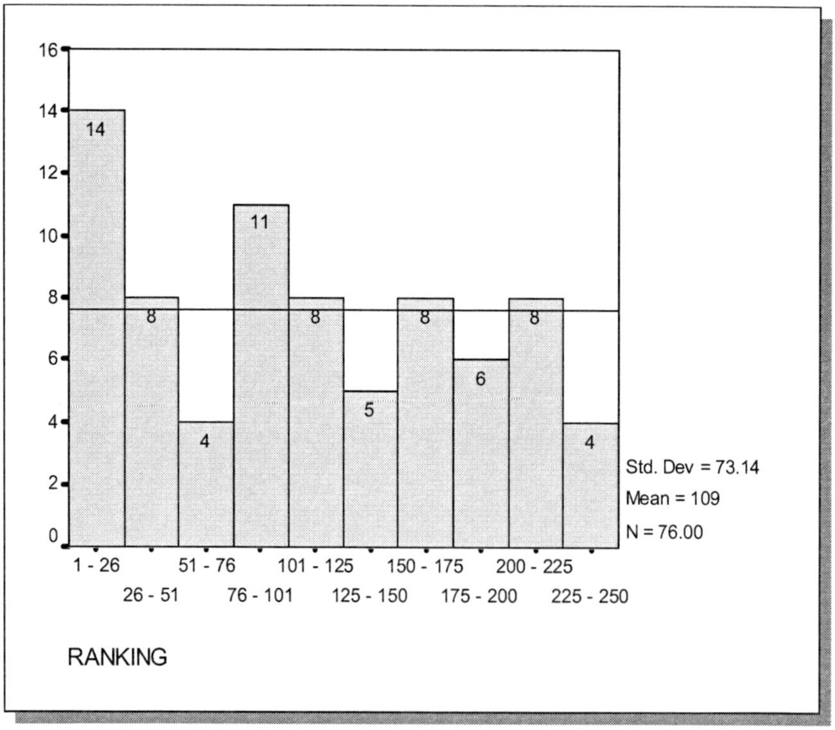


**Figure 21: Ranking distribution of responses across target 250 leading Austrian industrial corporations**

A series of three chi square tests were conducted to further strengthen the assumption that the survey responds were evenly spread across the top 250 Austrian industrial corporations. The first chi square test was performed using the same 10 sub-groups as above. In order to increase the likelihood of receiving a significant chi square, a more conservative approach was taken for the remaining two chi square tests. Five sub-groups were defined for the second chi square test and three sub-groups were defined for the third chi square test. Each of the three chi square tests resulted in minimum expected frequencies of respondents per sub-group.

The null hypothesis for all three chi square tests was $H_0$: Responses are equally spread across the top 250 Austrian industrial corporations sample. The alternative hypothesis was $H_A$: Responses are not equally spread across the top 250 Austrian industrial corporations sample. Results of the chi square tests were as follows:

- Chi square test 1: $X_1^2 = 11.632$ and df – value = 9,
- Chi square test 2: $X_2^2 = 4.132$ and df – value = 4, and
- Chi square test 3: $X_3^2 = .974$ and df – value = 2.

All of the observed values for the three chi square tests were not significant ($p < .001$). Therefore, the null hypotheses for all three chi square tests cannot be rejected. The consistent result across all three chi square tests indicates that the responsive companies are evenly spread across the top 250 Austrian industrial corporations sample (Bleymüller et al., 1996: 127-133; Kachigan, 1991: 295). Table 5 to Table 7 show the chi square test results.

**Frequencies**

| | RANKING | | | |
|---|---|---|---|---|
| | Category | Observed N | Expected N | Residual |
| 1 | 1 | 14 | 7.6 | 6.4 |
| 2 | 2 | 8 | 7.6 | .4 |
| 3 | 3 | 4 | 7.6 | -3.6 |
| 4 | 4 | 11 | 7.6 | 3.4 |
| 5 | 5 | 8 | 7.6 | .4 |
| 6 | 6 | 5 | 7.6 | -2.6 |
| 7 | 7 | 8 | 7.6 | .4 |
| 8 | 8 | 6 | 7.6 | -1.6 |
| 9 | 9 | 8 | 7.6 | .4 |
| 10 | 10 | 4 | 7.6 | -3.6 |
| Total | | 76 | | |

**Table 5: Chi square test results of ranking distribution with ten sub-groups**

**Test Statistics**

| | RANKING |
|---|---|
| Chi-Square[a] | 11.632 |
| df | 9 |
| Asymp. Sig. | .235 |

a. 0 cells (.0%) have expected frequencies less than 5. The minimum expected cell frequency is 7.6.

**Table 5: Chi square test results of ranking distribution with ten sub-groups (continued)**

**RANKING**

| | Observed N | Expected N | Residual |
|---|---|---|---|
| 1.00 | 22 | 15.2 | 6.8 |
| 2.00 | 15 | 15.2 | -.2 |
| 3.00 | 13 | 15.2 | -2.2 |
| 4.00 | 14 | 15.2 | -1.2 |
| 5.00 | 12 | 15.2 | -3.2 |
| Total | 76 | | |

**Table 6: Chi square test results of ranking distribution with five sub-groups**

**Test Statistics**

| | RANKING |
|---|---|
| Chi-Square[a] | 4.132 |
| df | 4 |
| Asymp. Sig. | .388 |

a. 0 cells (.0%) have expected frequencies less than 5. The minimum expected cell frequency is 15.2.

**Table 6: Chi square test results of ranking distribution with five sub-groups (continued)**

**RANKING**

| | Observed N | Expected N | Residual |
|---|---|---|---|
| 1 | 29 | 25.3 | 3.7 |
| 2 | 25 | 25.3 | -.3 |
| 3 | 22 | 25.3 | -3.3 |
| Total | 76 | | |

**Table 7: Chi square test results of ranking distribution with three sub-groups**

**Test Statistics**

| | RANK3 |
|---|---|
| Chi-Square[a] | .974 |
| df | 2 |
| Asymp. Sig. | .615 |

a. 0 cells (.0%) have expected frequencies less than 5. The minimum expected cell frequency is 25.3.

**Table 7: Chi square test results of ranking distribution with three sub-groups (continued)**

## Responses in terms of industry

Respondents answering the online risk & knowledge management survey were expected to provide general information about themselves, as well as about their company. This information included the selection of their industry, which was classified according to the top level SIC structure (EPA, 2004; OSHA, 2003; SSO, 2003). Table 8: Distribution of participating companies across industries displays the company classification for the completed surveys.

Manufacturing clearly sticks out with 49 replies or 64.5% of the overall population. Apart from public administration, each of the ten top level SIC industry sectors were represented

**SIC Code**

| | | Frequency | Percent | Valid Percent | Cumulative Percent |
|---|---|---|---|---|---|
| Valid | Agriculture, Forestry, And Fishing | 3 | 3.9 | 3.9 | 3.9 |
| | Mining | 1 | 1.3 | 1.3 | 5.3 |
| | Construction | 5 | 6.6 | 6.6 | 11.8 |
| | Manufacturing | 49 | 64.5 | 64.5 | 76.3 |
| | Transportation, Communications, Electric, Gas, Sanitary | 1 | 1.3 | 1.3 | 77.6 |
| | Wholesale Trade | 6 | 7.9 | 7.9 | 85.5 |
| | Retail Trade | 6 | 7.9 | 7.9 | 93.4 |
| | Finance, Insurance, And Real Estate | 2 | 2.6 | 2.6 | 96.1 |
| | Services | 3 | 3.9 | 3.9 | 100.0 |
| | Total | 76 | 100.0 | 100.0 | |

**Table 8: Distribution of participating companies across industries**

### *5.1.3 Sample description & Execution*

Both quantitative and qualitative analyses are performed to examine the main hypotheses outlined in following section, 5.2 Hypotheses. Answers obtained from the 76 respondents out of the target group consisting of the 250 leading Austrian industrial corporations laid the foundation for these analyses. Quantitative analyses are conducted first and are then followed by qualitative analyses. In the quantitative analyses, 16 initial hypotheses are posed. However, as a result of the examination of frequencies, these 16 hypotheses are collapsed to eight. How and why these hypotheses are collapsed is clarified below. Results of the quantitative analyses conducted on the eight collapsed hypotheses are presented. In the qualitative analyses, comments of the survey respondents are summarised and graphically displayed. Reasons for the approval and rejection of quantitative results are also discussed.

## 5.2 Hypotheses

The initial sixteen hypotheses tested in this research are depicted in Table 9: Hypotheses – survey questions matrix. These hypotheses are derived from the questions posed in 5.1 Aim and description of Risk & Knowledge management survey. Table 9 consists of four columns. Column one contains the numbered hypotheses. Column two names the trend and characteristics which are related to the bordering hypothesis. Column three includes the trend / characteristic survey questions, which are relevant to test the hypotheses located in the same row. Column four includes the risk knowledge management part of the hypotheses evaluation. Hypotheses are verified through a combination of the results of column three and four as demonstrated in the following analyses. Respondents rated their answers for questions in column one on a scale from one to 10. Thus, overall score per risk trend ranged from five to 50 and across all three risk trends from 15 to 150. Respondents answered with either "Yes" or "No" for questions in column four. The answer "Yes" was coded as one, the answer "No" was coded as two.

| Hypothesis | Trend / Characteristics | Trend / characteristic cluster of hypothesis evaluation | Risk knowledge management cluster of hypothesis evaluation |
|---|---|---|---|
| (1) Corporations that are highly affected by "complexity and large size" *possess low extent* of Risk management (RM) knowledge for this risk trend | Emergence of increasingly complex and bigger corporate structures<br>• Networked economy<br>• Shareholder Value<br>• Multiple Economic systems<br>• Globalisation<br>• Mergers & Acquisitions | From my company's perspective as an insurance customer and …<br>… with regard to increasingly complex and bigger company structures, I am …<br>• negatively affected by the *networked economy*<br>• feel an increasing focus on *shareholder value*<br>• dealing with challenges of *multiple economic systems*<br>• challenged by the effects of *globalisation*<br>• influenced by *Mergers & Acquisitions* | Questions regarding increasingly bigger and complex company structures:<br>• Do you have lessons learned on how to deal with this topic?<br>• Do you have applicable best practices? |
| (2) Corporations that are hardly affected by "complexity and large size" *possess extensive* RM knowledge for this risk trend | | | |
| (3) Corporations that are highly affected by "complexity and large size" *do not have extensive use of* RM knowledge for this risk trend | | | Questions regarding increasingly bigger and complex company structures:<br>• Do you make use of these lessons learned?<br>• Do you make use of these best practices? |
| (4) Corporations that are hardly affected by "complexity and large size" *make extensive use of* RM knowledge for this risk trend | | | |
| (5) Corporations that are highly affected by development of risk potential *possess a low extent* of Risk Management (RM) knowledge for this risk trend | Development of risk potential in positive and negative direction<br>• Natural catastrophes<br>• Industrial pollution<br>• Terrorism<br>• Technological advancement and failure<br>• Societal, political, cultural change | From my company's perspective as an insurance customer and …<br>…with regard to the development of risk potential in positive and negative direction, I am …<br>• concerned about the threat of *natural catastrophes*<br>• worried about the risk of *industrial pollution*<br>• troubled about potential *terrorist action*<br>• bothered about *technological advancements and failures*<br>• monitoring the effects of *societal, political and cultural changes* | Questions regarding growing risk potential in both positive and negative direction:<br>• Do you have lessons learned on how to deal with this topic?<br>• Do you have applicable best practices? |
| (6) Corporations that are hardly affected by "development of risk potential" *possess extensive* RM knowledge for this risk trend | | | |
| (7) Corporations that are highly affected by "development of risk potential" *do not have extensive use of* Risk Management (RM) knowledge for this risk trend | | | Questions regarding growing risk potential in both positive and negative direction:<br>• Do you make use of these lessons learned?<br>• Do you make use of these best practices? |
| (8) Corporations that are hardly affected by "development of risk potential" *make extensive use of* RM knowledge for this risk trend | | | |
| (9) Corporations that are highly affected by " the problems of the P&C market" *possess a low extent* of Risk Management (RM) knowledge for this risk trend | Problems of the Property and Casualty insurance market<br>• Price & capacity cycles<br>• Competitive disadvantages of the industry sector<br>• Legal changes<br>• Larger catastrophes<br>• New risks | From my company's perspective as an insurance customer and …<br>…with regard to the Problems of the Property & Casualty insurance market, I am …<br>• negatively affected by the industry's *price and capacity cycles*<br>• threatened by the *competitive disadvantages of the industry sector*<br>• negatively influenced by the *legal changes* of the insurance industry<br>• impacted by the *larger catastrophes* the industry has to deal with<br>• threatened by the *emergence of new, undefined risks* | Questions regarding the Problems of the Property & Casualty insurance market<br>• Do you have lessons learned on how to deal with this topic?<br>• Do you have applicable best practices? |
| (10) Corporations that are hardly affected by "the problems of the P&C market" *possess extensive* RM knowledge for this risk trend | | | |
| (11) Corporations that are highly affected by "the problems of the P&C market" *do not have extensive use of* RM knowledge for this risk trend | | | Questions regarding the Problems of the Property & Casualty insurance market<br>• Do you make use of these lessons learned?<br>• Do you make use of these best practices? |
| (12) Corporations that are hardly affected by "the problems of the P&C market" *make extensive use of* RM knowledge for this risk trend | | | |

**Table 9: Hypotheses – survey questions matrix**

<table>
<tr><th>Hypothesis</th><th>Trends / Characteristics</th><th>Trend / characteristic cluster of hypothesis evaluation</th><th>Risk knowledge management cluster of hypothesis evaluation</th></tr>
<tr><td>(13) Corporations that are highly affected by "complexity and large size, development of risk potential, and the problems of the P&C market" possess a low extent of Risk management (RM) knowledge for these risk trends</td><td rowspan="4">Emergence of increasingly complex and bigger corporate structures<br>• Networked economy<br>• Shareholder Value<br>• Multiple Economic systems<br>• Globalisation<br>• Mergers & Acquisitions<br><br>Development of risk potential in positive and negative direction<br>• Natural catastrophes<br>• Industrial pollution<br>• Terrorism<br>• Technological advancement and failure<br>• Societal, political, cultural change<br><br>Problems of the Property and Casualty insurance market<br>• Price & capacity cycles<br>• Competitive disadvantages of the industry sector<br>• Legal changes<br>• Larger catastrophes<br>• New risks</td><td rowspan="4">From my company's perspective as an insurance customer and …<br>… with regard to increasingly complex and bigger company structures, I am ...<br>• negatively affected by the networked economy<br>• feel an increasing focus on shareholder value<br>• dealing with challenges of multiple economic systems<br>• challenged by the effects of globalisation<br>• influenced by Mergers & Acquisitions<br><br>…with regard to the development of risk potential in positive and negative direction, I am …<br>• concerned about the threat of natural catastrophes<br>• worried about the risk of industrial pollution<br>• troubled about potential terrorist action<br>• bothered about technological advancements and failures<br>• monitoring the effects of societal, political and cultural changes<br><br>…with regard to the Problems of the Property & Casualty insurance market, I am …<br>• negatively affected by the industry's price and capacity cycles<br>• threatened by the competitive disadvantages of the industry sector<br>• negatively influenced by the legal changes of the insurance industry<br>• impacted by the larger catastrophes the industry has to deal with<br>• threatened by the emergence of new, undefined risks</td><td rowspan="2">Questions regarding increasingly bigger and complex company structures:<br>• Do you have lessons learned on how to deal with this topic?<br>• Do you have applicable best practices?<br><br>Questions regarding growing risk potential in both positive and negative direction:<br>• Do you have lessons learned on how to deal with this topic?<br>• Do you have applicable best practices?<br><br>Questions regarding the Problems of the Property & Casualty insurance market<br>• Do you have lessons learned on how to deal with this topic?<br>• Do you have applicable best practices?</td></tr>
<tr><td>(14) Corporations that are hardly affected by "complexity and large size, development of risk potential, and the problems of the P&C market" possess extensive RM knowledge for these risk trends</td></tr>
<tr><td>(15) Corporations that are highly affected by "complexity and large size, development of risk potential, and the problems of the P&C market" do not have extensive use of RM knowledge for these risk trends</td><td rowspan="2">Questions regarding increasingly bigger and complex company structures:<br>• Do you make use of these lessons learned?<br>• Do you make use of these best practices?<br><br>Questions regarding growing risk potential in both positive and negative direction:<br>• Do you make use of these lessons learned?<br>• Do you make use of these best practices?<br><br>Questions regarding the Problems of the Property & Casualty insurance market:<br>• Do you make use of these lessons learned?<br>• Do you make use of these best practices?</td></tr>
<tr><td>(16) Corporations that are hardly affected by "complexity and large size, development of risk potential, and the problems of the P&C market" make extensive use of RM knowledge for these risk trends</td></tr>
</table>

**Table 9: Hypotheses – survey questions matrix (continued)**

- Hypotheses and their related knowledge management questions
- Hypotheses and their related knowledge management questions
- Trend / Characteristic Questions applied to all hypotheses in neighbouring rows

**Figure 22: Hypotheses – survey questions matrix legend**

## 5.3 Quantitative analysis results

The following paragraphs illustrate the results from the quantitative part of the empirical analysis. Abbreviations for the statistical results used in this chapter can be found in 5.3.8 Legend for SPSS result tables.

### *5.3.1 Application of steps two and three of knowledge-based risk management process*

Over and above testing the research questions, the empirical analysis successfully demonstrates the practicability of steps two and three of the knowledge-based risk management process. Steps one, three and four of the process were not the focus of this examination, since they depend on good project management practice within the corporation. For the purpose of demonstrating the practicability of the knowledge-based risk management process, the risk & knowledge management survey questions were posed in the same structured way as explained in 4.2.2 Risk assessment and 4.2.3 Risk analysis. Part one of the risk & knowledge management survey requested respondents to rate each of the five questions pertaining to the three risk trends on a scale from one to ten. The overall score per risk trend therefore ranges from five to 50. Part two of the survey focused on knowledge management. Respondents had to indicate their possession and use of lessons learned and best practices associated with the three risk trends. Answers to the knowledge management questions were coded as "0" for no possession, "1" for possession but no use and "2" for possession and use of knowledge management.

Figure 23 through Figure 28 show how the risk & knowledge management survey results can be graphically displayed. Both the x- and y-axis represent one risk trend. For example in Figure 23, trend one, emergence of increasingly complex and bigger corporate structures is depicted on the x-axis and trend two, development of risk potential in positive and negative direction is depicted on the y-axis. Each dot in the matrix represents the risk perception of one of the 76 responding industrial corporations in Austria. In addition to the corporation's risk perception, the dot incorporates two more interesting pieces of information. First, the shape of the dot represents the availability and use of lessons learned or best practices for the risk trend on the x-axis. Possible dot shapes include a diamond (◊), a square (□) and a star (*). A diamond represents neither availability nor use of lessons learned or best practices. A square stands for availability but no use of lessons learned or best practices. Finally, a star represents availability and use of lessons learned or best practices. In Figure 23, for example, the shape of the dot represents lessons learned for risk trend one on the x-axis, i.e. T1LESSN. Secondly, the figure next to each dot represents the availability and use of lessons learned or best practices for the risk trend on the y-axis. A "0" represents neither availability nor use of lessons learned or best practices. A "1" stands for availability but no use of lessons learned or best practices. Lastly, a "2" represents availability and use of lessons learned or best practices. In Figure 23, for instance, the value next to the dot represents lessons learned for risk trend two on the y-axis, i.e. T2LESSN. A detailed legend of the following Figure 23 through Figure 28 is provided in Table 10: Legend of applied knowledge-based risk management process display.

Complete survey results of the examined corporation's risk perception as well their possession and use of lessons learned and best practices are depicted in Figure 23 through Figure 28 below:

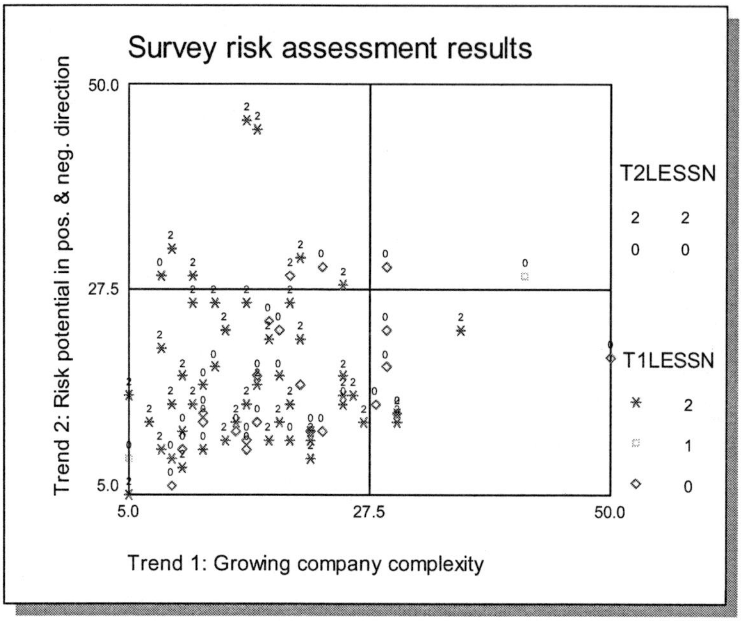


**Figure 23: Risk assessment with vs. without possession & use of lessons learned - Trends 1 & 2**

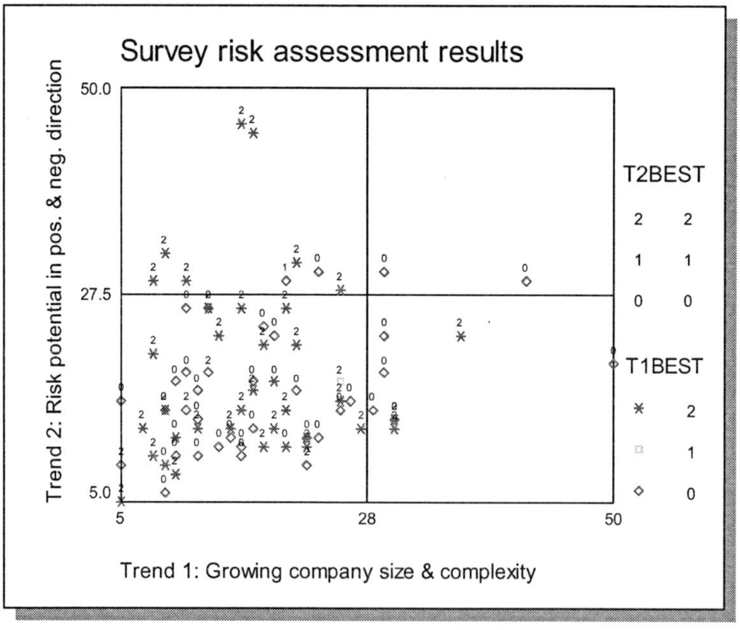


**Figure 24: Risk assessment with vs. without possession & use of best practices - Trends 1 & 2**

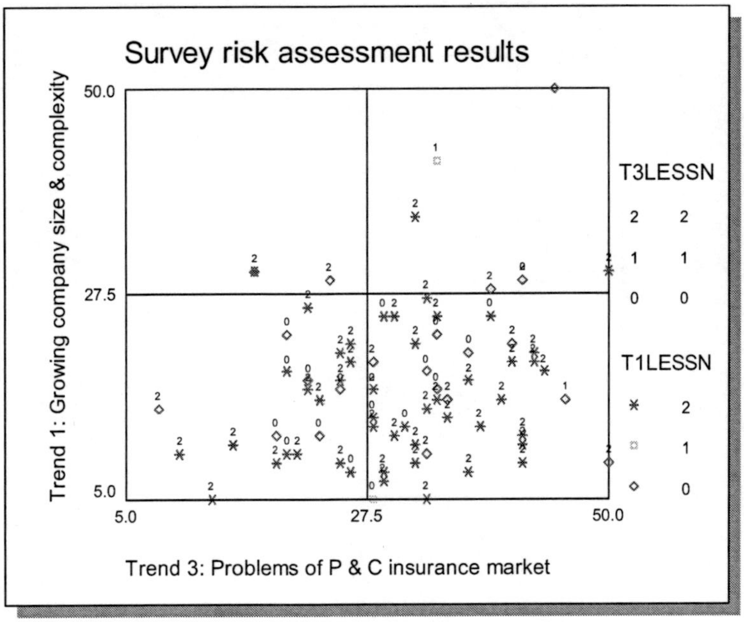


**Figure 25: Risk assessment with vs. without possession & use of lessons learned - Trends 1 & 3**

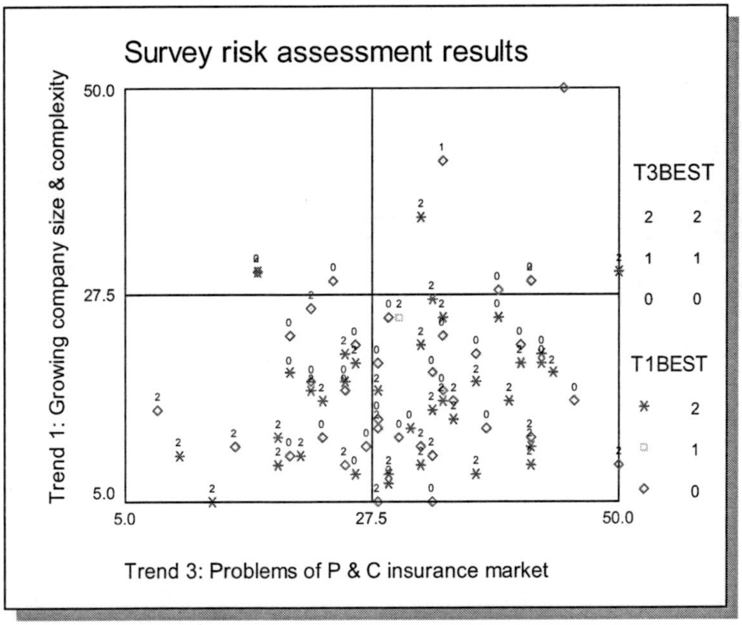


**Figure 26: Risk assessment with vs. without possession & use of best practices - Trends 1 & 3**

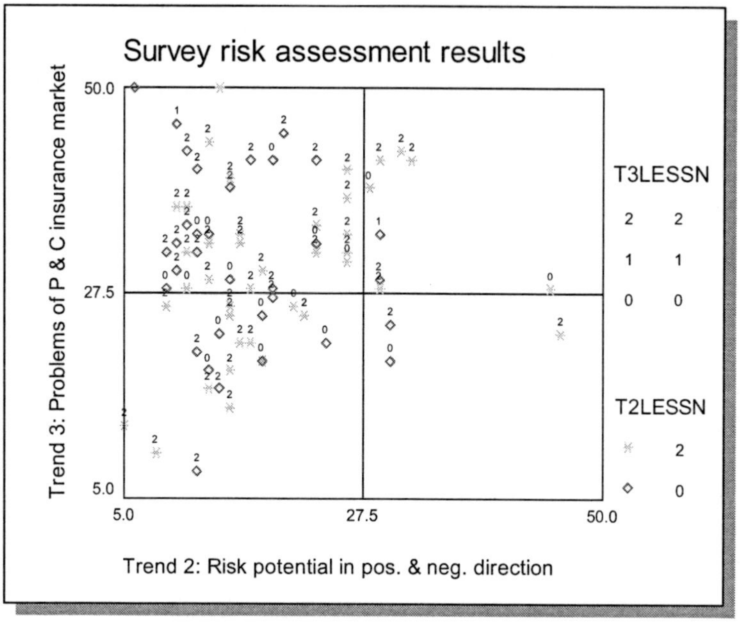


**Figure 27: Risk assessment with vs. without possession & use of lessons learned - Trends 2 & 3**

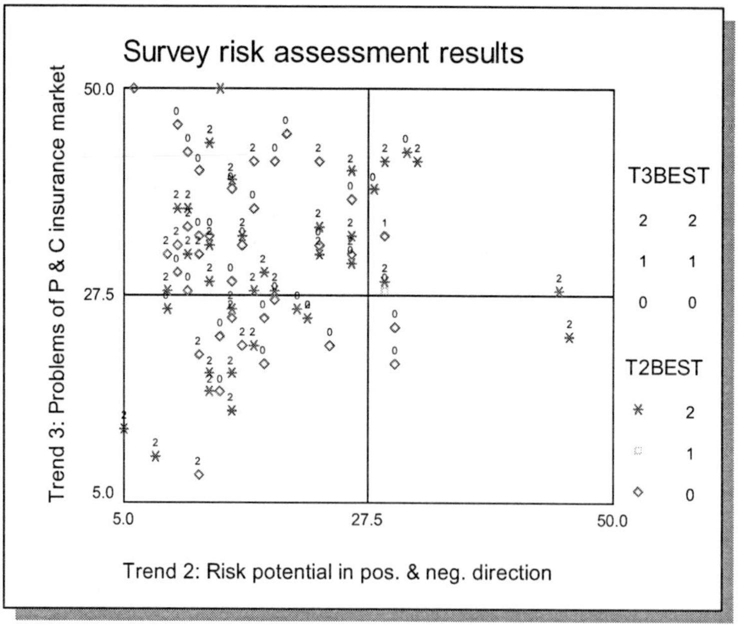


**Figure 28: Risk assessment with vs. without possession & use of best practices - Trends 2 & 3**

| SPSS table abbreviation | Short explanation | Full explanation | Values |
|---|---|---|---|
| | *Case label / Legend* (*) | | |
| **T1LESSN** | Trend 1 / Lessons learned | No availability vs. availability vs. availability & use of Lessons learned | 0 / 1 / 2 |
| **T1BEST** | Trend 1 / Best practices | No availability vs. availability vs. availability & use of Best practices | 0 / 1 / 2 |
| **T2LESSN** | Trend 2 / Lessons learned | No availability vs. availability vs. availability & use of Lessons learned | 0 / 1 / 2 |
| **T2BEST** | Trend 2 / Best practices | No availability vs. availability vs. availability & use of Best practices | 0 / 1 / 2 |
| **T3LESSN** | Trend 3 / Lessons learned | No availability vs. availability vs. availability & use of Lessons learned | 0 / 1 / 2 |
| **T3BEST** | Trend 3 / Best practices | No availability vs. availability vs. availability & use of Best practices | 0 / 1 / 2 |
| (*) *Case labels, i.e. the numbers 0,1,2 and the legend (◊ = 0, □ = 1, * = 2) represent a company's availability and use of lessons learned or best practices. For example x-axis Trend 1, y-axis Trend 2 corresponds with case labels for T2LESSN and legend for T1LESSN.* | | | |
| | *X – Y axis* | | |
| **Trend 1: ...** | Σ Characteristics for Trend 1 | Σ of characteristic values 1-5 for Trend 1: Growing company complexity & size | 5-50 |
| **Trend 2: ...** | Σ Characteristics for Trend 2 | Σ of characteristic values 1-5 for Trend 2: Risk potential in positive & negative direction | 5-50 |
| **Trend 3: ...** | Σ Characteristics for Trend 3 | Σ of characteristic values 1-5 for Trend 3: Problems of P & C insurance market | 5-50 |

**Table 10: Legend of applied knowledge-based risk management process displays**

### *5.3.2 Coefficient alpha reliabilities*

In the current investigation, three risk trends were identified in the literature. These risk trends have been shown to influence a company's overall risk (risk that is typically absorbed by the insurance industry). The three risk trends were (1) the emergence of increasingly complex and bigger corporate structures, (2) the development of risk potential in positive and negative direction and (3) the problems of the Property and Casualty insurance market. For each trend, five characteristics were selected which principally defined the trend. Each characteristic was again based on evidence in the literature. Characteristics identified for trend one were (1) Networked economy, (2) Shareholder value, (3) Multiple economic systems, (4) Globalisation and (5) Mergers & Acquisitions. Characteristics selected for trend two were (1) Natural catastrophes, (2) Industrial pollution, (3) Terrorism, (4) Technological advancement and failure and (5) Societal, political, cultural change. Characteristics chosen for trend three were (1) Price & capacity cycles, (2) Competitive disadvantages of the industry sector, (3) Legal changes, (4) Larger catastrophes and (5) New risks. Since the characteristics were derived from the literature, it was important to establish whether they were indeed consistently related to the corresponding risk trend. To this end, coefficient alpha reliabilities were conducted for each set of five characteristics. The coefficient alpha index ensures that survey respondents interpret the questions similarly. Coefficient alphas results are influenced primarily by two factors. Factor one is individual response rates, i.e., coefficient alphas would get lower if one or more respondents were just putting down random responses. Factor two is how individuals collectively interpret each of the characteristics. Outcomes of the coefficient alpha tests demonstrate high internal reliability. The coefficient alpha was 0.8236 for the first risk trend, 0.7379 for the second risk trend, and 0.8160 for the third risk trend. Coefficient alphas above 0.70 are generally considered acceptable (George and Mallery, 2003). All trends' coefficient alphas were above this conventional mark. Therefore, it can be concluded that each of the selected characteristics was consistent with the overall trend. The highly satisfactory coefficient alpha results for all three risk trends show that neither of the above two influencing factors (individual response rates and individuals collectively interpreting each of the characteristics) are problematic in respect to the answers provided by the survey respondents. Thus, it can be concluded that survey respondents took their time to fill out the questionnaire accurately and at the same time responded to the various different characteristics in similar ways. This conclusion is statistically driven, rather than how the author and others think people might be responding to the survey questions. Therefore, the coefficient alpha results are stronger than a conceptually backed argument alone, i.e., the "face validity" or what we think the items mean to people.

### *5.3.3 Boxplots for characteristics of the three risk trends*

The boxplots in Figure 29 provide a brief overview of the "median, quartiles, smallest and largest value, quartile range" (Bleymüller et al., 1996: 23-24) for each of the three risk trends' five characteristics.

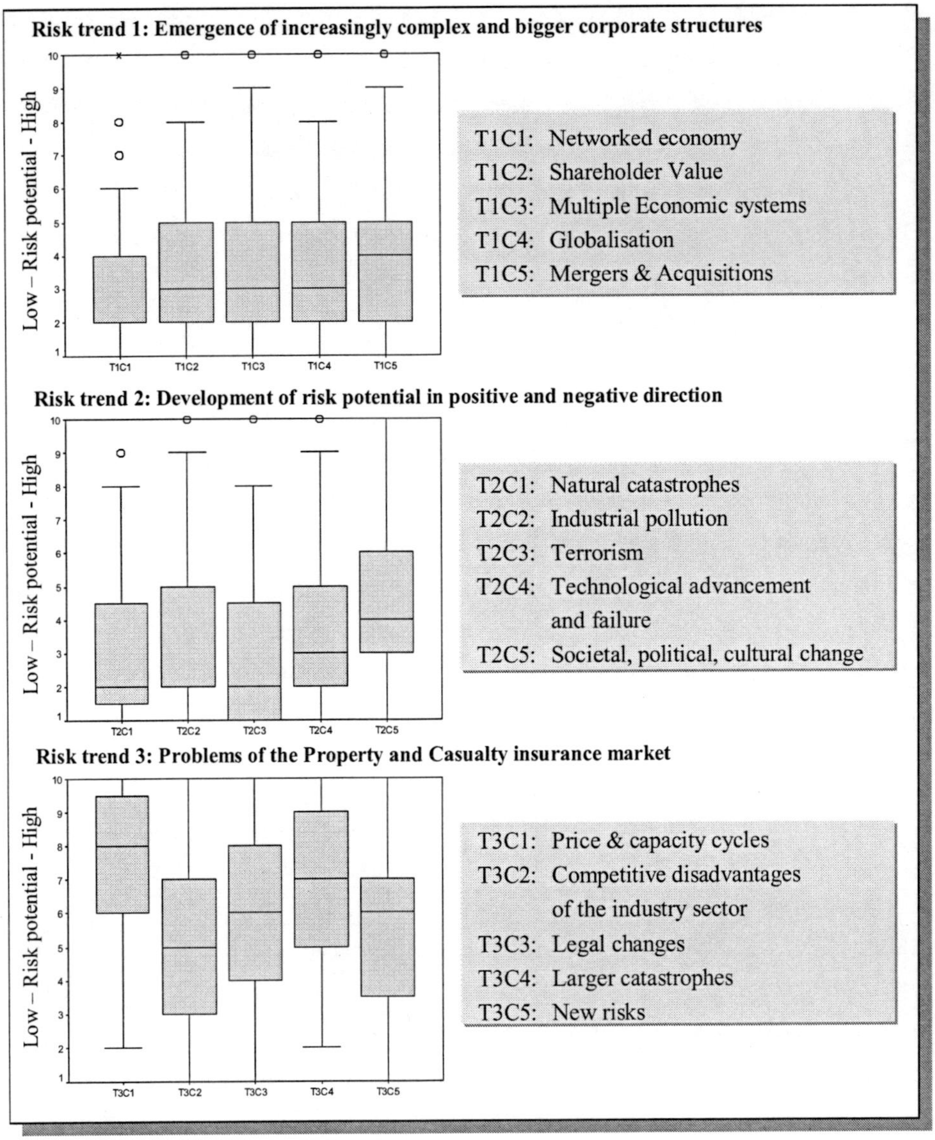


**Figure 29: Boxplots for the five characteristics of the three risk trends**

Potential score for each of the trend's characteristics addressed in the quantitative questions of risk & knowledge management survey ranged from one, meaning very low risk exposure, to ten, meaning high risk exposure. Boxplot results show that risk trend one and two are rated less threatening than risk trend three across all characteristics by the corporations responding to the survey. Thus, problems of the Property and Casualty insurance market seem to be a predominant concern for corporate risk managers. Additionally, the boxplots illustrate that the full range of possible answers (on the risk potential scale from one to ten) was obtained for most characteristics. Exceptions were T2C1, Natural catastrophes, which ranged from one to nine, T3C1, Price & capacity cycles, and T3C4, Larger catastrophes, which both ranged from two to ten. This finding suggests that the posed survey questions were not biased but led to meaningful results for the subsequent analysis.

### 5.3.4 *Examination of frequencies*

Frequencies were examined for companies' responses to possession and use of both lessons learned and best practices knowledge in order to set up the basis for the preceding primary analyses. Frequency analysis revealed that nearly all companies who had knowledge also claimed to put that knowledge to use. Therefore, companies were subsequently categorised as either having knowledge and use or as not having knowledge nor use. This finding is graphically depicted in Table 11: Answer combinations for possession and use of lessons learned and best practices.

| | | No knowledge | Possession of knowledge but no use | Possession & Use of knowledge | Wrong combination (No knowledge but use) |
|---|---|---|---|---|---|
| **Trend 1** | Lessons learned | 22 | 2 | 51 | 1 |
| | Best practices | 37 | 1 | 38 | 0 |
| **Trend 2** | Lessons learned | 33 | 1 | 42 | 0 |
| | Best practices | 37 | 1 | 38 | 0 |
| **Trend 3** | Lessons learned | 19 | 2 | 55 | 0 |
| | Best practices | 31 | 1 | 44 | 0 |

**Table 11: Answer combinations for possession and use of lessons learned and best practices**

A single wrong answer was provided for trend one, i.e. there was no possession of knowledge but use of that knowledge. Since this error only occurred once, a random mistake can be assumed. This invalid response was subsequently filtered out for the quantitative analysis. The rather insignificant size of the "possession of knowledge" group (1 or 2 responses per risk trend) versus the large groups of "no knowledge" and "possession & use of knowledge" shows corporations possessing knowledge generally also claim to put it to use. This finding allows the group “possession of knowledge but no use” to be overlooked altogether. Thus only two groups are relevant for the subsequent primary analysis. Group one is “no knowledge”, i.e. those companies who have no lessons learned and best practices knowledge. Group two is “possession & use of knowledge”, i.e. those companies who possess and use lessons learned and best practices knowledge. In addition, this results permits the collapsing of the initially proposed sixteen hypotheses depicted in Table 9: Hypotheses – survey questions matrix to eight hypotheses, shown in Table 12: Collapsed hypotheses – survey questions matrix. Only these eight collapsed hypotheses are examined in the following paragraphs.

| Hypothesis | Trend / Characteristics | Trend / characteristic cluster of hypothesis evaluation | Risk knowledge management cluster of hypothesis evaluation |
|---|---|---|---|
| (1) Corporations that are highly affected by "complexity and large size" *do not have extensive possession and use of* Risk management (RM) knowledge for this risk trend<br>(2) Corporations that are hardly affected by "complexity and large size" *possess and make extensive use of* RM knowledge for this risk trend | Emergence of increasingly complex and bigger corporate structures<br>• Networked economy<br>• Shareholder Value<br>• Multiple Economic systems<br>• Globalisation<br>• Mergers & Acquisitions | From my company's perspective as an insurance customer and …<br>… with regard to increasingly complex and bigger company structures, I am ...<br>• negatively affected by the *networked economy*<br>• feel an increasing focus on *shareholder value*<br>• dealing with challenges of *multiple economic systems*<br>• challenged by the effects of *globalisation*<br>• influenced by *Mergers & Acquisitions* | Questions regarding increasingly bigger and complex company structures:<br>• Do you possess and make use of these lessons learned on how to deal with this topic?<br>• Do you possess and make use of these best practices? |
| (3) Corporations that are highly affected by development of risk potential *do not have extensive possession and use of* RM knowledge for this risk trend<br>(4) Corporations that are hardly affected by "development of risk potential," *possess and make extensive use of* RM knowledge for this risk trend | Development of risk potential in positive and negative direction<br>• Natural catastrophes<br>• Industrial pollution<br>• Terrorism<br>• Technological advancement and failure<br>• Societal, political, cultural change | From my company's perspective as an insurance customer and …<br>…with regard to the development of risk potential in positive and negative direction, I am …<br>• concerned about the threat of *natural catastrophes*<br>• worried about the risk of *industrial pollution*<br>• troubled about potential *terrorist action*<br>• bothered about *technological advancements and failures*<br>• monitoring the effects of *societal, political and cultural changes* | Questions regarding growing risk potential in both positive and negative direction:<br>• Do you possess and make use of these lessons learned on how to deal with this topic?<br>• Do you possess and make use of these best practices? |
| (5) Corporations that are highly affected by " the problems of the P&C market" *do not have extensive possession and use of* a low extent of RM knowledge for this risk trend<br>(6) Corporations that are hardly affected by "the problems of the P&C market" *possess and make extensive use of* extensive RM knowledge for this risk trend | Problems of the Property and Casualty insurance market<br>• Price & capacity cycles<br>• Competitive disadvantages of the industry sector<br>• Legal changes<br>• Larger catastrophes<br>• New risks | From my company's perspective as an insurance customer and …<br>…with regard to the Problems of the Property & Casualty insurance market, I am …<br>• negatively affected by the industry's *price and capacity cycles*<br>• threatened by the *competitive disadvantages of the industry sector*<br>• negatively influenced by the *legal changes* of the insurance industry<br>• impacted by the *larger catastrophes* the industry has to deal with<br>• threatened by the *emergence of new, undefined risks* | Questions regarding the Problems of the Property & Casualty insurance market<br>• Do you possess and make use of these lessons learned on how to deal with this topic?<br>• Do you possess and make use of these best practices? |

**Table 12: Collapsed hypotheses – survey questions matrix**

<table>
<tr><th>Hypothesis</th><th>Trends / Characteristics</th><th>Trend / characteristic cluster of hypothesis evaluation</th><th>Risk knowledge management cluster of hypothesis evaluation</th></tr>
<tr><td>(7) Corporations that are highly affected by “complexity and large size, development of risk potential, and the problems of the P&C market” do not have extensive possession and use of RM knowledge for these risk trends</td>
<td rowspan="2">Emergence of increasingly complex and bigger corporate structures<br>• Networked economy<br>• Shareholder Value<br>• Multiple Economic systems<br>• Globalisation<br>• Mergers & Acquisitions<br><br>Development of risk potential in positive and negative direction<br>• Natural catastrophes<br>• Industrial pollution<br>• Terrorism<br>• Technological advancement and failure<br>• Societal, political, cultural change<br><br>Problems of the Property and Casualty insurance market<br>• Price & capacity cycles<br>• Competitive disadvantages of the industry sector<br>• Legal changes<br>• Larger catastrophes<br>• New risks</td>
<td rowspan="2">From my company’s perspective as an insurance customer and …<br>… with regard to increasingly complex and bigger company structures, I am ...<br>• negatively affected by the networked economy<br>• feel an increasing focus on shareholder value<br>• dealing with challenges of multiple economic systems<br>• challenged by the effects of globalisation<br>• influenced by Mergers & Acquisitions<br><br>…with regard to the development of risk potential in positive and negative direction, I am …<br>• concerned about the threat of natural catastrophes<br>• worried about the risk of industrial pollution<br>• troubled about potential terrorist action<br>• bothered about technological advancements and failures<br>• monitoring the effects of societal, political and cultural changes<br><br>…with regard to the Problems of the Property & Casualty insurance market, I am …<br>• negatively affected by the industry’s price and capacity cycles<br>• threatened by the competitive disadvantages of the industry sector<br>• negatively influenced by the legal changes of the insurance industry<br>• impacted by the larger catastrophes the industry has to deal with<br>• threatened by the emergence of new, undefined risks</td>
<td rowspan="2">Questions regarding increasingly bigger and complex company structures:<br>• Do you possess and make use of these lessons learned on how to deal with this topic?<br>• Do you possess and make use of these best practices?<br><br>Questions regarding growing risk potential in both positive and negative direction:<br>• Do you possess and make use of these lessons learned on how to deal with this topic?<br>• Do you possess and make use of these best practices?<br><br>Questions regarding the Problems of the Property & Casualty insurance market:<br>• Do you possess and make use of these lessons learned on how to deal with this topic?<br>• Do you possess and make use of these best practices?</td></tr>
<tr><td>(8) Corporations that are hardly affected by “complexity and large size, development of risk potential, and the problems of the P&C market” possess and make extensive use of RM knowledge for these risk trends</td></tr>
</table>

**Table 12: Collapsed hypotheses – survey questions matrix (continued)**

☐ Hypotheses and their related knowledge management questions

☐ Trend / Characteristic Questions applied to all hypotheses in neighbouring rows

**Figure 30: Collapsed hypotheses – survey questions matrix legend**

### 5.3.5 Pearson correlations

Correlation analysis between the availability and use of lessons learned (LESSNTOT), best practices (BESTTOT) and overall risk assessment (TS) resulted in another interesting finding regarding the examined survey results. Results of this analysis are portrayed in Table 13: Pearson correlations results for lessons learned, best practices and total risk score.

**Correlations**

| | | LESSNTOT | BESTTOT | TS |
|---|---|---|---|---|
| LESSNTOT | Pearson Correlation | 1 | .703** | -.051 |
| | Sig. (2-tailed) | . | .000 | .663 |
| | N | 76 | 76 | 76 |
| BESTTOT | Pearson Correlation | .703** | 1 | -.078 |
| | Sig. (2-tailed) | .000 | . | .502 |
| | N | 76 | 76 | 76 |
| TS | Pearson Correlation | -.051 | -.078 | 1 |
| | Sig. (2-tailed) | .663 | .502 | . |
| | N | 76 | 76 | 76 |

**. Correlation is significant at the 0.01 level (2-tailed).

**Table 13: Pearson correlations results for lessons learned, best practices and total risk score**

Companies' possession and use of lessons learned was positively correlated to companies' possession and use of best practices, $r(75) = .703$, $p < .01$. Thus, companies having and using lessons learned also have and use best practices. Likewise, companies not having and not using lessons learned also do not have and use best practices. A relationship between possession and use of lessons learned or best practices and the overall risk score can not however be positively tested through correlation analysis. Result of the correlation analysis seems to emphasize that lessons learned and best practices are both related and equally important components of knowledge.

### *5.3.6 Multivariate Analyses of Variance*

The primary analyses focuses on the examination of those companies having and using knowledge (i.e. lessons learned or best practices) compared to those companies with neither knowledge nor use, and whether these companies differed with regard to their perceived risk across the three trends and their characteristics. For these analyses, a series of Multivariate Analyses of Variance (MANOVA) tests were conducted. MANOVA were performed with company types (no possession nor use of knowledge vs. possession and use of knowledge) as the primary independent variable (both for lessons learned and for best practices) and the five characteristics of a given trend as the repeated dependent variables. Thus in total, six MANOVA tests were performed. Background theory for these analyses was derived from Kachigan (1991: 194-215) and Bleymüller et al. (1996: 119-125). MANOVA test was selected due to its unique ability to compare the "differences among two or more sample means" as well its usefulness in finding "relationships among variables" (Kachigan, 1991: 215).

#### *5.3.6.1 MANOVA 1 for risk trend 1 and lessons learned*

The first MANOVA compared companies who possessed and used knowledge of lessons learned for the first trend (emergence of increasingly complex and bigger corporate structures) with companies who did not[1]. The five characteristics of the first risk trend were used as repeated dependent variables[2]. An overall significant multivariate effect, $F(5,67) = 3.75$, $p < .05$[3] was ascertain. As shown in Table 14, companies possessing and using knowledge of lessons learned for the first risk trend, emergence of increasingly complex and bigger corporate structures,

[1] In the MANOVA results, a value of 0 for T1LESSN means "No possession nor use of lessons learned knowledge" whereas a value of 2 means "Possession and use of lessons learned knowledge"

[2] Original German survey questions: a) Risk Management: „Hinsichtlich des Trends ‚Entstehung komplexerer und größerer Unternehmensstrukturen', sieht sich Ihr Unternehmen bedroht bzw. negativ beeinflußt durch (1) die stärker vernetzte Wirtschaft (Digitalisierung, neue Geschäftsprozesse u. -modelle, zusammenhängende Produktions- und Logistikabläufe), (2) den wachsenden Fokus auf die Unternehmenswertsteigerung (Privatisierung, Gewinnmaximierung, Aktionärsstruktur, Börsenentwicklung, Risiko-minimierung, (3) die Herausforderungen unterschiedlicher Wirtschaftssysteme (Rechnungslegungsvorschriften, Anforderungen, (4) die Effekte der Globalisierung and (5) die Tendenz zu Fusionen & Übernahmen und der damit verbundene Anstieg von Risikokumul und Wechselwirkungen?" b) Knowledge management: „Besitzen Sie in Ihrem Unternehmen Lessons Learned (gemachte Erfahrungen), um mit diesem Trend umzugehen? Nutzen Sie diese Lessons Learned?"

[3] The significance of the overall multivariate effect for $F(5,67) = 3.75$, $p < .05$ can be seen in the statistical F distribution table (Kachigan 1991: 293).

indicate they are less at risk compared to companies who do not have possession nor use of lessons learned knowledge. This result supports hypotheses one and two in Table 12: Collapsed hypotheses – survey questions matrix. An investigation of the univariate analyses reveals that the overall multivariate effect appears to be primarily driven by the first characteristic, networked economy, $F(1,71) = 4.20, p < .05$, and the fourth characteristic, globalisation, $F(1,71) = 14.56, p < .001$[1]. Table 14: MANOVA results for Risk trend 1 shows that all characteristic means for risk trend one are in the same direction (i.e., companies with possession and use of lessons learned knowledge feel they are less at risk than companies with no possession or use of lessons learned knowledge). The only significant F values existed for characteristic (1) Networked economy (T1C1) and characteristic (4) Globalisation (T1C4).

**Between-Subjects Factors**

| | | N |
|---|---|---|
| T1LESSN | .00 | 22 |
| | 2.00 | 51 |

**Table 14: MANOVA results for Risk trend 1, Lessons learned**

[1] The critical value of F for 1 and 71 degrees of freedom is above 3.92 at the .05 significance level. This value is only reached for characteristic one (Networked economy) with F = 4.20 and characteristic four (Globalisation) with F = 14.56. The value for characteristic four (Globalisation) with F = 14.56 being greater than 6.85 even reaches .01 significance level. Based on the output from SPSS in Table 14, we can determine that the F - value is even significant at the .001 level. All other characteristics' F-values fall below .05 significance level (Kachigan 1991: 293).

**Descriptive Statistics**

| | T1LESSN | Mean | Std. Deviation | N |
|---|---|---|---|---|
| T1C1 | .00 | 3.73 | 2.548 | 22 |
| | 2.00 | 2.71 | 1.641 | 51 |
| | Total | 3.01 | 1.996 | 73 |
| T1C2 | .00 | 3.73 | 2.313 | 22 |
| | 2.00 | 3.61 | 2.299 | 51 |
| | Total | 3.64 | 2.287 | 73 |
| T1C3 | .00 | 4.23 | 2.369 | 22 |
| | 2.00 | 3.37 | 1.969 | 51 |
| | Total | 3.63 | 2.118 | 73 |
| T1C4 | .00 | 4.82 | 2.383 | 22 |
| | 2.00 | 2.94 | 1.702 | 51 |
| | Total | 3.51 | 2.102 | 73 |
| T1C5 | .00 | 4.64 | 2.498 | 22 |
| | 2.00 | 3.76 | 2.065 | 51 |
| | Total | 4.03 | 2.223 | 73 |

**Table 14: MANOVA results for Risk trend 1, Lessons learned (continued)**

**Multivariate Tests[b]**

| Effect | | Value | F | Hypothesis df | Error df | Sig. |
|---|---|---|---|---|---|---|
| Intercept | Pillai's Trace | .851 | 76.242[a] | 5.000 | 67.000 | .000 |
| | Wilks' Lambda | .149 | 76.242[a] | 5.000 | 67.000 | .000 |
| | Hotelling's Trace | 5.690 | 76.242[a] | 5.000 | 67.000 | .000 |
| | Roy's Largest Root | 5.690 | 76.242[a] | 5.000 | 67.000 | .000 |
| T1LESSN | Pillai's Trace | .219 | 3.753[a] | 5.000 | 67.000 | .005 |
| | Wilks' Lambda | .781 | 3.753[a] | 5.000 | 67.000 | .005 |
| | Hotelling's Trace | .280 | 3.753[a] | 5.000 | 67.000 | .005 |
| | Roy's Largest Root | .280 | 3.753[a] | 5.000 | 67.000 | .005 |

a. Exact statistic

b. Design: Intercept+T1LESSN

**Table 14: MANOVA results for Risk trend 1, Lessons learned (continued)**

**Tests of Between-Subjects Effects**

| Source | Dependent Variable | Type III Sum of Squares | df | Mean Square | F | Sig. |
|---|---|---|---|---|---|---|
| Corrected Model | T1C1 | 16.034[a] | 1 | 16.034 | 4.202 | .044 |
| | T1C2 | .219[b] | 1 | .219 | .041 | .839 |
| | T1C3 | 11.228[c] | 1 | 11.228 | 2.557 | .114 |
| | T1C4 | 54.150[d] | 1 | 54.150 | 14.558 | .000 |
| | T1C5 | 11.678[e] | 1 | 11.678 | 2.408 | .125 |
| Intercept | T1C1 | 636.089 | 1 | 636.089 | 166.680 | .000 |
| | T1C2 | 826.959 | 1 | 826.959 | 155.939 | .000 |
| | T1C3 | 887.722 | 1 | 887.722 | 202.153 | .000 |
| | T1C4 | 925.383 | 1 | 925.383 | 248.781 | .000 |
| | T1C5 | 1084.774 | 1 | 1084.774 | 223.718 | .000 |
| T1LESSN | T1C1 | 16.034 | 1 | 16.034 | 4.202 | .044 |
| | T1C2 | .219 | 1 | .219 | .041 | .839 |
| | T1C3 | 11.228 | 1 | 11.228 | 2.557 | .114 |
| | T1C4 | 54.150 | 1 | 54.150 | 14.558 | .000 |
| | T1C5 | 11.678 | 1 | 11.678 | 2.408 | .125 |
| Error | T1C1 | 270.952 | 71 | 3.816 | | |
| | T1C2 | 376.520 | 71 | 5.303 | | |
| | T1C3 | 311.785 | 71 | 4.391 | | |
| | T1C4 | 264.096 | 71 | 3.720 | | |
| | T1C5 | 344.267 | 71 | 4.849 | | |
| Total | T1C1 | 950.000 | 73 | | | |
| | T1C2 | 1346.000 | 73 | | | |
| | T1C3 | 1285.000 | 73 | | | |
| | T1C4 | 1216.000 | 73 | | | |
| | T1C5 | 1540.000 | 73 | | | |
| Corrected Total | T1C1 | 286.986 | 72 | | | |
| | T1C2 | 376.740 | 72 | | | |
| | T1C3 | 323.014 | 72 | | | |
| | T1C4 | 318.247 | 72 | | | |
| | T1C5 | 355.945 | 72 | | | |

a. R Squared = .056 (Adjusted R Squared = .043)

b. R Squared = .001 (Adjusted R Squared = -.013)

c. R Squared = .035 (Adjusted R Squared = .021)

d. R Squared = .170 (Adjusted R Squared = .158)

e. R Squared = .033 (Adjusted R Squared = .019)

**Table 14: MANOVA results for Risk trend 1, Lessons learned (continued)**

**1. Grand Mean**

| Dependent Variable | Mean | Std. Error | 95% Confidence Interval | |
|---|---|---|---|---|
| | | | Lower Bound | Upper Bound |
| T1C1 | 3.217 | .249 | 2.720 | 3.713 |
| T1C2 | 3.668 | .294 | 3.082 | 4.253 |
| T1C3 | 3.800 | .267 | 3.267 | 4.333 |
| T1C4 | 3.880 | .246 | 3.389 | 4.370 |
| T1C5 | 4.201 | .281 | 3.641 | 4.761 |

**Table 14: MANOVA results for Risk trend 1, Lessons learned (continued)**

**2. T1LESSN**

| Dependent Variable | T1LESSN | Mean | Std. Error | 95% Confidence Interval Lower Bound | 95% Confidence Interval Upper Bound |
|---|---|---|---|---|---|
| T1C1 | .00 | 3.727 | .416 | 2.897 | 4.558 |
| | 2.00 | 2.706 | .274 | 2.160 | 3.251 |
| T1C2 | .00 | 3.727 | .491 | 2.748 | 4.706 |
| | 2.00 | 3.608 | .322 | 2.965 | 4.251 |
| T1C3 | .00 | 4.227 | .447 | 3.336 | 5.118 |
| | 2.00 | 3.373 | .293 | 2.787 | 3.958 |
| T1C4 | .00 | 4.818 | .411 | 3.998 | 5.638 |
| | 2.00 | 2.941 | .270 | 2.403 | 3.480 |
| T1C5 | .00 | 4.636 | .469 | 3.700 | 5.572 |
| | 2.00 | 3.765 | .308 | 3.150 | 4.380 |

**Table 14: MANOVA results for Risk trend 1, Lessons learned (continued)**

### *5.3.6.2 MANOVA 2 for risk trend 1 and best practices*

The second MANOVA compared companies who possessed and used knowledge of best practices for the first risk trend (emergence of increasingly complex and bigger corporate structures) with companies who did not[1]. The five characteristics of the first risk trend were used as repeated dependent variables[2]. An overall insignificant multivariate effect was determined, $F(5,69) = 1.06$, $p < .05$[3], see Table 15. This result does not substantiate hypotheses one and two in Table 12: Collapsed hypotheses – survey questions matrix. However, as can be seen in Table 15: MANOVA results for Risk trend 1, Best practices, all the characteristic means except for the second characteristic, shareholder value, are in the same direction. Thus,

[1] In the MANOVA results, a value of 0 for T1BEST means "No possession nor use of best practices knowledge" whereas a value of 2 means "Possession and use of best practices knowledge"

[2] Original German survey questions: a) Risk Management: „Hinsichtlich des Trends ‚Entstehung komplexerer und größerer Unternehmensstrukturen', sieht sich Ihr Unternehmen bedroht bzw. negativ beeinflußt durch (1) die stärker vernetzte Wirtschaft (Digitalisierung, neue Geschäftsprozesse u. -modelle, zusammenhängende Produktions- und Logistikabläufe), (2) den wachsenden Fokus auf die Unternehmenswertsteigerung (Privatisierung, Gewinnmaximierung, Aktionärsstruktur, Börsenentwicklung, Risikominimierung, (3) die Herausforderungen unterschiedlicher Wirtschaftssysteme (Rechnungslegungsvorschriften, Anforderungen, (4) die Effekte der Globalisierung and (5) die Tendenz zu Fusionen & Übernahmen und der damit verbundene Anstieg von Risikokumul und Wechselwirkungen?" b) Knowledge management: „Besitzen Sie in Ihrem Unternehmen Best Practices (positive Musterbeispiele), um mit diesem Trend umzugehen? Nutzen Sie diese Best Practices?"

[3] The insignificance of the overall multivariate effect for $F(5,69) = 1.06$, $p < .05$ can be seen in the statistical F distribution table (Kachigan 1991: 293). The critical value of F for 5 and 69 degrees of freedom is above 1.9, which is greater than 1.06, at the .05 significance level.

companies with possession and use of best practices knowledge feel they are less at risk than companies with no possession or use of best practices knowledge.

**Between-Subjects Factors**

| | | N |
|---|---|---|
| T1BEST | .00 | 37 |
| | 2.00 | 38 |

**Table 15: MANOVA results for Risk trend 1, Best practices**

**Descriptive Statistics**

| | T1BEST | Mean | Std. Deviation | N |
|---|---|---|---|---|
| T1C1 | .00 | 3.35 | 2.418 | 37 |
| | 2.00 | 2.74 | 1.554 | 38 |
| | Total | 3.04 | 2.036 | 75 |
| T1C2 | .00 | 3.62 | 2.442 | 37 |
| | 2.00 | 3.66 | 2.408 | 38 |
| | Total | 3.64 | 2.409 | 75 |
| T1C3 | .00 | 4.00 | 2.449 | 37 |
| | 2.00 | 3.29 | 1.829 | 38 |
| | Total | 3.64 | 2.173 | 75 |
| T1C4 | .00 | 3.76 | 2.532 | 37 |
| | 2.00 | 3.18 | 1.706 | 38 |
| | Total | 3.47 | 2.158 | 75 |
| T1C5 | .00 | 4.03 | 2.630 | 37 |
| | 2.00 | 3.97 | 2.007 | 38 |
| | Total | 4.00 | 2.319 | 75 |

**Table 15: MANOVA results for Risk trend 1, Best practices (continued)**

**Multivariate Tests[b]**

| Effect | | Value | F | Hypothesis df | Error df | Sig. |
|---|---|---|---|---|---|---|
| Intercept | Pillai's Trace | .831 | 67.801[a] | 5.000 | 69.000 | .000 |
| | Wilks' Lambda | .169 | 67.801[a] | 5.000 | 69.000 | .000 |
| | Hotelling's Trace | 4.913 | 67.801[a] | 5.000 | 69.000 | .000 |
| | Roy's Largest Root | 4.913 | 67.801[a] | 5.000 | 69.000 | .000 |
| T1BEST | Pillai's Trace | .071 | 1.056[a] | 5.000 | 69.000 | .392 |
| | Wilks' Lambda | .929 | 1.056[a] | 5.000 | 69.000 | .392 |
| | Hotelling's Trace | .077 | 1.056[a] | 5.000 | 69.000 | .392 |
| | Roy's Largest Root | .077 | 1.056[a] | 5.000 | 69.000 | .392 |

a. Exact statistic

b. Design: Intercept+T1BEST

**Table 15: MANOVA results for Risk trend 1, Best practices (continued)**

**Tests of Between-Subjects Effects**

| Source | Dependent Variable | Type III Sum of Squares | df | Mean Square | F | Sig. |
|---|---|---|---|---|---|---|
| Corrected Model | T1C1 | 7.079[a] | 1 | 7.079 | 1.724 | .193 |
| | T1C2 | 2.467E-02[b] | 1 | 2.467E-02 | .004 | .949 |
| | T1C3 | 9.464[c] | 1 | 9.464 | 2.033 | .158 |
| | T1C4 | 6.145[d] | 1 | 6.145 | 1.325 | .253 |
| | T1C5 | 5.334E-02[b] | 1 | 5.334E-02 | .010 | .921 |
| Intercept | T1C1 | 694.866 | 1 | 694.866 | 169.196 | .000 |
| | T1C2 | 993.411 | 1 | 993.411 | 168.941 | .000 |
| | T1C3 | 996.131 | 1 | 996.131 | 213.991 | .000 |
| | T1C4 | 903.159 | 1 | 903.159 | 194.760 | .000 |
| | T1C5 | 1200.000 | 1 | 1200.000 | 220.130 | .000 |
| T1BEST | T1C1 | 7.079 | 1 | 7.079 | 1.724 | .193 |
| | T1C2 | 2.467E-02 | 1 | 2.467E-02 | .004 | .949 |
| | T1C3 | 9.464 | 1 | 9.464 | 2.033 | .158 |
| | T1C4 | 6.145 | 1 | 6.145 | 1.325 | .253 |
| | T1C5 | 5.334E-02 | 1 | 5.334E-02 | .010 | .921 |
| Error | T1C1 | 299.801 | 73 | 4.107 | | |
| | T1C2 | 429.255 | 73 | 5.880 | | |
| | T1C3 | 339.816 | 73 | 4.655 | | |
| | T1C4 | 338.521 | 73 | 4.637 | | |
| | T1C5 | 397.947 | 73 | 5.451 | | |
| Total | T1C1 | 1000.000 | 75 | | | |
| | T1C2 | 1423.000 | 75 | | | |
| | T1C3 | 1343.000 | 75 | | | |
| | T1C4 | 1246.000 | 75 | | | |
| | T1C5 | 1598.000 | 75 | | | |
| Corrected Total | T1C1 | 306.880 | 74 | | | |
| | T1C2 | 429.280 | 74 | | | |
| | T1C3 | 349.280 | 74 | | | |
| | T1C4 | 344.667 | 74 | | | |
| | T1C5 | 398.000 | 74 | | | |

a. R Squared = .023 (Adjusted R Squared = .010)
b. R Squared = .000 (Adjusted R Squared = -.014)
c. R Squared = .027 (Adjusted R Squared = .014)
d. R Squared = .018 (Adjusted R Squared = .004)

**Table 15: MANOVA results for Risk trend 1, Best practices (continued)**

### *5.3.6.3 MANOVA 3 for risk trend 2 and lessons learned*

The third MANOVA compares companies who possessed and used knowledge of lessons learned for the second risk trend (development of risk potential in positive and negative direction) were with companies who did not[1]. The five characteristics of the second risk trend

[1] In the MANOVA results, a value of 0 for T2LESSN means "No possession nor use of lessons learned knowledge" whereas a value of 2 means "Possession and use of lessons learned knowledge"

were used as repeated dependent variables[1]. There was an overall insignificant multivariate effect, $F(5,69) = 0.87$, $p < .05$[2]. It is interesting to note that companies possessing and using knowledge of lessons learned for the second risk trend, development of risk potential in positive and negative direction, indicate that they are higher at risk compared to companies who do not have possession nor use of lessons learned knowledge (see Table 16). This outcome, however, does not substantiate hypotheses three and four in Table 12: Collapsed hypotheses – survey questions matrix. As shown in Table 16: MANOVA results for Risk trend 2, Lessons learned, all the characteristic means are in the same direction. Therefore, companies with possession and use of lessons learned knowledge feel they are higher at risk than companies with no possession or use of lessons learned knowledge.

**Between-Subjects Factors**

| | | N |
|---|---|---|
| T2LESSN | .00 | 33 |
| | 2.00 | 42 |

**Table 16: MANOVA results for Risk trend 2, Lessons learned**

[1] Original German survey questions: a) Risk Management: „Hinsichtlich des Trends ‚Entwicklung des Risikopotentials in negativer und positiver Richtung' wird Ihr Unternehmen beeinflußt durch (1) die Bedrohung durch Naturkatastrophen (Klimaveränderung, Stürme, Erdbeben, Überflutung, Brände), (2) das Risiko industrieller Umweltverschmutzung (durch reguläre Geschäftsprozesse, z.B. $CO_2$-Ausstoß, oder Unfälle, z.B. Freisetzung von Chemikalien bei Betriebsstörungen), (3) mögliche terroristische Aktionen (gegen industrielle Einrichtungen bzw. Anschläge mit Auswirkungen auf Absatzmärkte und Handelswege), (4) unkontrollierten wissenschaftlichen Fortschritt und technisches Versagen (Genprodukte, elektromagnetische Strahlung, Internettechnologie (Viren, Hacker etc.)) und (5) die Auswirkungen gesellschaftlicher, politischer, kultureller Veränderungen (in den verschiedenen Produktions- bzw. Absatzregionen)?" b) Knowledge management: „Besitzen Sie in Ihrem Unternehmen Lessons Learned (gemachte Erfahrungen), um mit diesem Trend umzugehen? Nutzen Sie diese Lessons Learned?"

[2] The insignificance of the overall multivariate effect for $F(5,69) = 0.87$, $p < .05$ can be seen in the statistical F distribution table (Kachigan 1991: 293). The critical value of F for 5 and 69 degrees of freedom is above 1.9, which is greater than 0.87, at the .05 significance level.

**Descriptive Statistics**

| | T2LESSN | Mean | Std. Deviation | N |
|---|---|---|---|---|
| T2C1 | .00 | 2.55 | 1.622 | 33 |
| | 2.00 | 3.48 | 2.340 | 42 |
| | Total | 3.07 | 2.095 | 75 |
| T2C2 | .00 | 3.15 | 2.386 | 33 |
| | 2.00 | 3.74 | 2.586 | 42 |
| | Total | 3.48 | 2.501 | 75 |
| T2C3 | .00 | 3.03 | 2.352 | 33 |
| | 2.00 | 3.45 | 2.510 | 42 |
| | Total | 3.27 | 2.435 | 75 |
| T2C4 | .00 | 3.39 | 2.150 | 33 |
| | 2.00 | 3.98 | 2.384 | 42 |
| | Total | 3.72 | 2.287 | 75 |
| T2C5 | .00 | 4.18 | 1.991 | 33 |
| | 2.00 | 4.83 | 2.469 | 42 |
| | Total | 4.55 | 2.280 | 75 |

**Table 16: MANOVA results for Risk trend 2, Lessons learned (continued)**

**Multivariate Tests[b]**

| Effect | | Value | F | Hypothesis df | Error df | Sig. |
|---|---|---|---|---|---|---|
| Intercept | Pillai's Trace | .848 | 77.072[a] | 5.000 | 69.000 | .000 |
| | Wilks' Lambda | .152 | 77.072[a] | 5.000 | 69.000 | .000 |
| | Hotelling's Trace | 5.585 | 77.072[a] | 5.000 | 69.000 | .000 |
| | Roy's Largest Root | 5.585 | 77.072[a] | 5.000 | 69.000 | .000 |
| T2LESSN | Pillai's Trace | .059 | .866[a] | 5.000 | 69.000 | .508 |
| | Wilks' Lambda | .941 | .866[a] | 5.000 | 69.000 | .508 |
| | Hotelling's Trace | .063 | .866[a] | 5.000 | 69.000 | .508 |
| | Roy's Largest Root | .063 | .866[a] | 5.000 | 69.000 | .508 |

a. Exact statistic

b. Design: Intercept+T2LESSN

**Table 16: MANOVA results for Risk trend 2, Lessons learned (continued)**

**Tests of Between-Subjects Effects**

| Source | Dependent Variable | Type III Sum of Squares | df | Mean Square | F | Sig. |
|---|---|---|---|---|---|---|
| Corrected Model | T2C1 | 16.009[a] | 1 | 16.009 | 3.786 | .056 |
| | T2C2 | 6.359[b] | 1 | 6.359 | 1.017 | .317 |
| | T2C3 | 3.292[c] | 1 | 3.292 | .552 | .460 |
| | T2C4 | 6.265[d] | 1 | 6.265 | 1.201 | .277 |
| | T2C5 | 7.844[e] | 1 | 7.844 | 1.520 | .222 |
| Intercept | T2C1 | 670.089 | 1 | 670.089 | 158.481 | .000 |
| | T2C2 | 877.185 | 1 | 877.185 | 140.315 | .000 |
| | T2C3 | 776.626 | 1 | 776.626 | 130.218 | .000 |
| | T2C4 | 1003.812 | 1 | 1003.812 | 192.405 | .000 |
| | T2C5 | 1501.924 | 1 | 1501.924 | 291.022 | .000 |
| T2LESSN | T2C1 | 16.009 | 1 | 16.009 | 3.786 | .056 |
| | T2C2 | 6.359 | 1 | 6.359 | 1.017 | .317 |
| | T2C3 | 3.292 | 1 | 3.292 | .552 | .460 |
| | T2C4 | 6.265 | 1 | 6.265 | 1.201 | .277 |
| | T2C5 | 7.844 | 1 | 7.844 | 1.520 | .222 |
| Error | T2C1 | 308.658 | 73 | 4.228 | | |
| | T2C2 | 456.361 | 73 | 6.252 | | |
| | T2C3 | 435.374 | 73 | 5.964 | | |
| | T2C4 | 380.855 | 73 | 5.217 | | |
| | T2C5 | 376.742 | 73 | 5.161 | | |
| Total | T2C1 | 1030.000 | 75 | | | |
| | T2C2 | 1371.000 | 75 | | | |
| | T2C3 | 1239.000 | 75 | | | |
| | T2C4 | 1425.000 | 75 | | | |
| | T2C5 | 1935.000 | 75 | | | |
| Corrected Total | T2C1 | 324.667 | 74 | | | |
| | T2C2 | 462.720 | 74 | | | |
| | T2C3 | 438.667 | 74 | | | |
| | T2C4 | 387.120 | 74 | | | |
| | T2C5 | 384.587 | 74 | | | |

a. R Squared = .049 (Adjusted R Squared = .036)

b. R Squared = .014 (Adjusted R Squared = .000)

c. R Squared = .008 (Adjusted R Squared = -.006)

d. R Squared = .016 (Adjusted R Squared = .003)

e. R Squared = .020 (Adjusted R Squared = .007)

**Table 16: MANOVA results for Risk trend 2, Lessons learned (continued)**

### *5.3.6.4 MANOVA 4 for risk trend 2 and best practices*

The fourth MANOVA compares companies who possess and use knowledge of best practices for the second risk trend (development of risk potential in positive and negative direction) with companies who did not[1]. The five characteristics of the second risk trend were used as repeated

---

[1] In the MANOVA results, a value of 0 for T2BEST means "No possession nor use of best practices knowledge" whereas a value of 2 means "Possession and use of best practices knowledge"

dependent variables[1]. An overall insignificant multivariate effect, $F(5,69) = 0.472$, $p < .05$[2] was established. In accordance with the results of MANOVA three, companies which possess and use knowledge of best practices for the second risk trend, development of risk potential in positive and negative direction, indicate that they are higher at risk compared to companies who do not have possession nor use of best practices knowledge, as shown in Table 17. Again, this result does not substantiate hypotheses three and four in Table 12: Collapsed hypotheses – survey questions matrix. As shown in Table 17: MANOVA results for Risk trend 2, Best practices, all the characteristic means for the second risk trend are in the same direction. Hence, companies with possession and use of best practices knowledge feel they are higher at risk than companies with no possession or use of best practices knowledge.

**Between-Subjects Factors**

| | | N |
|---|---|---|
| T2BEST | .00 | 37 |
| | 2.00 | 38 |

**Table 17: MANOVA results for Risk trend 2, Best practices**

1 Original German survey questions: a) Risk Management: „Hinsichtlich des Trends ‚Entwicklung des Risikopotentials in negativer und positiver Richtung' wird Ihr Unternehmen beeinflußt durch (1) die Bedrohung durch Naturkatastrophen (Klimaveränderung, Stürme, Erdbeben, Überflutung, Brände), (2) das Risiko industrieller Umweltverschmutzung (durch reguläre Geschäftsprozesse, z.B. $CO_2$-Ausstoß, oder Unfälle, z.B. Freisetzung von Chemikalien bei Betriebsstörungen), (3) mögliche terroristische Aktionen (gegen industrielle Einrichtungen bzw. Anschläge mit Auswirkungen auf Absatzmärkte und Handelswege), (4) unkontrollierten wissenschaftlichen Fortschritt und technisches Versagen (Genprodukte, elektromagnetische Strahlung, Internettechnologie (Viren, Hacker etc.)) und (5) die Auswirkungen gesellschaftlicher, politischer, kultureller Veränderungen (in den verschiedenen Produktions- bzw. Absatzregionen)?" b) Knowledge management: „Besitzen Sie in Ihrem Unternehmen Best Practices (positive Musterbeispiele), um mit diesem Trend umzugehen? Nutzen Sie diese Best Practices?"

2 The insignificance of the overall multivariate effect for $F(5,69) = 0.472$, $p < .05$ can be seen in the statistical F distribution table (Kachigan 1991: 293). The critical value of F for 5 and 69 degrees of freedom is above 1.9, which is greater than 0.472, at the .05 significance level.

**Descriptive Statistics**

| | T2BEST | Mean | Std. Deviation | N |
|---|---|---|---|---|
| T2C1 | .00 | 2.81 | 1.793 | 37 |
| | 2.00 | 3.39 | 2.320 | 38 |
| | Total | 3.11 | 2.083 | 75 |
| T2C2 | .00 | 3.08 | 2.216 | 37 |
| | 2.00 | 3.74 | 2.688 | 38 |
| | Total | 3.41 | 2.472 | 75 |
| T2C3 | .00 | 2.95 | 2.160 | 37 |
| | 2.00 | 3.42 | 2.575 | 38 |
| | Total | 3.19 | 2.375 | 75 |
| T2C4 | .00 | 3.38 | 2.032 | 37 |
| | 2.00 | 4.05 | 2.493 | 38 |
| | Total | 3.72 | 2.287 | 75 |
| T2C5 | .00 | 4.35 | 1.903 | 37 |
| | 2.00 | 4.63 | 2.551 | 38 |
| | Total | 4.49 | 2.244 | 75 |

**Table 17: MANOVA results for Risk trend 2, Best practices (continued)**

**Multivariate Tests[b]**

| Effect | | Value | F | Hypothesis df | Error df | Sig. |
|---|---|---|---|---|---|---|
| Intercept | Pillai's Trace | .851 | 78.536[a] | 5.000 | 69.000 | .000 |
| | Wilks' Lambda | .149 | 78.536[a] | 5.000 | 69.000 | .000 |
| | Hotelling's Trace | 5.691 | 78.536[a] | 5.000 | 69.000 | .000 |
| | Roy's Largest Root | 5.691 | 78.536[a] | 5.000 | 69.000 | .000 |
| T2BEST | Pillai's Trace | .033 | .472[a] | 5.000 | 69.000 | .796 |
| | Wilks' Lambda | .967 | .472[a] | 5.000 | 69.000 | .796 |
| | Hotelling's Trace | .034 | .472[a] | 5.000 | 69.000 | .796 |
| | Roy's Largest Root | .034 | .472[a] | 5.000 | 69.000 | .796 |

a. Exact statistic

b. Design: Intercept+T2BEST

**Table 17: MANOVA results for Risk trend 2, Best practices (continued)**

**Tests of Between-Subjects Effects**

| Source | Dependent Variable | Type III Sum of Squares | df | Mean Square | F | Sig. |
|---|---|---|---|---|---|---|
| Corrected Model | T2C1 | 6.392[a] | 1 | 6.392 | 1.482 | .227 |
| | T2C2 | 8.061[b] | 1 | 8.061 | 1.325 | .253 |
| | T2C3 | 4.232[c] | 1 | 4.232 | .748 | .390 |
| | T2C4 | 8.523[d] | 1 | 8.523 | 1.643 | .204 |
| | T2C5 | 1.472[e] | 1 | 1.472 | .289 | .592 |
| Intercept | T2C1 | 721.912 | 1 | 721.912 | 167.431 | .000 |
| | T2C2 | 871.421 | 1 | 871.421 | 143.234 | .000 |
| | T2C3 | 759.965 | 1 | 759.965 | 134.278 | .000 |
| | T2C4 | 1035.189 | 1 | 1035.189 | 199.602 | .000 |
| | T2C5 | 1512.725 | 1 | 1512.725 | 297.432 | .000 |
| T2BEST | T2C1 | 6.392 | 1 | 6.392 | 1.482 | .227 |
| | T2C2 | 8.061 | 1 | 8.061 | 1.325 | .253 |
| | T2C3 | 4.232 | 1 | 4.232 | .748 | .390 |
| | T2C4 | 8.523 | 1 | 8.523 | 1.643 | .204 |
| | T2C5 | 1.472 | 1 | 1.472 | .289 | .592 |
| Error | T2C1 | 314.755 | 73 | 4.312 | | |
| | T2C2 | 444.125 | 73 | 6.084 | | |
| | T2C3 | 413.155 | 73 | 5.660 | | |
| | T2C4 | 378.597 | 73 | 5.186 | | |
| | T2C5 | 371.275 | 73 | 5.086 | | |
| Total | T2C1 | 1045.000 | 75 | | | |
| | T2C2 | 1326.000 | 75 | | | |
| | T2C3 | 1179.000 | 75 | | | |
| | T2C4 | 1425.000 | 75 | | | |
| | T2C5 | 1887.000 | 75 | | | |
| Corrected Total | T2C1 | 321.147 | 74 | | | |
| | T2C2 | 452.187 | 74 | | | |
| | T2C3 | 417.387 | 74 | | | |
| | T2C4 | 387.120 | 74 | | | |
| | T2C5 | 372.747 | 74 | | | |

a. R Squared = .020 (Adjusted R Squared = .006)
b. R Squared = .018 (Adjusted R Squared = .004)
c. R Squared = .010 (Adjusted R Squared = -.003)
d. R Squared = .022 (Adjusted R Squared = .009)
e. R Squared = .004 (Adjusted R Squared = -.010)

**Table 17: MANOVA results for Risk trend 2, Best practices (continued)**

### *5.3.6.5 MANOVA 5 for risk trend 3 and lessons learned*

The fifth MANOVA compares companies who possessed and used knowledge of lessons learned for the third risk trend (problems of the Property and Casualty insurance market) with companies who did not[1]. The five characteristics of the third risk trend were used as repeated dependent

[1] In the MANOVA results, a value of 0 for T3LESSN means "No possession nor use of lessons learned knowledge" whereas a value of 2 means "Possession and use of lessons learned knowledge"

variables[1]. An overall insignificant multivariate effect was established, $F(5,68) = 0.71$, $p < .05$[2]. This result indicates that companies possessing and using knowledge of lessons learned for the third risk trend, problems of the Property and Casualty insurance market, are not necessarily less at risk compared to companies who do not have possession nor use of lessons learned knowledge, see Table 18. This outcome does not substantiate hypotheses five and six in Table 12: Collapsed hypotheses – survey questions matrix. However, as can be seen in Table 18: MANOVA results for Risk trend 3, Lessons learned, all the characteristic means for the third risk trend are in the same direction. Thus, companies with possession and use of lessons learned knowledge feel they are slightly higher at risk than companies with no possession or use of lessons learned knowledge.

**Between-Subjects Factors**

| | | N |
|---|---|---|
| T3LESSN | .00 | 19 |
| | 2.00 | 55 |

**Table 18: MANOVA results for Risk trend 3, Lessons learned**

[1] Original German survey questions: a) Risk Management: „Hinsichtlich des Trends ‚Probleme des Sach- / Haftpflicht-Versicherungsmarktes' ist Ihr Unternehmen (1) negativ beeinflußt von Preis- und Kapazitätszyklen der Versicherungsbranche, (2) bedroht durch die langsame Modernisierung der Versicherungsbranche, (3) beeinflußt durch die Änderungen der Kapitalstruktur der Versicherungsbranche (Eigenkapital, Rating, Kapazitäten), (4) betroffen von den die Versicherungsindustrie belastenden wachsenden Katastrophenschäden, (5) bedroht durch das Entstehen neuer, bislang unbekannter Risiken für den Versicherer (z.B. Asbest, Genprodukte in der Produkthaftpflicht, Elektrosmog in der Umwelthaftpflicht)?" b) Knowledge management: „Besitzen Sie in Ihrem Unternehmen Lessons Learned (gemachte Erfahrungen), um mit diesem Trend umzugehen? Nutzen Sie diese Lessons Learned?"

[2] The insignificance of the overall multivariate effect for $F(5,68) = 0.71$, $p < .05$ can be seen in the statistical F distribution table (Kachigan 1991: 293). The critical value of F for 5 and 68 degrees of freedom is above 1.9, which is greater than 0.71, at the .05 significance level.

**Descriptive Statistics**

| | T3LESSN | Mean | Std. Deviation | N |
|---|---|---|---|---|
| T3C1 | .00 | 7.26 | 2.023 | 19 |
| | 2.00 | 7.47 | 2.340 | 55 |
| | Total | 7.42 | 2.251 | 74 |
| T3C2 | .00 | 4.21 | 2.016 | 19 |
| | 2.00 | 5.15 | 2.422 | 55 |
| | Total | 4.91 | 2.348 | 74 |
| T3C3 | .00 | 5.32 | 2.335 | 19 |
| | 2.00 | 6.24 | 2.502 | 55 |
| | Total | 6.00 | 2.477 | 74 |
| T3C4 | .00 | 6.42 | 2.194 | 19 |
| | 2.00 | 6.73 | 2.571 | 55 |
| | Total | 6.65 | 2.469 | 74 |
| T3C5 | .00 | 5.11 | 2.183 | 19 |
| | 2.00 | 5.56 | 2.616 | 55 |
| | Total | 5.45 | 2.506 | 74 |

**Table 18: MANOVA results for Risk trend 3, Lessons learned (continued)**

**Multivariate Tests[b]**

| Effect | | Value | F | Hypothesis df | Error df | Sig. |
|---|---|---|---|---|---|---|
| Intercept | Pillai's Trace | .911 | 139.001[a] | 5.000 | 68.000 | .000 |
| | Wilks' Lambda | .089 | 139.001[a] | 5.000 | 68.000 | .000 |
| | Hotelling's Trace | 10.221 | 139.001[a] | 5.000 | 68.000 | .000 |
| | Roy's Largest Root | 10.221 | 139.001[a] | 5.000 | 68.000 | .000 |
| T3LESSN | Pillai's Trace | .049 | .708[a] | 5.000 | 68.000 | .619 |
| | Wilks' Lambda | .951 | .708[a] | 5.000 | 68.000 | .619 |
| | Hotelling's Trace | .052 | .708[a] | 5.000 | 68.000 | .619 |
| | Roy's Largest Root | .052 | .708[a] | 5.000 | 68.000 | .619 |

a. Exact statistic

b. Design: Intercept+T3LESSN

**Table 18: MANOVA results for Risk trend 3, Lessons learned (continued)**

**Tests of Between-Subjects Effects**

| Source | Dependent Variable | Type III Sum of Squares | df | Mean Square | F | Sig. |
|---|---|---|---|---|---|---|
| Corrected Model | T3C1 | .620[a] | 1 | .620 | .121 | .729 |
| | T3C2 | 12.344[b] | 1 | 12.344 | 2.279 | .136 |
| | T3C3 | 11.967[c] | 1 | 11.967 | 1.976 | .164 |
| | T3C4 | 1.324[d] | 1 | 1.324 | .215 | .644 |
| | T3C5 | 2.967[e] | 1 | 2.967 | .469 | .496 |
| Intercept | T3C1 | 3066.458 | 1 | 3066.458 | 597.696 | .000 |
| | T3C2 | 1236.127 | 1 | 1236.127 | 228.211 | .000 |
| | T3C3 | 1884.562 | 1 | 1884.562 | 311.189 | .000 |
| | T3C4 | 2441.324 | 1 | 2441.324 | 396.300 | .000 |
| | T3C5 | 1607.399 | 1 | 1607.399 | 254.181 | .000 |
| T3LESSN | T3C1 | .620 | 1 | .620 | .121 | .729 |
| | T3C2 | 12.344 | 1 | 12.344 | 2.279 | .136 |
| | T3C3 | 11.967 | 1 | 11.967 | 1.976 | .164 |
| | T3C4 | 1.324 | 1 | 1.324 | .215 | .644 |
| | T3C5 | 2.967 | 1 | 2.967 | .469 | .496 |
| Error | T3C1 | 369.393 | 72 | 5.130 | | |
| | T3C2 | 389.994 | 72 | 5.417 | | |
| | T3C3 | 436.033 | 72 | 6.056 | | |
| | T3C4 | 443.541 | 72 | 6.160 | | |
| | T3C5 | 455.317 | 72 | 6.324 | | |
| Total | T3C1 | 4443.000 | 74 | | | |
| | T3C2 | 2183.000 | 74 | | | |
| | T3C3 | 3112.000 | 74 | | | |
| | T3C4 | 3716.000 | 74 | | | |
| | T3C5 | 2653.000 | 74 | | | |
| Corrected Total | T3C1 | 370.014 | 73 | | | |
| | T3C2 | 402.338 | 73 | | | |
| | T3C3 | 448.000 | 73 | | | |
| | T3C4 | 444.865 | 73 | | | |
| | T3C5 | 458.284 | 73 | | | |

a. R Squared = .002 (Adjusted R Squared = -.012)

b. R Squared = .031 (Adjusted R Squared = .017)

c. R Squared = .027 (Adjusted R Squared = .013)

d. R Squared = .003 (Adjusted R Squared = -.011)

e. R Squared = .006 (Adjusted R Squared = -.007)

**Table 18: MANOVA results for Risk trend 3, Lessons learned (continued)**

### *5.3.6.6 MANOVA 6 for risk trend 3 and best practices*

The sixth MANOVA compares companies who possessed and used knowledge of best practices for the third risk trend (problems of the Property and Casualty insurance market) with companies who did not[1]. The five characteristics of the third risk trend used as repeated dependent

[1] In the MANOVA results, a value of 0 for T3BEST means "No possession nor use of best practices knowledge" whereas a value of 2 means "Possession and use of best practices knowledge"

variables[1]. There was an overall insignificant multivariate effect, $F(5,69) = 1.06$, $p < .05$[2]. This indicates that companies possessing and using knowledge of best practices for the third risk trend, problems of the Property and Casualty insurance market, are not necessarily less at risk compared to companies who do not have possession nor use of best practices knowledge, as shown in Table 19. This outcome, however, does not substantiate hypotheses five and six in Table 12: Collapsed hypotheses – survey questions matrix. As shown in Table 19: MANOVA results for Risk trend 3, Best practices, all the characteristic means expect for the third characteristic, legal changes, are in the same direction. Hence, companies with possession and use of best practices knowledge feel they are higher at risk than companies with no possession or use of best practices knowledge. This result is in line with the slightly higher means reported in the fifth MANOVA.

**Between-Subjects Factors**

| | | N |
|---|---|---|
| T3BEST | .00 | 31 |
| | 2.00 | 44 |

**Table 19: MANOVA results for Risk trend 3, Best practices**

[1] Original German survey questions: a) Risk Management: „Hinsichtlich des Trends ‚Probleme des Sach- / Haftpflicht-Versicherungsmarktes' ist Ihr Unternehmen (1) negativ beeinflußt von Preis- und Kapazitätszyklen der Versicherungsbranche, (2) bedroht durch die langsame Modernisierung der Versicherungsbranche, (3) beeinflußt durch die Änderungen der Kapitalstruktur der Versicherungsbranche (Eigenkapital, Rating, Kapazitäten), (4) betroffen von den die Versicherungsindustrie belastenden wachsenden Katastrophenschäden, (5) bedroht durch das Entstehen neuer, bislang unbekannter Risiken für den Versicherer (z.B. Asbest, Genprodukte in der Produkthaftpflicht, Elektrosmog in der Umwelthaftpflicht)?" b) Knowledge management: „Besitzen Sie in Ihrem Unternehmen Best Practices (positive Musterbeispiele), um mit diesem Trend umzugehen? Nutzen Sie diese Best Practices?"

[2] The insignificance of the overall multivariate effect for $F(5,69) = 0.81$, $p < .05$ can be seen in the statistical F distribution table (Kachigan 1991: 293). The critical value of F for 5 and 69 degrees of freedom is above 1.9, which is greater than 0.81, at the .05 significance level.

**Descriptive Statistics**

| | T3BEST | Mean | Std. Deviation | N |
|---|---|---|---|---|
| T3C1 | .00 | 7.48 | 2.407 | 31 |
| | 2.00 | 7.43 | 2.172 | 44 |
| | Total | 7.45 | 2.256 | 75 |
| T3C2 | .00 | 5.00 | 1.880 | 31 |
| | 2.00 | 4.89 | 2.643 | 44 |
| | Total | 4.93 | 2.344 | 75 |
| T3C3 | .00 | 5.84 | 2.570 | 31 |
| | 2.00 | 6.18 | 2.443 | 44 |
| | Total | 6.04 | 2.485 | 75 |
| T3C4 | .00 | 6.97 | 2.213 | 31 |
| | 2.00 | 6.50 | 2.663 | 44 |
| | Total | 6.69 | 2.482 | 75 |
| T3C5 | .00 | 5.94 | 2.542 | 31 |
| | 2.00 | 5.20 | 2.530 | 44 |
| | Total | 5.51 | 2.544 | 75 |

**Table 19: MANOVA results for Risk trend 3, Best practices (continued)**

**Multivariate Tests[b]**

| Effect | | Value | F | Hypothesis df | Error df | Sig. |
|---|---|---|---|---|---|---|
| Intercept | Pillai's Trace | .929 | 181.913[a] | 5.000 | 69.000 | .000 |
| | Wilks' Lambda | .071 | 181.913[a] | 5.000 | 69.000 | .000 |
| | Hotelling's Trace | 13.182 | 181.913[a] | 5.000 | 69.000 | .000 |
| | Roy's Largest Root | 13.182 | 181.913[a] | 5.000 | 69.000 | .000 |
| T3BEST | Pillai's Trace | .055 | .809[a] | 5.000 | 69.000 | .547 |
| | Wilks' Lambda | .945 | .809[a] | 5.000 | 69.000 | .547 |
| | Hotelling's Trace | .059 | .809[a] | 5.000 | 69.000 | .547 |
| | Roy's Largest Root | .059 | .809[a] | 5.000 | 69.000 | .547 |

a. Exact statistic

b. Design: Intercept+T3BEST

**Table 19: MANOVA results for Risk trend 3, Best practices (continued)**

**Tests of Between-Subjects Effects**

| Source | Dependent Variable | Type III Sum of Squares | df | Mean Square | F | Sig. |
|---|---|---|---|---|---|---|
| Corrected Model | T3C1 | 4.928E-02[a] | 1 | 4.928E-02 | .010 | .922 |
| | T3C2 | .235[b] | 1 | .235 | .042 | .838 |
| | T3C3 | 2.141[c] | 1 | 2.141 | .344 | .560 |
| | T3C4 | 3.979[d] | 1 | 3.979 | .643 | .425 |
| | T3C5 | 9.717[e] | 1 | 9.717 | 1.512 | .223 |
| Intercept | T3C1 | 4046.129 | 1 | 4046.129 | 784.431 | .000 |
| | T3C2 | 1777.568 | 1 | 1777.568 | 319.272 | .000 |
| | T3C3 | 2627.848 | 1 | 2627.848 | 421.853 | .000 |
| | T3C4 | 3298.699 | 1 | 3298.699 | 532.792 | .000 |
| | T3C5 | 2256.970 | 1 | 2256.970 | 351.276 | .000 |
| T3BEST | T3C1 | 4.928E-02 | 1 | 4.928E-02 | .010 | .922 |
| | T3C2 | .235 | 1 | .235 | .042 | .838 |
| | T3C3 | 2.141 | 1 | 2.141 | .344 | .560 |
| | T3C4 | 3.979 | 1 | 3.979 | .643 | .425 |
| | T3C5 | 9.717 | 1 | 9.717 | 1.512 | .223 |
| Error | T3C1 | 376.537 | 73 | 5.158 | | |
| | T3C2 | 406.432 | 73 | 5.568 | | |
| | T3C3 | 454.739 | 73 | 6.229 | | |
| | T3C4 | 451.968 | 73 | 6.191 | | |
| | T3C5 | 469.030 | 73 | 6.425 | | |
| Total | T3C1 | 4543.000 | 75 | | | |
| | T3C2 | 2232.000 | 75 | | | |
| | T3C3 | 3193.000 | 75 | | | |
| | T3C4 | 3816.000 | 75 | | | |
| | T3C5 | 2753.000 | 75 | | | |
| Corrected Total | T3C1 | 376.587 | 74 | | | |
| | T3C2 | 406.667 | 74 | | | |
| | T3C3 | 456.880 | 74 | | | |
| | T3C4 | 455.947 | 74 | | | |
| | T3C5 | 478.747 | 74 | | | |

a. R Squared = .000 (Adjusted R Squared = -.014)

b. R Squared = .001 (Adjusted R Squared = -.013)

c. R Squared = .005 (Adjusted R Squared = -.009)

d. R Squared = .009 (Adjusted R Squared = -.005)

e. R Squared = .020 (Adjusted R Squared = .007)

**Table 19: MANOVA results for Risk trend 3, Best practices (continued)**

### *5.3.7 Z-score Analysis*

Two final z-score analyses were conducted with the purpose of testing hypotheses seven and eight in Table 12. Similar to the MANOVA analyses, companies without possession and use of risk management knowledge were compared with those companies with extensive possession and use of risk management knowledge. Therefore, companies having only possession but no use of knowledge for any one risk trend were filtered out. Five out of the 76 companies were filtered out for the lessons learned z-score analysis. Three out of 76 companies were filtered out for the best practices z-score analysis. For the remaining valid responses, a score of zero for not possessing nor using knowledge and a score of one for possessing and using knowledge was given for each company and risk trend. Hence, a company's combined score across all three risk trends ranges from zero to three. Next, the respondents' risk assessment answers for each characteristic based on a scale of one to ten were converted to z-scores. Finally, the means for the z-scores was calculated. Advantage of this conversion lies in the z-score's inclusion of "both the mean and the standard deviation" (Kachigan, 1991: 51), thus making the characteristics assessments across the three risk trends comparable. Subsequently, two regression analyses between z-scores means and lessons learned and best practices were performed. The results are displayed in Table 20: Results for Lessons learned z-scores analysis and Table 21: Results for Best practices z-scores analysis.

**Variables Entered/Removed[b]**

| Model | Variables Entered | Variables Removed | Method |
|---|---|---|---|
| 1 | ZTOT[a] | . | Enter |

a. All requested variables entered.

b. Dependent Variable: LESSNTO2

**Table 20: Results for Lessons learned z-scores analysis**

**Model Summary**

| Model | R | R Square | Adjusted R Square | Std. Error of the Estimate |
|---|---|---|---|---|
| 1 | .051[a] | .003 | -.012 | 1.09304 |

a. Predictors: (Constant), ZTOT

**Table 20: Results for Lessons learned z-scores analysis (continued)**

**ANOVA[b]**

| Model | | Sum of Squares | df | Mean Square | F | Sig. |
|---|---|---|---|---|---|---|
| 1 | Regression | .211 | 1 | .211 | .176 | .676[a] |
| | Residual | 82.437 | 69 | 1.195 | | |
| | Total | 82.648 | 70 | | | |

a. Predictors: (Constant), ZTOT

b. Dependent Variable: LESSNTO2

**Table 20: Results for Lessons learned z-scores analysis (continued)**

**Coefficients[a]**

| Model | | Unstandardized Coefficients | | Standardized Coefficients | t | Sig. |
|---|---|---|---|---|---|---|
| | | B | Std. Error | Beta | | |
| 1 | (Constant) | 2.070 | .130 | | 15.961 | .000 |
| | ZTOT | -.114 | .272 | -.051 | -.420 | .676 |

a. Dependent Variable: LESSNTO2

**Table 20: Results for Lessons learned z-scores analysis (continued)**

**Variables Entered/Removed[b]**

| Model | Variables Entered | Variables Removed | Method |
|---|---|---|---|
| 1 | ZTOT[a] | . | Enter |

a. All requested variables entered.

b. Dependent Variable: BESTTO2

**Table 21: Results for Best practices z-scores analysis**

**Model Summary**

| Model | R | R Square | Adjusted R Square | Std. Error of the Estimate |
|---|---|---|---|---|
| 1 | .050[a] | .003 | -.012 | 1.27379 |

a. Predictors: (Constant), ZTOT

**Table 21: Results for Best practices z-scores analysis (continued)**

**ANOVA[b]**

| Model | | Sum of Squares | df | Mean Square | F | Sig. |
|---|---|---|---|---|---|---|
| 1 | Regression | .275 | 1 | .275 | .169 | .682[a] |
| | Residual | 108.711 | 67 | 1.623 | | |
| | Total | 108.986 | 68 | | | |

a. Predictors: (Constant), ZTOT

b. Dependent Variable: BESTTO2

**Table 21: Results for Best practices z-scores analysis (continued)**

**Coefficients[a]**

| Model | | Unstandardized Coefficients | | Standardized Coefficients | t | Sig. |
|---|---|---|---|---|---|---|
| | | B | Std. Error | Beta | | |
| 1 | (Constant) | 1.680 | .153 | | 10.956 | .000 |
| | ZTOT | -.131 | .318 | -.050 | -.411 | .682 |

a. Dependent Variable: BESTTO2

**Table 21: Results for Best practices z-scores analysis (continued)**

Following the stronger MANOVA analyses for testing hypotheses one to six, the weaker z-score analyses do not substantiate hypotheses seven and eight described in Table 12: Collapsed hypotheses – survey questions matrix. Thus, a relationship between the overall risk assessment and the general possession and use of risk management knowledge cannot be established. This result was expected and is in line with the preceding MANOVA results, where only a significant relationship could be established for lessons learned of risk trend one, emergence of increasingly complex and bigger corporate structures.

### *5.3.8 Legend for SPSS result tables*

The table below illustrates the abbreviations which were used for the statistical analysis performed with SPSS, Version 11.0.

| SPSS table abbreviation | Short explanation | Full explanation | Range |
|---|---|---|---|
| Trend 1: Emergence of increasingly complex and bigger corporate structures / | | | |
| **T1C1** | Trend 1 / Characteristic 1 | Characteristic 1: Networked economy | 1-10 |
| **T1C2** | Trend 1 / Characteristic 2 | Characteristic 2: Shareholder value | 1-10 |
| **T1C3** | Trend 1 / Characteristic 3 | Characteristic 3: Multiple economic systems | 1-10 |
| **T1C4** | Trend 1 / Characteristic 4 | Characteristic 4: Globalisation | 1-10 |
| **T1C5** | Trend 1 / Characteristic 5 | Characteristic 5: Mergers & Acquisitions | 1-10 |
| Trend 2: Development of risk potential in positive and negative direction / | | | |
| **T2C1** | Trend 2 / Characteristic 1 | Characteristic 1: Natural catastrophes | 1-10 |
| **T2C2** | Trend 2 / Characteristic 2 | Characteristic 2: Industrial pollution | 1-10 |
| **T2C3** | Trend 2 / Characteristic 3 | Characteristic 3: Terrorism | 1-10 |
| **T2C4** | Trend 2 / Characteristic 4 | Characteristic 4: Technological advancement and failure | 1-10 |
| **T2C5** | Trend 2 / Characteristic 5 | Characteristic 5: Societal, political, cultural change | 1-10 |
| Trend 3: Problems of Property & Casualty insurance market / | | | |
| **T3C1** | Trend 3 / Characteristic 1 | Characteristic 1: Price & capacity cycles | 1-10 |
| **T3C2** | Trend 3 / Characteristic 2 | Characteristic 2: Competitive disadvantages of the industry sector | 1-10 |
| **T3C3** | Trend 3 / Characteristic 3 | Characteristic 3: Legal changes | 1-10 |
| **T3C4** | Trend 3 / Characteristic 4 | Characteristic 4: Larger catastrophes | 1-10 |
| **T3C5** | Trend 3 / Characteristic 5 | Characteristic 5: New risks | 1-10 |
| Trend 1: Emergence of increasingly complex and bigger corporate structures/ | | | |
| **T1Lessn** | Trend 1, Lessons learned | No possession/possession/possession & use of lessons learned | 0/1/2 |
| **T1Best** | Trend 1, Best practices | No possession/possession/possession & use of best practices | 0/1/2 |
| Trend 2: Development of risk potential in positive and negative direction/ | | | |
| **T2Lessn** | Trend 2, Lessons learned | No possession/possession/possession & use of lessons learned | 0/1/2 |
| **T2Best** | Trend 2, Best practices | No possession/use vs. possession/use of best practices | 0/1/2 |
| Trend 3: Problems of Property & Casualty insurance market / | | | |
| **T3Lessn** | Trend 3, Lessons learned | No possession/possession/possession & use of lessons learned | 0/1/2 |
| **T3Lessn** | Trend 3, Best practices | No possession/use vs. possession/use of best practices | 0/1/2 |
| Trends 1 – 3 | | | |
| **LESSNTOT** | Score for Lessons learned | Score for availability and use of lessons learned across Trends 1–3 | 0-6 |
| **BESTTOT** | Score for Best practices | Score for availability and use of best practices across Trends 1–3 | 0-6 |
| **TS** | Score for all risk trends | Score for overall risk perception (sum of all characteristics) | 15-150 |
| **LESSNTO2** | Score for Lessons learned | Score for availability and use of lessons learned across Trends 1–3 | 0-3 |
| **BESTTO2** | Score for Best practices | Score for availability and use of best practices across Trends 1–3 | 0-3 |
| **ZTOT** | Characteristics' z-score means | Means of the z-scores of Characteristics 1–15 | |

**Table 22: Legend of SPSS results tables**

## 5.4 Qualitative analysis results

Section 5.4 presents the results of the qualitative survey questions. Results build upon the previous quantitative analysis. The risk & knowledge management survey consisted of a pair of open questions for each risk trend and finished with one open feedback question. Thus in total, seven qualitative questions were incorporated. The first, third and fifth qualitative question asked about the corporations' strategic thoughts and measures dealing with the specific risk trend. The second, fourth and sixth qualitative question asked about the necessary lessons learned and best practices knowledge dealing with the particular risk trend.

Qualitative analysis results section is structured in four parts. Part one summarises the replies supporting the substantiated hypotheses for the first trend. Part two presents answers supporting the hypotheses for trend two and three and possible reasons for their approval or non-approval gathered. In part three, general findings supporting the overall theory are extracted. Finally, ideas for future research questions are presented in part four.

### *5.4.1 Supportive findings for substantiated hypotheses for the first risk trend*

Findings of the first MANOVA in the quantitative analysis in 5.3 suggest that companies possessing and using knowledge of lessons learned for the first risk trend, emergence of increasingly complex and bigger corporate structures, indicate they are less at risk compared to companies who do not have possession nor use of lessons learned knowledge. This result supports hypotheses one and two described in Table 12: Collapsed hypotheses – survey questions matrix. Quantitative support for these hypotheses seems to be primarily driven by two out of five characteristics, namely globalisation and networked economy.

The following summary of the two qualitative answers for risk trend one provides further support for the quantitative results.

#### *5.4.1.1 Strategies and measures to deal with emergence of increasingly complex and bigger corporate structures*

The first qualitative question regarding risk trend one asked respondents about their company's strategic thoughts and derived measures to deal with the first risk trend, emergence of increasingly complex and bigger corporate structures[1]. The following 13 answers were provided:

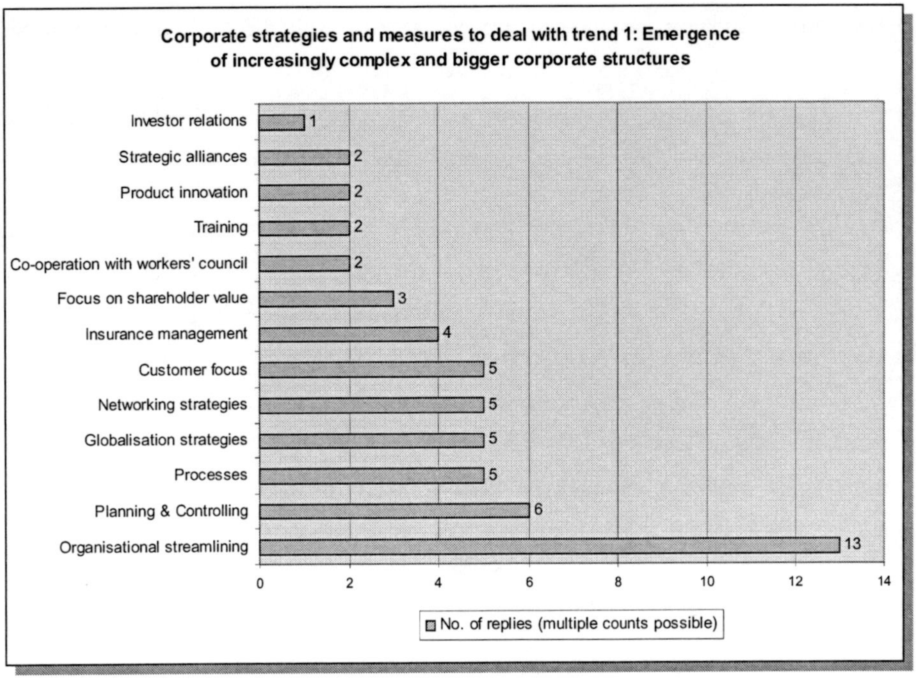


**Figure 31: Corporate strategies and derived measures dealing with Risk trend 1**

*Organisational streamlining* was named by thirteen respondents as being part of their strategic thoughts and derived measures in order to prevent the risks of trend one. This issue clearly exceeded the second most important point, planning & controlling. Corporations seem to rethink regularly the necessary organisational structures, leading to new, simpler structures and adaptations where necessary. One way to achieve a streamlined organisation is by inter-company mergers instead of complex inter-woven structures. Other possibilities are the introduction of quick decision-making processes and small, coordinated product oriented units. This organisational change requires the reduction of hierarchies, clear competencies and a

[1] Original German survey question: „Welche strategischen Überlegungen werden angestellt und welche Maßnahmen daraus abgeleitet, um mit der wachsenden Komplexität und Größe Ihres Unternehmens umzugehen?“

structured knowledge-flow within the corporation. One respondent stated that decisions about organisational structures were generally made by the headquarter abroad. This answer suggests a strong, imposed organisational structure exists behind the local operations in Austria. Another large corporation claimed to have already put group structures in place so that its organisational complexity would not lead to a fuzzy picture. Thus, allowing a detailed view and full manageability of the whole group. The same company is taking a centralised approach towards risk management in order to determine the possible negative results.

*Planning & Controlling* was designated by six corporations with regards to strategic thoughts and measures about risk trend one. An efficient reporting system with precise rules and useful guidelines seems to be very important. This reporting system – where necessary - needs to be consolidated, i.e. the planning horizon widened and the planning tools improved. In addition, a clear cost structure and a recurring strategic planning, including a focus on insurance risks, is required. Establishment of an efficient reporting system is supported by the definition of clear targets and functioning management supervision. Finally, the adaptation of international accounting standards is seen as important.

*Processes* were identified by five corporations' survey respondents as strategic thoughts and measures to deal with risk trend one. Generally, new business processes and the introduction of a process organisation are needed. Corporations try to increase transparency of processes and optimise their performance in different areas such as sales, logistics and production. This development could be supported through the creation of uniform standards in order to save time and improve customer service. Lastly, one response even asks for modular process system which can be extended to the steering of all business functions.

*Globalisation strategies* are important for five survey respondents in dealing with risk trend one. Some of the examined corporations seem to be striving for geographic diversification and global leadership in their market segment. Diversification, as was noted, can be supported by proactive behaviour, using international opportunities and learning from different cultures. In addition, a clear strategy of the target markets and which personnel and technology is required in order to access those markets is necessary. Risks of globalisation were also recognised as an opportunity in one instance. Due to the many M & A's in the respondent's particular industry sector, the company was able to play out its niche role and gain new customers who did not want to rely exclusively on one supplier. In the context of globalisation, one respondent only accepts an industry insurer which is large enough to follow its international development. This prerequisite means the industry insurer needs a global network, either through direct sales representation or through fronting partners.

*Networking strategies* were named by five participating corporations in handling risk trend one. The main challenge here seems to lie in the proactive use and exploitation of networking capabilities. The phenomenon of an increasingly networked business environment can either occur within the company or externally, e.g. with customers or both. Up-to-date IT systems seem to support the networked approach, helping the introduction of transparent processes.

*Customer focus* is identified by five corporations with regards to strategic thoughts and measures against risk trend one. While one company tries to widen its customer base, another one seeks to focus on its core market. Each alternative seems to be appropriate, as long as the market segment and a viable growth plan is clearly defined. Another main step towards customer focus seems to lie in the improvement of service and quality. Improvement of service and quality could be achieved by increasing professionalism across all business levels and functions.

*Insurance management* is designated by four respondents in the strategic thoughts and measures against risk trend one. Insurance management includes the concentration of insurance activities, bundling of policies and the introduction of cross national covers. One respondent calls for insurance management to be an integral part of each corporation's strategic planning. Setting high quality standards might enable risk managers to identify the most appropriate industrial insurer. The suggested criteria for choosing an appropriate insurer are financial strength, international representation and independence of the reinsurance market. Finally, corporations should start a critical dialogue with credit insurers in particular, finding an improved way to deal with uninsured customers.

*Focus on shareholder value* is mentioned by three corporations as their strategic thoughts and measures against risk trend one. A relatively high rating of this answer would support the acceptance of the quantitative analysis of characteristic two, shareholder value. All three companies proclaim growth of company value as a corporate goal. Two companies even provide details about how to achieve this goal. The first company tries to grow company value while at the same time not growing in company size. The second company realises the importance of increasing company value for further investments in promising projects and capital injections. Continuity of investments can only be achieved through sustained results and financial stability.

*Co-operation with workers' council* is seen by two respondents as important strategic thought and measure to deal with the growing corporate complexity by two corporations. This movement can be attributed to the growing international competition. For that purpose, agreements with the workers' council are made in order to bridge periods of full production. These agreements attempt a more liberal, flexible working schedule such as longer working hours in periods when larger orders are waiting.

*Training* is acknowledged by two companies in order to deal with risk trend one. The improvement of the training programmes is suggested in order to obtain a well trained, highly motivated work force.

*Product innovation* is named by two respondents in order to handle risk trend one. Product innovation includes the joint development of new products in co-operation with customers and the continuous search for and realisation of new, creative ideas.

*Strategic alliances* are mentioned by two corporations as part of their strategic thoughts and measures against growing corporate complexity. Strategic alliances include knowledge of how to search for and select the right strategic partnerships and financial investment.

*Investor relations* are identified by one corporation to deal with risk trend one. The respondent suggests continuous communication with capital markets and banks is part of the strategies and measures for managing the negative effects of risk trend one.

In summary, the qualitative responses presented seem to support the findings of the quantitative study. Particularly the strong qualitative answers regarding globalisation and networking strategies further support the strong quantitative results for the two characteristics of risk trend one, networked economy and globalisation. These characteristics were the key drivers of the positively tested hypothesis one "Corporations that are highly affected by complexity and large size do not have extensive possession and use of risk management knowledge for this risk trend" and hypothesis two "Corporations that are hardly affected by complexity and large size possess and make extensive use of risk management knowledge for this risk trend". The number of replies pertaining to organisational streamlining clearly exceeds all other categories. This result shows the respondents' need to constantly improve the corporation's structures in order to deal with risk trend one. Organisational streamlining is supported by planning & controlling, processes and customer focus, which can be seen as prerequisites for an ideal corporate structure. Finally, the effective addressing of these topics seems to be very important for corporations to take an effective networked, global business approach, which is requested by risk managers.

#### *5.4.1.2 Required lessons learned and best practices for emergence of increasingly complex and bigger corporate structures*

The second qualitative question regarding risk trend one asked respondents about the necessary lessons learned and best practices for their company to prevent the risks of emergence of increasingly complex and bigger corporate structures[1]. The following nine replies were given:

[1] Original German survey question: „Welche Lessons Learned bzw. Best Practices wären aus Sicht Ihres Unternehmens erforderlich, um den Risiken aus der Entstehung komplexerer und größerer Unternehmensstrukturen vorzubeugen?"

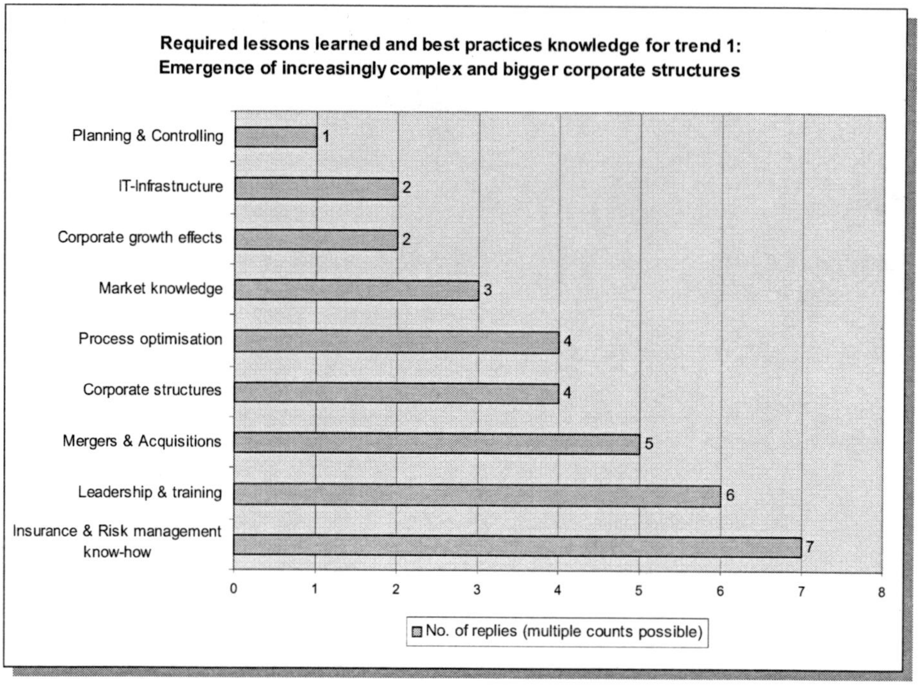


**Figure 32: Necessary lessons learned and best practices dealing with Risk trend 1**

*Insurance & Risk management know-how* is identified by seven corporations as the required lessons learned and best practices knowledge dealing with risk trend one. This finding is surprising since the questions for the risk trend of emergence of increasingly complex and bigger corporate structures did not focus on insurance topics. Respondents require knowledge and experience about international insurance programmes as well as the creation and implementation of risk analyses. One way to achieve this goal could be through know-how transfer with global insurance brokers. Industrial insurance brokers support insurers in achieving thorough claims analyses and deriving necessary risk management measures which benefit not only the specific corporate unit, but also the entire corporation. Another possibility is bundling insurance contracts in spite of inhomogeneous corporate structures to limit risk exposure for both the corporation and the insurer. One respondent argues that the company's choice of insurer is constantly reviewed in view of the company's growth and size. Therefore, only yearly insurance contracts are made. Yearly contracts are negotiated through corporate wide insurance meetings.

An additional benefit of the yearly price negotiation procedure is the risk knowledge transfer which occurs.

*Leadership and training* is suggested by six corporations for dealing with risk trend one. It seems evident that the creation of a common identity within the organisation, beginning with management, can be supported by using lessons learned and best practices knowledge. Creating a common identity requires common goals and measures in all parts of the organisation as well as swift reactions by a loyal management. Other reasons for the high ranking of this criterion might be because corporate risk managers assume lessons learned and best practices can be best transferred within a highly qualified work force. Know-how transfer can be done either by training sessions or by training on the job, including job rotations. One goal of the introduction of lessons learned and best practices is to lower or to eliminate entirely the possibility of costly second errors.

*Mergers & Acquisitions* is identified by five respondents as important knowledge with regard to risk trend one. Corporations seem to require in depth knowledge about acquiring companies and how to integrate them successfully into the existing group structures. The most effective means is by learning from previous M & A transaction experiences and the due diligence process. M & A and due diligence know-how seems to be more important for companies which try to grow through Mergers and Acquisitions rather than organically. Industries such as the automobile and food sector which have already gone through the consolidating process might provide good examples of lessons learned and best practices for other industries.

*Corporate structures* are mentioned by four corporations as required lessons learned and best practices knowledge for risk trend one. The corporate strategy must be first defined, before designing corporate structures and not vice versa. Larger corporations require more knowledge about individual's competencies. Failing to establish a well functioning organisation seems to be swiftly punished by the industry market. One respondent explains the important control mechanism of the cascade principle of corporate management. According to the cascade principle, management of the upper corporate level must be in the supervisory board of the next lower level of the corporate structure. For instance, the top management of the holding company should be on the supervisory board of the subsidiary companies. Finally, only constant change bringing in new lessons learned and best practices knowledge can avoid the stand-still of the organisation.

*Process optimisation* is mentioned by four respondents as necessary lessons learned and best practices knowledge for coping with risk trend one. The importance of process knowledge seems to be driven by globalisation, which increases competition and permits price increases in order to offset production cost. To deal with globalisation effects, it is suggested that processes should be documented and continuously monitored within the organisation. Therefore, process knowledge must be codified and internalised by the employees in order to become reusable.

*Market knowledge* is required by three respondents to manage risk trend one. Corporations acknowledge the requirement of lessons learned and best practices in their search for strategic partnerships, new products and markets. Business development could be, for instance, supported by using knowledge from customer credit ratings. Also, early forecast and establishment of reaction alternatives for market changes is seen as critical.

*Corporate growth effects* are named by two respondents with respect to risk trend one. These companies suggest the growth of company structures needs to be actively monitored in order to learn from the growth process. Monitoring might lead to the creation of reusable best practices which enables a controllable rather than chaotic growth process. One company claims to have acquired past lessons learned from having large, unmanageable units. These lessons learned were transformed into best practices by introducing a new process, creating new manageable business units when the size of individual units becomes uncontrollable.

*IT-Infrastructure* is important for two corporations for dealing with risk trend one. Knowledge about successfully introducing, applying and improving IT-systems (in this particular case the reporting systems SAP) are important in dealing with risk trend one, emergence of increasingly complex and bigger corporate structures.

*Planning & Controlling* is named by one corporation for handling risk trend one. In this case, the knowledge from existing and successful reporting structures should be better exploited. The risk knowledge transfer might be achieved by benchmarking against other successful parts of the corporations or learning from partners, suppliers and customers.

The overall findings for the question regarding the necessary knowledge dealing with risk trend one show that those corporations which responded are already actively addressing this topic. Insurance and risk management know-how was the leading answer and is seen as a cornerstone towards dealing with the emergence of increasingly complex and bigger corporate structures. Even though this outcome can be partially attributed to the fact that a large portion of the respondents were risk and insurance managers, the quantity of answers for this issue is still an unexpectedly large number. Results also show that insurance and risk management plays an important role in dealing with the complexity and large size of corporate structures. The second most important answer, leadership and training, is not surprising, since only a highly qualified workforce is able to deal with the challenges as well as the specialisation of today's business world. Leadership and training seems to be the general method for transferring lessons learned and best practices knowledge within the organisation. Answers three to five, Mergers & Acquisitions, Corporate structures and Process optimisation demonstrate the examined companies' need for knowledge regarding these topics. Expertise in the areas of Mergers & Acquisitions, Corporate structures and Process optimisation could help with the need for organisational streamlining reported in the first survey question regarding the necessary strategies and measures associated with risk trend one. Additionally, this expertise supports a globalised, networked business approach.

### *5.4.2 Possible reasons for substantiation and rejection of hypotheses for the second risk trend*

The following two paragraphs summarise the answers regarding risk trend two, development of risk potential in both positive and negative direction. First the strategies and measures to deal with the risk trend are mentioned. Second the necessary lessons learned and best practices knowledge in order to deal with trend two are presented. Hypotheses relating to risk trend two were not tested positive. Therefore the summary of this portion of the qualitative analysis sheds light on the possible reasons for the rejection of these hypotheses.

#### *5.4.2.1 Strategies and measures to deal with development of risk potential in both positive and negative direction*

The first qualitative question regarding risk trend two asked respondents about their company's strategic thoughts and derived measures to deal with the second trend, development of risk potential in both positive and negative direction[1]. The following eight answers were provided:

[1] Original German survey question: „Welche strategischen Überlegungen werden angestellt und welche Maßnahmen daraus abgeleitet, um mit diesem wachsenden Katastrophenpotential umzugehen?“

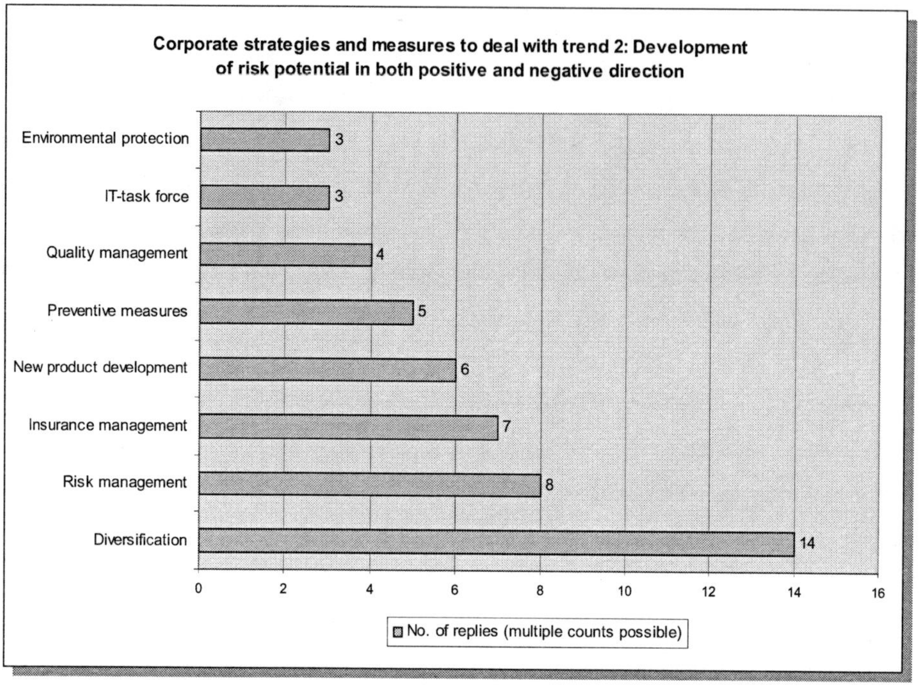


**Figure 33: Corporate strategies and derived measures against Risk trend 2**

*Diversification* is mentioned by fourteen companies as part of their strategic thoughts concerning risk trend two, increasing risk potential in negative and positive direction. Diversification includes entry into new markets in order to spread risk of existing products and markets. In addition, diversification involves the establishment of a geographically evenly spread customer base. Several respondents distribute their products via multiple locations worldwide to lower risk and dependency. To lower risk for the overall group, each unit should be able to run as a standalone, independent unit if necessary. Another suggestion for diversification to be realized is to carefully select product sites and processes. One way to begin diversification is to establish sales representations in foreign countries, which can then be followed by production sites. Co-operation within the group helps to reduce risk and offers alternatives. Several corporations indicated they were unaffected by risk trend two. One corporation claimed its business processes were unaffected by risk trend two, due to the company's focus on safe products and countries. Another corporation sees only limited political risks in the European products sites and possesses a well diversified distribution market with a global presence. One respondent has only recently started thinking about strategies and measures against societal, political and cultural change. These changes are successfully tackled with the help of the local companies. Local companies constantly monitor the developments abroad and provide constant feedback to the headquarters, allowing quick reactions of the parent company. Lastly, it is interesting to note with regard to diversification, numerous respondents stated they were not directly threatened by the risk trend two's characteristic terrorism, mainly due to their ownership structure and nationality.

*Risk management* is identified by eight of the questioned corporations for managing risk trend two. Emphasis was on the requirement for a stronger, better organised and regular risk management. One company calls for preventive or damage reducing measures against risk trend two. Another company acknowledges the importance of the five characteristics in general, but perceives a relatively low threat to the company's specific risk situation. In spite of the low perception of risk potential amongst respondents, business processes are adapted and risks reduced in preparation of the environmental changes. Adaptations might be the introduction of a production and sales buffer, the shortening of transportation distances, and alternative suppliers. Additionally, respondents suggest risk prevention, following local risk evaluation through independent third parties, such as loss adjusters or insurance brokers. Finally, one company seems to take advantage of its headquarters' risk management capabilities, rather than having to develop its own thoughts and strategies locally in the Austria branch organisation.

*Insurance management* closely follows risk management with seven corporations acknowledging its importance for risk trend two, increasing risk potential. Corporations surveyed seem to focus on insurance cover for only the major, existence threatening risks, instead of small damages as an important part of their strategy. As a result, three respondents mention an all risk insurance policy[1] with high deductibles. Apart from property insurance, the insurance cover should also include business interruption and liability insurance. Finally, the

[1] According to Hölzl (2004), an all risk insurance means a comprehensive property cover, excluding the classic cover of the engineering insurance, such as handling error or operating damage, as well as war, terror and similar events

existing insurance cover needs to be adapted whenever necessary to meet the corporate requirements.

*New product development* is incorporated in six corporations' strategic thoughts and measures for combating risk trend two. These companies claim to constantly and thoroughly monitor their product line as well as their supporting marketing activities. One company argued that it tries to capture societal changes at an early stage in order to take advantage of these changes economically. Another company which develops security systems for airplanes gathers necessary know-how in a European knowledge and development pool.

*Preventive measures* are named by five responsive corporations to manage increasing political risk. In all cases, the replies were mainly focused on physical buildings and not on intangible assets. Suggestions consisted of organisational precautions in the case of business interruptions and physical barriers against the damage through possible natural catastrophes, e.g. floods. Possible precautions need to be taken into account at the initial choice of the company location, where possible. One company is in the process of upgrading the security status of its buildings and premises. These security improvements are being realized in a project framework with concrete investments taken afterwards to prevent future damages.

*Quality management* is mentioned by four corporations as being part of their strategic thoughts and measures for dealing with risk trend two. A top quality standard is seen as reducing risk. High quality standards require modern equipment and machinery and clean production processes. Production machinery needs to be constantly monitored and if necessary the production processes optimised in order to maintain the high quality standard. This continuous improvement process might prevent major catastrophes while at the same time helping the constant product innovation.

*IT-task force* is stated by three respondents to handle risk trend two. These companies advise establishing very strict internal IT rules. In addition, precautions against virus attacks and hackers have to be constantly implemented and renewed. These necessary precautions could be achieved by introducing an IT-task force, as recommended by these corporations.

*Environmental protection* is proposed by three corporations as being part of their strategic thoughts and measures against risk trend two. One respondent claimed its company tries to work with, not against nature. Another respondent argued that industrial pollution has already been reduced due to heavy investments into environmental protection. One corporation acknowledged the risk of environmental pollution but does not see at this point in time a high vulnerability of its own corporation for this threat.

Analysis for the qualitative replies clearly shows that corporate risk managers concentrate on trying to avoid the risks of trend two such as natural catastrophes, industrial pollution and terrorism. The most important and extensively explained means of avoiding the risks of trend two is by diversifying business operations, markets and products. Therefore, one of the reasons why hypotheses three and four in Table 12 were rejected might lie in the respondents' greater awareness regarding the real threat of risk trend two, as apposed to corporations which do not possess knowledge in this area. Thus, companies unaware of the risk threats of growing risk potential are not inclined to gather knowledge and develop measures against this risk trend. The prior quantitative analysis for risk trend two consistently indicated that both companies with lessons learned as well as with best practices knowledge tended to rate their risk threat higher than companies without knowledge. However, companies with a higher risk threat rating tend to focus more on avoiding the risks of trend two. The qualitative answers demonstrate that the corporations examined have already established measures against risk trend two.

#### *5.4.2.2 Required lessons learned and best practices for development of risk potential in both positive and negative direction*

The second qualitative question regarding risk trend two asked respondents about the necessary lessons learned and best practices for their company, in order to prevent the risks of development of risk potential in both positive and negative direction[1]. The following six replies were provided:

[1] Original German survey question: „Welche Lessons Learned bzw. Best Practices wären aus Sicht Ihres Unternehmens erforderlich, um bei der Bewältigung des Risikopotentials in negativer und positiver Richtung mitzuwirken?“

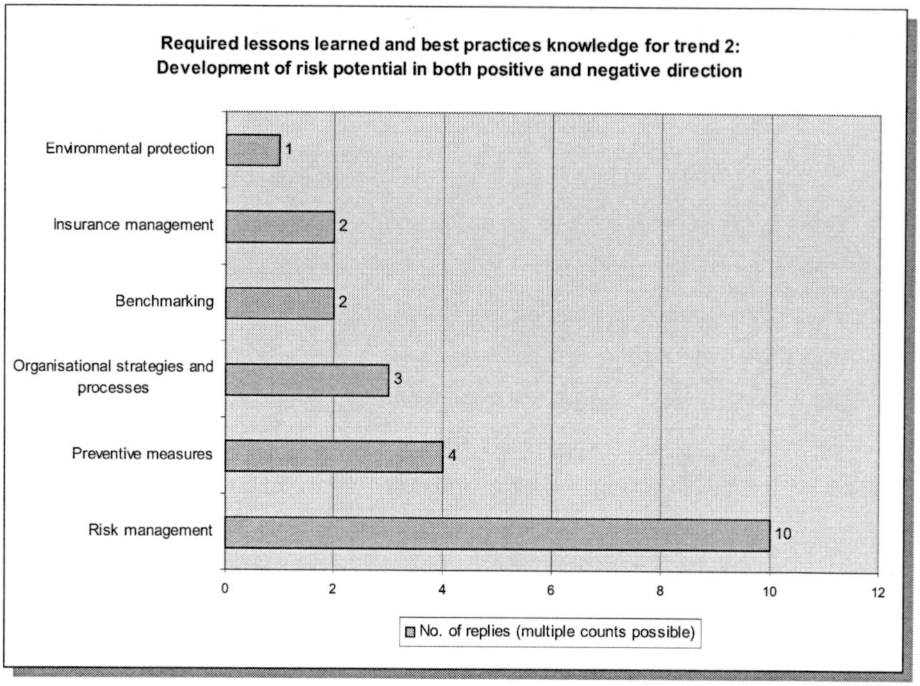


**Figure 34: Necessary lessons learned and best practices dealing with Risk trend 2**

*Risk management* was mentioned by ten companies as necessary lessons learned and best practices with regard to risk trend two. Respondents argue that the growing risk potential of natural catastrophes, terrorism and others could be met with risk management and adequate insurance covers. However, they also admit an insurance solution does not exist for every risk and not everything is insurable. Certain risks always need to be carried by the corporation itself and can not be rolled over to a third party. One way to limit the overall risk seems to be through recurring risk analyses, which display, evaluate and project the risks according to importance, occurrence probability and risk potential. Defined and assessed risks require emergency scenarios while at the same time methods for reducing the risk must be developed and pursued. If damage has occurred, corporations should rely on third party knowledge such as a professional loss adjuster, in order to reduce the arising costs. One company uses risk management knowledge gathered from its corporate headquarters abroad. Two respondents pointed out the successful introduction of the described risk management knowledge and processes into the organisation. Useful application of this knowledge requires a well trained staff.

*Preventive measures* are seen by four respondents as necessary knowledge against risk trend two. Even though it could be argued that this point is part of risk management which is mentioned above, this point was left separate due to its importance in dealing with risk trend two. Respondents argued that lessons learned and best practices should include action alternatives in the case of catastrophes. One company points out that it focuses on the establishment of action alternatives, because it assumes major catastrophes in many cases can not be fully prevented. Another company however claims prevention steps often are left out, leading to higher damages and problems in the long run. One way to gather knowledge about preventive measures might be by using a prevention manual, including a detailed description on how to protect tangible and intangible assets in the case of a catastrophe.

*Organisational strategies and processes* are relevant for three respondents to handle risk trend two. Organisational strategies and processes include clear guidelines and regulations for the organisation and a constant supervision of the defined rules. Also, knowledge about the right co-operation with public authorities might be helpful in order to prevent misunderstandings and prejudices. Partnering with public authorities could even lead to the organisations' active shaping of the legal framework rather than having to react to imposed rules and structures. Organisational strategies and processes knowledge also seems helpful for the entry into new, risky markets.

*Benchmarking* was named by two corporations as necessary lessons learned and best practices knowledge in order to deal with risk trend two. The positive and negative experiences by third parties within the industry need to be introduced into and leveraged within the organisation in order to lead to risk reduction. Implementation of lessons learned and best practices could be supported by constantly monitoring the market and a continuous dialogue with all relevant market participants.

*Insurance management* is noted by two of the examined companies as helping to deal with the second risk trend. Respondents note that every company has to build up an individual set of lessons learned and best practices for the right insurance solution. If insurance cover cannot be obtained, alternatives such as captives or risk prevention should be developed and pursued. In some cases, the lack of or the very limited availability of coverage for natural hazards such as floods and earthquake could affect the decision regarding a new or even existing location.

*Environmental protection* was noticed by one corporation as part of required knowledge to cope with risk trend two. Due to occurred damages affecting the environment, flooding and several fires, the company now possesses a set of lessons learned for this risk potential. However, what is still lacking is the necessary knowledge for preventing and if necessary handling environmental catastrophes.

Risk management was clearly the leading answer for this qualitative question. Contributing to this outcome could be the fact that respondents were primarily risk and insurance experts. For these experts, risk management is seen as the primary means of collecting the necessary lessons learned and best practices knowledge about the growing risk potential. This outcome supports the assumption of the previous qualitative question regarding strategies and measures for risk trend two. Companies with more extensive knowledge about the development of risk potential seem to react to the growing risk potential by developing and establishing a risk management function. Greater awareness regarding risk trend two, growing risk potential, seems to lead to the appropriate risk management measures. Thus, these results could be one of the contributing factors why hypotheses three and four were rejected. The robust replies for preventive measures show that by choosing the right business structure and strategy, companies do not rely only on insurance coverage in order to deal with risks financially, but instead steps are described in order to avoid large catastrophes. Benchmarking assures these steps are guided in the right direction.

### *5.4.3 Possible reasons for substantiation and rejection of hypotheses for the third risk trend*

The following two paragraphs summarise the qualitative answers regarding risk trend three. First, the strategies and measures to deal with the risk trend are mentioned. Secondly, the necessary lessons learned and best practices knowledge in order to deal with this particular trend are presented. Hypotheses relating to risk trend three were not tested positive. The summary of this portion of the qualitative analysis sheds light on the possible reasons for the rejection of these hypotheses.

### *5.4.3.1 Corporate strategies and measures to deal with the problems of the Property & Casualty insurance market*

The first qualitative question regarding risk trend three asked respondents about their company's strategic thoughts and derived measures to deal with the third trend, problems of the Property & Casualty insurance market[1]. The following nine answers were provided:

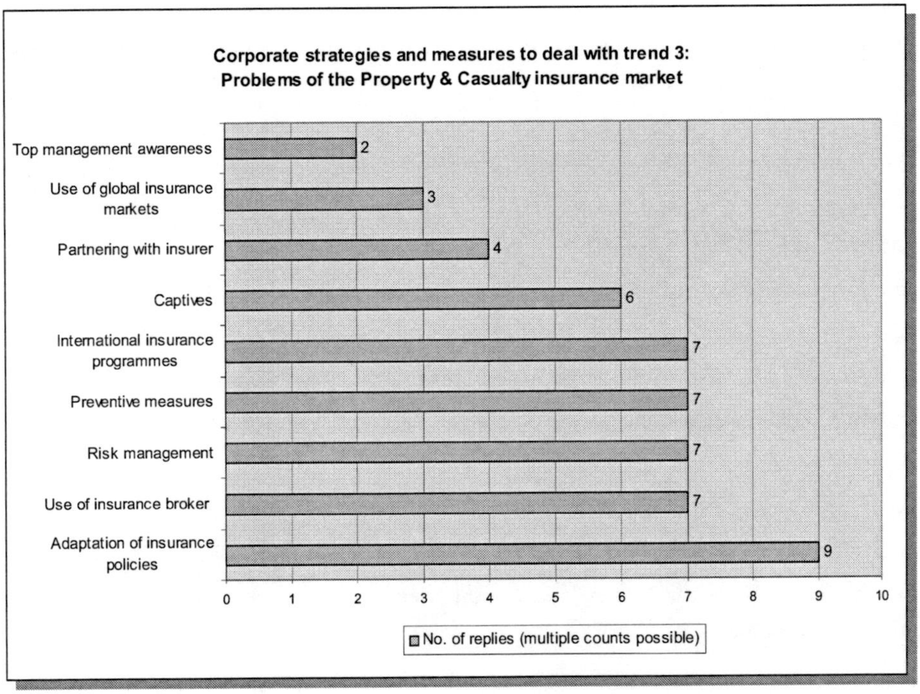


**Figure 35: Corporate strategies and derived measures against Risk trend 3**

*Adaptation of insurance policies* was named by nine corporations as part of their strategic thoughts and measures against risk trend three, problems of the P & C insurance market. Over half of the respondents claimed they would favour higher deductibles in their insurance policies.

[1] Original German survey question: „Welche strategischen Überlegungen werden angestellt und welche Maßnahmen daraus abgeleitet, um mit den Problemen der Versicherungsbranche, die Ihr Unternehmen beeinflussen können, umzugehen?"

A tendency towards only insuring worst-case scenarios while at the same time striving for reasonably affordable premiums seems to exist. Although not mentioned, it could also be argued that industrial insurers push for higher deductibles to eliminate frequent losses and thus lower their administration costs. Adaptation of insurance policies should be supported with the introduction of risk management, which helps with the identification of improvement potential and the corporation's vulnerabilities. While one respondent collects several quotes from differing insurers and achieves long term insurance contracts, another respondent prefers the freedom and flexibility of short-term contracts. A third corporation tries to diversify its insurance policies via several insurers in order to reduce risk of premium increases, insurer default and lacking competition.

*Use of insurance broker* is mentioned by seven corporations as part of their strategic thoughts and measures against risk trend three. Widespread penetration of insurance brokers is in line with the estimation of Krebs (2003), that roughly 80% of the Austrian industrial corporations already use an insurance broker vs. 20% direct business. An important reason for the use of an insurance broker seems to be its relative independence. Unlike most industrial corporations, the insurance broker is an expert on the local insurance market. Insurance brokers constantly monitor changes in the local insurance market and therefore can act swiftly and accordingly for their clients' needs. Thus, the use of insurance brokers could also be seen as an effective outsourcing of a competency which was previously held within the corporation. Another reason which speaks in favour of the use of an insurance broker is the improved negotiation skills, since the broker knows the current conditions and prices of the insurance market. Additionally, brokers help with the bidding as well as the adaptation process of insurance policies. Although not mentioned, another reason for the use of insurance brokers might be the brokers' understanding of both the insureds', as well as the insurers' concerns, thus facilitating the negotiation process. One corporation mentions the change of its group's insurance broker. The reason for this change was the broker's failure to achieve the insurance solution requested by the corporation. This statement shows that insured corporations are not tied to one broker but can also make independent choices. Another respondent points out that brokers are not used in order to provide the choice of the cheapest, but rather the most adequate insurance offers.

*Risk management* was identified by seven corporations in order to deal with risk trend three. An important first step in risk management is the establishment of a group wide risk management function. In several instances, formation of this group wide risk management function seems to have been already accomplished. Risk assessment and analyses can be pursued in cooperation with the insurance broker. The derived identified risk minimising measures should be implemented in a constant optimisation process. One method for achieving an accurate risk assessment is conducting regular risk surveys. Risk surveys stimulate the risk awareness of the corporation and lead to preventive measures. In addition, the necessary risk knowledge transfer between insured corporation, broker and insurer is achieved. Finally, one corporation uses risk management even for the risk assessment of new product introductions.

*Preventive measures* were named by seven respondents as being part of their strategic thoughts and measures to handle risk trend three. Similar to risk trend two, related, preventive measures are listed separately from risk management due to its importance in dealing with risk trend three. Corporations acknowledge an increase in evaluation of and investments in risk prevention and quality improvements. Preventive measures support the attempted reduction of insurance claims, e.g. in liability.

*International insurance programmes* (IPs) are mentioned by seven respondents as being an integral part of their strategic thoughts and measures against the P & C market problems. International insurance programmes include the concept of bundling all corporate insurance policies in one, global, group-wide cover. In addition, corporations are no longer relying solely on traditional, local industry insurers but rather tap the international insurance market for new insurance alternatives and risk capacity. Gaining access to international markets might be facilitated by and further support the first risk trend characteristics one and four, networked economy and globalisation. One respondent argues that the insurance cover is already provided through an IP and therefore the local company in Austria is only issuing the respective local policies. Advantage of an IP and the bundling of insurance policies could be seen in the decreased vulnerability to single events for both insured corporation as well as insurer.

*Captives* are identified by six corporations as part of the strategies and measures against trend three. A captive is a corporate in-house insurer which is already established by numerous global corporations. The captive gives corporations direct access to reinsurance markets, thus increasing their freedom of action. Some corporations are in the process of evaluating the possible formation of a captive in order to make their own provisions and to become self-sufficient. Establishing a captive is supported by using the lessons learned and best practices from already existing captives in other industries.

*Partnering with insurer* is pointed out by four corporations to manage risk trend three. In an economic period where the number of qualified industrial insurers in Austria has been dramatically reduced[1], sustained and long-term partnerships between industrial corporation and insurer has become very important. Corporations tend to bundle insurance policies with few insurers and try to maintain a continuous dialogue to overcome difficulties in price negotiations.

*Use of global insurance markets* is named by three respondents and further supports the thoughts about captives. In this case, corporations try to stimulate competitive bidding of the available insurers, in particular from the United States. Aim is to achieve a larger number of qualified offers instead of being limited to the small local range of industry insurers.

*Top management awareness* is mentioned by two corporations as being part of their strategic thoughts and measures against the problems of the P & C insurance market. It is suggested that a mindset change has occurred in the recent past regarding the importance of risk management. While the risk management function was previously seen as merely a supportive function of insurance management, it has now become top priority for the whole group. Reasons for this development have been the dramatic increase in insurance premiums and training.

The strong and substantial replies for strategies and measures against risk trend three are in line with the overall high characteristic mean results of the quantitative analysis of the problems of the P & C insurance market risk trend. Although hypotheses five and six could not be tested positively, risk management knowledge seems to be a viable way to limit the threats of the P & C insurance market. One way to apply this knowledge is by adapting the existing insurance policies, which is the answer most often given. It looks like the corporate insurance know-how is complemented by or even outsourced to insurance brokers. Establishment of IPs or captives is described in detail and seen as a very important step towards handling risks of the industry insurance market. Importance of IPs and captives in combination with use of global insurance markets seem to be highly connected to risk trend one's characteristics globalisation and networked economy, which where positively tested in the quantitative analysis.

---

[1] Recent exits of industry insurers in Austria include Basler in 2000, Anker in 2001, Axa in 2002 and nearly Gerling in 2002 according to Krebs (2003)

### 5.4.3.2 Required lessons learned and best practices for the problems of the Property & Casualty insurance market

The second qualitative question regarding risk trend three asked respondents about the necessary lessons learned and best practices for their company, in order to prevent the risks of Property & Casualty insurance market[1]. Results of this question are presented below:

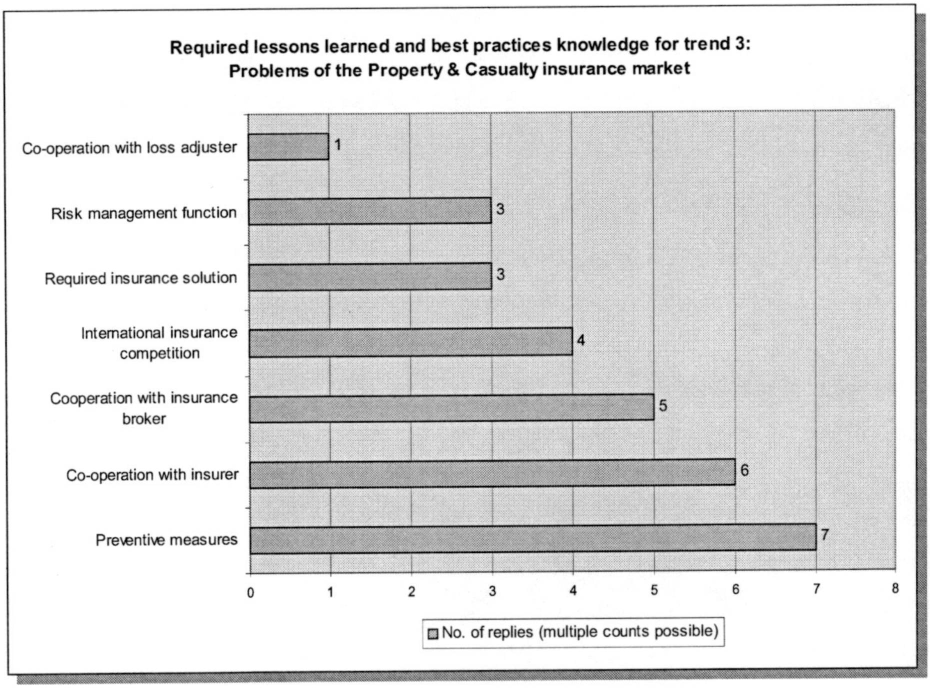


**Figure 36: Necessary lessons learned and best practices dealing with Risk trend 3**

*Preventive measures* were identified by seven respondents as important lessons learned and best practices to deal with risk trend three. In most corporations, preventive measures includes

[1] Original German survey question: „Welche Lessons Learned bzw. Best Practices wären aus Sicht Ihres Unternehmens erforderlich, um eine negative Beeinflussung Ihres Unternehmens durch die Entwicklungen in der Versicherungsbranche zu verhindern?"

knowledge about fire prevention and protection such as fire protection equipment, alarm & detection systems, and sprinkling systems as well as corporate fire brigades. Additionally, corporate wide credit risk and liability claims knowledge are required in order to lower the negative effects of the P & C insurance market problems. Corporations should also be better prepared for unavoidable claims and be aware beforehand of all relevant legal aspects. Preparation might also include knowledge about process redesign in order to improve the risk situation swiftly in a time of crisis. One corporation claims it had acquired lessons learned to facilitate the reduction of the risk potential by constantly monitoring the risk threat. A second corporation says it requires knowledge about product development and process engineering in order to reduce costs and risks. Finally, one respondent is trying to prevent damages to the car fleet through driver checks and trainings, while at the same time investing in modern, intelligent driver supporting safety equipment.

*Co-operation with insurer* is seen by six respondents as important lessons learned and best practices knowledge for handling risk trend three. Working effectively together means existing corporation–insurer partnerships need to be frequently evaluated and when necessary rearranged. Each company must decide whether one or multiple relationships with insures are required. A best practice could be the active collaboration between the insured corporation, insurer and loss adjuster in loss prevention. Collaboration might lead to a better understanding of the corporation's risk improvements and thus to a positive impact on premiums. Furthermore, collaboration might promote knowledge transfer between the three parties. One company points out that the sharp rise of liability premiums forces corporations to constantly rethink the insurance cover. Adaptations in the scope of the cover or the chosen insurer can be supported, where necessary, with lessons learned and best practices knowledge.

*Co-operation with insurance broker* is named by five respondents and thus closely following co-operation with insurer to deal with risk trend three. Corporations mentioning this point acknowledge the positive effect of the knowledge and support provided by the industrial insurance brokers involved. These companies do not rely exclusively on their internal capabilities to monitor the insurance market but rather build upon the expertise of a third party. Know-how provided by insurance brokers seems not to be exclusively focused on Austria but also has an internationally perspective. In order to limit the problems of the P & C insurance market, one company has established a mutually beneficial partnership with the whole insurance industry, including their insurance brokers. Such an insurance network seems to be helpful both within the organisation, as well as with the price negotiations with the insurer.

*International insurance competition* was identified by four respondents as relevant lessons learned and best practices knowledge in regards to risk trend three. One corporation, for instance, experienced European industrial insurers' pricing as being highly dependent on very few reinsurers. This corporation also expects US insurers to enter the European market very soon. Entrance of US insurers in the European market would lead to a high capacity surplus. The knowledge about new insurance capacity providers might be beneficial for Europe based companies. However, to benefit from lower premiums, corporations would have to accept higher precaution as well as the risk management provisions demanded by US insurers. Furthermore, knowledge about the developments of the global insurance markets might lead to the formation of captives, i.e. in-house insurance companies or international insurance programmes with umbrella policies covering multiple countries.

*Required insurance solution* is mentioned by three corporations as necessary knowledge in order to limit the P & C insurance market problems. Respondents highly value information obtained concerning the appropriate and required insurance cover for their corporation. Hence, relationships with professional brokers are pursued in order to increase transparency regarding the insurance services provided and their bottom line benefits. Better knowledge about the necessary insurance solution might assist the corporation in deciding how much risk it can carry itself and what it has to transfer to the insurer.

*Risk management function* is named by three corporations to manage risk trend three. Knowledge about the appropriate organisational structure to capture, assess and analyse the risks appears to be lacking. In addition, constant improvement of the claims handling process is an important step towards lowering the risks of the P & C insurance market problems.

*Cooperation with loss adjuster* is identified by one respondent in order to deal with the problems of the P & C insurance market. The corporation acknowledges the fact that the above mentioned risk management function can be very well supported by using the lessons learned and best practices of loss adjusters and insurers.

Foremost results for preventive measures for dealing with the problems of the P & C insurance market are not unexpected since avoidance is obviously the best way for corporations to deal with the industry's external problems. P & C insurance market problems seem to drive more co-operation between industrial corporations and insurers, brokers and other parties, such as loss adjusters. Increase in co-operation appears to support another general assumption that in a time of crisis, various groups of people tend to work more effectively together than in a period of stability. Corporations might even benefit from globalisation through increased competition between industry insurers, thus limiting the negative effects of the P & C insurance market. Like the previously mentioned strategies and measures against risk trend one, emergence of increasingly complex and bigger corporate structures, answers given regarding risk trend three underline the strong quantitative findings for the characteristics globalisation and networked economy.

### *5.4.4 Answers to final open comments & feedback question*

Seven respondents, in total, took advantage of the opportunity to answer the last qualitative question found at the end of the risk & knowledge management survey. This question requested comments and feedback regarding the study being conducted[1]. Responses can be categorised into four groups: (1) one answer regarding risk trend two, (2) four answers about risk trend three, (3) one answer concerning the use of the SIC code and finally (4) two general answers regarding the survey questions.

Answers regarding risk trend two, the development of risk potential in both positive and negative direction, came from a company which mentioned they institutionalised a set of risk management manuals aimed at dealing with the risk trends. Vulnerability against the risk trends is seen differently across the various sectors of the corporation.

Answers pertaining to risk trend three, problems of the Property & Casualty insurance market, were as follows. First, a company argued that in their industry sector no shortage of insurance cover exists but a visible increase in the risk threat has taken place. A second company pointed out that the insurance prices had dramatically increased over the last year. As a consequence, the company is now in the process of installing an in-house insurer in order to deal with the predicament of increasing insurance prices. A third company mentions the EU

---

[1] Original German survey question: „Anregungen, Fragen, Kommentare"

extension in 2005 and calls upon the insurances to play a vital part in the new members' integration process. A fourth corporation states they are an industrial corporation supported by an insurance broker in their insurance affairs.

Regarding the industrial classification at the beginning of the survey, one corporation states that it was unable to select a suitable SIC code due to the corporate structure as a conglomerate. Consequently, the selection was made for the holding company. Feedback on the SIC code could be used to further refine the industrial differentiation between companies examined in future studies.

Finally, two out of the seven companies responding to the feedback question mentioned they found some of the survey questions difficult to answer. Thus, it can be assumed the majority of the respondents understood and answered appropriately the risk & knowledge management survey.

### *5.4.5 Findings supporting the theoretical analysis*

Qualitative and quantitative answers provided by the risk & knowledge management survey respondents substantiate the theoretical part of this research in several cases. These cases are summarised as follows.

Correct selection of the characteristics described for each risk trend in the state of the field analysis is supported by the quantitative coefficient alpha reliabilities analysis. Calculated coefficient alpha for each risk trend was above the acceptable level of 0.70 (0.8236 for risk trend one, 0.7379 for risk trend two, and 0.8160 for risk trend three). Thus, the selected characteristics are consistent for each risk trend. Most characteristics are also mentioned several times by the survey respondents in the qualitative analysis. In particular, characteristic one, two and four of risk trend one, i.e. networked economy, shareholder value and globalisation are frequently named. Characteristics one, two and five of risk trend two, i.e. natural catastrophes, industrial pollution and societal, political and cultural change were mentioned. Characteristics one and two of risk trend three, i.e. price and capacity cycles and competitive disadvantages of the industry sector were highlighted. Also, MANOVA analysis performed in the quantitative analysis further substantiates the selection of the characteristic networked economy ($F(1,71) = 4.20$, $p < .05$) and globalisation ($F(1,71) = 14.56$, $p < .001$) for risk trend one.

Qualitative question answers emphasize both risk and insurance management as an integral part of the responsive corporations' strategy in order to deal with the change in the overall risk environment. As a result, companies have already established and institutionalised the risk management function. The strong qualitative answers might have been influenced partly by the target group's work-related focus on risk and insurance management. However, the establishment and institutionalisation of the risk management function is consistent with the proposed and developed knowledge-based risk management process, which is directed at corporate and insurance risk managers. Role description of the corporate and the insurance risk manager for this new process match in principal the desired structures provided in the qualitative survey answers. However, none of the respondents have or were able to suggest a structured approach. This fact validates the research needed in this field and thus this book.

Benchmarking, which is an important part of steps three and four (risk assessment and analysis) of the described knowledge-based risk management process, is specifically identified in the qualitative analysis for risk trend two. Similar answers are provided for the other risk trends, such as knowledge about the required insurance solutions and preventive measures. This finding suggests that the corporations examined require external knowledge about comparable corporations in order to assess their own improvement potential, thus, validating the inclusion of benchmarking in the knowledge-based risk management process.

Theoretically, the knowledge-based risk management process could be applied manually. However, only a web based platform would facilitate and enable a global, networked approach. To test this assumption and the examined corporations' co-operation, the risk & knowledge management survey was conducted online. The online survey was a success. Survey results arrived in a surprisingly fast and comprehensive manner, even though only a very simple survey form was utilized. Furthermore, the reusability factor of the gathered answers was much higher and faster than with conventional examinations such as paper surveys.

### *5.4.6 Suggestions for further empirical studies*

The qualitative analysis leads to numerous possibilities for further research. One important follow-up study to the existing risk & knowledge management survey could be the re-conducting of the qualitative parts of the survey in a more structured way. For example, each risk trend characteristic could be verified with an open question. An enhanced qualitative structure might shed light on further reasons for approval or disapproval of the hypotheses in Table 12. The extended risk & knowledge management survey could be conducted by either sticking to the same survey target group or by extending it to a wider spectrum. While the choice of the same target group would allow a better comparison with the existing study, a wider target group insures inclusion of new knowledge and opinions.

The richness of the qualitative answers provided shows that risk managers are willing to share existing knowledge regarding the three examined risk trends and even beyond. The question now is how to most effectively collect and transfer this knowledge not only within the corporation but also between corporations. Answering this question could be the aim of further research. A starting point for this examination could be the knowledge-based risk management process concept in combination with the online risk & knowledge management survey. The next step could be the architecture design for an online risk management platform for corporate and insurance risk managers. Next, existing internal barriers against knowledge management within the examined corporations should be examined and necessary measures derived from current organisational theory in order to achieve the required results.

## 5.5 Discussion

The final section of chapter five discusses some of the major findings of the empirical analysis and their implications for the scientific field.

**High coefficient alpha reliabilities**

The coefficient alpha analysis conducted for each risk trend demonstrated high internal reliability for each risk trend. Importance of this finding lies in the proof that the characteristics extracted from the state of the field analysis are consistent for each risk trend. Hence, chosen characteristics well define the given risk trends. As Kachigan (1991: 140) points out, the coefficient alpha analysis is the most important step in analysing empirical data because it tests the significance of the answers provided. In addition, Kachigan (1991: 141) states that "measurements can be reliable without being valid, but cannot be valid without being reliable". Results of the performed coefficient alpha analysis established that the provided answers were reliable and understood in a similar and consistent way by the survey respondents. These results enabled the subsequent data analyses. However, the selected characteristics describing each risk trend might not be exclusive. Further research projects could adapt as well as extend the list of characteristics for each risk trend. In particular, if the literature suggests a change in the risk environment. An extended risk trend characteristics matrix is graphically displayed in Figure 37. Possibility to extend the risk trend description by adding or replacing new characteristics beyond the currently five existing characteristics is another positive feature of the knowledge-based risk management process. Validity of the new set of characteristics can again be tested through coefficient alpha reliabilities.

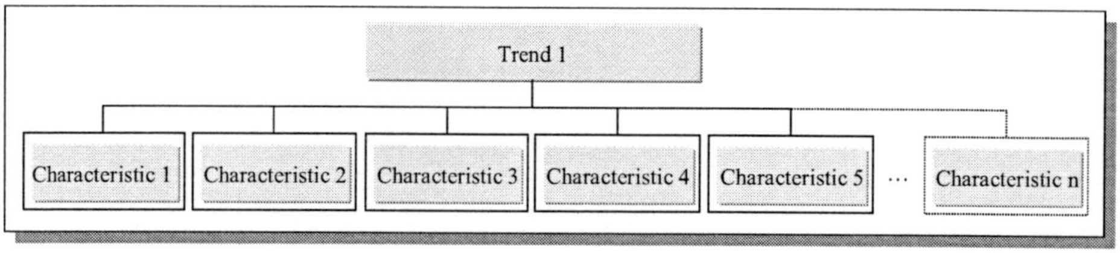


**Figure 37: Extended trend and characteristics matrix**

### Possession and use of knowledge identical amongst corporations

Examination of frequencies discovered a distinction cannot be made between possession and usage of risk management knowledge. Hence, companies possessing risk management knowledge claim to put this risk knowledge to use. According to the survey respondents, all the existing knowledge within the corporation is either fully used or it does not exist. An area of further investigation could be conducted in companies claiming to possess and use risk management knowledge. The central question to be examined would be whether all risk knowledge available within the organisation is truly leveraged. If risk knowledge is not yet being leveraged, which is the common assumption by experts on knowledge management such as Bollinger and Smith (2001: 18), necessary measures on how to tap this risk management knowledge need to be developed and introduced within the organisations.

### High correlation between usage of lessons learned with usage of best practices

Results of the state of the field analysis suggested knowledge management can be applied by using lessons learned and best practices (Patton, 2002: 329-336; Bhatt, 2001: 65-68). Therefore, the risk & knowledge management survey questions were separated in these two categories, so as to more precisely examine risk knowledge management. The correlation analysis pursued shows a highly significant correlation between answers for lessons learned and best practices questions. People acknowledging the existence of lessons learned also tend to recognize the existence of best practices. This finding suggests corporate knowledge is indeed a combination of all the lessons learned and best practices which lie within its employees or which have been explicitly written down within the company.

### Globalisation and networked economy are key risk trend drivers

MANOVA tests pursued across all three risk trends showed that significance could only be established for risk trend one, growing complexity and corporate size. This finding shows companies which possess and use risk management knowledge regarding risk trend one rate their risk exposure lower than companies without knowledge. Thorough examination of this finding reveals that all characteristic means are consistent with this result. However, the key drivers for the positive MANOVA test are two characteristics, namely globalisation and networked economy. Subsequent qualitative analysis showed similar results in that globalisation and networking strategies are key strategies and measures in dealing with company size and complexity. Future studies should therefore examine why these two characteristics currently play such a dominant role for corporate risk managers. This investigation might lead to a better understanding of the current risk environment and help to handle this risk environment by applying the appropriate risk management knowledge and expertise.

### Corporations possessing and using knowledge see greater threat of growing risk potential

Quantitative analysis for risk trend two indicated that both companies possessing and using lessons learned as well as possessing and using best practices knowledge tended to rate their risk threat higher than companies without knowledge. Consequently, the hypotheses for risk trend two were rejected. One reasons for this rejection could be that companies with more knowledge can better assess the true risk menace. These companies might have realised how important and dangerous the growing risk potential of natural catastrophes, industrial pollution, terrorism, technological advancement and failure and societal, political and cultural change could be for their company. The perceived higher risk threat could be the reason for the higher score for this risk trend. If this is the case, it is an interesting finding, since only known risk can be dealt with and preventative measures integrated, as opposed to unknown risk. Research should therefore be conducted on whether companies tend to rate risk higher when they are aware of the risk threat. Additionally, tools could be developed and implemented for revealing unknown risk and taking appropriate action in order to handle the risk.

**Respondents rate P & C insurance market problems as highest overall risk threat**

Comparison of the characteristic means for each risk trend reveal that risk trend three, P & C insurance market problems, are rated consistently the highest. Furthermore, the characteristic mean values for risk trend three sometimes even doubled those of the other two risk trends. Questions for risk trend three were located in the third section of the risk & knowledge management survey. Due to this fact, it seems very unlikely the higher characteristic mean values are a coincidence. Rather, results suggest an external, unrelated risk trend is posing a serious problem to industrial corporations today. The strong results could be driven by the risk and insurance managers' helplessness in having to accept the drastic rise in insurance prices and reduced risk coverage, as mentioned by several respondents. A future study could examine why the danger of this risk trend was consistently rated higher than the other two risk trends and what the possible implications for risk and insurance managers might be in order to deal with the risk trend three, P & C insurance market problems.

**Qualitative analysis supports quantitative results**

Qualitative questions proved to be an effective way to support the qualitative results and gain additional in depth information about all three risk trends from the responding corporations.

Globalisation and networking strategies were frequently identified by respondents for risk trend one. This result is fully in line with the two positively tested risk trend one's characteristics globalisation and networked economy. Organisational streamlining, the top answer, seems to be an important step towards preparing an industrial corporation for the competitive landscape that emerges due to globalisation and a fully networked economy.

Insurance and risk management know-how, the leading answer for risk trend two, shows that corporate risk managers are still relying on industrial insurers' expertise to deal with the growing risk potential. How this dependency could be leveraged by both industrial insurers as well as industrial companies would be an interesting field of further study.

Responses demonstrate that the corporations' high dependence on the P & C insurance market problems can only be tackled by proactive risk and insurance management.

A potential future study in the field of risk and knowledge management could refine the quantitative questions regarding the risk trends. More in-depth expert knowledge might lead to a better understanding of the nature of the risk trends and thus help to develop effective risk reducing measures.

**Limitations of empirical analysis**

Several limitations of the empirical analysis should be acknowledged. Firstly, the target group for the risk and knowledge management survey consisted of the 250 largest industrial corporations in Austria. It was demonstrated that this group represents the industrial sector of the Austrian economy and it was supposed that larger industrial corporations are more likely to possess and use risk management concepts than smaller ones. However, it could be assumed that other industrial corporations exist in Austria. These companies were not addressed as part of the survey and therefore could not contribute to the research performed.

Secondly, respondents had to be open to phone, email and Internet contact, in order to respond to the risk and knowledge management survey. The risk and knowledge management survey was conducted fully online rather than using traditional mail services. Thus, by opting for this non-traditional method for conducting the survey, the author had the expectation that the respondent did not have any barriers either to email or to Internet. This expectation could have impacted the overall response rate. Although all 250 companies did provide a high-level insurance or risk management decision maker as recipient for the invitation email, not all of these target group members were responsive. This unresponsiveness might indicate that interest in surveys, even when supported from the Vienna University of Economics and Business Administration is generally never 100%. Survey return results suggest that the responses are limited to those members of the target group who were open minded towards the topic and who were also able to use the new media email and Internet for the survey answering process.

Thirdly, the risk and knowledge management survey questions had to be translated from English into German. This translation was necessary due to the fact that the survey was performed in Austria and the business language in Austria is German. To assure the quality of the translation, an English - German language expert reviewed the translation. However, minor changes to the meaning of specific survey questions could occur during the course of any translation. Likewise, minor modifications to particular statements need to be considered in 5.4 Qualitative analysis results, since the qualitative answers of the survey respondents were also translated from German into English and summarised. Again, translation of the qualitative answers was supported with a language expert.

**Self – reflection**

One of the key learnings during the course of this book proved to be the process of conducting the risk and knowledge management survey. In the early stages of this research, it became clear that the survey design and implementation were a corner stone for the successful completion of the book. A re-run of the survey would have been impossible due to the structure of the target group. Consequently, no mistakes could be made without jeopardising the completion of this book and without a possible loss of reputation for the university and involved advisors. The input, experience and support brought forward by both advisors insured that no mistakes were made with regard to the survey questions, i.e. questions were posed in the right way and that no questions were left out. In addition, the advisors' support enabled the pursuit of a new method of conducting a survey via email and Internet. Pursuing an online survey proved to be an important learning experience and know-how generation for both parties. Further success of the survey also hinged on obtaining support from Hoppenstedt and Zahel winery. Hoppenstedt provided an Austrian company database, which was used to extract general information about the 250 leading Austrian industrial companies. Zahel winery provided support in the form of prizes for the survey respondents. Gathering the support of these external sources required new negotiation and sales skills.

Several additional key learnings were gained during the survey process. Firstly, it proved to be very important to remind the target group. Reminders were achieved in a friendly manner via email. Maintaining a balance between pushing the target group towards filling out the survey and still being polite was a difficult task, but in the end proved to be very successful. As illustrated in Figure 19, the number of responses increased after each reminder email. Secondly, incorporating incentives into the survey process was significant. Responses were higher when incentives were announced. Completing a survey does not necessarily require a prize for everybody but if odds are high for winning something then more people will participate. Thirdly, decision makers answering the survey questions seemed to be in favour of short, informative mailings rather than long explanations. What seems to be more important is that the survey source is a secure, trusted organisation, which in this study was the case with the Vienna University of Economics and Business Administration.

Several interesting findings and learnings occurred during the analysis of the quantitative and qualitative answers. Obtaining a significant response rate was important to the overall success of the risk and knowledge management survey results. Another important outcome was statistically determining that the selected characteristics consistently described each of the three risk trends and that the respondents collectively interpreted the survey question similarly. The high quality of the survey answers shows that corporate risk managers in Austria take research studies seriously. The finding that those company possessing lessons learned and best practices also put them to use was noteworthy. However, a structured risk management approach incorporating knowledge management concepts seemed to be lacking in all the companies responding. Therefore, these companies could benefit from the introduction of the knowledge-based risk management process.

# 6 Conclusions

Chapters two through four examine from a theoretic point of view the following three risk trends: (1) the emergence of increasingly complex and bigger corporate structures, (2) the development of risk potential in positive and negative direction and (3) the problems of the Property and Casualty insurance market. Application of knowledge management in the form of lessons learned and best practices for handling these risk trends was examined and explained by two benchmarks. As a consequence of this investigation, a need for incorporating knowledge management into the current risk management processes was discovered.

On this basis a new knowledge-based risk management process was proposed. This new knowledge-based risk management process does not replace but enhances existing risk management processes. Chapter five provides results of the empirical analysis conducted. Aim of this analysis was to substantiate the theoretic results as well as to demonstrate the practicability of steps two and three of the knowledge-based risk management process. Chapter six presents the comparison between the theoretical and empirical results achieved and the possible reasons for resulting similarities and differences. In addition, conclusions for the scientific as well as the business community are drawn.

## 6.1 Comparison of theoretical and empirical results

The following sections contrast the findings for the theoretic and empirical parts of this research.

### *6.1.1 Risk trends and characteristics*

An extensive review of the current international literature on risk and insurance management brought to light three major risk trends which today threaten industrial corporations. These three risk trends were namely: (1) the emergence of increasingly complex and bigger corporate structures, (2) the development of risk potential in positive and negative direction and (3) the problems of the Property and Casualty insurance market.

Using the same literature sources, a description of every risk trend was formulated through five main characteristics. Selection of the five characteristics for each risk trend was based on their frequency and detailed appearance in the literature. Each of the chosen fifteen characteristics was assigned the same weight for the theoretic description of the three risk trends. Identically weighted characteristics assure the comparability of characteristics within a trend and between trends, even though differences in importance among the characteristics could have been assumed.

A risk & knowledge management survey was developed and conducted to test the theoretical assumptions. The risk trend part of the survey consisted of five questions per risk trend. Each question asked the leading experts on risk and insurance management in Austria to rate a particular risk trend's characteristic. As expected, results were not consistent across all fifteen characteristics. Yet, every risk trend was determined by the coefficient alpha analysis as being well defined by the chosen characteristics. This finding shows that a thorough literature review is key in gathering suitable results for a risk trend description. However, the experiences of a very specific survey target group might result in a differentiated view on the importance of the state of the field analysis. Risk & knowledge management survey results encourage further empirical research studies, which might be time consuming, but could lead to interesting first hand experience to further support theoretic results.

### *6.1.2 Linking knowledge management with risk management*

The theory brought forward in the state of the field analysis suggests that knowledge management can play an important role in the improvement of risk management. Knowledge management for this book is defined as the successful application of lessons learned and best practices in the industrial corporation, in order to avoid, compensate or mitigate risks. Exemplary sources from the current scientific literature, as well as two practical cases of Austrian industrial corporations are provided to illustrate the opportunities for linking knowledge and risk management.

The empirical analysis uses the risk & knowledge management survey to test the linkage between knowledge and risk management. As previously mentioned, the survey consists of two main parts. Part one asks industrial corporations about their perceived risk exposure. Part two asks about the availability and use of lessons learned and best practices. Each of the two survey parts is divided into a quantitative and qualitative section. The statistical analysis focuses on the relationship of the answers of the two main parts, i.e. risk management and knowledge management. Further refinement of the statistical analysis was made due to the separation of knowledge management in applying lessons learned and best practices. Companies were consequently categorised as either having knowledge and use or as not having knowledge nor use. In principle, the quantitative tests can be seen as a scientific check of the theory brought forward in the first part of the research.

A connection between risk management and knowledge management could only be established for one out of the three risk trends. For risk trend one, emergence of increasingly complex and bigger corporate structures, companies who possessed and used risk management lessons learned rated their overall risk exposure lower than those without lessons learned. The positive results for risk trend one and lessons learned are mainly driven by two out of the five risk trend one characteristics, specifically globalisation and networked economy. A positive relationship could not be established for risk trends two and three in relationship to lessons learned or for all three risk trends in relationship to best practices. Empirical findings seem to suggest that availability and use of risk management knowledge does not necessarily lead to a lower perception of the risk threat. Moreover, companies having and using knowledge tend to be more aware of the possible dangers. As a consequence, respondents tended to rate the risk threat for their companies higher than those without possession and use of knowledge. Additionally, companies with high use of lessons learned and best practices provided detailed answers on how to deal with their risk threats. Hence even though a statistical correlation between knowledge management and risk management can not be verified, both the quantitative and the qualitative answers suggest that companies can highly benefit from the use and application of risk management lessons learned and best practices.

### *6.1.3 Lessons learned and best practices are both knowledge components*

Research on knowledge management divides knowledge into two parts, explicit and implicit knowledge. The focus of this book however was only on explicit knowledge, hence structured, codified knowledge within the survey target group corporations. Researchers examining the most effective exploitation of explicit knowledge argue that it can be best applied by using lessons learned and best practices. Lessons learned for this book are defined as reusable examples of how industrial corporations were unable to avoid, compensate or mitigate damage before its occurrence. On the hand, best practices for this book are reusable examples of avoidance, compensation or mitigation of risks to the industrial corporation.

Structuring of part two of the risk & knowledge management survey in questions for lessons learned and best practices allowed the testing of correlation between these two knowledge components. A highly significant relationship between the availability of lessons learned and best practices in the corporations examined could be identified. Hence, companies claiming possession and use of lessons learned tend to claim possession and use of best practices. This finding supports the assumption made in the theoretic part of the research that lessons learned and best practices are both equal parts of knowledge. Introduction of knowledge-based risk management within industrial corporations should therefore focus on both aspects of knowledge management, i.e. lessons learned and best practices, in order to be successful.

### *6.1.4 Knowledge-based risk management process in theory and practice*

Chapter four describes a new knowledge-based risk management process in order to handle the threats of three risk trends identified in the state of the field analysis. Part of this process is to graphically display the current risk positioning of the corporation. This display allows the comparison with a desired future risk positioning after the successful completion of the knowledge-based risk management process. Form of repositioning depends on the onset risk positioning of the company. A detailed description on how the new process could be applied by industrial corporations with the help of industry insurers is provided in chapter 5. The knowledge-based risk management process consists of five steps: (1) risk identification, (2) risk assessment, (3) risk analysis, (4) risk handling and (5) risk monitoring. Description of the process points out that a sustained, long-term application of the knowledge-based risk management process can help to improve the corporation's overall risk exposure and limit the negative effects of the three risk trends.

Description of the knowledge-based risk management process maintains companies possessing and using risk management lessons learned and best practices for a risk trend pair are likely to be found in the lower left quadrant of the risk trend matrix. On the contrary, companies with no possession and use of risk management knowledge for a risk trend pair are expected to be in the upper right corner of the matrix. Figure 38 through Figure 40 demonstrate the differences and similarities between theory and practice of the risk trend one – risk trend two combination. Most of the 76 responsive corporations find themselves in the lower left corner of the matrix. According to the theory, this would suggest all of these companies possess lessons learned and best practices. Validity of this statement can be confirmed by comparing the shape of and the figure next to each dot. The legend for the following figures can be found in Table 20: Legend of comparison of theoretical and empirical results graphical display. The following four examples illustrated in Figure 40 show how the assumption in the theory can be verified by using the results of the Risk & Knowledge management survey:

*Example 1* shows four companies which, according to the theory of the knowledge-based risk management process, find themselves in the correct position within the risk trend matrix. Company one is in the top left quadrant. Company one's star shape dot and "0" case label indicate lessons learned for risk trend one are available and in use (star shape) but not for risk trend two ("0" case label). Company two is in the lower left quadrant due to its star shape and "2" case label. This indicator signifies that lessons learned are available and in use for both risk trends. Company three and four are in the upper right quadrant. Company three has a diamond shape and a "0" case label, meaning that lessons learned are neither available nor used for both risk trends. Company four has a "0" case label and a box shape. The "0" case label represents the lacking availability and use of lessons learned for risk trend two, while the box shape means the availability but no use of lessons learned for risk trend one.

*Example 2* depicts a company in the lower left corner. This positioning would suggest possession and use of lessons learned for both risk trend one and risk trend two. However, the company has a star shape dot and only a "0" case label, thus indicating lessons learned for risk trend one are available and in use but not for risk trend two. Therefore the expected positioning according to the theory would be in the upper left quadrant of the matrix.

*Example 3* portrays a company in the lower right quadrant. Yet, this company has a diamond shape and a "0" case label. Therefore, its position should be in the top right quadrant, since it has neither availability nor use of lessons learned for trend one and for trend two.

*Example 4* shows two companies in the upper left corner and one in the lower right corner of the risk trend matrix. All three companies possess and use both lessons learned for risk trend one (star shape) and risk trend two ("2" as case label). Therefore, these three companies according to the theory would have been expected to be in the lower left corner of the matrix.

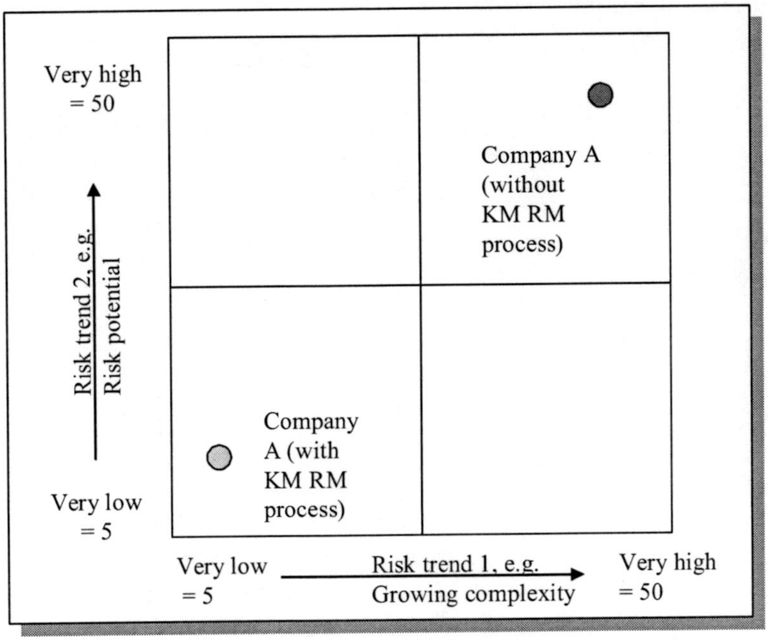


**Figure 38: Exemplary theoretically expected outcome of risk assessment**

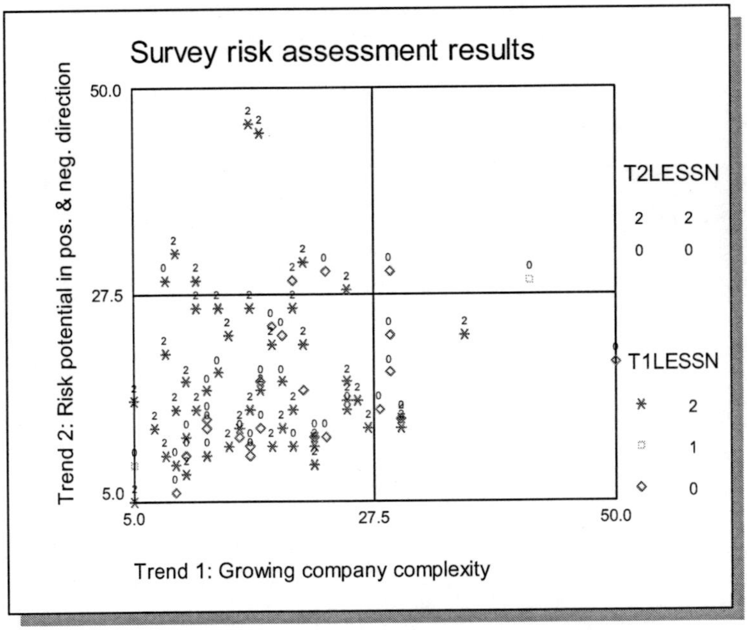


**Figure 39: Exemplary empirical outcome of risk assessment**

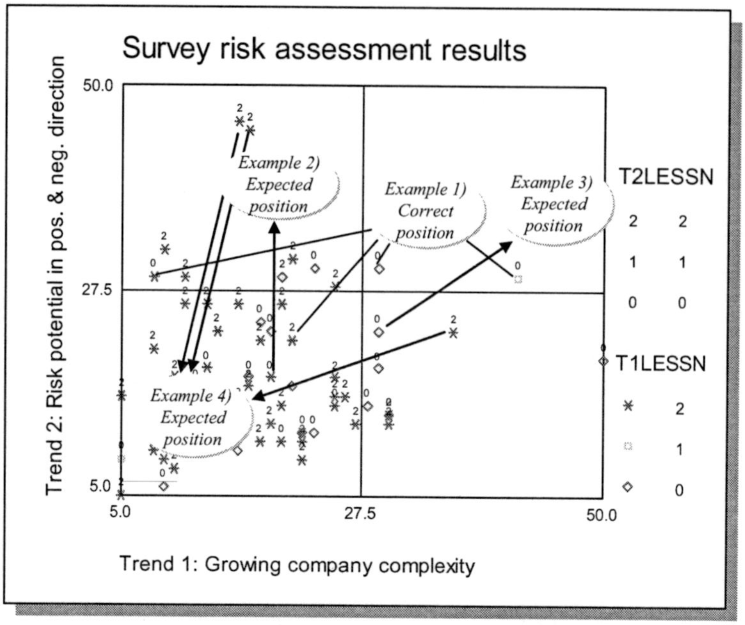


**Figure 40: Risk assessment theory & practice comparison – Trends 1 and 2, Lessons learned**

Remaining risk trend – lessons learned and best practices combinations could also be analysed using the above mentioned method. Figure 40 illustrates the results of these risk trend combinations. As depicted in these diagrams, several outcomes are not as expected, thus leading to the unsubstantiated hypotheses.

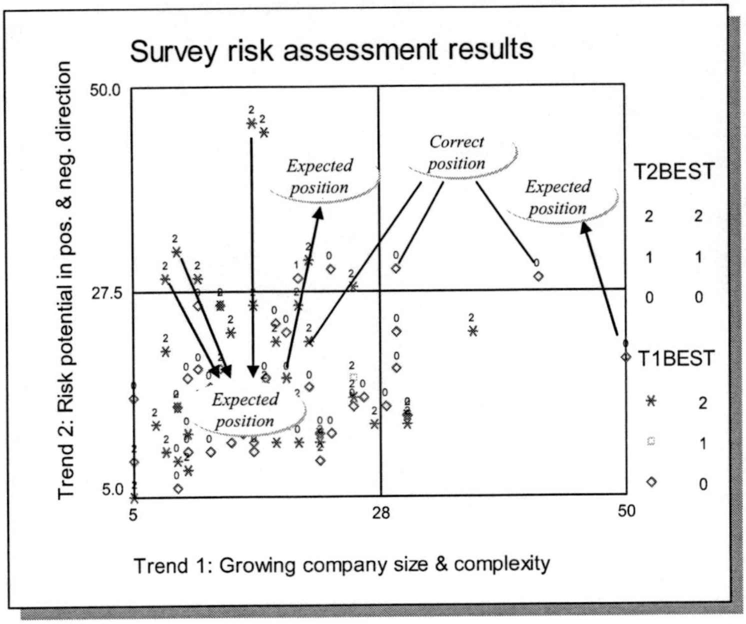


**Figure 41: Risk assessment theory & practice comparison – Trends 1 and 2, Best practices**

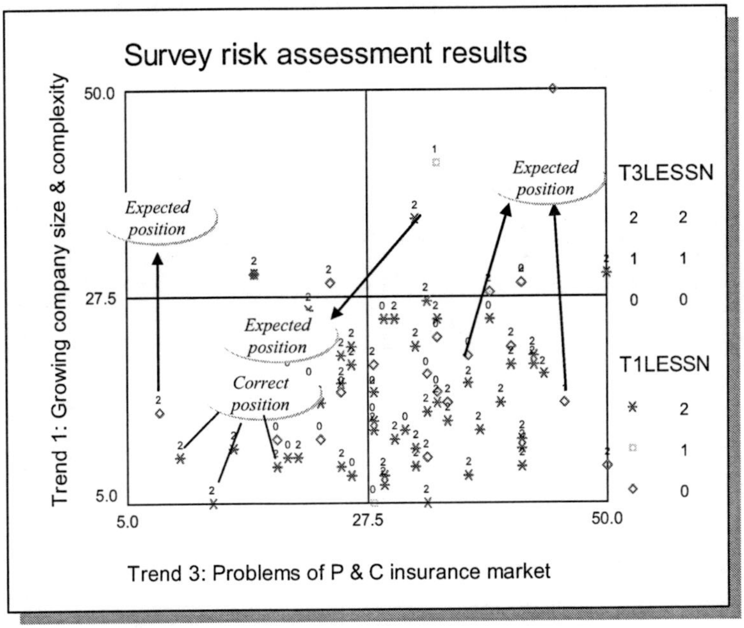


**Figure 42: Risk assessment theory & practice comparison – Trends 1 and 3, Lessons learned**

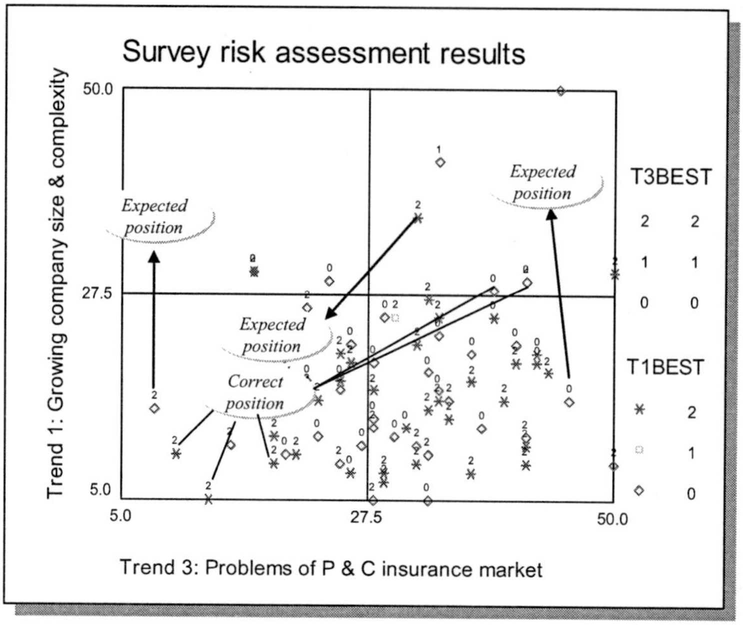


**Figure 43: Risk assessment theory & practice comparison – Trends 1 and 3, Best practices**

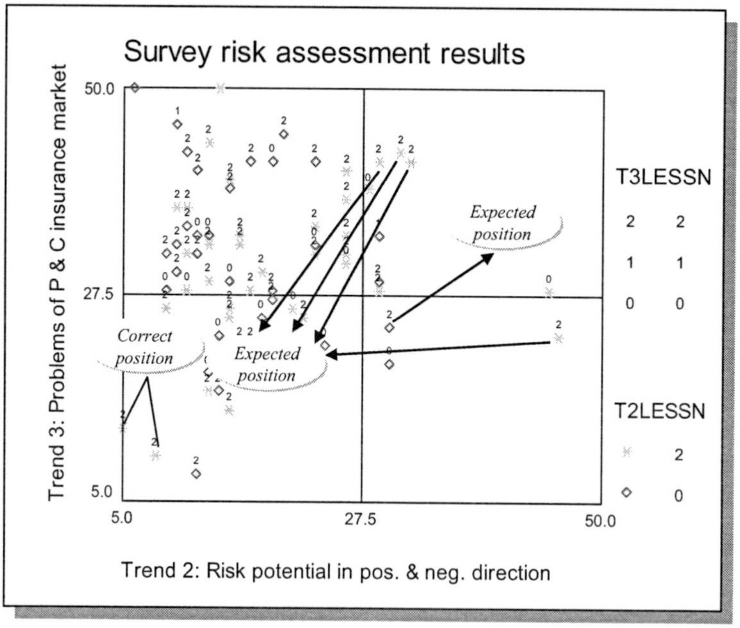


**Figure 44: Risk assessment theory & practice comparison – Trends 2 and 3, Lessons learned**

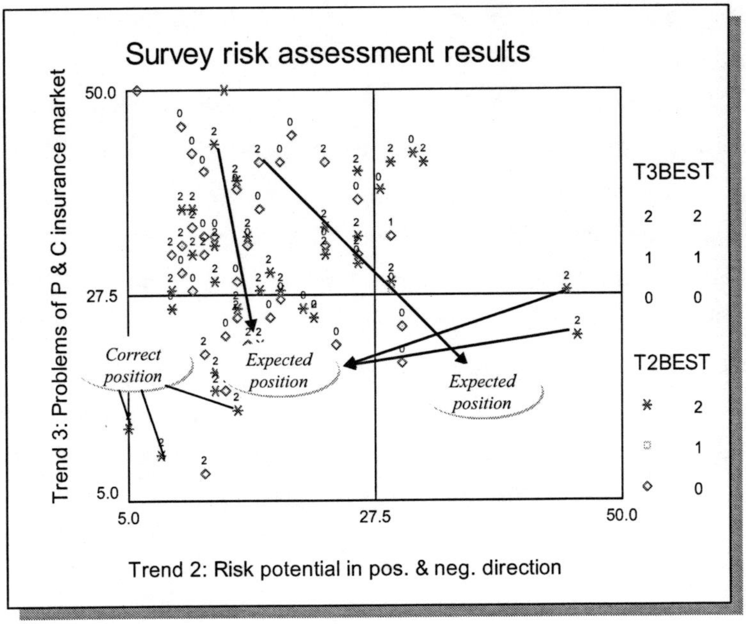


**Figure 45: Risk assessment theory & practice comparison – Trends 2 and 3, Best practices**

| SPSS table abbreviation | Short explanation | Full explanation | Values |
|---|---|---|---|
| | *Case label / Legend* (*) | | |
| **T1LESSN** | Trend 1 / Lessons learned | No availability vs. availability vs. availability & use of Lessons learned | 0 / 1 / 2 |
| **T1BEST** | Trend 1 / Best practices | No availability vs. availability vs. availability & use of Best practices | 0 / 1 / 2 |
| **T2LESSN** | Trend 2 / Lessons learned | No availability vs. availability vs. availability & use of Lessons learned | 0 / 1 / 2 |
| **T2BEST** | Trend 2 / Best practices | No availability vs. availability vs. availability & use of Best practices | 0 / 1 / 2 |
| **T3LESSN** | Trend 3 / Lessons learned | No availability vs. availability vs. availability & use of Lessons learned | 0 / 1 / 2 |
| **T3BEST** | Trend 3 / Best practices | No availability vs. availability vs. availability & use of Best practices | 0 / 1 / 2 |
| *(*) Case labels, i.e. the numbers 0,1,2 and the legend (◊ = 0, □ = 1, * = 2) represent a company's availability and use of lessons learned or best practices. For example x-axis Trend 1, y-axis Trend 2 corresponds with case labels for T2LESSN and legend for T1LESSN.* | | | |
| | *X – Y axis* | | |
| **Trend 1: …** | Σ Characteristics for Trend 1 | Σ of characteristic values 1-5 for Trend 1: Growing company complexity & size | 5-50 |
| **Trend 2: …** | Σ Characteristics for Trend 2 | Σ of characteristic values 1-5 for Trend 2: Risk potential in positive & negative direction | 5-50 |
| **Trend 3: …** | Σ Characteristics for Trend 3 | Σ of characteristic values 1-5 for Trend 3: Problems of P & C insurance market | 5-50 |

**Table 23: Legend of comparison of theoretical and empirical results graphical display**

The knowledge-based risk management process assumes that the goal position for all companies is the lower left quadrant of the matrix. Therefore, companies situated in the upper right hand corner of the graph should try to move to the lower left hand corner of the graph. The proposed method for achieving this goal is by learning from the examples of the benchmark companies in the low-risk quadrant. Implementation of lessons learned and best practices suggested by the benchmark companies should move companies in the low-risk quadrant direction. Lessons learned and best practices were gathered effectively in the qualitative questions of the risk & knowledge management survey and summarised in 5.4 Qualitative analysis results. In a thorough and in-depth application of the knowledge-based risk management process, this important knowledge gathering step should be further refined. Refinement could involve incorporating a structured method for explicitly writing down the important aspects and elements of the risk management knowledge.

Companies positioned in the lower right corner in Figure 40 need lessons learned in order to deal with risk trend one. According to the qualitative analysis, required lessons learned for risk trend one include topics such as insurance & risk management know-how, leadership & training, and M & A expertise. Companies situated in the top left corner in Figure 40 need lessons learned in order to deal with risk trend two. Suggested lessons learned for risk trend two from the examined benchmark corporations are comprised of, for instance, risk management, preventive measures as well as organisational strategies and processes. Companies in the upper right corner need a combination of the previously mentioned lessons learned for both risk trend one and risk trend two. Implementation of all suggested lessons learned and best practices is clearly not practical. However, it can be assumed that the application of a carefully selected group of the identified lessons learned and best practices can be highly beneficial for the company. One way to make that right selection for the appropriate lessons learned and best practices is by using the SIC code as proposed in the theoretical part in 4.2.3 Risk analysis. As shown in Table 8: Distribution of participating companies across industries, most corporations responding to the survey were manufacturing companies (SIC code 4, 49 out of 76), followed by wholesale trade and retail trade (SIC codes 6 and 7, both 6 out of 76). Therefore the most likely area for finding benchmark examples would be in the manufacturing, wholesale and retail trade.

Companies three and four mentioned in *Example 1* of Figure 40 are positioned in the upper right matrix quadrant. *Company three* is from the manufacturing sector (SIC code 4) and *company four* is from the wholesale sector (SIC code 9). Both companies rate themselves high on the threats against risk trends one, increasing company complexity and size and risk trend two, growing risk potential in negative and positive direction. Companies' qualitative answers in addition to the quantitative answers in the risk & knowledge management survey illustrate a lack of lessons learned for risk trends one and two. Hence, these companies could benefit from lessons learned knowledge gathered from benchmark companies. Successful implementation of the appropriate lessons learned knowledge could move these companies from the high risk to the low risk quadrant. Step III (risk analysis) of knowledge-based risk management process determines appropriate benchmarks. Practical execution of this process step for the high risk manufacturing and wholesale companies is outlined below.

*Company three:* A total of 41 out of 49 companies for the manufacturing sector rated themselves low for risk threat one, increasing size and complexity of corporations. A total of 45 out of the 49 manufacturing companies rated themselves low for risk threat two, growing risk potential in negative and positive direction. Low rated companies are companies having a score of 27 or lower and therefore are located in the lower section of the matrix. Seven manufacturing companies have a risk trend one score of 9 and below (2×score 9, 1×score 8, 1×score 7, 3×score 5). Five manufacturing companies have a risk trend two score of 9 and below (1×score 5, 1×score 6, 3×score 9). These low risk manufacturing companies are potential benchmarks for other manufacturing companies with a high risk threat for risk trend one and two. Hence, these companies are providers of lessons learned knowledge. Selected benchmark manufacturing corporations argue for example that they are adjusting their business processes constantly to meet the changing environment and to reduce and limit the risk potential. In addition, constant monitoring of the risk situation and development of suitable alternative scenarios is very important. These suggestions could be put forward to *company three*, the manufacturing company, situated in the upper right quadrant during the application of the knowledge-based risk management process. Assuming the suggestions are taken seriously and are well introduced in the corporation, *company three* should improve its risk positioning.

*Company four:* Five related wholesale companies exist in the sample for the high risk wholesale company. All five wholesale companies rate their risk exposure for risk trend one and two low (1×score 21, 19 and 18, 2×score 17 for risk trend one; 1×score 24, 22, 18, 17 and 13 for risk trend two). Thus, all five of the related wholesale companies could act as potential benchmark companies for *company four*. A closer look at *company four* and the five potential benchmark companies leads to an interesting finding. *Company four* and two out of the five potential benchmarks are all Austrian subsidiaries of international pharmaceuticals corporations (corporations' names are not disclosed for confidentiality reasons). Thus, lessons learned for *company four* are most likely to come from these two highly related corporations. Only one of the two benchmark pharmaceuticals companies could provide lessons learned for risk trends one and two. Suggestions from this benchmark corporation could be beneficial for *company four*. For instance, the benchmark pharmaceuticals corporation suggests the introduction of new organisational structures, faster marketing decisions, strict IT regimes and product controls, benchmarking with other companies and installation of an insurance captive. These suggestions could be put forward to *company four*, the pharmaceuticals wholesale company, situated in the upper right quadrant during the application of the knowledge-based risk management process. Assuming the suggestions are taken seriously and are well introduced in the corporation, *company four* might improve its risk positioning towards its two rivals in the low risk positions.

Preceding examples from the risk & knowledge management survey have proven that the steps two - Risk assessment and three - Risk analysis of the knowledge-based risk management process work in practice. Therefore the application of the overall process could be suggested to support the work of risk managers in industrial corporations.

## 6.2 Possible reasons for similarities and differences

The following four sections provide reasons for the correlations and discrepancies between theoretic and empirical analysis.

### *6.2.1 Global research sources vs. local survey target group*

One of the reasons for target groups' differences in the rating of severity of the three risk trends and their describing characteristics could lie in the nature of the state of the field study. International journals with renowned authors from around the world were selected in order to get an up-to-date picture of the literature on risk and knowledge management. The resulting description of the three risk trends and each risk trend's five characteristics represents the views and thoughts of these representatives of the scientific community. Their view might not necessarily always match the views of Austrian risk & insurance managers, the target group of the risk & knowledge management survey. Consequently, some of the risk trend characteristics might be rated more relevant than others due to the specific conditions of the Austrian overall market environment. On the other hand, global literature had to be selected since the study was directed at leading Austrian industrial corporations, which are mostly acting as global players. Therefore, the study can be seen as good way to evaluate Austria's position in a global and networked economy setting.

### *6.2.2 Lacking disclosure of risk & knowledge management expertise in surveys*

Results of the empirical analysis can be counted as a success, because of the relatively high return rate and the extraordinary profile of the responsive companies. The rich content of the qualitative questions shows that the target group were indeed experts and decision makers in risk & insurance management within their corporations. However, it can be assumed companies answering the survey provided only examples of risk management lessons learned and best practices and in most instances possess an even greater extent of risk management knowledge than what they admitted. In addition, corporations completing the survey but not answering the qualitative questions might possess risk management knowledge which was not reported. Likewise corporations not participating in the study might possess valuable risk management knowledge which could not be collected. In all three cases, a lack of disclosure of valuable risk management know-how can be assumed.

A reason for lacking disclosure might be the reluctance of decision makers to give away confidential information. Even though, the receptor of this information, the Institute of Risk Management and Insurance, Vienna University of Economics and Business Administration, is an accredited and trustworthy institution. Furthermore, certainly not all of the respondents see a personal benefit in sharing knowledge with others. While this attitude can be found amongst most research projects, the rich findings for the qualitative results show companies were still quite willing to share their knowledge and expertise. Providing additional bottom line benefits for participating in the knowledge-based risk management process might influence corporations to fully share their existing and highly valuable lessons learned and best practices on risk and insurance management. Plus, corporations might have a stronger motive to participate in the process.

### *6.2.3 Knowledge gap in corporate risk management*

Results of both the quantitative and qualitative part of the risk & knowledge management survey provided suitable answers with rich content for the empirical analysis. The extensive content of results leads to the conclusion that in many cases knowledge management is already a part of risk management in industrial corporations. The finding, however, does not answer how systematic knowledge management in the form of lessons learned and best practices is applied within each individual corporation. In addition, knowledge management might be at a different development level depending on each of the three risk trends and their describing five characteristics. Difference in risk management development could have impacted the answers of both the quantitative and qualitative questions, leading to a rejection of some of the proposed hypotheses. In future studies, a possible way to determine whether a knowledge gap exists is by pursuing focus interviews with the targeted companies in order to collect background reasons for their replies.

### *6.2.4 Dominance of single threats vs. holistic risk view*

State of the field analysis resulted in a view on a wide range of possible risks threatening industrial organisations. Three most dominating risk threats were selected to perform this study. The subsequent risk & knowledge management survey utilised these three risk threats and examined corporate risk manager's perception about each risk threat. Responsive corporations tended to answer the survey questions depending on their background and bearing their own risk situation in mind. Risk and insurance managers' individual focus on certain risks was for instance revealed by the strong results for globalisation and networked economy, in comparison to the relatively lower results for the remaining risks. Answers provided by individual respondents demonstrate most of the respondents do not take into account the sum of all risk threats. Thus, respondents did not apply an overall view. In many cases, respondents seem to focus on a few distinct risks which might have already occurred in their previous work experience or be important in their current situation. One suggestion might be that even though risks might differ in importance depending on the specific company situation, all risks need to be taken seriously into account in order to insure a long-term protection. Only by constantly monitoring the development of the entire risk environment can new developments be successfully detected and dealt with.

## 6.3 Outlook

Improvement of corporate risk management through the help of knowledge management is the primary research area of this book. Risk management improvement becomes necessary due to the changing risk environment. Three major risk trends, namely the emergence of increasingly complex and bigger corporate structures, the development of risk potential in positive and negative direction and the problems of the Property and Casualty insurance market are identified as threatening industrial corporations today. Available risk management processes are no longer dealing successfully with the changing risk environment. Knowledge management seems to be a key component missing in the existing risk management processes. As a result, a new knowledge-based risk management process was designed and explained. In a subsequent empirical analysis, feasibility of parts of the knowledge-based risk management process was demonstrated through a web-based risk & knowledge management survey. Results of the survey were used to examine the connection between risk and knowledge management while at the same time demonstrating the practicability of the knowledge-based risk management process.

The final chapter debates the possible future developments of the three risk trends, provides areas of further research, sketches out the knowledge-based risk management process and discusses the possible impact of globalisation and networking on the risk management discipline.

### Development of the three risk trends and risk perception

One of the research boundaries lies in the study's restriction on a given moment in time. This limitation is necessary and allows the examination of the three risk trends at a certain stage in their development. In addition, practical application and test of the knowledge-based risk management process is enabled. Without the limitation, monitoring the risk trend development would have been required across several periods in order to arrive at useful conclusions. A possible long-term research project could be the examination of the three risk trends and their changing perception of corporate risk managers over time. The study could examine how the three risk trends found in this study are developing over time and why the perception of the risk importance changes. As a result, risk management scientists could determine whether the negative impact of the three risk trends on the industrial corporation is indeed increasing over time. A long term study could also examine, refine and adjust the underlying characteristics describing the three risk trends.

**Areas of further research**

Since the risk & knowledge management survey was pursued only in Austria, one suggested area for further research is to confirm whether this same study can be repeated with identical or similar results in another industrialised country. A validation of the identified risk trends and their underlying characteristics could be reached by repeating the study in another industrialised country. Concurrently, similarities and differences between the Austrian industrial environment in comparison to other markets could be discovered. A repetition of the study could show how risk management lessons learned and best practices are transferable across borders. Possible target countries for a repeated study could be Germany, other EU states, the USA or several Asian states. Reasons for choosing Germany or other EU states could lie in a relatively comparable economic structure and similar cultural background. In Germany and Switzerland, the risk and knowledge management survey could even be pursued in the same language. On the contrary, the United States offers some of the world's largest companies which seem to be predestined for a repeated risk and knowledge management study. Extending the geographic area of the risk & knowledge management survey would show whether the Austrian risk and insurance trends are in line with the global risk and insurance trends. Proved alignment of the risk and insurance trends would further support the fact that risk trends are no longer limited to small boundaries but rather present in a global, networked fashion.

Another possible research question is how far advanced industrial corporations are in institutionalising risk management in their business processes. Companies considering risk management as a top management priority are certainly dealing with the threat of the three risk trends in a much more professional way than companies without a risk management focus. Such a study will be difficult to achieve due to the companies' reluctance to reveal organisational shortfalls. Success of the study depends on the research team's ability to get inside several different organisations and study how risk management is pursued. In addition to industrial corporations, industry insurers should be examined and how risk management knowledge is successfully transferred to their customer. Results of the study could lead to a further improvement of the knowledge-based risk management process as proposed in this book.

Finally, a future study could examine in further detail the nature of the required risk management knowledge by industrial corporations. The study in this book has already identified numerous lessons learned and best practices in dealing with the three risk trends emergence of increasingly complex and bigger corporate structures, the development of risk potential in positive and negative direction and the problems of the Property and Casualty insurance market. Due to the natural limitations of research surveys, the provided lessons learned and best practices examples are not always comprehensively described. A future study could gather lessons learned and best practices in the form of detailed, in-depth and anonymous benchmarks. Recorded benchmarks allow the examined corporation to gain the full benefit from their own experience while at the same time providing other companies with the same knowledge.

**Future of the knowledge-based risk management process**

The focus of this book is step two and three of the knowledge-based risk management process. Application of the risk & knowledge management survey provided basis for the exploration of these two process steps. The survey conducted was a success. As a result, these two process steps are feasible within corporations. Follow on task would be the practical test of the overall process within one or more industrial corporations.

Application of the knowledge-based risk management process should be facilitated by a professional industry insurer, possessing the necessary risk management know-how. The learning from a practical application could possible lead to an adaptation and extension of risk trends and characteristics, in order to more fully meet the risk threats. Apart from the proof that the knowledge-based risk management works in practice, the involved industry insurer could learn from the practical application of the process in how to digitise parts of the process. Digitisation would make the knowledge-based risk process more efficient and usable for globally acting corporate customers. Industry insurers using the process might be able to differentiate themselves from their competitors' risk management services while at the same time providing and building risk management know-how.

### Impact of globalisation and networked economy on risk management

Both the theoretical and empirical analysis come to the conclusion that globalisation and networked economy play a dominant role for industrial corporations today. Risk managers have to acknowledge the continuously growing importance of these two risk trend characteristics. Prior to the occurrence of globalised and networked economy, major industrial companies were primarily dealing with few national or sometimes regional competitors. Nowadays, industrial corporations find themselves in a global market place with numerous large and strong competitors. Those companies realising the opportunities of a globalised, networked economy while at the same time being prepared against its threats can succeed in the future.

A structured approach can support corporate and insurance risk managers in identifying, analysing, assessing, handling and monitoring the threats of globalisation and networked economy. Apart from that, globalisation and networked economy can have a positive effect on risk management. First of all, globalisation can help risk to be diversified across many countries, thus reducing the overall risk of the company. Secondly, the networked economy can help to gather risk management knowledge and expertise from global benchmarks. Subsequently, benchmark know-how can be introduced within the whole corporate network at relatively low cost due to the available networking technologies. Risk managers could grasp this opportunity and extend their available risk and knowledge management capabilities beyond their current scope. This paradigm shift would increase the overall importance of both the individual risk manager and risk management within the organisation.

In summary, this study validates Theil's postulation (1996: 218) that risk management has actually grown in importance, rather than becoming old fashioned. As shown, certain industrial corporations are affected by the dramatic change of risk environment and the increasing threat of major risk trends. Avoidance, compensation or mitigation of major risk threats continues to be a joint endeavour between corporations and industry insurers. For companies, Kloman (1992: 311) is right by pointing out that the past merits of risk management will be small in comparison to their future impact. Concluding, three additional suggestions need to be made. First of all, in order to meet the change in risk environment, corporate and insurance risk managers have to constantly improve their current risk management processes. A networked economy seems to provide totally new means for process improvements. Secondly, corporate "not invented here syndromes" need to be exchanged with an open attitude towards learning from past negative examples as well as from positive benchmarks. Actively exchanging risk management ideas and knowledge is a key towards lowering the overall risk exposure while at the same time stimulating the evolvement of the risk management discipline. Finally, risk management services are likely to become the key differentiator between more successful and less successful industry insurers. Those insurers realising the opportunity in becoming both a provider of risk capacity and risk knowledge will earn a sustainable competitive advantage from long-term customer partnerships.

# 7 Bibliography


Aarsteinsen, Barbara (2002): *New Risks in the Wired World.* In: *Canadian Insurance*, August 2002, 10-15.

Achleitner Paul M.; Biebel Jörg H. and Wichels Daniel (2002): *Does WTC Matter for the Investment Policy of P / C Insurance Companies?*. In: *The Geneva Papers on Risk and Insurance – Issues and Practice*, Vol. 27, No. 2, April 2002, 275-282.

Adams, William James (2000): *International Trade in Risky Foods: The Policies of the European Community and the World Trade Organisation.* In Frenkel, M.; Hommel, U. and Rudolf, M., eds: *Risk Management – Challenge and Opportunity.* Heidelberg and New York: Springer-Verlag Berlin, 313-332.

Albrecht, Peter (1992): *Zur Risikotransformationstheorie der Versicherung: Grundlagen und ökonomische Konsequenzen.* Karlsruhe: Verlag Versicherungswirtschaft.

Alff, Gregory (2002): *Returning from a Deep Soft Market and the Largest Catastrophe in History.* In: *Risk Management*, January 2002, 18-26.

Alff, Gregory (2004): *Nearing Recovery.* In: *Risk Management*, January 2004, 8-14.

Anderson, Dan R. (2003): *Environmental Risk Management: A Critical Part of Corporate Strategy.* In: *The Geneva Papers on Risk and Insurance – Issues and Practice*, Vol. 27, No. 2, April 2003, 152-180.

Angwin, Duncan (2001): *Mergers and acquisitions across European borders: National perspectives on preacquisition due diligence and the use of professional advisers.* In: *Journal of World Business*, Vol. 36, Iss. 1, 2001, 32-57.

Aon (2002): *AONNEWS Frühjahr 2002.* Hamburg: Aon Jauch & Hübener GmbH, 2002.

Apfelthaler, Gerhard; Muller, Helen J. and Rehder, Robert R. (2002): *Corporate global culture as competitive advantage: learning from Germany and Japan in Alabama and Austria?*. In: *Journal of World Business*, Vol. 37, 2002, 108-118.

Baker, Tom (2002): *Liability and Insurance after September 11: Embracing Risk Meets the Precautionary Principle*. In: *The Geneva Papers on Risk and Insurance – Issues and Practice*, Vol. 27, No. 3, July 2002, 349-357.

Batabyal, A. A. and Beladi, H. (2001): *Aspects of the Theory of Financial Risk Management for Natural Disasters*. In: *Applied Mathematics Letters*, Vol. 14, 2001, 875-880.

Bate, Paul (1997): *Cultural Change: Strategien zur Änderung der Unternehmenskultur*. München: Gerling Akademie Verlag.

Bellmann, Matthias; Krcmar, Helmut and Sommerlatte, Tom, eds (2002): *Wissensmanagement: Strategien-Methoden-Fallbeispiele*. Düsseldorf: Symposion.

Best Practices (2004): *Benchmarking - Research and Consulting*. In: Best Practices LLC, www.bestpracticedatabase.com, 14th April 2004.

Bhatt, Ganesh D. (2001): *Knowledge management in organizations: examining the interaction between technologies, techniques, and people*. In: *Journal of Knowledge Management*, Kempston, Vol. 5, Iss. 1, 2001, 68-75.

Bleymüller, Josef; Gehlert, Günther and Gülicher, Herbert (1996): *Statistik für Wirtschaftswissenschaftler*. 10th ed., München: Vahlen.

Blondeau, Jacques (2001): *Insurance and Reinsurance at the Dawn of the 21st Century*. In: *The Geneva Papers on Risk and Insurance – Issues and Practice*, Vol. 26, No. 2, April 2001, 145-155.

Bloomer, Jonathan (2004): *The Impact of Insurance Accounting on Business Reality and Financial Stability*. In: *The Geneva Papers on Risk and Insurance – Issues and Practice*, Vol. 29, No. 1, January 2004, 56-62.

Bollinger, Audrey S. and Smith, Robert D. (2001): *Managing organizational knowledge as a strategic asset*. In: *Journal of Knowledge Management*, Kempston; Vol. 5, Iss. 1, 2001, 8-18.

Börse Express (2003): *The story behind...RHI*. In: Drastil, Christian, ed: Wirtschafts Blatt online, No. 420b, 27th November 2003, www.wirtschaftsblatt.at, 28th January 2004.

Brealey, Richard A. and Myers, Stewart C. (1996): *Principles of Corporate Finance*. New York: McGraw-Hill.

Brühwiler, Bruno (1994): *Internationale Industrieversicherung: Risk-Management, Unternehmensführung, Erfolgsstrategien*. Karlsruhe: Verlag Versicherungswirtschaft.

Büchel, Bettina and Raub, Steffen (2002): *Building Knowledge-creating Value Networks*. In: *European Management Journal*, Vol. 20, No. 6, December 2002, 587-596.

Carayannis, Elias G. and Alexander, Jeffrey (1999): *Winning by Co-Opeting in Strategic Government-University-Industry R & D Partnerships: The Power of Complex Dynamic Knowledge Networks*. In: *Journal of Technology Transfer*. Boston: Kluwer Academic Publishers, Vol. 24, 1999, 197-210.

Conrad, Klaus (1988): *Geophysik und Rückversicherung*, in: Geratewohl et al., eds: *Beiträge zur Rückversicherung*. Karlsruhe: Verlag Versicherungswirtschaft, 133-164.

Coster, Michael N. and Hankin, Robin K. S. (2003): *Risk assessment of antagonistic hazards*. In: *Journal of Loss Prevention in the process industries*, Vol. 16, 2003, 545-550.

Covello, Vincent T. and Merkhofer, Miley W. (1993): *Risk Assessment Methods – Approaches for assessing health and environmental risks*. New York and London: Plenum Press.

Cummins J. David and Doherty Neil A. (2002): *Capitalisation of the Property–Liability Insurance Industry: Overview*. In: *Journal of Financial Services Research*, 21:1/2, 2002, 5-14.

Daniel, Jean-Pierre (2003): *The Broader Cultural Context of Insurance: Insurance and Religions*. In: *The Geneva Papers on Risk and Insurance – Issues and Practice*, Vol. 28, No. 1, January 2003, 102-110.

Davies, N. J. (2000): *Knowledge Management*. In: *BT Technology Journal*, Vol. 18, No. 1, 62-63.

de Castries, Henri (2004): *Ethics, Governance, Trust, Transparency, and Customer Relations*. In: *The Geneva Papers on Risk and Insurance – Issues and Practice*, Vol. 29 No. 1, January 2004, 36-39.

de la Martinière, Gérard (2003): *The Complexity of Managing a Global Company: Regional Exposure vs. Global Exposure.* In: *The Geneva Papers on Risk and Insurance – Issues and Practice*, Vol. 28, No. 1, January 2003, 87-93.

De Mey, Jozef (2003): *The Aftermath of September 11: The Impact on and Systematic Risk to the Insurance Industry.* In: *The Geneva Papers on Risk and Insurance – Issues and Practice*, Vol. 28, No. 1, January 2003, 65-70.

Dickinson, Gerry (2001): *Enterprise Risk Management: Its Origins and Conceptual Foundation.* In: *The Geneva Papers on Risk and Insurance – Issues and Practice*, Vol. 26, No. 3, July 2001, 360-366.

Doherty, Neil A.; Lamm-Tennant, Joan and Starks, Laura T. (2003): *Insuring September 11th: Market Recovery and Transparency.* In: *The Journal of Risk and Uncertainty*, Vol. 26:2/3, 2003, 179-199.

Dorfman, Mark S. (2002): *Introduction to Risk Management and Insurance.* 7th ed., New Jersey: Prentice Hall.

Drew, Stephen A. W. (1997): *From Knowledge to Action: the Impact of Benchmarking on Organisational Performance.* In: *Long Range Planning*, Vol. 30, June 1997, 427-441.

Duarte, Deborah and Snyder, Nancy (1997): *Facilitating Global Organisational Learning in Product Development at Whirlpool Corporation.* In: *Journal of Production Innovation Management.* New York, NY, Vol. 14, 1997, 48-55.

Eickstädt, Jan (2001): *Alternative Risiko-Finanzierungsinstrumente.* Diss. *Universität Karlsruhe.* München: Gerling Akademie Verlag.

Ennsfellner, Karl C. and Gassner-Möstl, Elke (2000): *Versicherungsprodukte in Österreich – Grundlagen der Personen-, Sach- und Vermögensversicherung.* Wien: Linde Verlag.

EPA (2004): *U.S. Environmental Protection Agency*, www.epa.gov/edr/fsicnaic.pdf, 14th April 2004.

Farny, Dieter (1996): *Globalisierungsstrategien in der Versicherungswirtschaft? Zugleich eine Betrachtung über nationale Versicherungskulturen.* In: Mugler J. and Nitsche, M., eds: *Versicherung, Risiko und Internationalisierung: Herausforderungen für Unternehmensführung und Politik.* Wien: Linde Verlag, 265-276.

Farny, Dieter (1999): *The Development of European Private Sector Insurance over the Last 25 Years and the Conclusions that Can be Drawn for Business Management Theory of Insurance Companies*. In: *The Geneva Papers on Risk and Insurance – Issues and Practice*, Vol. 24, April 1999, 145-162.

Farny, Dieter (2000): *Versicherungsbetriebslehre.* 3rd ed., Karlsruhe: Verlag Versicherungswirtschaft.

Farny, Dieter et al. (1978): *Meinungsspiegel Risk Management.* BFuP 4/78, 324-340.

Fatemi, Ali and Luft, Carl (2002): *Corporate risk management – Cost and benefits*. In: *Global Finance Journal,* 13, 2002, 29-38.

Fellhuber, Martin (2004): *RHI hat Krise fast gemeistert.* In: Wirtschafts Blatt online, www.wirtschaftsblatt.at, 24th March 2004.

Fields, Joseph A.; Klein, Linda S. and Myskowski, Edward G. (1998): *Lloyd's Financial Distress and Contagion within the US Property and Liability Insurance Industry*. In: *Journal of Risk and Uncertainty*, 16:2, 1998, 173-185.

Flanigan, George B. (2004): *Insurance Coverage for Environmental Claims*. In: *Risk Management Magazine*, January 2004, 28-31.

Forstmann, S. (1998): *Managing cultural differences in cross-cultural mergers and acquisitions*. In: Torp, J. E.; Gertsen, M. C. and Soderberg, A.-M., eds: *Cultural dimensions of international mergers and acquisitions*. Berlin: Walter de Gruyter, 57-83.

Garven, James R. (2002): *On the Implications of the Internet for Insurance Markets and Institutions*. In: *Risk Management and Insurance Review*, Vol. 5, No. 2, 2002, 105-116.

Geipel-Kern, Anke (2004): *Wie Nanotechnologie das Unmögliche möglich macht*. In: *Das Österreichische Industriemagazin*, March 2004, 72-78.

George, D. and Mallery, P. (2003): *SPSS for Windows step by step: A simple guide and reference - 11.0 update*. 4th ed., Boston: Allyn & Bacon.

Geratewohl, Klaus (1988): *Schicksalsteilung in der Rückversicherung aus heutiger Sicht*, in: Geratewohl et al., eds: *Beiträge zur Rückversicherung*. Karlsruhe: Verlag Versicherungswirtschaft, 13-68.

Gerling, Rolf (1986): *Ein Marketing-Konzept für Industrieversicherer.* Bern and Stuttgart, Verlag Paul Haupt.

Glanzstoff (1999): *Glanzstoff Austria GmbH & Co KG gestern und heute.* St. Pölten: Glanzstoff Austria GmbH & Co KG, June 1999.

Glanzstoff (2001): *Abluftsituation der Firma Glanzstoff.* St. Pölten: Glanzstoff Austria GmbH & Co KG, June 2001.

Glanzstoff (2004): *Firmenhistorie und Umweltinformationen auf Internetseite.* www.glanzstoff.at, 30th January 2004.

Gleason, James T. (2001): *Risiko-Management – Wie Unternehmen finanzielle Risiken messen, steuern und optimieren.* Frankfurt and New York: Campus Verlag.

Gouillart, Francis J. and Kelly, James N. (1995): *Transforming the Organization: Reframing corporate direction, Restructuring the company, Revitalizing the enterprise, Renewing people.* New York: MacGraw-Hill.

Grace, Martin F. et al. (2003): *Catastrophe Insurance: Consumer demand, markets and regulation.* Boston, Dordecht and London: Kluwer Academic Publishers.

Güldenberg, Stefan (2001): *Wissensmanagement und Wissenscontrolling in lernenden Organisationen-Ein systemtheoretischer Ansatz.* 3rd ed., Wiesbaden: DUV Wirtschaftswissenschaft, Edition Österreichisches Controller-Institut.

Haase, Claudia (1997): *Glanzstoff: Der Weg aus dem Elend zum Erfolg.* In: Wirtschafts Blatt online, www.wirtschaftsblatt.at, 6th November 1997.

Hall, Brian P. (2001): *Values development and learning organizations.* In: *Journal of Knowledge Management*, Kempston, Vol. 5, Iss. 1, 19-32.

Haller, Matthias (1975): *Sicherheit durch Versicherung – Gedanken zur künftigen Rolle der Versicherung.* Bern and Frankfurt a. M.: Herbert Lang.

Haller, Matthias (1990): *Risiko-Management und Risiko-Dialog.* In: Schüz, Mathias, ed: *Risiko und Wagnis: Die Herausforderung der industriellen Welt.* Pfullingen: Gerling Akademie Verlag, Vol. 1, 229-256.

Haller, Matthias (1991): *Risiko-Management und Versicherung*. In: Versicherungsenzyklopädie, 4th ed., Vol. 1, 523-568.

Haller, Matthias (1995a): *Die Entwicklung des industriellen Risikos und die künftige Rolle des Risk Managers*. Published speech held for the meeting of the BfV, 26-27th October 1995 in Mainz, St. Gallen, 1-22.

Haller, Matthias (1995b): *Zukunft des Versicherungs-Marketing: Vom Produkt zur Institution*. In: Bach, P., ed: *Aktuelle Entwicklungen im Versicherungsmarketing*, Köln, 1-12.

Haller, Matthias (1996): *Gesellschaftliche Risikoprobleme - Frühwarnfunktion der Versicherung?!*. In: Mugler J. and Nitsche, M., eds: *Versicherung, Risiko und Internationalisierung: Herausforderungen für Unternehmensführung und Politik*. Wien: Linde Verlag, 331-342.

Hallikas, Jukka; Virolainen, Veli-Matti and Tuominen, Markku (2002): *Risk analysis and assessment in network environments: A dyadic case study*. In: *International Journal of Production Economics*, Vol. 78, 2002, 45-55.

Happel, Elke and Liebwein, Peter (2000): *Risikofrüherkennung des Risk-Managements nach KonTraG*. In: *Versicherungswirtschaft*, Vol. 55, No. 4, 15th February 2000, 228.

Hargassner, Sabine (1990): *Risiken im Industriebetrieb, „Sichern und Versichern" an Hand der Gerling Versicherung und der Gerling Consult*. Accepted thesis *Wirtschaftsuniversität Wien*.

Harland, Christine; Brenchley, Richard; Walker, Helen (2003): *Risk in supply networks*. In: *Journal of Purchasing and Supply Management*, Vol. 9, 2003, 51-62.

Harrington, Scott E. and Niehaus, Gregory, R. (2003): *Risk Management & Insurance*, 2nd ed., New York: McGraw-Hill.

Heidenhain, Detmar (2001): *Managing Technological Risks: A Challenge for Professional Engineering Insurers*. In: *The Geneva Papers on Risk and Insurance – Issues and Practice*, Vol. 26, April 2001, 268-276.

Help (2003a): *Information on the Austrian commercial register*, www.help.gv.at/76/760007_f.html, 6th April 2003.

Help (2003b): *Information on the Austrian commercial register*, www.help.gv.at/76/760008_f.html, 6th April 2003.

Hilton, P.A. and Marlin, T.A. (1997): *The Role of the Nonprofit in Rating Environmental Performance.* In: *Corporate Environmental Strategy*, Vol. 3, spring 1996, 21-30

Himmelbauer, Leo (2002): *Cornelius Grupp legt Erfolgsbilanz vor.* In: Wirtschafts Blatt online, www.wirtschaftsblatt.at, 27th September 2002.

Himmelbauer, Leo (2004): *RHI hängt die Konkurrenz ab.* In: Wirtschafts Blatt online, www.wirtschaftsblatt.at, 16th January 2004.

Hoffmann, Klaus (1985): *Risk Management – Neue Wege der betrieblichen Risikopolitik.* Karlsruhe: Verlag Versicherungswirtschaft.

Hohlfeld, Knut (2002): *Auf dem Weg zu weltweiten Grundsätzen und Standards der Versicherungswirtschaft.* In: *Versicherungswirtschaft*, Vol. 57, No. 1, 1st January 2002, 6.

Hohlfeld, Knut (2004): *Current Priorities in International Standard Setting on Insurance Supervision.* In: *The Geneva Papers on Risk and Insurance – Issues and Practice*, Vol. 29, No. 1, 2004, 78-86.

Hölscher, Reinhold (2002): *Von der Versicherung zur integrativen Risikobewältigung.* In: Hölscher, R. and Elfgen, R., eds: *Herausforderung Risikomanagement – Identifikation, Bewertung und Steuerung industrieller Risiken.* Wiesbaden: Gabler Verlag, 3-31.

Hommel, Ulrich (2000): *Managing Catastrophic Risk with Financial Instruments.* In: Frenkel, M.; Hommel, U. and Rudolf, M., eds: *Risk Management – Challenge and Opportunity.* Berlin, Heidelberg and New York: Springer-Verlag, 39-62.

Hoppenstedt (2003): *Firmen-Datenbank „Österreich".* Hoppenstedt & Co. Wirtschaftsverlag, CD-ROM, Iss. 1-2003, Wien.

Hörmann, Oliver (1999): *Die Internationalisierung des Industrieversicherungsgeschäfts von in Österreich zugelassenen Unternehmen.* Accepted thesis *Wirtschaftsuniversität Wien.*

Industriemagazin (2003): *Die 250 größten Industriebetriebe.* In: *Das Österreichische Industriemagazin*, July/August 2003, 42-67.

IRMBA (2004): *International Risk Management Benchmarking Association™*, www.irmba.com, 12th April 2004.

Jablonowski, Mark (2002): *Are Formal Risk Assessments of Any Use?*. In: *Risk Management*, August 2002, 24-27.

Jaiswal, Rajeev Kumar et al. (2002): *Forest fire risk zone mapping from satellite imagery and GIS.* In: *International Journal of Applied Earth Observation and Geoinformation*, Elsevier Science, Vol. 4, 2002, 1-10.

Jirsa, Vera; Oppl, Christian (1988): *Versicherungslehre: Geld-, Kredit- und Versicherungswesen.* 4th ed., Wien: Manz.

Kachigan, Sam Kash (1991): *Multivariate Statistical Analysis – A conceptual Introduction.* 2nd ed., New York: Radius Press.

Kaen, Fred R. (2000): *Risk Management, Corporate Governance And the Modern Corporation.* In Frenkel, M.; Hommel, U. and Rudolf, M., eds: *Risk Management – Challenge and Opportunity.* Berlin, Heidelberg and New York: Springer-Verlag, 248-262.

Karten, Walter (1972): *Die Unsicherheit des Risikobegriffes – Zur Terminologie der Versicherungsbetriebslehre.* In: Hesberg, D.; Nell, M.; Richter, A.; Schott, W., eds (2000): *Versicherungsbetriebslehre – Kernfragen aus entscheidungsorientierter Sicht von Walter Karten.* Karlsruhe: Verlag Versicherungswirtschaft, 3-28.

Karten, Walter (1978): *Aspekte des Risk Managements.* In: Hesberg, D.; Nell, M.; Richter, A.; Schott, W., eds (2000): *Versicherungsbetriebslehre – Kernfragen aus entscheidungsorientierter Sicht von Walter Karten.* Karlsruhe: Verlag Versicherungswirtschaft, 29-48.

Karten, Walter (1988): *Existenzrisiken der Gesellschaft – Herausforderungen für die Assekuranz.* In: Hesberg, D.; Nell, M.; Richter, A.; Schott, W., eds (2000): *Versicherungsbetriebslehre – Kernfragen aus entscheidungsorientierter Sicht von Walter Karten.* Karlsruhe: Verlag Versicherungswirtschaft, 197-218.

Karten, Walter (1991): *Risiken der Gentechnologie für die Assekuranz.* In: Hesberg, D.; Nell, M.; Richter, A.; Schott, W., eds (2000): *Versicherungsbetriebslehre – Kernfragen aus entscheidungsorientierter Sicht von Walter Karten.* Karlsruhe: Verlag Versicherungswirtschaft, 219-228.

Karten, Walter (1998): *Risiken aus Umwelthaftung – Risk Management und Versicherung*. In: Hesberg, D.; Nell, M.; Richter, A.; Schott, W., eds (2000): *Versicherungsbetriebslehre – Kernfragen aus entscheidungsorientierter Sicht von Walter Karten*. Karlsruhe: Verlag Versicherungswirtschaft, 227-280.

Kielholz, Walter B. and Murray, Richard H. (2004): *Insurance Economics and Legal Systems: The Treacherous Intersections of Insurance Economics and Today's Liability Systems*. In: *The Geneva Papers on Risk and Insurance – Issues and Practice*, Vol. 29, No. 1, 2004, 1-4.

Kirchsteiger, Christian (1999): *Trends in accidents, disasters and risk sources in Europe*. In: *Journal of Loss Prevention in the process industries*, Elsevier Science, Vol. 12, 1999, 7-17.

Kirkpatrick, Jeffrey S.; Howard, Jacqueline M.; Reed David A. (2002): *Assessing homeland chemical hazards outside the military gates: industrial hazard threat assessments for department of defense installation*. In: *The Science of the Total Environment* 288, 2002, 111–117.

Kleindorfer, Paul R.; Kunreuther, Howard C. and Schoemaker, Paul J. H. (1993): *Decision Sciences – An integrative perspective*. Cambridge: Cambridge University Press.

Kloman, H. F (1992): *Rethinking Risk Management*. In: *The Geneva Papers on Risk and Insurance – Issues and Practice*, No. 64, 1992, 299-313.

Kramer, W. Michael (2003): *Combating International Corruption and Fraud*. In: *Risk Management*, March 2003, 40.

Krebs, Michael (2000): *Die virtuelle Unternehmung als Wissensorganisation: Potenziale und Grenzen des Wissensmanagements*. In: Witt, F. H., ed: *Unternehmung und Informationsgesellschaft, Management-Organisation-Trends*. Wiesbaden: Gabler Verlag, 107-136.

Kromschröder, Bernhard (1994): *Zum Stand und zur Entwicklung der Versicherungsentscheidungstheorie*. In: Hesberg, D. et al., eds: *Risiko, Versicherung Markt*. Karlsruhe, 69-94.

Kromschröder, Bernhard et al. (1992): *Qualität und Qualitätsmanagement in der Versicherungswirtschaft*. In: *Zeitschrift für Betriebswirtschaft*. Wiesbaden: Gabler Verlag, 43-74.

Krüger, Andreas; Schmolke, Gernot and Vaupel, Ronald (1999): *Projektmanagement als kundenorientierte Führungskonzeption: Management mit Projekten und Management von Projekten*. In: Küpper, Hans-Ulrich, ed.: *Controlling Anwendungen*, Stuttgart.

Kunreuther, Howard (2002): *Risk Analysis and Risk Management in an Uncertain World, Perspectives*. In: *Risk Analysis*, Vol. 22, No. 4, 2002, 655-664.

Kunreuther, Howard and Pauly, Mark (2004): *Neglecting Disaster: Why Don't People Insure Against Large Losses?*. In: *The Journal of Risk and Uncertainty*, Vol. 28, No. 1, 2004, 5-21.

Lang, Josephine Chinying (2001): *Managerial concerns in knowledge management*. In: *Journal of Knowledge Management*, Kempston, Vol. 5, Iss. 43-57, 2001.

Lecomte G. and Gahagan, K. (1998): *Hurricane insurance protection in Florida*. In Kunreuther, H. and Roth, R. Sr., eds: *Paying the price: The status and role of insurance against natural disasters in the United States*. Ch. 5. Washington, DC: Joseph Henry Press.

Levene (2004): *Global economy, technology create new risks for businesses*. Delivered speech by chairman of Lloyd's at World Affairs Council, San Francisco on 21st April 2004, www.lloyds.com/index.asp?ItemId=7546, 3rd May 2004.

Lohse, Ute (2001): *Business excellence in Versicherungsunternehmen*. Diss. *Universität Hannover*. Karlsruhe: Verlag Versicherungswirtschaft.

Louisot, Jean-Paul (2004): *What Makes an Effective Risk Manager?*. In: *Risk Management Magazine*, www.rmmag.com/Magazine/PrintTemplate.cfm?AID=1990, 4th May 2004.

MacMinn, Richard D. (2002): *Value and Risk Comment*. In: *Journal of Banking and Finance*, Vol. 26, 2002, 297-301.

Main, J. (1992): *How to steal the best ideas around*. In: *Fortune*, 126, 8, 1992, 102-106.

Mair, Karin (2003): *RHI Versicherungsmeeting, Teil 3 – RHI Versicherungsmanagement*. Presentation to investors, 29th September 2003. Wien: RHI.

Manghetti, Giovanni (2002): *Multinational Insurance Groups: The Main Problems for Supervisors*. In: *The Geneva Papers on Risk and Insurance – Issues and Practice*, Vol. 27, No. 3, July 2002, 310-319.

Marsh (2003): *Haftpflicht 2003 – Europa: Welche Deckungssummen wurden abgeschlossen?*. Marsh & McLennan Companies.

Martin, Klaus (2001): *Auswirkungen des KonTraG auf das Risk Management.* In: *Versicherungswirtschaft*, Vol. 56, No. 18, 15th September 2001, 1460.

Mathmann, Wolfgang (2002): *Integriertes Risikomanagement.* In: *Versicherungswirtschaft*, Vol. 57, No. 24, 15th December 2002, 1930.

McBriar, Ian et al. (2003): *Risk, gap and strength: key concepts in knowledge management.* In: *Knowledge-Based Systems*, 16, 2003, 29-36.

Mehr, R. I. and Hedges, B. A. (1963): *Risk Management in the Business Enterprise.* In: Homewood III.

Mikosch, Carlheinz (1991): *Industrie-Versicherungen: ein Leitfaden für nationale und multinationale Unternehmen.* Wiesbaden: Gabler Verlag.

Mugler, Josef (1979): *Risk Management in der Unternehmung.* Wien: Orac.

Müller, Wolfgang (1993): *Risiko und Ungewissheit.* In: Wittmann, W., ed: *Handwörterbuch der Betriebswirtschaft*, Vol. 3, 5th ed., Stuttgart, 3813-3824.

Müller, Wolfgang (1994): *Informationsökonomische Grundlagen und empirische Überprüfung eines Beschreibungsmodells für Versicherungsprodukte.* In: Schwebler, R. et al., eds: *Dieter Farny und die Versicherungswissenschaft.* Karlsruhe, 363-380.

Neumann, Robert; Stingl, Alexandra and Grillitsch, Waltraud (2003): *Best Practices and Lessons Learned in Knowledge Management Projects.* Published during ECKM 2002, the 3rd European Conference on Knowledge Management, Trinity College Dublin, Ireland, 1-17, Universität Klagenfurt.

O'Rourke, Morgan (2003): *Cyberattacks Prompt Response to Security Threat.* In: *Risk Management*, January 2003, 8.

OECD (2002): *Economic Outlook.* Vol. 2002/1, No. 71, June 2002.

OSHA (2003): *U.S. Department of Labor, Occupational Safety & Health Administration.* www.osha.gov/oshstats/sicser.html, 5th April 2003.

Patton, Michael Q. (2002): *Evaluation, knowledge management, best practices, and high quality lessons learned.* In: *American Journal of Evaluation*, Vol. 22, No. 3, 329-336.

Pausenberger, Ehrenfried and Nassauer, Frank (2000): *Governing the Corporate Risk Management Function: Regulatory Issues.* In: Frenkel, M.; Hommel, U. and Rudolf, M., eds: *Risk Management – Challenge and Opportunity.* Berlin, Heidelberg and New York: Springer-Verlag, 263-276.

Peter, Christoph F. (2001): *Unternehmerisches Risikomanagement – Konsequenzen einer integrierten Risikobewältigung für die Versicherung.* Diss. *Hochschule St. Gallen (HSG)*, St. Gallen.

Pfeiffer, Christoph (1999): *Einführung in die Rückversicherung.* 5th ed., Wiesbaden: Gabler Verlag.

Pottier, Steven W. and Sommer, David W. (1999): *Property-Liability Insurer Financial Strength Ratings: Differences across Rating Agencies.* In: *The Journal of Risk and Insurance*, Vol. 66, No. 4, December 1999, 621-642.

Pressman, Ronald (2003): *Insurance Technology Strategy: Time to Re-evaluate.* In: *The Geneva Papers on Risk and Insurance – Issues and Practice*, Vol. 28, No. 1, January 2003, 39 – 64.

Property-Casualty (2001): Schroeder, A., Saqi, V. and Winans, C., eds: *World Trade Centre Special Issue.* Morgan Stanley Equity Research: *Insurance – Property-Casualty*, 17th September 2001.

PSBS (2004): *The Benchmarking Process.* In: Public Sector Benchmarking Service, www.benchmarking.gov.uk/about_bench/theprocess.asp#, 7th April 2004.

Raffler, Hans (1988): *Politische Risiken und Brandstiftung – ihre Auswirkungen auf die industrielle und gewerbliche Sachversicherung.* In: Geratewohl et al., eds: *Beiträge zur Rückversicherung.* Karlsruhe: Verlag Versicherungswirtschaft, 355-398.

Raphael, Adam (1994): *Unbegrenzte Haftung*, orig. engl. title: Ultimate risk. Wien: Zsolnay Verlag.

Reactions (2003): *The Reactions guide to terror risk insurance.* www.reactionsnet.com/index5.html?/index90ns.html?/contents/publications/reactions/books /header.html&/contents/publications/reactions/terrorrisk/contents.html, 28th February 2003.

Rejda, George E. (1992): *Principles of risk management and insurance.* 4th ed., New York: HarperCollins Publishers.

Renn, Ortwin (2002): *Die subjektive Wahrnehmung technischer Risiken.* In: Hölscher, R. and Elfgen, R., eds: *Herausforderung Risikomanagement – Identifikation, Bewertung und Steuerung industrieller Risiken.* Wiesbaden, Gabler Verlag, 73-89.

Renn, Ortwin (2004): *Perception of Risks.* In: *The Geneva Papers on Risk and Insurance – Issues and Practice*, Vol. 29, No. 1, January 2004, 102-114.

"RHI erreicht wichtige Vereinbarungen im Zusammenhang mit US Chapter 11 Verfahren". In: www.rhi.at/internet/de/corpsvc/ir/Alle_20News/13.04.04_20_20Vereinbarungen_ 20Ch_2011.html, 20th April 2004.

"RHI: Einigung im Asbeststreit". In: *Presse*, 14th April 2004.

Richter, Markus (2002): *RHI-Konzernergebnis 2001 von Neuausrichtung des Kerngeschäftes Feuerfest geprägt.* In: *RHI Investor Relations – News/PR*, www.rhi.at/DE/printir525.htm, 6th November 2003.

Richter, Markus (2003a): *RHI sieht Zahlungsansprüche im Zusammenhang mit US Chapter 11-Verfahren.* In: *RHI AD HOC*, www.rhi.at, 7th August 2003.

Richter, Markus (2003b): *RHI bestätigt auch im III. Quartal gute operative Performance.* In: *RHI AD HOC*, www.rhi.at, 6th November 2003.

Richter, Markus (2003c): *RHI Versicherungsmeeting, Teil 2 – Feuerfest & Heraklith.* Presentation to investors, 29th September 2003. Wien: RHI.

Risk Perception (2004): *Nanotechnology – Small matter, many unknowns.* Hett, Anabella, ed.: *Risk Perception.* Swiss Re: Zürich.

Ritchie, Bob and Marshall, David (1993): *Business Risk Management.* London: Chapman & Hall.

Rößl, Dietmar (1997): *Report for the LEONARDO DA VINCI project: Success factors and Training Resources – An industry specific analysis for Austria.* Wirtschaftsuniversität Wien.

Rößl, Dietmar (1999): *Die Gestaltung von Beziehungen als zentrale Marketingaufgabe im Klein – und Mittelbetrieb – Ein Diskussionspapier.* In: Mugler J., ed: *Materialien d. Instituts für BWL der Klein – und Mittelbetriebe and der WU Wien.* Wirtschaftsuniversität Wien.

Roth, R. Jr. (1998): *Earthquake insurance protection in California.* In Kunreuther, H. and Roth, R. Sr., eds: *Paying the price: The status and role of insurance against natural disasters in the United States.* Ch. 4. Washington, DC: Joseph Henry Press.

Sage, Andrew P. and Rouse, William B. (1999): *Information Systems Frontiers in Knowledge Management.* In: *Information Systems Frontiers*, 1:3, 205-219.

Sandner, Karl (1992): *Prozesse der Macht – Zur Entstehung, Stabilisierung und Veränderung der Macht von Akteuren in Unternehmen.* 2nd ed., Heidelberg: Physica-Verlag.

Schettler, Heinrich; Wieczorek, Martin J. and Philipp, Michael (2002): *Operational risks and business continuity: An Essayistic Overview.* In: Wieczorek, M.; Naujoks, U. and Bartlett, B., eds: *Business Continuity.* Heidelberg: Springer Verlag, 3-31.

Schinnerl, Elisabeth (2000): *Glanzstoff steigt aus der Krise aus und zum Global Player auf.* In: Wirtschafts Blatt online, www.wirtschaftsblatt.at, 5th May 2000.

Schinzler, Hans-Jürgen (2003): *Global Financial Architecture: Implications for Regulation, Supervision and Accountancy Issues.* In: *The Geneva Papers on Risk and Insurance – Issues and Practice*, Vol. 27, No. 1, January 2003, 1-15.

Schließer, Waldfried (1996): *Aktuelle Aspekte der Internationalisierung des Versicherungsgeschäfts – Ursachen, Aspekte, Trends.* In: Mugler J. and Nitsche, M., eds: *Versicherung, Risiko und Internationalisierung: Herausforderungen für Unternehmensführung und Politik.* Wien: Linde Verlag, 277-300.

Schradin, Heinrich R. (1994): *Erfolgsorientiertes Versicherungsmanagement – Betriebswirtschaftliche Steuerungskonzepte auf risikotheoretischer Grundlage.* Diss. *Universität Mannheim*, Karlsruhe: Verlag Versicherungswirtschaft.

Schüz, Mathias (2002): *Ganzheitliche Betrachtung und Bewältigung unternehmerischer Risiken.* In: Hölscher, R. and Elfgen, R., eds: *Herausforderung Risikomanagement – Identifikation, Bewertung und Steuerung industrieller Risiken.* Wiesbaden: Gabler Verlag, 51-71.

SEC (2004): *What every investor should know....* U.S. Securities and Exchange Commission, www.sec.gov/investor/pubs/bankrupt.htm, 30th January 2004.

Senge, Peter M. (1990): *The Firth Discipline – The art and practice of the learning organisation*. New York: Doubleday Currency.

Seufert, Andreas; Back, Andrea and von Krogh, Georg (2002): *Wissensnetzwerke: Vision – Referenzmodell – Archetypen und Fallbeispiele.* In: Götz, K., ed: *Wissensmanagement – Zwischen Wissen und Nichtwissen.* 4th ed., München and Mering: Rainer Hampp Verlag, 129-151.

Shah, Rachna and Ward, Peter T. (2003): *Lean manufacturing: context, practice bundles, and performance.* In: *Journal of Operations Management*, 21, 2003, 129-149.

Shleifer, Andrei and Vishney, Robert W. (1996): *A survey of corporate governance.* Working Paper, National Bureau of Economic Research, April 1996.

Sigma (2002): *Global non-life insurance in a time of capacity shortage.* Hess, Thomas, ed.: *sigma*, 04/2002. Zürich: Swiss Re.

Sigma (2003a): *Natural catastrophes and man-made disasters in 2002: high flood loss burden.* Hess, Thomas, ed.: *sigma*, 02/2003. Zürich: Swiss Re.

Sigma (2003b): *Insurance company ratings.* Hess, Thomas, ed.: *sigma*, 04/2003. Zürich, Swiss Re.

Smith, K. W. and Quella, J. A. (1995): *Seizing the moment to capture value in a strategic deal.* In: *Mergers and Acquisitions*, Vol. 29, No. 4, 1995, 25-30.

SSO (2003): *State Services Organisation.* www.sso.org/ecos/DSS/sicnads.htm, 5th April 2003.

Stahel, Walter R. (2002): *Insurance, Risk Management and Culture.* In: *The Geneva Papers on Risk and Insurance – Issues and Practice*, Vol. 27, No. 2, April 2002, 268 – 274.

Stam, G. J., Bottelberghs, P. H. and Post, J. G. (1998): *Environmental risk: towards an integrated assessment of industrial activities.* In: *Journal of Hazardous Materials*, Vol. 61, 1998, 371-374.

Statistik Austria (2004): *Statistisches Jahrbuch 2004.* 11th January 2004, www.statistik.at/jahrbuch/pdf/k21.pdf, 319-329.

Steward, Gordon (2002): *The Public Role of Insurers in Man-Made Catastrophes.* In: *The Geneva Papers on Risk and Insurance – Issues and Practice*, Vol. 27, No. 2, April 2002, 288-294.

Steward, Simon; Callaghan, James and Rea, Tim (1999): *The eCommerce revolution.* In: *BT Technology Journal*, Vol. 17, No. 3, July 1999, 124-132.

Strejcek, Gerhard and Theil, Michael (2002): *Technology push, legislation pull? E-government in the European Union.* In: *Decision Support Systems*, 34, 2002, 305-313.

Tah, J.H.M. and Carr, V. (2001a): *Towards a framework for project risk knowledge management in the construction supply chain.* In: *Advances in Engineering Software*, Vol. 32, 835-846.

Tah, J.H.M. and Carr, V. (2001b): *A fuzzy approach to construction project risk assessment and analysis: construction project risk management system.* In: *Advances in Engineering Software*, Vol. 32, 847-857.

TBE (2004): *What is benchmarking?.* The Benchmarking Exchange. www.benchnet.com/wib.htm, 7th April 2004.

Theil, Michael (1995): *Risikomanagement für Informationssysteme.* Wien: Service Fachverlag an der Wirtschaftsuniversität Wien. Accepted dissertation *Wirtschaftsuniversität Wien*, 1994.

Theil, Michael (1996): *Risikomanagement – Stand und Ansätze für eine Weiterentwicklung.* In: Mugler J. and Nitsche, M., eds: *Versicherung, Risiko und Internationalisierung: Herausforderungen für Unternehmensführung und Politik.* Wien: Linde Verlag, 205-220.

Theil, Michael (2003): *The value of personal contact in marketing insurance: Client judgments of representativeness and mental availability.* In: *Risk Management and Insurance Review*, Vol. 6, No. 2, 2003, 145-157.

Tuomi, Ilkka (2002): *The Future of Knowledge Management.* In: *Lifelong Learning in Europe (LLinE)*, Vol. 7, No. 2, May 2002, 69-79.

U.S. Congress (1995): *Federal disaster assistance. Report of the Senate task force on funding disaster relief.* Washington, DC: U.S. Government Printing Office.

Ullberg, Eskil; Rodriguez, Enrique and Stormby, Nils (2002): *Risk Management: From Portfolio Strategy to Value-creating Systems Strategy*. In: *The Geneva Papers on Risk and Insurance – Issues and Practice*, Vol. 27, No. 3, July 2002, 467-476.

USDOJ (2000): *Assessment of the increased risk of terrorist or other criminal activity associated with posting off-site consequence analysis information on the internet*. U.S. Department of Justice, 18th April 2000, www.usdoj.gov/criminal/april18final.pdf.

Van den Berghe, Lutgart (1996): *Der Wettlauf um die Zukunft in der Bank- und Versicherungsbranche – Welche strategischen Konzepte und Erkenntnisse sind nützlich oder sogar notwendig?*. In: Mugler J. and Nitsche, M., eds: *Versicherung, Risiko und Internationalisierung: Herausforderungen für Unternehmensführung und Politik*. Wien: Linde Verlag, 53-65.

Van den Berghe, Lutgart and Verweire, Kurt (2001): *Convergence in the Financial Services Industry*. In: *The Geneva Papers on Risk and Insurance – Issues and Practice*, Vol. 26, No. 2, April 2001, 173-183.

Venohr, Bernd (1995): *Strategisches Kundenbindungsmanagement – Leitmotiv für Versicherungsunternehmen*. In: Bach, P., ed: *Aktuelle Entwicklungen im Versicherungsmarketing*. Köln, 61-72.

Waagner-Biro (2004): *Firmeninformation auf Internetseite*. www.waagner-biro.at, 30th January 2004.

Wagner, Fred (2000): *Risk Management im Erstversicherungsunternehmen – Modelle, Strategie, Ziele, Mittel*. Karlsruhe: Verlag Versicherungswirtschaft.

Ward, Damian and Zurbruegg, Ralf (2000): *Does Insurance Promote Economic Growth? Evidence from OECD Countries*. In: *The Journal of Risk and Insurance*, Vol. 67, No. 4, December 2000, 489-506.

Weber, Jürgen and Liekweg, Arnim (2000): *Statutory Regulation of the Risk-Management Function in Germany: Implementation Issues for the Non-Financial Sector*. In: Frenkel, M.; Hommel, U. and Rudolf, M., eds: *Risk Management – Challenge and Opportunity*. Berlin, Heidelberg and New York: Springer-Verlag, 277-294.

Weber, Y. (2000): *Measuring cultural fit in mergers and acquisitions*. In: Ashkanasy, N. M.; Wilderom, C. P. M. and Peterson, M. F., eds: *Handbook of organisational culture and climate*. Thousand Oaks: Sage, 309-319.

White, Rodney and Etkin, David (1997): *Climate Change, Extreme Events and the Canadian Insurance Industry*. In: *Natural Hazards* 16, 1997, 135-163.

Widmayer, Reinhold C. (1996): *Glanzstoff reinigt St. Pöltens Luft*. In: Wirtschafts Blatt online, www.wirtschaftsblatt.at, 12th October 1996.

Wiedenlübbert, Reiner (2001): *Assekuranz, Ökologie und Risiko: Versicherungen als Mitgestalter des ökologischen Generationenvertrages*. Diss. *Universität in Oldenburg*, Wiesbaden: Deutscher Universitäts-Verlag.

Willis (2003): *Reinsurance Market Review – Spring 2003*. London: Willis Re.

Witt, Frank H. (2000): *Management und „New Economy"*. In: Witt, F. H., ed: *Unternehmung und Informationsgesellschaft, Management-Organisation-Trends*. Wiesbaden: Gabler Verlag, 3-7.

Wopperer, Wolfgang (2002): *Fraud Risks in E-commerce Transactions*. In: *The Geneva Papers on Risk and Insurance – Issues and Practice*, Vol. 27, No. 3, July 2002, 383-394.

Yasin, M.M.; Small, M. and Wafa, M.A. (1997): *An Empirical Investigation of JIT Effectiveness: an Organisational Perspective*. In: *International Journal of Management Science*, Vol. 25, No. 4, 1997, 461-471.

Zech, Jürgen (2001): *Rethinking Risk Management: The Combination of Financial and Industrial Risk*. In: *The Geneva Papers on Risk and Insurance – Issues and Practice*, Vol. 26, No. 1, January 2001, 71-82.

Zehetner, Eduard (2003): *RHI Versicherungsmeeting, Teil 1 – RHI nach der Krise*. Presentation to investors, 29th September 2003. Wien: RHI.

**Interviews:**

Hölzl, Franz (2004), (Director Property insurance, Gerling Allgemeine Versicherungs-AG). Personal interview, 9th January 2004.

Krebs, Andreas (2003), (Head of sales, Gerling Allgemeine Versicherungs-AG). Personal interview, 15th October 2003.

Mazanek, Rudolf (2004), (Amtsdirektor, Statistik Austria). Personal interview, 13th January 2004.

Plank, Alfred (2003), (Head of technology, Glanzstoff Austria GmbH & Co. KG). Personal interview, 30th October 2003.

# Appendix 1: Risk & Knowledge Management online survey design

Appendix one describes the web-based risk & knowledge management survey targeted at the insurance and risk managers of the 250 leading Austrian industrial corporations.

The risk & knowledge management survey was integrated in a new website of the chair of Institute of Risk Management and Insurance of the Vienna University of Economics and Business Administration. The internet domain www.wu-wien-ivw.com[1] was registered for the purpose of conduction the online risk & knowledge management survey as well as for future online research projects for the department. Therefore, an important milestone in the research development of the Institute of Risk Management and Insurance of the Vienna University of Economics and Business Administration was reached.

Appropriate contacts and their correct email addresses were gathered in six steps with the purpose of guiding the risk and insurance experts of the targeted companies to the survey website.

Due to the execution of the survey in Austrian industrial corporations, the German language was used for the correspondence with respondents as well as the content of the survey web site. Therefore, some of the following parts are in their authentic German version.

Step one - selection of the 250 largest industrial corporations in Austria from the current ranking of Industriemagazin (2003), a leading Austrian industrial magazine. Corporations included in this ranking are a representative portion of Austrian industrial corporations. Combined revenues of these corporations in 2002 account for 65% of the total production revenues of Austrian corporations in 2001 (Statistik Austria, 2004: 329). Another reason why this target group was selected was because of the availability of a dedicated risk- / insurance-management function. Finally, the corporations' perceived vulnerability by the three risk trends (1) the emergence of increasingly complex and bigger corporate structures, (2) the development

[1] The author is indebted to the Institute of Risk Management and Insurance, Vienna University of Economics and Business Administration for funding the survey website

of risk potential in positive and negative direction and (3) the problems of the Property and Casualty insurance market.

Step two – extraction of all available contact persons from the selected 250 corporations and the corporations' core business data such as company name, address, email, telephone, fax, no. of employees, business area etc. from the current version of Hoppenstedt (2003) company database[1]. Extraction resulted in 4467 (!) data sets. One main advantage of Hoppenstedt versus other company databases is its connection with the official Austrian company register (Firmenbuch). Therefore, the information is very reliable and up-to-date, especially since corporations are required by law to keep their records up-to-date. In addition, Hoppenstedt contains numerous contact persons for each corporation. Information per contact person includes items such as their individual job description.

Step three – reduction of the 4467 extracted data sets to 250 data sets by selecting one appropriate contact person for each of the 250 corporations. Position of insurance or risk manager was explicitly marked in several instances and therefore all other contact persons could be eliminated. In other cases, several potential contact persons were extracted and the remaining contacts deleted.

Step four- sending first email to the remaining corporations, where no dedicated insurance or risk manager was previously identified. Aim of this announcement email was to receive the right contact person for each company and to also raise interest in the upcoming survey. The email was sent out on the 28th October 2003 and had the following content:

Sehr geehrte Damen und Herren,

für eine Studie an der Wirtschaftsuniversität Wien über die führenden Industrieunternehmen Österreichs benötigen wir den Ansprechpartner Ihres Unternehmens im Bereich Versicherungen bzw. Risikomanagement.

Über die Zusendung des Namens, der Funktion sowie der Emailadresse dieser Person wären wir Ihnen sehr dankbar, damit wir diese für eine kurze Onlinebefragung inklusive Gewinnspiel kontaktieren können. Ihre Angaben werden selbstverständlich vertraulich behandelt.

---

[1] The Austrian company database was kindly provided by Mag. Nikolaus Futter and Karin Wild of Verlag Hoppenstedt & Co Wirtschaftsverlag Ges.m.b.H., Matznergasse 17, A-1141 Wien, Austria for this study

Schon jetzt bedanken wir uns recht herzlich für Ihre Mühe und verbleiben

mit freundlichen Grüßen

ao. Univ.-Prof. Mag. Dr. Michael Theil

Institut für Versicherungswirtschaft / Wirtschaftsuniversität Wien Institute of Risk Management and Insurance / Vienna University of Economics and Business Administration
A-1090 Wien, Augasse 2-6
Tel. (+ 43-1) 31336 4947, Fax (+ 43-1) 31336 90 4947
http://www.wu-wien.ac.at/usr/versich/theil/local.html

Step five – further reduction of the number of corporations with open contact due to the generally very quick email replies by the in step four addressed companies. The remaining open companies were directly contacted via phone. Name, role and email address of the responsible contact person was requested and received.

Step six – actual mailing to the 250 targeted industrial corporations about the risk & knowledge management survey being conducted took place. This mailing occurred three times, first on the 4th September, then on the 15th September and finally on the 7th October 2003. Mailing included the link to the survey website and information about a prize[1] for the 1st, 10th, 50th, 100th, 150th, 200th, 250th received survey replies. Email content of the first mailing was as follows:

Sehr geehrte Damen und Herren,

als eines von 250 führenden österreichischen Unternehmen möchte ich Sie heute herzlich zur Teilnahme an einer Studie der Wirtschaftsuniversität Wien einladen.

Die Studie mit dem Schwerpunkt "Versicherungen und Risikomanagement" wird in Form eines Onlinefragebogens durchgeführt, den Sie unter http://www.wu-wien-ivw.com finden. Klicken Sie hier bitte auf den Menüpunkt "Fragebogen". Die Dauer der Befragung liegt zwischen 5 und 10 Minuten.

[1] The prizes for the survey, one bottle of Cabernet Merlot 2001 per winner, were kindly sponsored by Weingut Zahel, Maurer Hauptplatz 9, 1230 Vienna, Austria.

Jeder Teilnehmer erhält als Dankeschön eine Zusammenfassung der Ergebnisse. Darüber hinaus gewinnt die 1., 10., 50., 100., 150., 200. sowie 250. Einsendung je eine Flasche Zahel Cabernet Merlot 2001. Ihre Angaben werden selbstverständlich vertraulich und anonymisiert behandelt. Der Befragungszeitraum ist bis zum 15. Oktober 2003.

Schon jetzt bedanken wir uns recht herzlich für Ihre Mühe und verbleiben

mit freundlichen Grüßen

ao. Univ.-Prof. Mag. Dr. Michael Theil

Institut für Versicherungswirtschaft / Wirtschaftsuniversität Wien
Institute of Risk Management and Insurance / Vienna University of Economics and Business Administration
A-1090 Wien, Augasse 2-6
Tel. (+ 43-1) 31336 4947, Fax (+ 43-1) 31336 90 494

Incoming replies are graphically displayed in Figure 19: Survey time frame, mailing dates and reception of replies over time. The three peaks show the dependency between reception of emails and the subsequent replies. The third peak on the 7th October was stimulated by proposing an additional prize for the first, second and third answers, which directly followed this mailing.

76 respondents accessed the risk & knowledge management survey website. The website consists of four parts:

- Welcome area
- Survey area
- Download area
- Contacts area

Each of the four parts is explained in detail below and the corresponding screenshots displayed.

"Welcome area" consists of a welcome letter, signed both by the advisor and co-advisor of this book. The welcome letter explains the nature of the study, i.e. the examination of the relationship between risk management and knowledge management, in addition to providing a direct link to the survey. Also the opportunity of winning a prize by submitting the survey is mentioned and the sponsor of this prize is acknowledged.

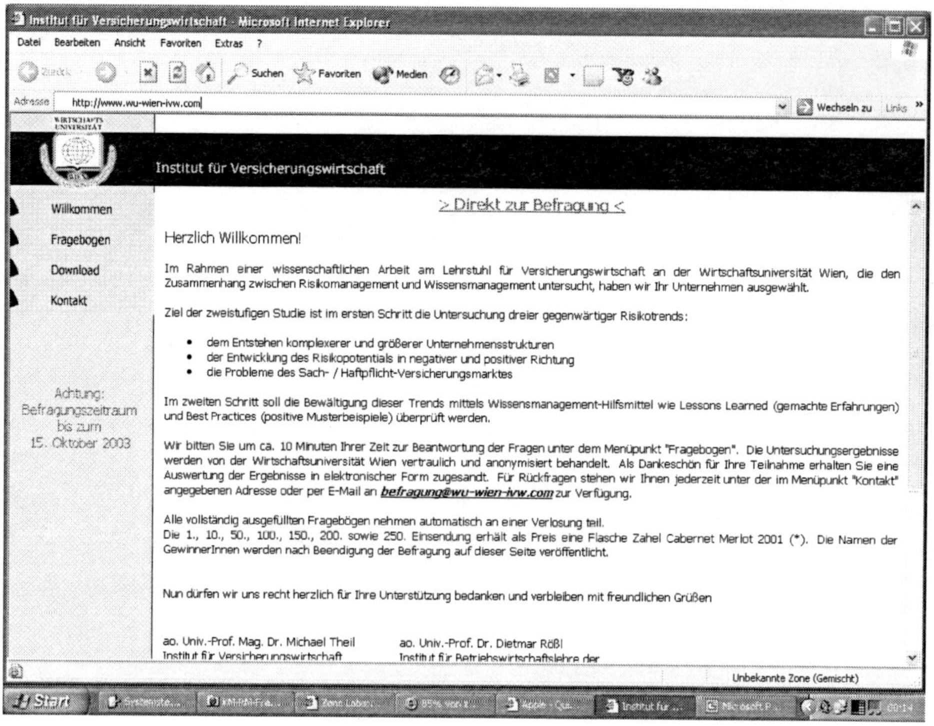


**Figure 46: Online survey – Welcome area**

"Survey" is the second part of the website. The survey is structured in four easy to answer and graphically highlighted sections. Content of the survey is presented in detail in Appendix 2: Risk & Knowledge management survey content. The four sections of the survey are:

- General information
- Influence by risk trends
- Handling of risk trends through knowledge management
- Questions, Comments

Only fully completed surveys are accepted. Hence, no survey field can be left blank by a respondent. Incomplete surveys are rejected with an error message, indicating the missing fields. This direct field indication allows respondents to quickly fill in the missing data and then resubmit the survey. Positive effect for the conducted study is that only fully completed surveys are received, thus lowering the uncertainties of the statistical analyses.

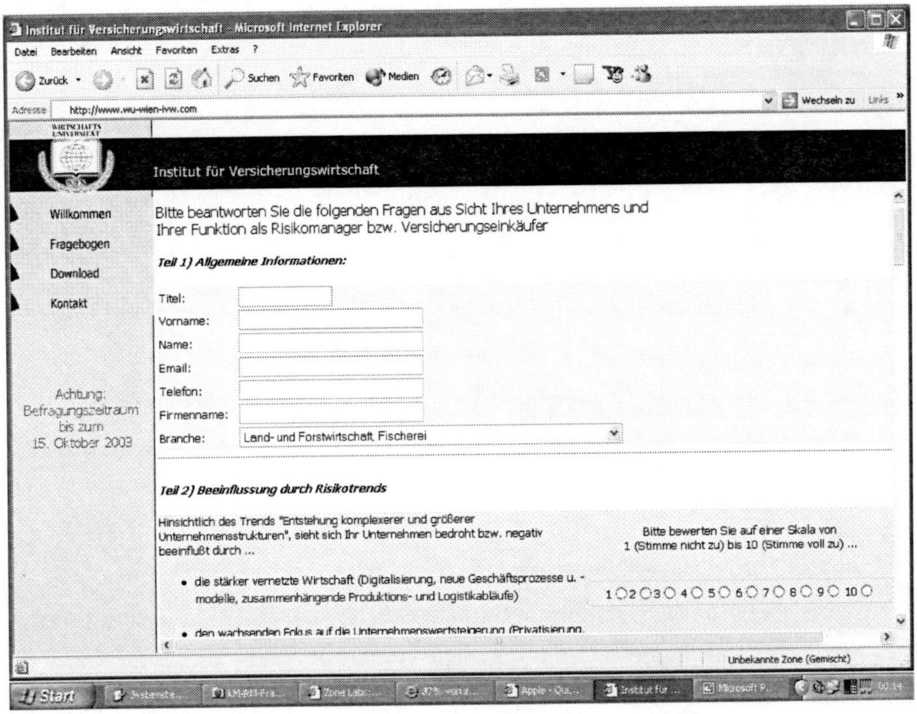


**Figure 47: Online survey – Survey area**

A confirmation window, depicted in Figure 48, appears after pressing the submit button as confirmation for a successful survey submission. In addition to a friendly thank you greeting to the respondent, the opportunity to connect to the website of the Institute of Risk Management and Insurance is provided.

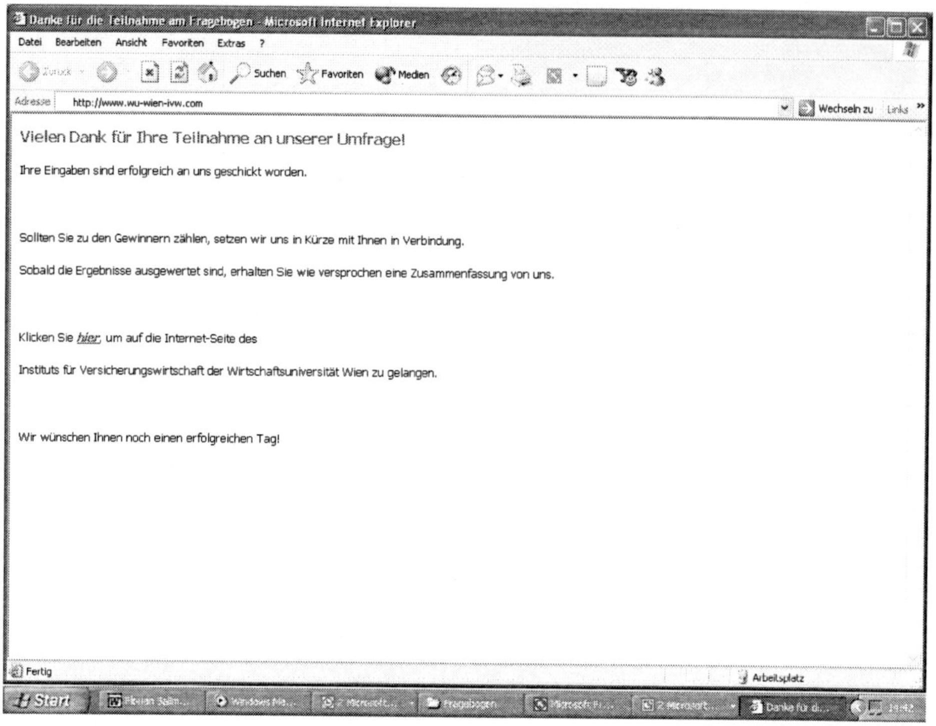


**Figure 48: Online survey – Successful submission feedback**

"Download area" offers an additional way to submit the risk & knowledge management survey. Under this option, an identical copy of the online risk & knowledge management survey is provided in a Microsoft Word™ form. A copy of the provided survey form can be downloaded to the respondent's computer by selecting this option. Thereby, the respondents can complete the survey offline and at their convenience. Furthermore, respondents answering questions on this form find a simple way to fill in and save their entered information. Completed survey forms can be submitted via email, fax or mail. Reasons for using this path can be either the malfunctioning of the online survey due the incompatibility of the web browser or the target group's reluctance to submit confidential company data via the internet. Only one respondent exploited the possibility of sending the word survey in this study. Supplied answers for this case were manually typed in the online form and resubmitted, so that results were included in the results file.

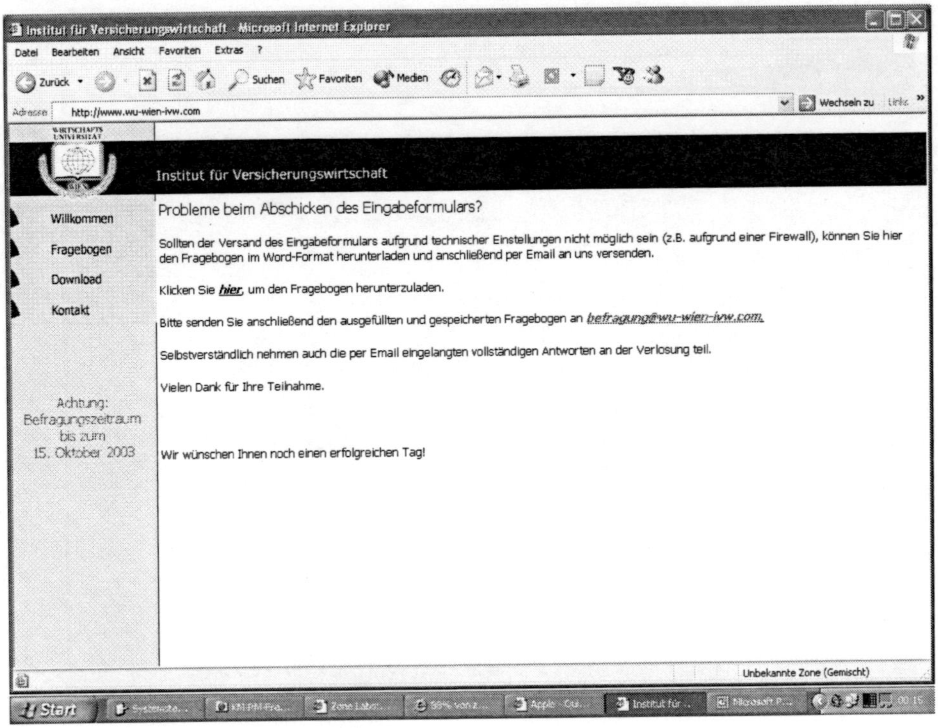


**Figure 49: Online survey – Download area**

"Contact details" provide targeted risk and insurance managers a quick overview of who is responsible for the survey and how a contact can be established if required. In most cases, the responses arrived directly via email, therefore this part of the website retained more of an informative character.

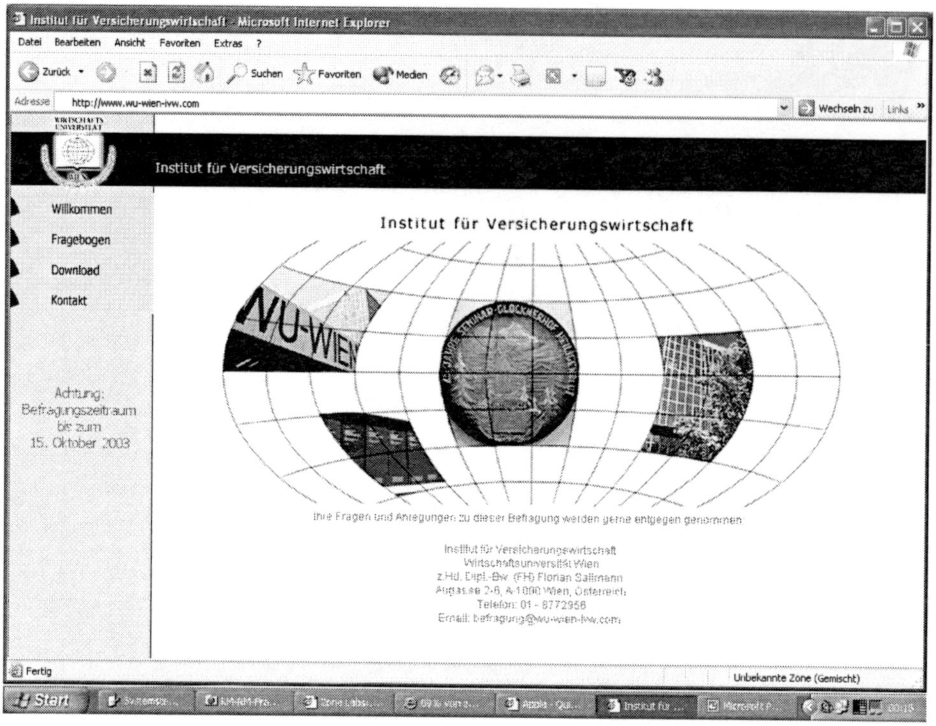


**Figure 50: Online survey – Contacts area details**

In summary, the online survey for this book proved to be very efficient and useful. Main benefits of the online survey were:

- Only complete surveys could be submitted
- Data was received in a structured text file which could be easily imported in Microsoft Excel™, thus avoiding all double entry and potential typing errors
- Once a survey was submitted successfully, an email containing all data was sent to the web site's email account
- All questions and comments from the target group were received electronically, saving time
- Respondents receive an immediate feedback if their submitted survey is complete and has safely arrived
- Answers required a minimum of time by the targeted corporations avoiding frustration by the high profile structure of the target group (CEOs, CFOs, Head of human resources, risk management, insurance management etc.)

- Promotion of the University's institute of risk management and insurance
- Reusability of the survey website for further research projects
- Overall speed of the internet technology, allowing two follow-up cycles during the normal time of a traditional feedback loop of three to five weeks
- The possibility to precisely track the arrival time of survey, insuring prizes were fairly awarded

Utilising an online survey is highly recommended for a sample size of 250 corporations. If the necessary programming skills are available, the initial up-front investment for the creation and testing of an online survey is highly likely to pay off in the second half of the project.

# Appendix 2: Risk & Knowledge management survey content

The following appendix contains the Microsoft Word™ version of the online risk & knowledge management survey. The survey was created, using the questions as stated in 5.1 Aim and description of Risk & Knowledge management survey and the hypotheses 5.2 Hypotheses. One question testing the corporations' vulnerability towards each trend – characteristics pair was formulated. Each question was assigned a scale from one to ten. An additional question regarding the availability and use of the knowledge management tools "lessons learned" and "best practices" was posed regarding each trend – characteristics pair. Questions were translated into German and tested with both language and risk-management experts.

Content of the web-based survey was identical with the Microsoft Word™ survey. Only one out of the 76 respondents used the word form. Nevertheless, the easy readability of the word version of the form offers its use for presenting the survey content for this appendix.

*Versicherungs-Risikomanagement Studie des Instituts für Versicherungswirtschaft, WU Wien*

Den ausgefüllten Fragebogen bitten wir Sie an befragung@wu-wien-ivw.com zu senden.

Bitte beantworten Sie die folgenden Fragen aus Sicht Ihres Unternehmens und
Ihrer Funktion als Risikomanager bzw. Versicherungseinkäufer

***Teil 1) Allgemeine Informationen:***

Titel:

Vorname:

Name:

Email:

Telefon:

Firmenname:

Branche: Land- und Forstwirtschaft (zur Auswahl bitte anklicken)

### Teil 2) Beeinflussung durch Risikotrends

Hinsichtlich des Trends "Entstehung komplexerer und größerer Unternehmensstrukturen", sieht sich Ihr Unternehmen bedroht bzw. negativ beeinflußt durch ...

Bitte bewerten Sie auf einer Skala von 1 (Stimme nicht zu) bis 10 (Stimme voll zu) ...

| | 1 | 2 | 3 | 4 | 5 | 6 | 7 | 8 | 9 | 10 |
|---|---|---|---|---|---|---|---|---|---|---|
| • die stärker vernetzte Wirtschaft (Digitalisierung, neue Geschäftsprozesse u. -modelle, zusammenhängende Produktions- und Logistikabläufe) | □ | □ | □ | □ | □ | □ | □ | □ | □ | □ |
| • den wachsenden Fokus auf die Unternehmenswertsteigerung (Privatisierung, Gewinnmaximierung, Aktionärsstruktur, Börsenentwicklung, Risikominimierung) | □ | □ | □ | □ | □ | □ | □ | □ | □ | □ |
| • die Herausforderungen unterschiedlicher Wirtschaftssysteme (Rechnungslegungsvorschriften, Anforderungen | □ | □ | □ | □ | □ | □ | □ | □ | □ | □ |
| • die Effekte der Globalisierung | □ | □ | □ | □ | □ | □ | □ | □ | □ | □ |
| • die Tendenz zu Fusionen & Übernahmen und der damit verbundene Anstieg von Risikokumul und Wechselwirkungen | □ | □ | □ | □ | □ | □ | □ | □ | □ | □ |

Welche strategischen Überlegungen werden angestellt und welche Maßnahmen daraus abgeleitet, um mit der wachsenden Komplexität und Größe Ihres Unternehmens umzugehen?

Hinsichtlich des Trends "Entwicklung des Risikopotentials in negativer und positiver Richtung" wird Ihr Unternehmen beeinflußt durch ...

1 (Stimme nicht zu) - 10 (Stimme voll zu)

| | 1 | 2 | 3 | 4 | 5 | 6 | 7 | 8 | 9 | 10 |
|---|---|---|---|---|---|---|---|---|---|---|
| • die Bedrohung durch Naturkatastrophen (Klimaveränderung, Stürme, Erdbeben, Überflutung, Brände) | □ | □ | □ | □ | □ | □ | □ | □ | □ | □ |
| • das Risiko industrieller Umweltverschmutzung (durch reguläre Geschäftsprozesse, z.B. $CO_2$-Ausstoß, oder Unfälle, z.B. Freisetzung von Chemikalien bei Betriebsstörungen) | □ | □ | □ | □ | □ | □ | □ | □ | □ | □ |
| • mögliche terroristische Aktionen (gegen industrielle Einrichtungen bzw. Anschläge mit Auswirkungen auf Absatzmärkte und Handelswege) | □ | □ | □ | □ | □ | □ | □ | □ | □ | □ |
| • unkontrollierten wissenschaftlichen Fortschritt und technisches Versagen (Genprodukte, elektromagnetische Strahlung, Internettechnologie (Viren, Hacker etc.)) | □ | □ | □ | □ | □ | □ | □ | □ | □ | □ |

| | |
|---|---|
| • die Auswirkungen gesellschaftlicher, politischer, kultureller Veränderungen (in den verschiedenen Produktions- bzw. Absatzregionen) | 1 2 3 4 5 6 7 8 9 10<br>□ □ □ □ □ □ □ □ □ □ |

Welche strategischen Überlegungen werden angestellt und welche Maßnahmen daraus abgeleitet, um mit diesem wachsenden Katastrophenpotential umzugehen?

| Hinsichtlich des Trends "Probleme des Sach- / Haftpflicht-Versicherungsmarktes" ist Ihr Unternehmen ... | 1 (Stimme nicht zu) - 10 (Stimme voll zu) |
|---|---|
| • negativ beeinflußt von Preis- und Kapazitätszyklen der Versicherungsbranche | 1 2 3 4 5 6 7 8 9 10<br>□ □ □ □ □ □ □ □ □ □ |
| • bedroht durch die langsame Modernisierung der Versicherungsbranche | 1 2 3 4 5 6 7 8 9 10<br>□ □ □ □ □ □ □ □ □ □ |
| • beeinflußt durch die Änderungen der Kapitalstruktur der Versicherungsbranche (Eigenkapital, Rating, Kapazitäten) | 1 2 3 4 5 6 7 8 9 10<br>□ □ □ □ □ □ □ □ □ □ |
| • betroffen von den die Versicherungsindustrie belastenden wachsenden Katastrophenschäden | 1 2 3 4 5 6 7 8 9 10<br>□ □ □ □ □ □ □ □ □ □ |
| • bedroht durch das Entstehen neuer, bislang unbekannter Risiken für den Versicherer (z.B. Asbest, Genprodukte in der Produkthaftpflicht, Elektrosmog in der Umwelthaft-pflicht) | 1 2 3 4 5 6 7 8 9 10<br>□ □ □ □ □ □ □ □ □ □ |

Welche strategischen Überlegungen werden angestellt und welche Maßnahmen daraus abgeleitet, um mit den Problemen der Versicherungsbranche, die Ihr Unternehmen beeinflussen können, umzugehen?

### Teil 3) Risikotrendbewältigung durch Wissensmanagement

Bitte wählen Sie die zutreffende Antwort:

Fragen bezüglich des Trends "Entstehen komplexerer und größerer Unternehmensstrukturen":

- Besitzen Sie in Ihrem Unternehmen Lessons Learned (gemachte Erfahrungen), um mit diesem Trend umzugehen? Ja ☐ Nein ☐
- Nutzen Sie diese Lessons Learned? Ja ☐ Nein ☐
- Besitzen Sie in Ihrem Unternehmen Best Practices (positive Musterbeispiele), um mit diesem Trend umzugehen? Ja ☐ Nein ☐
- Nutzen Sie diese Best Practices? Ja ☐ Nein ☐

Welche Lessons Learned bzw. Best Practices wären aus Sicht Ihres Unternehmens erforderlich, um den Risiken aus der Entstehung komplexerer und größerer Unternehmensstrukturen vorzubeugen?

Fragen bezüglich des Trends "Entwicklung des Risikopotentials in negativer und positiver Richtung": Bitte wählen Sie die zutreffende Antwort:

- Besitzen Sie in Ihrem Unternehmen Lessons Learned (gemachte Erfahrungen), um mit diesem Trend umzugehen? Ja ☐ Nein ☐
- Nutzen Sie diese Lessons Learned? Ja ☐ Nein ☐
- Besitzen Sie in Ihrem Unternehmen Best Practices (positive Musterbeispiele), um mit diesem Trend umzugehen? Ja ☐ Nein ☐
- Nutzen Sie diese Best Practices? Ja ☐ Nein ☐

Welche Lessons Learned bzw. Best Practices wären aus Sicht Ihres Unternehmens erforderlich, um bei der Bewältigung des Risikopotentials in negativer und positiver Richtung mitzuwirken?

| Fragen bezüglich des Trends "Probleme des Sach- / Haftpflicht-Versicherungsmarktes": | Bitte wählen Sie die zutreffende Antwort: |
|---|---|
| • Besitzen Sie in Ihrem Unternehmen Lessons Learned (gemachte Erfahrungen), um mit diesem Trend umzugehen? | Ja ☐ Nein ☐ |
| • Nutzen Sie diese Lessons Learned? | Ja ☐ Nein ☐ |
| • Besitzen Sie in Ihrem Unternehmen Best Practices (positive Musterbeispiele), um mit diesem Trend umzugehen? | Ja ☐ Nein ☐ |
| • Nutzen Sie diese Best Practices? | Ja ☐ Nein ☐ |

Welche Lessons Learned bzw. Best Practices wären aus Sicht Ihres Unternehmens erforderlich, um eine negative Beeinflussung Ihres Unternehmens durch die Entwicklungen in der Versicherungsbranche zu verhindern?

***Teil 4) Anregungen, Fragen, Kommentare***

Vielen Dank für Ihre Teilname!

Bitte vergessen Sie nicht, den Fragebogen vor dem Versand abzuspeichern.

Alle vollständig beantwortete Einsendungen nehmen automatisch an der Wein-Verlosung teil.

# Appendix 3: State of the field research matrix for corporate risk trends

| | |
|---|---|
| **Article** | **Natural catastrophes and man-made disasters in 2002: high flood loss burden** |
| **Author** | Thomas Hess |
| **Journal / Publication** | Swiss Re, sigma No. 2/2003 |
| **Publication date** | 2003 |
| **Examined questions** | The major "losses from natural catastrophes and man-made losses" in the year 2002 are examined and consequences on the Property & Casualty insurance and reinsurance industry displayed, P. 3 |
| **Emergence of increasingly complex and bigger corporate structures** | |
| **Development of risk potential in positive and negative direction** | • "After 11 September 2001, terrorism took on a new dimension in the public mind. Although the insurance industry had a smaller burden to bear than in 2001, terrorist attacks claimed 800 victims in 2002. […]. The attacks in Bali and Djerba, in Tunisia, only underline the latent risk posed by international terrorism.", P. 8<br>• "The potential insured losses arising from terrorist attacks are considerably lower for insurers and reinsurers in the private sector today than they were prior to September 2001. While the scope of coverage for terrorism-related losses has been limited and reassessed, a number of markets – for example, the US, Germany and France – have introduced new forms of terrorism coverage in which the state carries a substantial share of the losses.", P. 8<br>• "Floods and the devastation that accompanies them are often underestimated. Floods have long played a subordinate role in the insurance industry – one rated far below earthquakes and storms on the loss scale. However, a new reality has set in the insurance industry. Given that no continent has remained untouched by major floods over the past few years and that direct insurers have had to contend with new loss records on an almost annual basis in this risk category, the industry has started to rethink this issue.", P. 8f<br>• "As climate is a statistical value – […] – individual events can in principle not be taken as proof or as disproof of a statement on climate change. Nevertheless, the increasing number of floods witnessed recently are consistent with developments that climatologists expect to find in a warmer climate.", P. 12<br>• "The main causes of the rise in insured losses that has been witnessed over the past 30 years are the increase in insured values, their concentration in highly exposed areas and their high susceptibility to external influences.", P. 13 |
| **Problems of P/C Insurance market** | |
| **Risk management measures** | • "In future the insurance industry should attribute just as much importance to cycles as it does to trends in its risk assessments.", P. 13<br>• "The insurance industry can make its own contribution – and at reasonably priced premiums – towards marshalling the financial burden presented by floods. However, the experience gained with existing solutions in a number of countries has shown that this is possible only as long as the conditions for insurability are in place. It falls within the remit of the state to create such conditions that allow the industry to offer comprehensive insurance protection. This includes the exclusion of risk zones in town planning, the introduction of construction regulations that reduce the risk to which properties are exposed in endangered areas, the erection of flood barriers and, if necessary, the creation of retention areas.", P. 9<br>• "Thanks to new methods and modern technology, the insurance industry's exposure to flooding can usually be assessed with a high degree of accuracy today, thereby fulfilling an essential condition for the insurability of flood risks. However, the risk analysis requires a lot of time and data. Furthermore, the necessary data for a lot of countries are available but are very often difficult to come by. For this reason, it is sometimes a good idea to finance such projects collectively, for example, in collaboration with national insurance associations.", P. 11<br>• "The insurance industry can also take control of this issue – via premiums that are commensurate with risk, for example – and thus contribute to the increase in the population's awareness of danger and thereby to the reduction in the loss burden.", P. 13 |
| **Open scientific questions** | |

| | |
|---|---|
| **Article** | **Global non-life insurance in a time of capacity shortage** |
| **Author** | Thomas Hess |
| **Journal / Publication** | Swiss Re, sigma No. 4/2002 |
| **Publication date** | 2002 |
| **Examined questions** | The prospects of "non-life insurance in a time of capacity shortage" are examined, P. 1 |
| **Emergence of increasingly complex and bigger corporate structures** | • "(3) The post-Enron world of accounting and regulation demands transparency and does not favor overly complex transactions.", P. 9<br>• "Although the non-life industry's overall exposure to credit risk appears to be manageable, the recent surge in highly visible corporate defaults (Enron, K-Mart, WorldCom, etc) has caused a reevaluation of the industry's credit exposure. This affects both insurers' bond portfolios as well as the credit risk embedded in their products, e.g., credit and surety insurance, derivatives, and the credit risk in finite (re) insurance deals.", P. 12 |
| **Development of risk potential in positive and negative direction** | • "Prior to September 11, the assumed maximum loss potentials attached to terrorist acts were of manageable size and were comparable to property losses resulting from fire and explosion. On this basis, terrorism was not explicitly excluded from property policies. However, the magnitude of the WTC [World Trade Centre] loss revealed a new scope and extent of the terrorist threat, forcing insurers to reconsider these assumptions and the insurability of terrorism risks altogether. Terrorism risks are increasingly meeting fewer of the important criteria of insurability, particularly as it is impossible to accurately assess the probability and severity of a terrorist attack. As a result, terrorism is insurable only on a very limited basis. Hence, it appears necessary for government and insurers to work together to develop solutions.", P. 3<br>• "..., spectacular corporate failures like Enron or WorldCom have increased the need for better corporate governance, more transparency, and improved reporting on risk.", P. 5<br>• "(4) International terrorism has become an additional exposure, challenging the limits of insurability.", P. 9<br>• "In addition to the financial impacts of the largest loss in the insurance history, the September 11 attack added a new dimension to insurance risk (substantial losses from terrorism).", P. 14<br>• "Traditional measures of loss severity – e.g., Probable Maximum Loss (PML), and Estimated Maximum Loss (EML) – are currently under discussion.", P. 14<br>• "The malice involved in the September 11 attack that destroyed the WTC and the complete disregard for human life it revealed were something new to insurers and called into question established insurance practice.", P. 14 |
| **Problems of P/C Insurance market** | • "Though September 11 clearly accelerated this trend [price increases], the hardening of the P/C insurance market began in late 2000, early 2001.", P. 3<br>• "The hardening of the market is expected to last longer than in previous cycles, given the global shortage of quality capital and increased risk exposures. Some years of above-average profitability are necessary to restore the balance sheets of many non-life insurers.", P. 3<br>• "The competitive environment in non-life insurance has dramatically changed over the last two to three years. The soft market and the decline in equity markets have reduced the industry's capital base in all major markets and turned excess capital into a tight capital base, particularly in commercial lines and reinsurance.", P. 3<br>• "During most of the last ten years, insurers could rely on the exceptional performance of global stock markets.", P. 3<br>• "..., recent financial scandals (e.g. Enron, WorldCom, and Xerox) are keeping investors away from the financial markets.", P. 3<br>• "During the second half of the 1990s, non-life insurers often leveraged their capital funds with substantial investment risks. The share of assets invested in equities increased accordingly from 1990 to 1999. However, equity shares are falling now due to declining valuations and asset sales made in order to realize badly needed capital gains. From a risk/return perspective, it is now more attractive to allocate capital to non-life insurance and the credit markets, where the prospects are good, rather than to investments in the stock market or business tied to stock-market or investment valuations, where prospects are very uncertain.", P. 4<br>• "During the soft market in the second half of the 1990s, the theme of alternative risk transfer (ART) for corporations was dominated by convergence and integrated risk management. New products helped expand the limits of insurability.", P. 4<br>• "The hardening of the market has changed the focus of the ART market towards increasing capacity. Now, with capacity tight, many limits are being placed on traditional insurance covers and the demand for ART solutions has shifted towards products that provide solutions for risks that are now hard to transfer.", P. 4<br>• "During the soft market, rising insurance capacity and fierce price and market-share competition led to widely available coverage and low premium rates. Underwriting results declined in all major markets. Net investment results, including realized capital gains, increased through 1998 in most major markets, bridging the gap between deteriorating underwriting profitability and providing a small improvement to net income. Investment returns worsened after 1999 as interest rates bottomed out and stock market stalled, setting the stage for the hardening of the market.", P. 6<br>• "The hardening started earlier in 2000 in some European property markets due to the losses from the winter storms Lothar and Martin in December 1999." P. 6 footnote<br>• "Non-life insurers have emerged from the recent soft market facing a different environment. (1) The industry's capital funds have diminished dramatically, probably by USD 180 billion, which implies a capital shortage in commercial-lines insurance and reinsurance. (2) The investment climate has changed for the foreseeable future from high yields during the 1990s to low yields that are not sufficient to support underwriting losses of the magnitude of the late 1990s.", P. 9<br>• "Hence, the main task for insurers remains to improve underwriting results.", P. 11<br>• "..., in the wake of accounting scandals, the attitude of clients, reinsurers and regulators towards finite solutions has changed. There will be lower demand from corporations and a greater focus on risk transfer and disclosure.", P. 13 |
| **Risk management measures** | • "It will be crucial, and a matter of urgency, for the insurance industry to develop models that are at least able to estimate the severity of loss resulting from terrorism risks. This would be a decisive step towards quantifying the risk and the most important condition for making terrorism risks insurable in the private market. Innovative solutions involving pools, new forms of insurance (e.g., finite treaties) and the financial markets are required to achieve a broad risk spread.", P. 15 |
| **Open scientific questions** | • "Before asking, whether new risk-management concepts are required to cover the threat of terrorism, it must be ascertained whether terrorism risks are insurable at all.", P. 14<br>• "..., terrorism is indeed uncorrelated with other risks.", P. 14 |

| | | |
|---|---|---|
| **Article** | **Risikomanagement – Stand und Ansätze für eine Weiterentwicklung** | **Rethinking Risk Management** |
| **Author** | Michael Theil | H. F. Kloman, |
| **Journal / Publication** | Versicherung, Risiko und Internationalisierung: Herausforderungen für Unternehmensführung und Politik, Mugler J. [Hrsg.], P. 205 – 220 | The Geneva Papers on Risk and Insurance – Issues and Practice No. 64, 1992, P. 299 – 313 |
| **Publication date** | 1996 | July 1992 |
| **Examined questions** | "Was bringt Individuen und Organisationen, also auch Unternehmungen dazu, sich mit Fragen des Risikos auseinanderzusetzen?". Fazit: "Das Unbehagen mit der Unsicherheit führt zu Bemühungen, dieses zu bewältigen", P. 207 | "Why rethinking risk management is so important today, in a period in which we are beset by uncertainties. If risk management can contribute to the larger goal of creating new confidence – reducing fear – it will be important to all of us both individually and in the organisations and management measure structures in which we participate", P. 300 |
| **Emergence of increasingly complex and bigger corporate structures** | „Die Komplexität von Risikosituationen hat Dimensionen erreicht [...], so daß Handlungsempfehlungen, die vielfach [...] lauten: 'erkenne die Risiken, bestimme Schadeneintrittswahrscheinlichkeiten und Schadensausmaße, setze die geeigneten risikopolitischen Instrumente ein' an Grenzen stoßen", P. 218 | "Corporate managers are now confronted with a much wider variety of economic, social, regulatory and competitive factors influencing performance", P.304 |
| **Development of risk potential in positive and negative direction** | | "The effect of catastrophes on risk management will be significant. Our belief in progress and the skill of technology to improve life is becoming more overshadowed by our inability to prevent catastrophes. The risk of technological catastrophes appears to be increasing, [...]. At the same time there are arguments that seismic risk is increasing as well, [...].", P. 309 |
| **Problems of P/C Insurance market** | • "'Risk Management is governed by insurance' wird aus der Beobachtung abgeleitet, daß Alternativen zu Versicherung erst (ernsthaft) in Erwägung gezogen werden, wenn Versicherungsschutz nicht mehr oder nur mehr zu hohen Preisen zu bekommen ist", P. 217<br>• "Niedrige Versicherungsprämien machen die Suche nach risikopolitischen Alternativen unattraktiv", P. 217 | "Part of the problem lies in the focus of the insurance industry. It has failed to put real emphasis on risk control and risk research [...]. It has perpetuated the "illusion that insurance has "solved" a risk problem, when in effect there is more risk sharing than risk transfer, particularly with larger organisations. Insurance underwriters have failed to develop strong risk assessment skills. [...], the volatility of the commercial insurance marketplace, leading to the current financial instability of property/casualty insurers in both the U.S. and London, argues that reduced, rather than increased, reliance on conventional insurance may well be necessary", P. 311 |
| **Risk management measures** | • "Nach der Analyse der Risiken gilt es, diese im Einklang mit den Zielen des risikobedrohten Systems zu gestalten", P. 216<br>• „Für die praktische Anwendung wurden [...] schadenvermindernde wie auch schadenausgleichende, bereits in aller Ausführlichkeit dargestellt", P. 217<br>• Entscheidend ist, „dass es jeweils auf die ‚Netto'-Wirkung der einzusetzenden risikopolitischen Instrumente ankommt, und nicht darauf, worauf gerade Augenmerk gelegt wird. Diese Aufgabe ist freilich viel zu komplex: Selbst für Risiken, zu deren Erfassung enormer Aufwand getrieben wird, erweisen sich die Kenntnisse über die Wirkungen von Sicherungsmaßnahmen als widersprüchlich und vielfach unzureichend", P. 217f | • Risk management should be "holistic endeavour: [...] looks at all risks and their inter-relationships including primary, secondary and tertiary effects", P. 306<br>• "Risk management function" should address operational, legal, management measure and financial / market risks. While there may be numerous other ways of looking at these areas of risk, there is no question but that risk management can no longer be defined as focusing on but one or two of these areas", P. 306<br>• "Proper and proactive risk management function should be able to act as early warning device, [...] for those who listen", P. 310<br>• Risk management within an organization should be integral part of both technology and management, in which the assessment, control, and financing of risks, costs and benefits become a continuing exercise of rational judgment", P. 311 |
| **Open scientific questions** | "Risikomanagement hat sich im Laufe der Zeit nicht überlebt – nach wie vor besteht Bedürfnis nach Grundlagen zur Risikobewältigung, womöglich ist dieses sogar gestiegen", P. 218 | "'Did it [Risk management] do any good?': Yes, risk management has done some good, but the full significance of its contribution is still to come." P. 311 |

| **Article** | **Lloyd's Financial Distress and Contagion within the US Property and Liability Insurance Industry** | **Enterprise Risk Management: Its Origins and Conceptual Foundation** |
|---|---|---|
| **Author** | Joseph A. Fields, Linda S. Klein and Edward G. Myskowski | Gerry Dickinson |
| **Journal / Publication** | Journal of Risk and Uncertainty, 16:2 P. 173-185 (1998) | The Geneva Papers on Risk and Insurance – Issues and Practice Vol. 26 No. 3, P. 360 – 366 |
| **Publication date** | 1998 | July 2001 |
| **Examined questions** | "The intra-industry effect of Lloyd's financial distress on publicly traded US insurance companies is examined.", P. 173 | "The origins and conceptual foundation" of "enterprise risk management", P. 360 |
| **Emergence of increasingly complex and bigger corporate structures** | | [...], following a number of high-profile company failures and preventable large losses, the scope of corporate governance has widened to embrace the risks that a company takes", P. 360<br>Because of the complexity of identifying, controlling and managing risks across a company, dedicated and specialist expertise is required. A new coordinating management role is now emerging – that of the chief risk officer (CRO).", P. 364 → **Dickinson draws a very interesting organizational chart, including the CRO – function on P. 365** |
| **Development of risk potential in positive and negative direction** | "Catastrophic events at one firm can impact the operations or financial results of other firms in either a positive or negative fashion.", P. 174 | "A range of external and internal factors can cause the outcomes of a company's activities to depart from those set down in its corporate objectives. Some external factors relate to those in the marketplace in which a company competes, such as new entrants into the market, changing consumer tastes or new product developments. Other external factors arise from a wider context, such as changes in the economy, changes in capital and financial market conditions, and changes in the management measure, legal, technological, demographic and other environments.", P. 361 |
| **Problems of P/C Insurance market** | • "Lloyd's financial distress raises concerns about a systematic disruption in the reinsurance industry. For example, reinsurance markets that provide coverage to insurers for large catastrophic exposures such as hurricanes, have never fully recovered from the Lloyd's crisis. Coastal areas in the eastern and southeastern United States still suffer from market failure as a result of the lack of available reinsurance coverage; the underlying primary homeowner's coverage is still largely unavailable from commercial carriers.", P. 173<br>• "Opler and Titman (1994) [...] find that major crisis allows companies to make organizations changes that would not be feasible under normal operating circumstances.", P. 174<br>• "The financial crisis at Lloyd's has fundamentally affected the marketplace because trust in the unlimited liability form has been undermined.", P. 175<br>• "Lloyd's role in the United States market has been particularly pronounced", P. 175<br>• "...reinsurance supply is a particular obstacle to the efficient functioning of the primary markets for insurance (see Berger, Cummins, and Tennyson (1992)). When a major reinsurer experiences a financial crisis, primary insurers may be negatively affected if they are unable to adequately diversify large exposures or if they must revaluate loss reserve estimates", P. 177 | "For many years, companies have been able to transfer certain types of risks to insurance companies. These transferred risks related to natural catastrophes, accidents, human error or fraud, but as the scope of insurance markets expanded, some types of commercial risks could be transferred, such as credit risks. The existence of these insurance markets forced managers to consider alternatives to the purchase of insurance.", P. 360 |
| **Risk management measures** | | • "Enterprise risk management must be a top-down process", P. 363<br>• "Most of the risks that a company faces cannot be insured or hedged, and so they must be retained and financed internally. Other mechanisms also exist for reducing risk, apart from the purchase of insurance and hedging with financial derivatives.", P. 363<br>• "Divestments of corporate activities and the outsourcing of operating functions provide other mechanisms for risk transfer.", P. 363<br>• "Risk retention decisions on insurable risks [...] and risk retention decisions for financial risks [...] should be determined jointly;...", P. 364 |
| **Open scientific questions** | "The study raises important issues concerning the potential for a systematic disruption in the domestic supply of insurance resulting from financial problems at foreign reinsurers." P. 183 | Enterprise risk management has not developed its full potential yet but is likely to due to the increased accountability of the corporate leadership teams for companies' risk taking. It is however not answered how this process will look like (Author's comment). |

| **Article** | **Rethinking Risk Management: The Combination of Financial and Industrial Risk** | **Insurance and Reinsurance at the Dawn of the 21st Century** |
|---|---|---|
| **Author** | Jürgen Zech | Jacques Blondeau |
| **Journal / Publication** | The Geneva Papers on Risk and Insurance – Issues and Practice Vol. 26 No. 1, P. 71 – 82 | The Geneva Papers on Risk and Insurance – Issues and Practice Vol. 26 No. 2, P. 145 – 155 |
| **Publication date** | January 2001 | April 2001 |
| **Examined questions** | "[…] new challenges that arise from integrating […] financial and industrial risks", P. 72 | Future of Insurance and Reinsurance in the 21st century |
| **Emergence of increasingly complex and bigger corporate structures** | • "The recent development and the expected increase in alternative risk financing allow large multinational corporations to choose freely from national and global markets and challenge industrial insurance companies to excel in the development of products which provide risk management solutions.", P. 71<br>• "International companies are exposed to various kinds of risk", P. 71<br>• "Companies have long had strategies for business issues such as growth or customer focus but there has been a gap in their strategic thinking in how they assume and manage risk. Progressive firms are trying to fill that gap", P. 72<br>• "One of the major influences that changed the global business environment at the end of the second millennium and is continuing to do so is the concentration of companies in the form of mergers and acquisitions. This development challenges not only the strategic positioning of a company in its market but also requires financial flexibility to respond to unforeseen changes.", P. 79<br>• "The focus on shareholder value and the ongoing global concentration through mergers and acquisitions will have a lasting influence on risk management for international corporations and for insurance companies", P. 81 | • "[…] the insurance values per risk are going to increase tremendously and we are heading towards a much more complex industrial world. […] our business [the reinsurance business] is going to change a lot in this respect", P. 151<br>• "[…] the state and the corporation embody imposed risks (pollution, natural catastrophes and so on)", P. 151 |
| **Development of risk potential in positive and negative direction** | • "Besides global risk, such as climate changes or changes in the legal environment over which an organization has only limited control, the company also faces the traditional risks, which refer to the organisation's industrial risks.", P. 72 | • "We are moving from a static to a dynamic approach. […], we are moving from the accidental to the gradual", P. 152<br>• "We are living with faster technological change and, as far as life spans are concerned, we have clearly moved from the mortality risks to the longevity risk.", P. 152<br>• "[…] we are clearly moving from known risks to hidden or unknown risks. Take for example, electromagnetic effects, GMOs, food safety, or cloning. There are all sorts of risks and we have no clue as to what the future is going to be.", P. 152 |
| **Problems of P/C Insurance market** | • "The industrial insurance market has experienced a transition from regulated national markets (product and price regulation) towards almost total deregulation.", P. 71<br>• "They [Product managers] need to understand the holistic approach of companies' risk managers, and structure products that reflect the changes in the legal, accounting, and tax environment of the different countries of operation of their international clients.", P. 81<br>• "Due to the radical changes in an insurance product's design, corresponding reinsurance might not yet exist or be too immature to provide sufficient cover. Insurance companies might therefore have to look for alternative solutions", P. 81 | "[…] we are in the process of moving from the classical model to a new mode, the virtual corporation. Each of the key elements in the value chains is going to be done by a specialized company. Distribution is more and more the key activity of insurance companies and MGAs. Back office administration is going to be completely outsourced via TPAs.", P. 152 |
| **Risk management measures** | Factors as of P. 72 are:<br>• Risk assessment<br>• Risk control<br>• Risk financing<br>• Administration<br>• Risk communication | "[…] reinsurers are going to take away from the insurer what insurers do not want: the volatility. To do this, we need to have streamlined organizations with very low costs and highly qualified teams", P. 153 |
| **Open scientific questions** | • "[…] the development of new products must reflect the companies' desire to maintain a reasonable cost of risk and result in optimized solutions applying a cost-benefit analysis. These changes will only be successful if companies and industrial insurers work closely together as a team to achieve solutions that combine financial as well as industrial risks.", P. 81 | "Are we going to see a real convergence between various businesses or are we going to keep the line of demarcation between banking, insurance and reinsurance?<br>What about the speed of change?<br>Are we going to experience a revolution or rather a very progressive evolution?", P. 155 |

| | |
|---|---|
| **Article** | **Convergence in the Financial Services Industry** |
| **Author** | Lutgart Van den Berghe and Kurt Verweire |
| **Journal / Publication** | The Geneva Papers on Risk and Insurance – Issues and Practice Vol. 26 No. 2, P. 173 - 183 |
| **Publication date** | April 2001 |
| **Examined questions** | "General observations and recommendations on the drastic changes the financial services industry is undergoing", P. 173 |
| **Emergence of increasingly complex and bigger corporate structures** | • "..., we consider a financial conglomerate as a group of enterprises which is formed by different types of financial institutions (banks, insurance companies and investment institutions.", P. 174<br>• "During the last couple of years, we also notice more integration between banking, insurance and investment in back-office activities. This is especially the case for asset management activities, but there are numerous examples which show that financial conglomerates try to integrate on other levels and activities as well.", P. 174<br>• "How diversified are the financial conglomerates? Some financial conglomerates combine substantial banking and insurance activities, while for others the diversification strategy is only marginal.", P. 174<br>• "..., it is our firm belief that the combination of banking and insurance products as is now done through bancassurance and assurfinance is just the first step of a more profound development.", P. 174<br>• "The complementarity in time and space between different financial and insurance products not only creates natural incentives for cross-selling and packaging but also for innovative product integration. Through unbundling (old traditional products) and re-bundling (in accordance with the real market needs) new service bundles are created.", P. 176<br>• "The supply of integrated services can be seen as a special application of the more general shift from product-oriented supply to a more client-oriented focus.", P. 176<br>• "Although the formation of financial conglomerates can lead to better conditions for integration, it is certainly no guarantee that (only) this route leads to the supply of integrated financial services.", P. 177f<br>• "Looking at the market scene today, we can state that one or another form of financial convergence can be witnessed in many, if not all developed markets. It is striking to observe that even the strongest opponents of financial convergence accept that this trend is irreversible.", P. 179 |
| **Development of risk potential in positive and negative direction** | • "Financial convergence hides advantages as well as disadvantages. At the outset, the general critique against diversification of business firms certainly influenced the sceptical evaluation of many types of financial convergence. Economic research and literature showed that, at least in the manufacturing industries, the large conglomerates, built up in the 1950s and 1960s, destroyed shareholder value in the subsequent years. Therefore, it was not surprising that quite a number of large conglomerates have been refocusing on their core business by either down-scaling or even by breaking up in the last decades. Despite the negative connotations of diversification in the business world, a more positive attitude is prevailing nowadays in the financial services industry. The main idea is that the diversification in the financial services industry is more of the related form. With related diversification, there is more potential for synergies at the different levels of the value chain, and a more operational integration instead of mere "portfolio diversification." P. 179f<br>• "Supervisors will have to address the potential disadvantages in a flexible way, without killing the flexibility and innovation in this industry. Risks that will have to be tackled by the supervisors are, for example, conflicts of interests, abuse of power, tied-in sales, etc.", P. 180<br>• "Although the supervisors have feared that conglomerates create extra risk, our research[1] showed that the risk profile of financial conglomerates is better than that of specialized suppliers (specialized banks and specialized insurance companies).", P. 182 |
| **Problems of P/C Insurance market** | • "An optimal regulation and supervision can only be guaranteed if there is a good balance between the measures to guarantee a stable and reliable financial sector on the one hand and the need for safeguarding sufficient competition and innovation on the other hand.", P. 173<br>• "A generalized trend towards multi-channel structures and multi-distribution has gained a difficult but a certain acceptance; this trend goes beyond the bancassurance movement, because many non-traditional competitors are entering the arena (and the same holds for the distribution of bank products);", P. 175<br>• "Quite a substantial number of the traditional insurance intermediaries that have survived this tough competition, have developed a new, innovative and offensive strategy in order to create their own competitive advantage.", P. 175<br>• "... in the U.S., providing financing arrangements for corporate risks is becoming big business in the investment banking industry. Virtually all large investment banks in the U.S. have now developed large risk management divisions that focus on new products that utilize capital market tools for financing a broad array of corporate financial risks. Investment banks, insurance companies, reinsurers and insurance brokers are also coming together to jointly form catastrophe property and liability insurance companies to write high limits of traditional insurance.", P. 176<br>• "...the traditional insurers focus their core business on a very small part of the whole risk management spectrum.", P. 176 |
| **Risk management measures** | |
| **Open scientific questions** | • "Up to now, most attention has been devoted to the question of reconciling the sectoral regulatory and supervisory approach with the creation of financial conglomerates. The solution has mainly been sought in the direction of the solo-plus supervision. However, this solo-plus supervision is probably only a temporary solution. The more financial convergence evolves, into the direction of integrated services, the more important the "plus" will have to be, creating the danger of double supervision.", P. 183<br>• "We therefore hope that academic institutions, regulatory authorities and supra-national organizations will collaborate to find a way to realize a better disclosure of this financial convergence in all its aspects.", P. 183 |

[1] Verweire, K., 1999, "Performance consequences of financial conglomeration with an empirical analysis in Belgium and the Netherlands", Doctoral thesis, Thesis Publishers Amsterdam, Amsterdam

| **Article** | **New Risks in the Wired World** | **Returning from a Deep Soft Market and the Largest Catastrophe in History** |
|---|---|---|
| **Author** | Barbara Aarsteinsen | Gregory Alff |
| **Journal / Publication** | Canadian Insurance, August 2002, P. 10-15 | Risk Management, January 2002, P. 18 - 26 |
| **Publication date** | August 2002 | January 2002 |
| **Examined questions** | "Technology holds out a universe of opportunities – and an unnerving world of emerging risks. The digital age has revolutionized the way in which business is conducted but with the advances have come new threats and vulnerabilities.", P. 10 | The article discusses the outlook of the insurance / reinsurance industry after a long and extremely soft market and the effects of the September 11 terror attacks. |
| **Emergence of increasingly complex and bigger corporate structures** | • "It is impossible to precisely quantify cyber crime and the extent of the damage being incurred. Many incidents go unreported – because they're not detected, because many companies don't want bad publicity, because there are worries about civil liability, and because there are fears that public exposure will set victims up as easy prey, prone to further violations.", P. 11<br>• "The electronic Internet backbone is the bricks and mortar of businesses today, every business.", P. 12 | "There will be, as has already been demonstrated, increased interest in the use of captives and self-insurance by large companies looking to avoid the second round of sharp price increases and have the ability to access reinsurance markets individually.", P. 26 |
| **Development of risk potential in positive and negative direction** | • "When you're a risk manager, there are a lot of scary possibilities to keep you up at night. Cybercrime is the latest nightmare.", P. 10<br>• "There are dramatic gaps in coverage that don't protect against all the emerging risks, which are, of course, increasing and evolving all the time.", P. 14 | "Now, the events of September 11 have resulted in the largest insurable losses in history, surpassing the $18 billion direct total losses for Hurricane Andrew.", P. 19 |
| **Problems of P/C Insurance market** | | • "The net underwriting losses for the U.S. property/casualty industry for calendar year 2000 were $31.2 billion. Only 1992 results driven by the enormous cost of Hurricane Andrew were worse.", P. 19<br>• "While the underwriting losses of 1992 were driven largely by natural catastrophes, the underwriting losses of 2000 were created by underpricing of the broad range of insurance products across the entire property/casualty industry.", P. 19<br>• "The premium increases achieved by the industry in 2001 will be large enough to offset the net losses of September 11, but not large enough to improve the industry's financial results. With much lower realized capital gains and unrealized capital losses likely to exceed those experienced during 2000, the policyholders' surplus for the property/casualty industry may fall by 8 percent or more when 2001 results are finalized.", P. 20<br>• "A very hard market will continue through 2002, with a second round of strong price increases.", P. 26<br>• "The hard market portion of the property/casualty pricing cycle will lengthen into 2003, with prices not beginning to plateau until the middle of 2003.", P. 26<br>• "The financial blow to reinsurers from September 11, which has resulted in lower reinsurance capacity available from individual reinsurers, will make it increasingly difficult to complete layers for the largest concentrated property and liability risks.", P. 26<br>• "The greatest threat at this time is the potential for a second major catastrophe, either from an act of terrorism or from a natural catastrophe, such as a level 4 or level 5 hurricane. Such an event, coming in the next six to twelve months, could trigger serious solvency concerns for some major carriers.", P. 26 |
| **Risk management measures** | • "There are two broad areas of cyber coverage. First-party coverage protects against losses suffered by the insured as a result of loss of damage to assets – downtime or systems damage arising from a virus, for example. Third-party coverage protects the insured against lawsuits arising when customers or trading partners are affected by first-party situations, such as theft of confidential information.", P. 15 | |
| **Open scientific questions** | • "A natural evolution will continue to take place, market participants predict. However, the intensifying spotlight on corporate governance is seen as boding particularly well for cyber insurance. As boards of directors are being held more accountable amidst a spate of scandals, senior managers are expected to feel greater urgency about cyber vulnerabilities.", P. 15 | |

| | |
|---|---|
| **Article** | **Managing Technological Risks: A Challenge for Professional Engineering Insurers** |
| **Author** | Detmar Heidenhain |
| **Journal / Publication** | The Geneva Papers on Risk and Insurance – Issues and Practice Vol. 26, P. 268 – 276 |
| **Publication date** | April 2001 |
| **Examined questions** | • "A huge number of technological developments are expected to become reality in the 21st century. Five basic areas can be identified to form the key technologies, which will be of great significance for the insurance and reinsurance industries during the next few decades:<br>o Information technology<br>o Energy and the environmental engineering<br>o Medicine and genetic engineering<br>o Micro-systems and new materials<br>o Transportation and traffic systems", P. 268 |
| **Emergence of increasingly complex and bigger corporate structures** | "The public sector is increasingly transferring to private investors its responsibilities for planning, financing and operating long-term infrastructure projects, such as transportation systems, utilities, waste disposal, communication systems and even correctional facilities. Contrary to the old days, where all risk in connection with such projects were usually "insured" by the taxpayer, private investors and lenders look for risk-minimization. This creates a new demand for extensive insurance cover.", P. 273 |
| **Development of risk potential in positive and negative direction** | "…there will be a marked increase in major engineering losses in the future.", P. 272 |
| **Problems of P/C Insurance market** | • "The speed of technological progress will continue to accelerate rapidly. It is of existential importance for insurers and reinsurers involved in the engineering insurance lines to keep a constant eye on this development, to track it and to understand it. In today's globally developing world of technology, it is of fundamental importance to successful business operations for the engineering insurer to keep pace with technological progress and to be just as aware of its successes and failures as of lessons to be learned from losses.", P. 271<br>• "Every merger of insurers means there is one insurer less. The groups are getting bigger, financially stronger and need less reinsurance, except in major-risk business, where the reinsured values and liabilities are constantly rising. This increases the risk of massive fluctuations in results and makes balancing with a portfolio more difficult. At the same time, global insurers often force their regional subsidiaries into a hard, turnover-oriented and price-driven competition, sometimes consciously accepting underwriting losses in the process. The old-established local insurers react accordingly in order to defend their market share.", P. 274 |
| **Risk management measures** | • "In the future, the management of technological risks will be linked more strongly than ever before to new developments and advancements in technology. In dealing with this subject, therefore, it is absolutely essential to consider the impact of technological developments on the insurance industry, and especially their impact on engineering insurers and their management of the risks in their portfolio.", P. 268<br>• "When accepting new technological risks, in particular major engineering and construction risks, careful risk assessment and expert control is a precondition. Thorough evaluation of comprehensive underwriting information, site inspections, loss prevention and research as well as claims handling are part of this process of risk management. This process attempts to reduce the probability and the magnitude of hazards, whilst at the same time trying to manage residual risks. Greater emphasis is recently placed on monitoring construction progress and physically inspecting larger, complex projects. Only through that active involvement can be ensured that engineering lines of business can be further pursued successfully, particularly in times of low premiums and extensive covers.", P. 272<br>• "Thus, locally operating global engineering insurers' benefit from special knowledge that newcomers to the market usually do not have. This knowledge is there to be used: Their longstanding risk and loss experience, evaluated intelligently, updated regularly, regionally diversified in connection with exposure-oriented, prospective pricing and the setting of conditions and of course readily available, i.e. IT-based with global networking, make specialist engineering insurers and reinsurers a sought-after partner for their local partners and independent insurers alike.", P. 274 |
| **Open scientific questions** | • "Technological development entails a risk of change! For engineers, change means challenge. The challenges for engineering insurers are to be found in the future development of technology! Therefore, professional engineering insurers and reinsurers should have a strong and deep interest in the potential technological developments of this century. This will enable them to offer substantial added value to their clients, assisting them to take advantage of the chances and opportunities offered through new technological developments.", P. 276 |

| | |
|---|---|
| **Article** | **World Trade Center Special Issue** |
| **Author** | Alice Schroeder, Vinay Saqi & Chris Winans |
| **Journal / Publication** | Insurance – Property-Casualty |
| **Publication date** | September 17, 2001 |
| **Examined questions** | "The Problem: How can this be the largest workers compensation loss in history (by multiples), the most expensive aviation disaster in history (by multiples), one of the largest property losses in history, the most expensive business interruption in history (by multiples), the largest life insurance catastrophic loss in history (by multiples), and one of the largest potential liability claims in history – yet every one of the 36 major companies that have reported, representing the vast majority of market exposures, says it is going to come out of it financially A-OK, with little more than a bad quarter or year to report? The answer: they can't - all the companies can't be above average. The sum of the losses has to add up to the total. Some of the numbers you are seeing reported by companies are likely significantly understated, mostly because they are net of reinsurance recoverables that in many cases will never be collected.", P. 2f |
| **Emergence of increasingly complex and bigger corporate structures** | |
| **Development of risk potential in positive and negative direction** | "Rising demand for property insurance - in fact for all types of insurance - is likely to be one of the consequences of the World Trade Centre disaster. For example, the replacement cost of the two Towers is estimated at $5 billion, but they were insured for only $3.3 billion. We understand that the owner has claimed the disaster was two separate events, apparently in an attempt to tap two coverage limits and collect the full replacement cost. We don't think this will be successful. We do think property owners will take note of the perils of under-insurance.", P. 11 |
| **Problems of P/C Insurance market** | • "The reinsurance market has not recovered from its weak financial condition of the late 1990s. Pricing began to turn up only in 2000 and many insurers were counting on 2001 as the down payment on a return to normalcy. A huge hole has just been gouged out of companies' balance sheets. Some companies that would not have otherwise been toppled by a large catastrophe probably just can't afford this one given its timing.", P. 4<br>• "We had already been hearing of requests for backup and replacement covers for smaller reinsurers, indicating the flight to quality was in full flow, before this event.", P. 5<br>• "Now, we believe this loss is a recipe for disaster for overleveraged reinsurers. We would call it close to a 100% probability that some reinsurers will fail and be unable to pay claims as a result of this event.", P. 5<br>• "What All This Means: The capacity of the reinsurance market worldwide to take risk, currently around $120 billion annually of premium, will shrink significantly - perhaps by one-third or even more. The shrinkage is a function not just of the losses - but of several other factors:<br>• 1) the perceived flight to quality and lack of faith in the credit-worthiness of lower-tier reinsurers;<br>• 2) underwriters' fear and greater recognition of higher risk factors will result in a lower willingness to assume and retain risk and greater allocations of capital to many types of risk;<br>• 3) fear of credit losses will cause buyers to shrink capacity allocated to some reinsurers and reduce their "approved lists";<br>• 4) despite some commentary to the contrary, we believe the capital markets will not be willing to restore the industry's capital with the exception of the largest and strongest players because of demand shifts.", P. 5<br>• "In general, we believe the attack will increase risk aversion and therefore, unlike a normal market when prices rise, we do not expect as dramatic an increase in self-insurance and rising deductibles as would otherwise have occurred. Rather, we believe that buyers will rediscover the value of insurance, and be less reluctant to pay for what is, in fact, a very valuable product. This could be helpful to insurers who badly need to charge more economic pricing at a time when the outlook for the economy is not good.", P. 11<br>• "The insurance business already suffers greatly from the fact that buyers do not discriminate adequately between companies with good and bad claims-paying ratings, and good and bad balance sheets. Now, a time has finally arrived in which the sheep and goats of the industry will be separated. It would be unfortunate if the sheep acquiesced with or even encouraged an effort by Congress to dress up the goats to look like sheep.", P. 13 |
| **Risk management measures** | |
| **Open scientific questions** | |

| | |
|---|---|
| **Article** | **Capitalisation of the Property–Liability Insurance Industry: Overview** |
| **Author** | J. David Cummins and Neil A. Doherty |
| **Journal / Publication** | Journal of Financial Services Research 21:1/2 5-14 |
| **Publication date** | 2002 |
| **Examined questions** | "What can explain the dramatic changes in capital structure in this [property-liability insurance] industry?", P. 5 |
| **Emergence of increasingly complex and bigger corporate structures** | |
| **Development of risk potential in positive and negative direction** | "An increased awareness by insurers of their exposure to catastrophic property losses coupled with inadequate supply of reinsurance for such losses also may have played a role in the leverage declines. Hurricane Andrew in 1992 and the Northridge earthquake in 1994 led insurers to revise upward their estimates of potential losses due to natural catastrophes. Simultaneously, it became apparent that reinsurance for these large events was inadequate (Swiss Re, 1997; Froot, 1999)", P. 6 |
| **Problems of P/C Insurance market** | • "The declines in leverage may have been triggered by the introduction of a risk-based capital (RBC) system by the National Association of Insurance Commissioners (NAIC) in 1994", P. 5<br>• "The 1990s bull market in corporate equities, combined with insurer reluctance to increase stockholder dividends also contributed to leverage declines.", P. 5<br>• "..., the run up in stock prices was the principal, but not the only, cause of the leverage declines", P. 5<br>• Another factor contributing the declining leverage in the industry is the decreasing importance of financial ratings and the influence of rating agencies. The insurance product market reacts quickly to changes in financial ratings firms such as A.M. Best company, Standard & Poor's, and Moody's. Especially in the commercial lines market, it is necessary for insurers to maintain at least an A rating in order to avoid losing customers to competitors.", P. 6<br>• "The growth in the market for alternative risk transfer products, which provide a substitute for conventional insurance provides another possible explanation for the capitalization trends. These include self-insurance programs, captive insurance companies, and securitized financial risk transfer instruments. These products have drained many of the more predictable risks out of insurance markets, increasing the overall volatility of insurer growth to stagnate, partially accounting for the gap between premium and equity growth.", P. 6<br>• "In many respects, the leverage declines of the 1990s can be interpreted as a particularly dramatic phase of the property-liability insurance underwriting cycle. Substantial evidence exists that a cycle is present in the underwriting profit ratio, defined as $r_u = \frac{P-L-E}{P}$ where P= Premiums, L = losses incurred, and E = expenses incurred.", P. 6<br>• "Leverage ratios in the property-liability insurance industry declined precipitously during the 1990s.", P. 12<br>• "It is clear that the decline in leverage (e.g., the premium revenues during the roughly fifteen years preceding 2001. More than half of the capital growth consisted of realized and unrealized capital gains on investments. About one-third of the capital growth was attributable to retained earnings form other sources, and the remainder represented new capital raised in securities markets or contributed by affiliated firms", P. 12<br>• "The theory of underwriting cycles predicts that insurers will be reluctant to pay out accumulated capital as dividends because of the costs of raising new capital following the next underwriting or investment shock. Hence, insurers tend to "hoard" capital during profitable times to provide internal funds to withstand the next crisis.", P. 12<br>• "..., there is evidence that ratings provide a reasonable accurate indication of insurer financial strength – private ratings tend to be more accurate in predicting insurer insolvencies than do regulatory risk measures.", P. 12<br>• "..., insurers held more capital in part to avoid ratings downgrades and the attendant loss of key customers, suppliers, and employees.", P. 12 |
| **Risk management measures** | |
| **Open scientific questions** | |

| **Article** | **Risiko-Management und Versicherung** |
|---|---|
| **Author** | Matthias Haller |
| **Journal/Publication** | Versicherungsenzyklopädie, 4. Auflage 1991, Band 1, S. 523-568 |
| **Publication date** | 1991 |
| **Examined questions** | „Aus diesem Grund steht am Anfang die Frage, wie Störungen sich im Gesamtzusammenhang der Unternehmung manifestieren, welche Folgerungen sich zunächst für das Management im Allgemeinen aufdrängen. Auf dieser Basis stellt sich sodann das Risikoproblem, zu dessen Lösung weit mehr als die logischen Instrumente der Entscheidungstheorie erforderlich sind.", P. 528 |
| **Emergence of increasingly complex and bigger corporate structures** | • „Es ist davon auszugehen, daß jedes in einer Unternehmung zu lösende Problem – somit auch jedes Risikoproblem – technologische, ökonomische und soziale Aspekte aufweist, wenn auch die relative Bedeutung von Fall zu Fall sehr verschieden ist. Im Hinblick auf das Risiko-Management weist die soziale Komponente einen deutlichen Nachholbedarf auf.", P. 532<br>• „Risiko läßt sich nur im Zusammenhang mit einem abgegrenzten System umschreiben. In unserem Falle ist dies die Unternehmung (evtl. auch ein Konzern oder ein Unternehmensbereich)", P. 536<br>• „Bei der Bewältigung des Unternehmensrisikos geht es daher zunächst nicht um die Beschäftigung mit Störungen, sondern mit Zielen und Plandaten, denn ohne Ziele bestehen auch keine Risiken. In der Praxis ist allerdings ein anderes Phänomen häufiger: Weil Ziele nicht ausdrücklich formuliert, werden, sind den Unternehmungsangehörigen die entsprechenden Risiken ebenfalls nicht bewußt. Im Schadenfalle wird man dann zur Erkenntnis gelangen, daß unbewußt vorausgesetzte Randbedingungen für den Erfolg der Unternehmung ebenso bedeutend waren wie die bewußten Pläne", P. 535 |
| **Development of risk potential in positive and negative direction** | • „... spektakuläre Folgen von Schadenfällen sind Zeichen dafür, daß es in den letzten Jahren stets schwieriger geworden ist, dieses „richtige Risiko" zu erkennen, zu bemessen und zu bewältigen.", P. 525<br>• „Es scheint sich vielmehr eine Lücke zu öffnen zwischen zunehmenden Sicherungsbemühungen in den Unternehmungen und noch rascher wachsenden Risiken.", P. 526<br>• „Wie die Analyse von Großschadenereignissen eindeutig gezeigt hat, kommt dem Bewußtseinsfaktor vor jeder rein logischen Erwägung im Risiko-Management die entscheidende Rolle zu. Es läßt sich nämlich feststellen, daß verletzte Randbedingugnen der Unternehmungsaktivität Ursprung und Ablauf von Störungen immer stärker beeinflussen, von den Führungsangehörigen jedoch nach wie vor vernachlässigt werden, weil man die Erörterung solcher Fragen als lästig empfindet. Damit nimmt die Entscheidungsqualität tendenziell ab. Angesichts einer zunehmenden Ungewißheit bezüglich der Umweltentwicklung und rasch zunehmender Schadenpotentiale ist es deshalb ein Hauptanliegen des Risiko-Managements, daß Risikofragen überhaupt gleichgewichtig in den Entscheidungsprozeß eingebracht werden", P. 536 |
| **Problems of P/C Insurance market** | • "Versicherung bleibt auch darum ein wichtiges Instrument des Risiko-Managements, weil jede Investition in die güterliche Sicherung ein relativ hohes Maß an Unsicherheit offen läßt. Bei abnehmenden Wachstumsraten und konjunktureller Anspannung wird die Tatsache wieder höher bewertet, dass die Versicherung das Sicherungsinstrument mit dem höchsten Zuverlässigkeitsgrad verkörpert. Dies ist umso wichtiger, als sich jede Störung letztlich im finanziellen Bereich auswirkt und das Überleben von Unternehmungen nach Störungsfällen entscheidend von der Ausgestaltung der finanziellen Sicherung abhängt. Indem sie die übrigen Sektoren von der Reservebildung im versicherbaren Bereich entlastet, trägt die Assekuranz somit zur direkten und indirekten Überlebenssicherung bei. In einer arbeitsteiligen Wirtschaft wird diese Funktion zweifellos noch gestärkt werden.", P. 563<br>• „Allerdings wäre es gefährlich, die Auswirkungen des Risiko-Managements einzig unter dem Aspekt des Prämienvolumens zu beurteilen. Längerfristige Perspektiven deuten vielmehr darauf hin, dass sich mit dem Risiko-Management ein qualitativer Umschwung vollzieht, auf dessen Basis sich die wirtschaftliche und gesellschaftliche Funktion der Assekuranz erheblich verändert.", P. 563<br>• „Weil Risk Management in der Praxis zunächst of als Reduktion des Prämienvolumens erfahren wurde, besteht bei Angehörigen der Assekuranz Misstrauen gegenüber dem Risiko-Management.", P. 561<br>• „Hier zeigt sich, wie eng Bedrohung und Chance der Versicherungsindustrie beieinander liegen. Wenn es gelingt, den Verkauf der herkömmlichen „Versicherungen" in eine Dienstleistung einzugliedern, welche auf das Bedürfnis nach Sicherheit ausgerichtet ist und einen Beitrag zur gesamten Problemlösung erbringt, wird sich der Wirkungsbereiche der Branche zweifellos noch erweitern. Sollte aber die Assekuranz dieser Herausforderung nicht begegnen, so werden andere Institutionen teilweise an ihren Platz treten: die Banken (Allfinanzdienste mit Sicherungsfunktion), die Sicherheitsindustrie (mit Konzepten statt Apparaten), nicht zuletzt aber auch der Staat und die öffentliche Sozialversicherung.", P. 564f<br>• „Die politische Diskussion um Flixborough, Seveso und Chiasso, aber auch die Auseinandersetzung um Sicherheit und Versicherung von Kernkraftwerken lässt die Tendenz erkennen, dass eine breite Öffentlichkeit kaum mehr geneigt ist, den Unterschied zwischen dem Gefährdungspotential (maximal possible loss) und dem durch Experten geschätzten „Restrisiko" von technischen oder logistischen Systemen allzu sehr anwachsen zu lassen. Diese Einsicht – eng verbunden mit dem Faktor „innere Sicherheit" – müsste die Versicherungsindustrie vermehrt veranlassen, nicht erst subsidiär in Erscheinung zu treten.", P. 565 |

| Article | Risiko-Management und Versicherung |
|---|---|
| **Risk management measures** | • „Der RM-Prozeß – erstmals ausführlich von Mehr / Heges (1963) beschrieben – ist eine Aufeinanderfolge von Identifikation, Analyse und Handhabung des Risikos; als Instrumente der Risikohandhabung dienen Vermeidung, Verminderung, Überwälzung und Selbstragen des Risikos. Der Verantwortliche oder Koordinator für die Versicherung (und zum Teil auch für die Risikoverminderung) wird als Risk Manager bezeichnet.", P. 526f<br>• „Mehren sich die Störfälle, so besteht natürlicherweise das Bestreben, auch die Früherkennung, Frühwarnung und anschließende Verhinderung einer ernsthaften Störung in den Sicherungsprozeß einzubeziehen. Damit schließt Risiko-Mangement das Krisen-Mangement mit ein, versucht aber nach Möglichkeit im Störprozeß in einer früheren Phase einzugreifen (Störungs-Management), ja nach Möglichkeit die Strukturen sogar so zu setzen, daß gewisse Störabläufe erst gar nicht möglich sind (Verletzbarkeits-Management)", P. 534<br>• „Risiko = Möglichkeit, daß sich Erwartungen des Systems Unternehmung aufgrund von Störprozessen nicht erfüllen", P. 534<br>• „Auf Basis der Sicherheit als Leitidee kann mit den Führungsmitteln der Sicherungsprozeß ausgelöst werden. Über Planung, Entscheidung, Durchführung und Kontrolle konkretisieren sich nach und nach die Risiken verschiedener Unternehmungsbereiche, während sich über die Maßnahmen das Sicherheitsniveau generell verbessert.", P. 541.<br>• „Wo sich aufgrund der Evaluation von Störungsketten ein außerordentlich hohes Störpotential ergibt, wird mit Vorteil eine wahrscheinlichkeitsfundierte Fehlerbaumanalyse oder Störfallanalyse vorgenommen. … .Der Schwerpunkt des Einsatzes solcher Analysen liegt naturgemäß bei technischen Systemen. Die außerordentlich hohen Kosten der Informationsgewinnung lassen eine Übertragung auf das umfassende Risiko-Management der Unternehmung nur begrenzt zu." P. 546. |
| **Open scientific questions** | • Der Faktor „Management" im Risiko-Management hat somit zu gewährleisten, daß die Führung unter dem Aspekt der Störpotentiale und der Störungsüberwindung in die „normale" Führung integriert wird: Einerseits ist der Sicherungsprozeß so zu gestalten, daß er in enger Verbindung mit der Führung erfolgt, andererseits sind die Führungsstrukturen so festzulegen, daß sie den existentiellen Sicherungsbedürfnissen von sich aus gerecht werden. Nicht zuletzt hat auch der verwendetet Risikobegriff solchen Anforderungen zu entsprechen", P. 534<br>• „In Zukunft wird weniger die Bewältigung des Risikos für den Kunden entscheidend sein. Entwicklungen ähnlich jenen in der Datenverarbeitung und im Fremdenverkehr weisen auf die Natur des Wandels: In der Marktleistung tritt an die Stelle des Produktes die Problemlösung.", P. 564<br>• „Es geht darum, die Kombination von Risikoinformation und Schaden-Know-How, wie sie sich bei den Versicherern anballt, vermehrt der Planung und Führung industrieller Systeme zugänglich zu machen.", P. 566<br>• „Vorerst bedarf es einer Annäherung von Konzept und Sprache zwischen Assekuranz und industrieller Führung. Hierzu mag das praxisorientierte Risiko-Management als Disziplin nützliche Dienste leisten.", P. 566 |

| **Article** | **Die Entwicklung des industriellen Risikos und die künftige Rolle des Risk Managers** |
|---|---|
| **Author** | Matthias Haller |
| **Journal / Publication** | Publikation eines Vortrages im Rahmen der Mitgliederversammlung des BfV vom 26. -27. Oktober 1995 in Mainz, St. Gallen 1995, P. 1 – 22 |
| **Publication date** | 1995 |
| **Examined questions** | • "Der tendenziell zunehmende Dissens, wie wir ihn zwischen Industrie und Assekuranz in den vergangenen Jahren beobachten, entspringt nicht einem ‚bösartigen' Verhalten der einen oder anderen Partei; er ist vielmehr die systemische Konsequenz aus Entwicklungen, deren Tendenzen seit den siebziger Jahren abzusehen sind, heute aber eine neue – und akzentuierte – Ausprägung erhalten. Falls die nachfolgenden Gedanken Zustimmung finden, ergibt sich auch für den Risk Manager eine zusätzliche, wichtige Rolle: Als Vermittler in einem Risiko-Dialog, den wir begründen und sorgfältig realisieren sollten.", P. 2 |
| **Emergence of increasingly complex and bigger corporate structures** | • "Seit ungefähr zwanzig Jahren, spätestens aber seit 1986 sind gesellschaftliche Risikoprobleme virulent geworden, welche einen strukturellen Konflikt zwischen der produzierenden Wirtschaft und der Öffentlichkeit spiegeln:<br>- Einerseits die Abhängigkeit der Öffentlichkeit von der Aktivität der Unternehmungen, weil diese die weitere Wohlstandsentwicklung garantieren (Chancenaspekt der Risiken).<br>- Andererseits zunehmende Widerstände und Ängste, weil die Unternehmungen – als Produzenten von Großunfällen und ökologischen Störungen – die Lebensbasis der Gesellschaft gefährden (Gefahrenaspekt, der zunehmend wahrgenommen und über die Medien verstärkt wird).", P. 2<br>• „Nun kann man aus Sicht der multilokal bzw. global orientierten Unternehmung den Standpunkt geltend machen, dass sie sich angesichts der Dezentralisierung der Aktivitäten solchen Gefährdungen in einem beträchtlichen Ausmaß entzieht und damit zwischen europäischen Industriestandorten und jenen in „emerging economies" ein günstiger Ausgleich zu erzielen ist. Zweifellos hat das Argument seine Berechtigung, doch sind auch aus der globalen Betrachtung heraus Einschränkungen geltend zu machen.", P. 8<br>• „Schließlich zeigen Untersuchungen zur Vernetzung der Risiken im multilokalen System, dass die steigende Komplexität, die divergierenden Sicherheitskulturen sowie die eingeschränkte Kommunikationsmöglichkeit das technologisch bedingte Großrisiko- in dem Masse erhöht, wie die Auslagerung zu einer Reduktion der sozialen Komponente geführt hat.", P. 8<br>„Für ein Industrieunternehmen ist Versicherung ein Instrument zur Gestaltung der eigenen Risikolage.", P. 13 |
| **Development of risk potential in positive and negative direction** | • "Unter dem Gefahrenaspekt Erhöhung der Verwundbarkeit der Systeme aufgrund zunehmender Vernetzung der Gesamtanlagen und der Vergrößerung der Kapazitäten: Größtunfälle, Systemzusammenbrüche und ökologische Störungen treten äußerst selten auf, können aber von katastrophaler Wirkung sein, falls es dennoch einmal zu einem derartigen Ereignis kommt.", P. 2<br>• „Ein verändertes Verständnis von ‚Risiko' ist darum gefordert, weil sich die Risikoveränderung in der modernen Industriegesellschaft durch schwergewichtig zwei Entwicklungen kennzeichnet:<br>1. Abnahme der Störanfälligkeit und Zunahme des Schadenpotentials aus wenigen ‚Dennoch-Unfällen' (Kleinstwahrscheinliche Größtschäden).<br>2. Abnahme der Zurechenbarkeit von Schäden auf klar definierbare Verursacher. Die exakte Zurechnung wird sowohl sachlich (Was ist passiert?) wie auch sozial (Wer ist/sind der/die Verursacher?) und zeitlich (Seit wann existiert die Schadenursache bzw. die Störung?) immer schwieriger.", P. 12<br>• „Wie die Vernetzte Analyse der Risikoentwicklung im multilokalen Management ergab, ist keinesfalls mit einer Beruhigung dieser Entwicklung zu rechnen: die entsprechenden Wirkungsgefüge führen tendenziell dahin, dass die Verwundbarkeit laufend zunimmt und relativ wenige, dennoch realisierte Störungen zum Teil weltumspannende Konsequenzen aufweisen werden.", P. 12 |
| **Problems of P/C Insurance market** | • „Im Rahmen des beschriebenen Gesamtzusammenhanges hat sich die Industrieversicherung neu zu positionieren", P. 9<br>• „Das überproportionale Wachstum der Gefährdungspotentiale führt zu einer erhöhten Bedeutung versicherbarer Risken: Damit erhält die Versicherungspolitik der Industrie grundsätzlich eine wichtigere Funktion.", P. 8<br>• „Es handelt sich hier um eine Situation, die aus der Perspektive beider Partner unbefriedigend erscheint: Aus Sicht der Industrieversicherer<br>• „- Die generell schlechte Ertragssituation der Branche, welche mit dem miserablen Geschäftsabschluss von 1991 ihren Tiefpunkt erreicht hat;<br>- Kapazitätsbeschränkungen und Preiserhöhungen der Rückversicherer, […];<br>- Vorläufiger Abschluss eines Kampfs um Marktanteile mit Blick auf einen europäischen Binnenmarkt, […];<br>- Reorganisation nach Kundengruppen in maßgebenden Versicherungshäusern, […];<br>- Damit und mit den übrigen Ertragsproblemen verbunden: Beendigung der (oft freiwilligen) Quersubventionierung des Industriegeschäfts aus dem Privatkundengeschäft.", P. 11<br>• „Für den Versicherer bedeutet Versicherung nicht Erfüllung irgendeiner besonderen Pflicht (z.B. Organisation der „Gefahrengemeinschaft"), sondern ist Ergebnis einer autonomen Versicherbarkeits-Entscheidung.", P. 13 |
| **Risk management measures** | „Daraus resultiert 4. eine vernetzte Betrachtung des erweiterten Risiko-Managements und der Risikogemeinkosten. Der grundsätzliche Wirkungszusammenhang für eine positive Entwicklung der Versicherung kommt in einem einfachen Basis-Wirkungsgefüge zum Ausdruck. Darauf aufbauend lassen sich die bisherigen Überlegungen schrittweise einbringen und ergänzen, bis ein differenziertes, erweitertes Wirkungsgefüge nach dem Ansatz des Vernetzten Denkens entsteht.", P. 16 |
| **Open scientific questions** | „Bisher hat sich die Arbeit im Risiko-Dialog vor allem an den Problemen zwischen Industrie und Öffentlichkeit orientiert. Es wäre erfreulich, wenn künftig auch die intimeren Probleme zwischen Industrie und der Assekuranz in einem solchen Dialog weitergeführt würden: Der Risk Manager ist zugleich die Schlüsselperson und die Nahtstelle dazu.", P. 21 |

| | |
|---|---|
| **Article** | **Gesellschaftliche Risikoprobleme - Frühwarnfunktion der Versicherung?!** |
| **Author** | Matthias Haller |
| **Journal / Publication** | Versicherung, Risiko und Internationalisierung: Herausforderungen für Unternehmensführung und Politik, Mugler J. / Nitsche, M. [Hrsg.], Wien 1996, P. 331 – 342 |
| **Publication date** | 1996 |
| **Examined questions** | • „Versicherung als Frühwarnsystem der Gesellschaft?", P. 341<br>• "Wenn es um gesellschaftliche Risikoprobleme geht, stehen Versicherer offenbar vor einem Dilemma:<br>o Einerseits kann es ihnen nicht egal sein, wie sich die Risiken in der Gesellschaft entwickeln, denn letztlich schlägt sich jede Veränderung in der einen oder anderen Form im Versicherungsgeschäft nieder;<br>o Andererseits weisen es – oder wiesen es? – Versicherer entschieden zurück, zur Lösung von gesellschaftlichen Risikoproblemen verantwortlich herangezogen zu werden: ‚Es kann nicht unsere Rolle sein, Risiken von diesem Ausmaß und Struktur in unsere Geschäftsbücher zu übernehmen, und noch viel mehr wehren wir uns im Zeichen der Marktwirtschaft dagegen, über Akzeptanz oder Ablehnung des Risikotransfers die Rolle des Risikopolizisten zu übernehmen.' (N.N., Tiefeninterview im Risiko-Dialog)", P. 333 |
| **Emergence of increasingly complex and bigger corporate structures** | "Andererseits zunehmende Widerstände und Ängste, weil die Unternehmungen als Produzenten von Großunfällen und ökologischen Störungen – die Lebensbasis der Gesellschaft gefährden (Gefahrenaspekt, der zunehmend wahrgenommen und über die Medien verstärkt wird).", P. 334 |
| **Development of risk potential in positive and negative direction** | • "Die Signalereignisse von 1986, im deutschen Sprachraum durch die Stichworte Tschernobyl, Challenger und Schweizerhalle (Brand von Basel) charakterisiert, haben die Debatte um die weitere Entwicklung der Risikopotentiale und der (möglichen) Größtschäden und Katastrophen stark angeheizt; …", P. 333f<br>• „Unter dem Druck von jährlichen Milliardenbelastungen sind die Sanierungsmaßnahmen in den einzelnen Versicherungsbranchen mit mehr oder weniger Erfolg eingeleitet, und es ist auch gelungen, im Zusammenhang mit den Größtrisiken in den vergangenen Jahren spezielle Risikoträger zu schaffen. Doch zeigt gerade die Begrenzung und die Ausgliederung solcher Risiken aus dem traditionellen Deckungsbereich, dass nach wie vor Ungewissheit darüber herrscht, inwiefern solche Risiken der Versicherung überhaupt zugänglich sind und – wenn ja – eine strategische Neuausrichtung aller Geschäftsfelder angesagt ist.", P. 334<br>• „…Relativ wenig Versicherungsfälle beanspruchen einen zunehmenden Anteil des Gesamtprämienvolumens einer (Teil-) Branche, wobei gleichzeitig immer weniger Industrieunternehmungen Erfahrungen im Umgang mit (Größt-) Schadenfällen gewinnen können.", P. 337 |
| **Problems of P/C Insurance market** | „In der Assekuranz selbst sind es vor allem zwei Faktoren, welche die generelle Risikoentwicklung zum geschäftlichen Traktandum erhoben:<br>• einerseits Milliardenverluste im Industriegeschäft, wo einige wenige ‚kleinstwahrscheinliche Größtschäden' den Hauptteil der Prämien konsumieren;<br>• andererseits enorme Kumulschäden im Privatkundenbereich, die sich vor allem als Folge zuvor nicht beobachteter Naturereignisse (insb. Stürme; Hagelzüge und Überschwemmungen) einstellten. Damit wurde die Assekuranz vollends in Interessenbereiche gerückt, die vormals eher von ökologisch orientierten Gruppierungen besetzt waren.", P. 334<br>• „Die Schere zwischen Wohlstands- und der Gefahrenentwicklung dürfte sich in den kommenden Jahren weiter öffnen, denn sowohl die Globalisierung des Wettbewerbs wie die Vergrößerung der Binnenmärkte sind von Wachstumshoffnungen getragen.", P. 335<br>• „Gleichzeitig nimmt die Gefahr von Systemzusammenbrüchen mit weitreichenden Auswirkungen (z.B. Volatilität der Börsen im Zeichen der Informatisierung und des globalen Geschäftsbetriebs, Zusammenbrücke der Verkehrssysteme) zu, während erste ökologische Störungen konkrete Signale für weit umfangreichere ökologische Katastrophen (Klimaveränderung, Ozon, Fremdenverkehr) setzen. Der Bereich de Gentechnologie nimmt insofern einen speziellen Stellenwert ein, als Chancen zur Lösung wichtiger gesellschaftlicher Probleme zweifelsfrei gegeben sind, während die Risikodimension sowohl vom Ansatz wie von der Auswirkung her bereits heftig umstritten ist. Die ‚Großunfälle' vergangener Jahre sind im Sinne der vorangegangenen Abbildung erst als Signalereignisse zu werten, die in technischer wie in ökonomischer Hinsicht nicht zu erratischen Erschütterungen führten, jedoch die Entwicklungstendenzen des Risikos offen legten.", P. 336<br>• „Während bis vor kurzem die Schadenabschätzung relativ leicht war und zudem das Ausmaß der Industrieschäden einigermaßen im Rahmen der BIP-Entwicklung zunahm, zeigt das letzte Jahrzehnt eine bedrohliche Verselbständigung der Großschäden: - Industrieschäden wachsen in gesellschaftlich relevante Größenordnungen hinein, und die Industrie frägt Versicherungssummen nach, welche volkswirtschaftliche Dimensionen erreichen. Trotz (oder wegen) erhöhten Sicherheitsinvestitionen ist der Risikoausgleich kaum mehr gewährleistet", P. 336f (→ 6. Complex Corp.) |
| **Risk management measures** | • „Im Zeichen dieser Frühwarn- und Mittlerfunktion sind drei „Hebelwirkungen" (Leverages) denkbar, welche den (relativ schwachen) Impulsen aus der Assekuranz einen relativ starken Einfluß auf die weitere Risikoentwicklung verleihen könnten:<br>o Der kognitive Hebel: […]<br>o Der Limitierungs-Hebel: […]<br>o Der Dialog-Hebel: […]", P. 339ff |
| **Open scientific questions** | „Es geht nicht nur darum, mit irgendwelchen Aktionen Wirkungen zu erzielen; vielmehr besteht das Anliegen, dass Versicherer sich mit Informationen folgenreich ‚Gehör verschaffen'", P. 341f |

| | |
|---|---|
| **Article** | **Environmental Risk Management: A Critical Part of Corporate Strategy** |
| **Author** | Dan R. Anderson |
| **Journal / Publication** | The Geneva Papers on Risk and Insurance – Issues and Practice Vol. 27 No. 2, P. 152 – 180 |
| **Publication date** | April 2002 |
| **Examined questions** | The article examines the trend that "environmental risk management" is becoming a critical component of corporate strategy", P. 152 |
| **Emergence of increasingly complex and bigger corporate structures** | "These two examples [Ford, Coca-Cola] also illustrate that the increased globalisation of the world economy and consolidations of corporations from different continents will increase the business risks of global warming", P. 173 |
| **Development of risk potential in positive and negative direction** | • "…environmental costs will be increasingly internalised to businesses. This increased internalisation of risk costs will result from increased litigation as well as from the broadening of risks into the reputation, business, regulatory, and ethical risk areas." , P. 153<br>• "To date environmental risk costs have derived mostly from fines from non-compliance, Superfund and asbestos liabilities, and individual incidents like the Exxon Valdez oil spill. While these costs have been substantial (see Anderson, 1996), it is the author's opinion that they are the tip of a potential iceberg of future environmental risk costs. If environmental risk management systems are not in place to assess and control these risks, property, liability, and other risk costs could be enormous.", P. 160<br>• "GM [genetically modified] crops have been marketed by seed companies and used by farmers for their superior characteristics over traditional crops. These characteristics included better yields, lower costs, less chemical use, and pest resistance.", P. 162<br>• "As the set of future potential benefits greatly exceeds the documented benefits of GMOs, so too does the set of future potential risk greatly exceed the documented risks of GMOs. With both benefits and risks we are working in the realm of the potential and the unknown. Huge uncertainty and unpredictability are present, which of course create risks within themselves. In addition to involving the typical risks of injuries and property damages, potential risk of GMOs include cultural, ethical and religious ramifications, the unpredictability and potential irreversibility of genetic pollution, as well as reputational and regulatory risks and the business risk that consumers may refuse to buy GMO products", P. 163<br>• "The rising concentrations of $CO_2$ which are causing global warming principally come from energy production, factories, homes, automobiles, and deforestation. Rising $CO_2$ concentrations are a symptom of expanding economies, jobs, and standards of living.", P. 170<br>• "As with GMOs, a wide variety of risks emanate from confirmed global warming. Most of the risks are potential or estimated. A considerable amount of uncertainty and unpredictability exists as to how precisely global warming risks will develop over the next century.", P. 170 |
| **Problems of P/C Insurance market** | • "The most obvious specific risk of global warming is the property risk. Risk mangers with properties in areas vulnerable to hurricanes, storms and floods, property insurers for both homeowners and commercial properties, federal flood insurance officials, catastrophe reinsurers, and property insurance brokers and consultants all need to be alert appropriate mitigation and financing strategies as well as disaster planning schemes need to be put in place. Capital markets dealing with catastrophe bonds, catastrophe options and exchanges, weather derivatives, and carbon trading mechanisms all will be affected by global climate change. Life and health insurers, healthcare providers, and government officials will need to adjust to changes in disease patterns and temperature stress conditions", P. 175 |
| **Risk management measures** | • "Union Carbide, following the Bhopal catastrophe, instituted a "Root Cause Analysis" on all significant spills and accidents to help prevent recurrence (Hilton and Marlin, 1997)", P. 157<br>• "…companies like International Paper and Westvaco that have eliminated elemental chlorine in their paper-bleaching mills (Hilton and Marlin, 1997). By eliminating the elemental chlorine environmental risk "upstream", it will not be present to cause environmental costs "downstream".<br>• "For instance, industries are developing new technologies to reduce the generation of hazardous waste, and more industries are treating hazardous wastes on site, rather than shipping wastes to disposal sites (Yuill, 1997)", P. 157<br>• "Chlorofluorocarbons (CFCs) and dichlorodiphenyltrichloroethane (DDT) are examples of environmentally harmful substances that have been removed from business processes and products in many countries. Their removal required direct regulation because it was so difficult to identify the specific responsible parties (manufacturers, users) with the environmental harm (ozone depletion, decreasing bird population). For those unregulated substances that are potentially harmful to the environment, loss-control expertise could be applied to assist in developing techniques for the removal or reduction of such substances from business processes.", P. 158<br>• "Avoidance is a risk management control tool that often cannot be utilised for obvious practical reasons. […]. On the other hand, avoidance can be a very practical tool for developers and users of GMO technology, as firms have a choice. For instance, earlier in this article, Gerber, Heinz, McDonald's, and Frito-Lay were discussed regarding their decisions to discontinue using GM ingredients in their foods. ", P. 168<br>• "Ford Motor Company belongs to an organisation called the U.S. Council for International Business, which supports Preident Bush's decision to reject the Kyoto accord. Volvo, which is now owned by Ford, has publicly supported the Kyoto Treaty before being acquired by Ford in 1999", P. 173 |
| **Open scientific questions** | "The increasing importance and development of environmental risk management will require the talents of individuals in the risk management and insurance industries. The business opportunities for risk managers, insurers, brokers, consultants, and academics are enormous. It will take some thinking outside of the box but risk management training and techniques are particularly well suited to developing effective and efficient environmental risk management strategies", P. 177 |

| | |
|---|---|
| **Article** | **Global Financial Architecture: Implications for Regulation, Supervision and Accountancy Issues** |
| **Author** | Hans-Jürgen Schinzler |
| **Journal / Publication** | The Geneva Papers on Risk and Insurance – Issues and Practice Vol. 27 No. 1, P. 1 – 15 |
| **Publication date** | January 2003 |
| **Examined questions** | "There are different aspects to the subject of international financial architecture: implications for regulation, supervision and accountancy. For that reason, it is all the more important to look at the background issues and to examine the point the discussion has reached so far.", P. 1 |
| **Emergence of increasingly complex and bigger corporate structures** | • "The widespread popularity and implementation of the "shareholder value approach" in corporate management, combined with a greater awareness of equity capital costs, is forcing market participants to engage in extremely opportunistic finance management practices", P. 2<br>• "The value chain in the global financial architecture is being redefined. On the one hand, specific market participants are concentrating on special segments, which they service using optimized structures for costs and performance. On the other hand, there is a process of market convergence and market transparency as a result of the alignment of finance management sectors. Commercial banks, investment banks, asset management and insurance companies are examining and implementing ways of jointly servicing the market.", P. 2<br>• "Standardisation and reporting requirements: if there is a standard approach for calculating group solvency, as in the European Union, then logically one report, e.g. from the parent company, should suffice and this report should be addressed to the supervisory authority in the home state (of the parent company); …", P. 3<br>• "As already mentioned, the subject of accounting standards is a crucial one: management, shareholders, analysts and supervisors all need reliable, up-to-date information to help them make decisions.", P. 3<br>• "For the fact is that fast close cannot function, at least not in large companies that operate on an international level, if the latter are confronted in every country with different accounting and valuation regulations, different disclosure rules and different supervisory requirements. In theory, it seems a perfectly simple process to record each set of information once on a uniform worldwide IT system and then to present it in different ledgers so as to meet requirements for local reporting, for the balance sheet, for tax purposes, for the various supervisory authorities and for group accounting purposes. In practice, however, it is an extremely complex, time-consuming and costly process. In my opinion, what we need is not just global standardisation, but also simplified accounting standards and a much more efficient reporting system to the supervisory authorities.", P. 4 |
| **Development of risk potential in positive and negative direction** | • "The number and dimension of global risks will continue to grow. The events of the past year have further underlined the importance of carrying out a professional evaluation, and of adopting a hedging strategy, for risks that were unknown up to now.", P. 2 |
| **Problems of P/C Insurance market** | • "Some of the developments that have an impact on the insurance side originate from banking supervision and relate to questions of financial stability, or else they stem from the supervision of financial conglomerates. If uniform standards are developed for banks (e.g. for capital adequacy), this often prompts the question of whether there is something similar for insurance companies. And if not, this is immediately seen as a shortcoming in the system and criticised accordingly.", P. 3<br>• "The WTC loss has cost the insurance industry an enormous amount of money. Can it be right to pay the money that is required to meet this loss from taxed reserves, even though we know from experience that large and very large losses, from whatever cause, always occur again, although fortunately not on a regular basis?", P. 5 |
| **Risk management measures** | "Following the Enron investigation, the SEC drastically reduced the accounting deadlines for filing quarterly and annual reports. Reporting duties which become too burdensome could have a detrimental effect on the quality of the data. I believe that there is an area of conflict, or even a conflict of interests between:<br>o the scope and complexity of reporting;<br>o the quality of the date; and<br>o the time that is available to draw up the reports.<br>The acceleration of reporting is certainly in the best interests of companies; in markets that change rapidly, the survivors will be those who know at all times how they stand andhow matters may develop. Fast close is, therefore, an understandable matter of concern. Fast close, however, means not just optimised processes and systems, and having the financial resources to create them. Fast close also requires well-trained staff who knows what they are doing. Above all, it demands the right prerequisites. Specifically, this means an appropriate and co-ordinated regulatory framework established by governments, standard-setting bodies and supervisory authorities.", P. 4 |
| **Open scientific questions** | |

| **Article** | **Insurance, Risk Management and Culture** |
|---|---|
| **Author** | Walter R. Stahel |
| **Journal / Publication** | The Geneva Papers on Risk and Insurance – Issues and Practice Vol. 27 No. 2, P. 268 – 274 |
| **Publication date** | April 2002 |
| **Examined questions** | "The third millennium has engraved itself in the history books right from the start under the heading RISKS. But what are the lessons from history that historians will draw 50 years from now?", P. 268 |
| **Emergence of increasingly complex and bigger corporate structures** | |
| **Development of risk potential in positive and negative direction** | • "11 September 2001, the date of "Attack on America", is one milestone. It has meant an unexpected and brutal discontinuity of life for New York and the U.S., but not only that. It has also shown the vulnerability of our Western society, which relies on high technology and fears violence.", P. 268<br>• "The old view that only nature can cause major catastrophes had to be revised over night, in the sense that it is people who are the biggest risk factor. The second lesson is that the biggest catastrophe imaginable has to be taken into account for future risk and technology assessment. It is no longer the biggest possible accident which needs to be considered in assessing possible losses; the worst possible case that can be imagined now has to be accepted as a potential reality", P. 269<br>• "Biological weapons, such as contamination with anthrax, are only a small example of homemade weapons open to any small laboratory worldwide involved in life sciences or biotechnology.", P. 270<br>• "It [the September 11th terror attack] has demonstrated the helplessness of modern technology in fighting cultural issues. Stealth bombers and tomahawk cruise missiles are of no use in combating the determination of people armed with pocket-knives.", P. 269<br>• "At stake are not only new technologies, but also the question of an upgrading of existing technology with high inherent vulnerability, such as nuclear power stations. The central issue is the quest for strategies for a safer world", P. 269<br>• "Similarly, the terrorists around Bin Laden used the internet for their communications, a technological development financed by the Pentagon during the Cold War with the specific objective that no one could control it", P. 271 |
| **Problems of P/C Insurance market** | |
| **Risk management measures** | • "One conclusion is therefore that the problem of culture, and promoting cultural ecology, should be given much greater attention by politicians.", P. 272 |
| **Open scientific questions** | "For insurance, financial services and risk management, this means that the discussion on sustainability has to be much broader than the present focus on sustainable investments and global warming.", P. 274 |

| | |
|---|---|
| **Article** | **Are Formal Risk Assessments of Any Use?** |
| **Author** | Mark Jablonowski |
| **Journal / Publication** | Risk Management, August 2002, P. 24 - 27 |
| **Publication date** | August 2002 |
| **Examined questions** | "The stakes of risk management decisions are higher than ever and thus these decisions need to be supported by a higher level of detail. Determining that appropriate level of detail is a matter of understanding and grappling with the uncertainties of probability that inevitably challenge the risk management profession.", P. 24 |
| **Emergence of increasingly complex and bigger corporate structures** | |
| **Development of risk potential in positive and negative direction** | |
| **Problems of P/C Insurance market** | |
| **Risk management measures** | • "To effectively use formal risk assessments, we must understand the numbers, any uncertainties surrounding them and what we can do about those uncertainties.", P. 26<br>• "A variety of risk assessment methods, in addition to intuition, can supplement statistical assessment of risk and support the much needed details of credibility to back a risk management decision.", P. 27<br>• "Scenario. Scenario-based methods construct a logical progression of loss event possibilities. For example, a fire exposure could be traced from its initiation (e.g., careless smoking) to possible outcomes. Along the way, probabilities of subevents (e.g., the functioning of sprinklers) are assessed. Ultimate fire damage outcomes are thus developed. The scenario-based approach avoids some of the problems of statistics because the probabilities of subevents can be calculated more accurately (e.g., there is considerable data for failure rates of sprinklers). Scenario-based assessments can push the credibility of our probability beyond the 10 percent threshold.", P. 27<br>• "Industry-wide data. Using industry-wide data in risk studies lends to their credibility. Greater statistical accuracy however, comes at the cost of relevance. As the range of the study grows, the similarity of generic data to that of the specific organization decreases. Few formal methods exist for enhancing an individual organisation's data to fit generic data. Those that do, such as Bayesian statistics, make strong theoretical assumptions that may or may not hold true.", P. 27<br>• "Consultants. In considering critical exposures and related risk management decisions, we may also seek outside help in both the methods of risk assessment and their application. We cannot, however, abrogate our responsibility for making adequate risk decisions on the part of the organization. That means knowing the weaknesses and strengths of outside consultants and their methods. The true value of an outside assessment of risk is in the genuine information it provides. This information should be considered an additional information source, to be combined with intuitive judgment. In judging the true worth of formal assessments, we must realize that such assessments do not supplant expert judgment, or vice versa.", P. 27<br>• "Treating Uncertainty. Formal assessments can be greatly improved if they explicitly incorporate uncertainty due to knowledge imperfections. This cannot be accomplished using the standard methods of probability and statistics. Confidence intervals assess uncertainty due to randomness in the sampling process; they do not address the idea of knowledge imperfection directly. The simplest way to suggest uncertainty due to knowledge imperfection is the use of intervals of uncertainty, suggested by the multiple plausible alternatives shown in Figure 2. The credibility of these intervals is judged by how well they let us deal with the real world. The balance is between specificity and truth. If data is scarce, and we create an exact estimate, it is less likely to be true.", P. 27 |
| **Open scientific questions** | • "A huge part of risk management is understanding and dealing with the unknown. Formal risk assessment methods help us realize what we do not know and what we do. The risk of being misled by false precision, however, remains very real.", P. 27 |

| | |
|---|---|
| **Article** | **The Complexity of Managing a Global Company: Regional Exposure vs. Global Exposure** |
| **Author** | Gérard de la Martinière |
| **Journal / Publication** | The Geneva Papers on Risk and Insurance – Issues and Practice Vol. 28 No. 1, P. 87 – 93 |
| **Publication date** | January 2003 |
| **Examined questions** | "The [insurance companies] experience of the last few years along with the combination of a very high technical loss and expense ratio and a serious financial crisis have raised new questions about the risks of globalisation", P. 87 |
| **Emergence of increasingly complex and bigger corporate structures** | |
| **Development of risk potential in positive and negative direction** | |
| **Problems of P/C Insurance market** | Insurance companies have to deal with the following benefits and threats:<br>• The benefits of globalisation<br>o Risk diversification […]<br>o The constitution of global business lines […]<br>o Optimisation of resource allocations […]<br>• The risks of globalisation<br>o The involuntary accumulation of exposure […]<br>o The risks of image contagion […]<br>o The complexity of global management […], P. 87 – 91 |
| **Risk management measures** | • "Insufficient recognition of group structures […] The follow-up of accumulated positions at group level, or the prevention of infectious and image risks, is such that new functions have to be created at the level of central HQ (ALM, risk management, fight against money laundering, etc.). Even if these functions are exercised in liaison with all the subsidiaries, the difficulty of assigning a specific service to each of them can make it difficult to cover the corresponding costs, whose sharing and justification must be very strict.", P. 91<br>• "Fragmentation of insurance supervision […] To avoid these drawbacks and prevent an increasing gap between the economic reality of international companies and the monitoring system which should assess the risks of their activities, in-depth reforms are necessary. In the European area, prudential legislation should be fully standardised and implemented in a closely co-ordinated way, as proposed for some time by the European Insurer's Committee. An additional stage would consist of devoting specialised teams to the supervision of insurance groups and, as such, exonerating them from the fragmentary supervision of each Member State.", P. 92<br>• "Adaptation of insurance accounting standards […] In view of economic globalisation, the need for a universal standard to report the results of insurance groups is becoming urgent:<br>• the effective comparability of performance conditions, access to the capital markets, and the best allocation of resources in terms of the specific quality of structures and profits.", P. 92 |
| **Open scientific questions** | "New economic and social prospects on a global scale, new company management in order to take on the challenge of internationalisation, and a new approach by politicians to the follow-up of multi-national groups will guarantee progress in optimising the allocation of resources to all clients and partners of the company.", P. 93 |

| | |
|---|---|
| **Article** | **Liability and Insurance after September 11: Embracing Risk Meets the Precautionary Principle** |
| **Author** | Tom Baker |
| **Journal / Publication** | The Geneva Papers on Risk and Insurance – Issues and Practice Vol. 27 No. 3, P. 349 – 357 |
| **Publication date** | July 2002 |
| **Examined questions** | "My goal in this essay is to suggest how it might be that the insurance state spawned these seemingly contradictory reactions [Precaution and Embracing risk], how those reactions are in fact less contradictory than they at first appear, and what the embracing risk thesis and the precautionary principle might portend for liability and insurance after September 11.", P. 349 |
| **Emergence of increasingly complex and bigger corporate structures** | |
| **Development of risk potential in positive and negative direction** | • "We also discovered that our efforts to prevent loss had created new kinds and magnitudes of loss. The asbestos nightmare that still threatens workers, employers and the insurance industry is a leading example. Remember, asbestos was so ubiquitous because it prevented harm. Other people might point to the case of thalidomide, the HIV blood transfusion crisis, made cow disease or the threat of nuclear winter. In the financial markets, we might refer to Long-term Capital, the S & L crisis, and perhaps even Enron, though the latter may be more a story about a classic "pump and dump" stock fraud than of financial risk reduction gone bad.", P. 352<br>• "Yet, not all risk are the same. No, the answer to every potential loss is not the spreading risk approach of the past", P. 354 |
| **Problems of P/C Insurance market** | • "We need to recognise that competition on the basis of risk selection, especially in personal lines of insurance and perhaps more broadly, is destructive and often pernicious, except when risk classification sends a useful signal that insureds can act upon to prevent loss, to their and society's benefits.<br>• "Because of this development risk, liability insurers design insurance contracts so that they can run away from the loss at the earliest possible moment. As a result, limited liability and bankruptcy come to play too large a role in the management of development risk, so that victims do not in fact have the protection against loss that the law claims to provide them (cf. LoPucki, 1996)", P. 356<br>• "…'development risk' – the risk that a product will produce a kind of harm that is not foreseeable at the time of design but for which the manufacturer is liable under the principle of strict liability. If the risk is not foreseeable to the manufacturer, then it is not foreseeable to insurers, either. This means that liability insurance pricing is at best an estimate, coupled to the fervent hope that the good bets cancel out the bad and that the future will not be too different from the past", P. 356 |
| **Risk management measures** | • "First, insurance companies should adapt to increase the incentives for individuals and institutions to prevent harm while at the same time working together, through government regulation, to prevent the destructive competition and de-pooling that may otherwise result.", P. 356f<br>• "Second, insurance institutions should adapt to provide coverage for unpredictable loss by increasing the ability of insurers, or the system as a whole, to make assessments. That assessment element can come in the form of a government backstop, as developed, for example, in Florida following Hurricane Andrew and as suggested for terrorism. Or perhaps it will come in more creative ways that social scientists and lawyers will invent.", P. 357<br>• "…, the massive liabilities imposed on Dow Chemical because of silicon breast implants, despite the almost complete lack of evidence meeting traditional scientific standards that the implants in fact caused the chronic fatigue syndrome and other ailments they were accused of causing", P. 355 |
| **Open scientific questions** | "Reinventing insurance to prevent destructive competition and to legitimate and facilitate assessment present real challenges. But those challenges are no more difficult than those successfully surmounted by the architects and engineers of the insurance state that served us so well in the last century. So, fellow architects and engineers, let's get to work!", P. 357 |

| **Article** | **Fraud Risks in E-commerce Transactions** |
|---|---|
| **Author** | Wolfgang Wopperer |
| **Journal / Publication** | The Geneva Papers on Risk and Insurance – Issues and Practice Vol. 27 No. 3, P. 383 – 394 |
| **Publication date** | July 2002 |
| **Examined questions** | "In Europe, the volume of e-commerce transactions has been constantly on the rise throughout the past years. […]. The continuation of this promising development is endangered by the fact that Internet security breaches cost U.S.$15 billion in 2001 with an upward tendency in the future.", P. 383 |
| **Emergence of increasingly complex and bigger corporate structures** | • "In fact, many enterprises are concerned about the wrong issues. While the application of well functioning firewalls, intrusion detection and other technological measures are important, business practices and a perfectly working security policy are even more vital. Rules concerning Internet use, such as when employees may use the Internet for private purposes, which sites or classes of site they can or cannot access, can be established. Unlimited use of the Internet can increase security risks.", P. 384 |
| **Development of risk potential in positive and negative direction** | • "Many companies have neglected the importance and application of the security technology available. Furthermore, too little control is usually exercised by companies over their IT landscape. Web hackers have no problem finding and using the weak points within commercial sites, and easily access customer card information and other personal financial details", P. 384f<br>• "While e-commerce continues to grow, few people fully understand the risks involved. In a survey conducted by the British Association of Insurance & Risk Managers, risk managers who responded said that neither employee users nor management boards understand the risks associated with e-commerce and IT. There is also a belief that the insurance market does not fully understand the risks, which is backed by the contention of insureds that they are unable to obtain adequate insurance cover from them.", P. 384<br>• "Variety of risks endangering the transaction process: Theft of components […], Manipulation of software in components […], Installation of contaminated software […], Weak points in hardware and software […], Loss of stored data […], Manipulation of stored data […], Misuse of distant maintenance access points […], Duplication of money units […], Re-entry of outdated data […], Pretence of being an authentic communication partner […], Pretence of being a serious communication partner […], Non-acknowledgement of data […], Risks that are inherent in the transmitter medium […], Faulty transmission […], Incoherence through faulty transaction finishing processes […], Spying out cryptographic codes […], P. 385 – 387<br>• "We are still on the brink of the e-commerce revolution, and Internet security and fraud are issues that will not go away. It is of vital importance that more and more effort is made to achieve security that is as perfect as possible, which in the long term could be more valuable than marketing and other expenditure spent on acquiring customers", P. 392f<br>• "The Internet is an open net and the principle that "nothing is secure on the Internet" continues to be valid. Encryption methods can substantially increase the security of money transactions on the Internet but cannot grant full security.", P. 393 |
| **Problems of P/C Insurance market** | • "Even if the insurance industry is increasingly making use of the Internet for marketing its products and some companies also offer the online conclusion of motor and accident policies, companies do not yet meet the insurance needs of customers using the net for their business transactions. Insurers are faced with two main problems. On the one hand, a statistical database is non-existent, while on the other the legal issue is not restricted to one country and moreover not clear.", P. 392 |
| **Risk management measures** | • "The following case was reported by the police in Heidelberg, Germany. Swindlers ordered from a computer company goods valued at some millions of euros. The company delivered at once and never received the payment due. The gangsters hardly left any trace. All information that they gave to the e-mail server was incorrect. Personal data mostly is not verified by the companies that offer online services. Many of them only check if the data given are plausible and could theoretically be correct. At the German police academy in Freiburg, the police are learning how they can trace the perpetrators in such cases through communication protocols of e-mail service companies and access providers.", P. 388<br>• "If consumers' data become accessible, for example, you need a rapid way of identifying what the fault is and where its origin lies. Regular testing of security systems is necessary to ensure that all systems are working properly and no violations have taken place. Encryption disguises data in a way that protects anyone from reading it without the respective key. In principle, an encrypted credit card number cannot be read without the key to unencrypted it. The most sophisticated type of encryption is Public Key Infrastructure as well as digital signatures.", P. 389<br>• "Amongst insurers, the Cologne-based Gerling Group has taken the position of a forerunner with its "Trusted Shops" which is a joint venture with a consulting company. "Trusted Shops" was created in late 1999 in close co-operation with consumer protection agencies and with the support of the European Commission. Amongst other features like certification of online-shops and various customer services, "Trusted Shops" offers a money-back guarantee (underwritten by Gerling) to online customers. All participating shops have to meet strict demands as to data security and delivery, and to refund payment to the customer in the event of non-delivery or return of goods within due time. Moreover, it requires the supplier to provide the customer with a contact person if problems should arise, price transparency, general terms and conditions of trade that are easy to understand, as well as prompt customer service. The concept is completed by a close co-operation with the French company "Paybox" which has developed a payment method on the Internet in which the online order is confirmed by an automatic telephone call-back carried out by "Paybox", which acts as an intermediary. The program is installed on the server of the supplier and ensures that there has been communication between the customer and the "Paybox" server validating the order and about the willingness of the customer to pay. "Paybox" applies data security and encryption standards coding the number of the supplier, the order number, amount and currency, and the customer's e-mail address, which are all transmitted in a secure process. The system of "Trusted Shops" is maybe the only one whose success can be proved by figures so far. Renowned international companies are members of "Trusted Shops". By October 2001, more than 250,000 customers had already used "Trusted Shops"; 250 online shops were already certified, and another 180 were in the process of certification. More than 1,000 buyers a day with a purchase volume of €130 on average register for the money-back guarantee. "Trusted Shops" is active at international level, among others in major European markets like the U.K., France and Germany.", P. 389f<br>• "In the middle of 2001, Visa International launched a program to increase Internet security by impeding access to stored data by hackers. The so-called "Account Information Security Programm" (AIS) defines strict security standards for the storage and use of customer data on Internet sites. Since 1 November 2001, all Internet dealers and service providers have had to match these new security standards which include, among other elements, the allocation of customer-related passwords, secure encryption of data, and the existence of firewalls for access to the Internet.", P. 391 |
| **Open scientific questions** | "It will be a vital challenge for the insurance industry to close the hopefully few remaining security gaps through specialised insurance covers that match the multiple demands of Internet traders and customers.", P. 393 |

| | |
|---|---|
| **Article** | **Does WTC Matter for the Investment Policy of P / C Insurance Companies?** |
| **Author** | Paul M. Achleitner, Jörg H. Biebel and Daniel Wichels |
| **Journal / Publication** | The Geneva Papers on Risk and Insurance – Issues and Practice Vol. 27 No. 2, P. 275 – 282 |
| **Publication date** | April 2002 |
| **Examined questions** | |
| **Emergence of increasingly complex and bigger corporate structures** | • "Due to globalisation, the world economy has become highly interconnected with production networks and supply chains around the world. Extraordinary natural catastrophes might also have the potential to indirectly disrupt economic activities on a significant global scale, in addition to their direct damage impact.", P. 279 |
| **Development of risk potential in positive and negative direction** | • "A major earthquake or hurricane in a region with clusters of globally interconnected businesses (e.g. Silicon Valley, the metropolitan area of Tokyo, or the semiconductor industry in Taiwan) could potentially have very similar effects on the capital markets. Being exposed to the residual risk via capital market investments creates the danger of cumulated risk towards single dramatic events, thereby increasing the probability of ruin. These risks would not be adequately captured by an independent analysis of underwriting and investment risks.", P. 279 |
| **Problems of P/C Insurance market** | • "The attack on the World Trade Center (WTC) had a serious double impact on insurance companies, revealing a significant correlation between the asset and liability sides of their balance sheets. Insurance companies that previously considered themselves well capitalised, suddenly felt vulnerable to simultaneous shocks to their risk-absorbing capital. The unprecedented simultaneous shock challenges the previous investment assumption of P/C insurers that there is no major relation between underwriting and investment risks.", P. 275<br>• "As with most catastrophic events, from a financial perspective the focus during the tragedy has been primarily on the impact on the liability side of the balance sheet.", P. 275<br>• "The unprecedented simultaneous shock on both the asset and liability sides has shown a degree of correlation between investment and underwriting risks that was previously unrecognised.", P. 275<br>• "As a consequence, a systematic asset liability management (ALM) has not played a key role in structuring investment portfolios [of P / C insurers] so far.", P. 276<br>• "As terrorist attacks unlike natural disasters may be frequent and incalculable, government intervention might also be required to this end in order to solve otherwise 'uninsurable risks' (e.g. in the airline industry).", P. 277<br>• "However, the combined effect of these two shocks led to a severe testing of their risk-absorbing capacity for many insurers. Insurance companies which previously considered themselves well capitalised suddenly felt vulnerable to simultaneous shocks to their absorbing capital from the investment and underwriting side. With respect to major catastrophes P / C insurers might have to review the relevant investment assumption to disregard a major relationship between their balance sheet sides and to restructure their current investment approaches.", P. 277f<br>• "In a sense, WTC can be seen as a catalyst bringing forward some of the changes already underway in the investment attitude of P / C insurance companies.", P. 279<br>• "However, the vulnerabilities revealed in the prevailing business model of P / C insurance companies might be more far reaching, increasing the potential for substantial consequences well beyond the pure underwriting of insurance coverage.", P. 282<br>• "There are plausible arguments that these considerations might eventually reduce the 'risk appetite' of P / C insurers, with potentially far-reaching implications. With respect to the industry, a lower portion of equity investments and corporate bonds and therefore a higher share of government bonds could lead to a more regular investment income. However, this will have a potential P & L impact by limiting the ability to counterbalance volatile underwriting results through the steering of realised investment income. With respect to the capital markets, the more conservative 'risk appetite' might reduce the overall demand for equity by insurance companies, thereby potentially changing the composition of the institutional ownership profile in the capital markets, both in general and for specific securities.", P. 282 |
| **Risk management measures** | • "The overall value proposition of any investment policy for P / C companies is to optimise capital management by explicitly considering any potential correlation between investments and underwriting. General principles have already been well established by extensive work on ALM procedures for life insurance companies. Those applications can principally be transferred to P / C insurance companies. In a general structure, underwriting insurance risk represents the core competence of an insurance company and should therefore constitute the starting point for the investment portfolio construction. The structure of the insurance portfolio yields the necessary risk capital and establishes a transfer portfolio representing the maturity structure of expected cash outflows. Any deviation from the transfer portfolio represents an ALM mismatch which has to be supported by risk capital that has to be charged correspondingly. The riskiness of the deviation has to be determined based on possible correlation between the mismatch and insurance events on the liability side.", P. 280<br>• "Likewise, the overall aim of investment management, to safeguard the fulfilment of insurance obligations, requires a deeper understanding of the risk structure underwritten. At the same time, the investment process becomes noticeably more complex as detailed investment guidelines are necessary to implement the allocation restrictions in a dynamic environment.", P. 282 |
| **Open scientific questions** | |

| Article | The Public Role of Insurers in Man-Made Catastrophes | OECD Economic Outlook |
|---|---|---|
| Author | Gordon Stewart | |
| Journal / Publication | The Geneva Papers on Risk and Insurance – Issues and Practice Vol. 27 No. 2, P. 288 – 294 | Volume 2002/1, No. 71, June |
| Publication date | April 2002 | June 2002 |
| Examined questions | "This paper looks at the enormity of this disaster primarily from the communications experience of the Insurance Information Institute.", P. 288 | "…the OECD Economic Outlook analyses prospective global and country-specific economic trends over the period 2002 to 2003 in the context of a world economy which is progressively returning to growth after a relatively short and shallow economic downturn.", P. iii |
| Emergence of increasingly complex and bigger corporate structures | | "An important risk arises from the implications of impaired profitability and highly-leveraged balance sheets for corporate investments. In the United States, despite easy monetary policy, many corporations appear to have been forced out of the commercial paper market into the bond market. While this helps to lock in rates and extends planning horizons, such a shift may also be raising the cost of capital, especially in circumstances where the Government is now competing more actively for funds.", P. 26 |
| Development of risk potential in positive and negative direction | | "A very different tension lurking in the background is that created by the risk of further terrorist attacks. As noted in the previous OECD Economic Outlook, policy-makers reacted promptly and vigorously to the 11 September aggression and, combined with the resilience of the private sector, this helped to limit the short-run impact of the shock. Further attacks cannot be ruled out, however, and despite the ongoing efforts to be better prepared fur such emergencies, they could have serious disruptive effects. Over the long run, the heightened terrorist threat may have some lasting, if diffuse, macroeconomic effects.", P. 29 |
| Problems of P/C Insurance market | "The experience of the Insurance Information Institute from Hurricane Andrew through September 11 demonstrates that the media's portrayal of insurance in a major crisis is the biggest single factor in the industry's public standing. This occurs because the insurance industry receives its highest amount of coverage during a period when the largest numbers of people are paying attention. Most important, it is the industry as a whole that is judged by the general public, not simply individual companies. If a particular firm or sector does poorly, it will drag down the perception of the whole, which is usually identical to the element with the lowest public approval. Therefore it is essential that a unified, organised, alert, aggressive and sustained communications effort be put in place. This cannot be summoned out of thin air when a catastrophe strikes. Since the news media is always among the first on the scene, crisis communications work must begin immediately and continue long after the initial drama. Acting quickly to explain a disaster's implications and reaching out to the victims and their families are important first steps.", P. 293 | • "Primary insurers and reinsurers are now facing the complex task of pricing the risks related to terrorism, which is difficult not least because it involves "correlated risk", i.e. the possibility that several catastrophic events occur simultaneously. With time, however, insurance companies will become better equipped to model "patterns" and risks of terrorist attacks, much as they already do for natural catastrophes.", P. 126<br>• "…, the use of mechanisms to transfer insurance risks to the financial markets could also play an important role in increasing coverage against terrorism. The market for insurance bonds – sometimes known as "catastrophe bonds" – launched in 1996, has remained thin, as the fear of information asymmetries reduced demand and the availability of cheaper sources of finance discouraged issuance from insurance companies.", P. 126<br>• "Overall, even though it has been hit by the largest amount of reimbursements ever recorded, the insurance industry has escaped bankruptcy, and some large reinsurers are still able to distribute dividends to their shareholders.", P. 127<br>• "More worrying is the shrinkage of coverage for commercial properties deemed too risky and for terrorism risk altogether.", P. 128<br>• "Government involvement is likely to be especially justified in the case of potential losses arising from mega-terrorism (such as a nuclear attack), which is typically excluded from standard insurance policies.", P. 128 |
| Risk management measures | "Problems also arise from not listening closely enough to critics and failing to communicate what is being done clearly enough and long enough. The industry learned this the hard way with poor response to disasters such as the 1991 Oakland, California fires. We also learned that if long-term strategic communications planning is combined with honest, aggressive implementation, then a disaster – man-made or natural – can affect insurance positively for many years.", P. 294 | • "Crisis management played a key role after 11 September to restore confidence, safeguard the financial system and avoid a self-fulfilling depression. Decisions taken by the Federal Reserve, other central banks and governments were essential in this respect. One lesson of this crisis is that when policymakers have to take rapid decisions in an environment of deep uncertainty and imperfect information, priority ought to be given to liquidity management.", P. 118<br>• "In reaction to the attacks, the insurance industry raised its premiums, reduced coverage and called on governments to step in and cover risks deemed too large for the private sector. Indeed, risks related to terrorism are difficult to price, not least because of the possibility that several catastrophic events occur at once (correlated risk). However, private sector initiatives specifically tailored to provide insurance for this type of risk are emerging.", P. 118<br>• "Mega-terrorism risk poses special challenges that cannot be fully addressed by the private sector and may require international action.", P. 118<br>• "In view of this [Mega-terrorism is a terrorist attack with the help of atomic or biological weapons in densely populated areas], preparedness should be seen as essential, even if the possibility of such an attack is considered as remote.", P. 120 |
| Open scientific questions | | |

| | |
|---|---|
| **Article** | **The Aftermath of September 11: The Impact on and Systematic Risk to the Insurance Industry** |
| **Author** | Jozef De Mey |
| **Journal / Publication** | The Geneva Papers on Risk and Insurance – Issues and Practice Vol. 28 No. 1, P. 65 – 70 |
| **Publication date** | January 2003 |
| **Examined questions** | • The article analysis the effects of the September 11 terror attacks on the insurance and reinsurance industry |
| **Emergence of increasingly complex and bigger corporate structures** | |
| **Development of risk potential in positive and negative direction** | • "The third effect on the insurance industry, and probably the most profound has been the change in perception of terrorism risk. Until September 11, risks associated with terrorism had not been considered very relevant by the industry. Cover for such risks was implicitly included in many types of policies without any explicit premium. This has changed, probably forever, due to the events of September 11.", P. 67<br>• "…, a more important and lasting effect of September 11 has been the discovery of a new type of terrorism. The scale of the terrorist acts of September 11 was not considered probable, and created new boundaries around insurable terrorism risks. Terrorism on a scale like that of September 11 does not meet two of the basic criteria of an insurable risk:<br>o both the probability (frequency) and the severity of losses (maximum possible and now probable loss) of events like these cannot be quantified; and<br>o terrorists acts are by nature not random.<br>• Furthermore, the potential damage of terrorism of a war-like scale is virtually unlimited, whereas as stated earlier the potential financial capacity of the private insurance industry is in principle limited.", P. 67 |
| **Problems of P/C Insurance market** | • "Although it has been demonstrated that the industry can absorb such a claim and that it is able to recapitalise itself back to, at least pre-September 11 levels, we should be aware that the industry is not capable to absorb multiple events such as those of September 11. The financial capacity of any industry is in principle limited.", P. 66<br>• "A second almost direct effect has been an increase of reinsurance premium across many lines of business. The sudden drop in capacity and the 'flight to high quality reinsurers' were the main drivers for the said increase.", P. 66<br>• "One could therefore conclude that indirectly September 11 has pushed general insurers to focus on their core business.", P. 68<br>• "September 11 has also reinforced the perception that due to the correlation of both insurance and financial risks, a sudden extreme event could set in motion a 'domino-like' collapse of a large segment of the insurance sector. This risk can be considered the systemic risk of the industry.", P. 68<br>• "It should also be mentioned that other problems which where dormant before September 11 have surfaced and been dealt with. The tragic events of September 11 served as an excuse. The structural problems of the airline industry are a clear illustration: if the industry had been financially sound before September 11, it could have dealt better with the sudden drop in air travel", P. 69<br>• "There are similar examples in the insurance industry. We have seen rate increases in direct insurance and reinsurance business lines that are basically unrelated to terrorism risk, but which had structure profitability problems. The events of September 11 have been the catalyst to revive much-needed disciplined underwriting and pricing.", P. 69 |
| **Risk management measures** | • "Industries like property development and air travel cannot function properly without cover against claims resulting from terrorism. The corporate sector has started to look for alternative solutions, an example being The Association of European Airlines which launched the idea to set up a terrorism insurance fund (Eurotime) to be financed by levying a small fee per ticket. Similar initiatives emerged in the chemical industry and elsewhere. But these types of industry-specific mutual schemes seem not to be an adequate long-term solution if they are not backed by public funds.", P. 67<br>• "In view of the uninsurability of this new form of extreme terrorism, the involvement in one form or another of governments as 'insurers of last resort' seems the only long-term solution. The 'Pool Re' solution implemented in the U.K. in 1993 after a series of IRA attacks, has pointed the way forward. Insurers providing cover in the U.K. on certain business lines can reinsure terrorism risks with Pool Re, which reinsurers itself with the U.K. Government. Now also France, the GAREAT, and Germany with Extremus AG, have introduced similar combined public / private schemes", P. 67<br>• "The fall of equity markets following September 11 and again during the second quarter of 2002 has done serious damage to the financial health of general insurers and reinsurers As profitability can no longer depend on continuous capital gains on their equity portfolios, insurers and reinsurers will need to focus again on their core underwriting and claims management skills while at the same time improving their efficiency.", P. 70 |
| **Open scientific questions** | |

| | |
|---|---|
| **Article** | **Risk Management: From Portfolio Strategy to Value-creating Systems Strategy** |
| **Author** | Eskil Ullberg, Enrique Rodriguez and Nils Stormby |
| **Journal / Publication** | The Geneva Papers on Risk and Insurance – Issues and Practice Vol. 27 No. 3, P. 467 – 476 |
| **Publication date** | July 2002 |
| **Examined questions** | • "In this article we will explore three issues that we have found increasingly relevant to managing risk in today's economies and businesses. We will end the article with some conclusions related to how to create customer value from managing opportunities today where risk management plays a key role in realising a profitable business.", P. 468 |
| **Emergence of increasingly complex and bigger corporate structures** | • "The driving factors for economic growth are today enabling and "forcing" change in value and wealth creation in a way that has not been seen since the early days of the industrial revolution. The most significant of theses factors are, as we know: new technologies, globalisation of markets and deregulation of markets. During the last two decades also Intellectual property rights (IP) have become key strategic issues for market access to many companies. All these represent new market opportunities for growth.", P. 468<br>• "Unfortunately there are also some more negative aspects connected to the new opportunities like possible climate changes and other macro factors that are a consequence of the industrial revolution and increased globalisation, but they also represent new markets like management of environmental systems.", P. 468<br>• "These driving forces put the actual value creation process under pressure for change in an increasingly complex situation: more and bigger actors, larger and freer markets, etc. than say, more than 100 years ago when the industrial revolution was steaming ahead.", P. 468<br>• "Investments in information technology, which also is a service enabler of high potential, have skyrocketed and accounted in 1999 for 4 to 5 per cent of GDP in the leading IT countries.", P. 469<br>• "The states become market actors in the knowledge economy by regulating an infrastructure that in turn enables new value-creating logic. This infrastructure is different from the industrial infrastructure regulations where the focus has been on the 'distribution of wealth created in factories' rather than on the creation of wealth in a co-production way with the clients or users", P. 469<br>• "The transition to a 'knowledge', 'information economy' or 'service economy' becomes more and more obvious and demands a serious approach theoretically, conceptually and with regard to risk.", P. 471<br>• "Driving forces (IT, globalisation and deregulation) force economic actors to take more risks to be competitive as well as to develop competencies to master them.", P. 476 → **See Kloman** |
| **Development of risk potential in positive and negative direction** | • "The challenge in taking advantage of the new opportunities for value and wealth creation thus force economic actors to take more risk to be competitive as well as to develop competencies to be competitive as well as to develop competencies to master them.", P. 468<br>• "A conclusion could be that to be successful in the new more competitive and performing economic system the macro driving forces bringing new opportunities to create value and wealth force market actors to take more risk with respect to:<br>o New technology and the 'information highway', which involves systems risk (such as availability and stability), security and information safety risks;<br>o Globalisation includes political risks, cultural risks, etc.;<br>o Deregulation means new market risks, bigger markets, etc.;<br>o Risk due to activities spread out physically, in space, between actors and co-production partners and in time (a change in business logic);<br>o Other factors like climate means that natural resources may be destroyed.", P. 472 |
| **Problems of P/C Insurance market** | |
| **Risk management measures** | • "This leads us to the conclusion that when increased uncertainty is introduced in the offering the potential of the knowledge economy can be harnessed using the service logic for value creation only of management of the risk becomes an integral part of the offering. This means that economic actors must include risk management as part of their offering. That means rethinking the business model. Risk management activities can be introduced in at least two ways: managing the client's risks by taking over full responsibility and control of the client's process (relieving the client), or enabling the client to manage its risks in its value creation for its customers. In the first case this could be done in the form of an outsourcing strategy or operator strategy. In the second you give tools, information, to the user of your products or services to better manage the risk involved in using them in creating value.", P. 474 |
| **Open scientific questions** | |

| | |
|---|---|
| **Article** | **Insurance Technology Strategy: Time to Re-evaluate** |
| **Author** | Ronald Pressman |
| **Journal / Publication** | The Geneva Papers on Risk and Insurance – Issues and Practice Vol. 28 No. 1, P. 39 – 64 |
| **Publication date** | January 2003 |
| **Examined questions** | "Are insurance companies positioned to take advantage of the latest advances in technology? In this mature industry, technology can be a significant lever for growth. The vital element to developing a technology strategy, and the using it to its utmost potential, is a continuous evaluation and alignment.", P. 39 |
| **Emergence of increasingly complex and bigger corporate structures** | |
| **Development of risk potential in positive and negative direction** | "Because of the constant patches and 'quick fixes', the mainframes create an environment rife with opportunity for potential hackers.", P. 40 |
| **Problems of P/C Insurance market** | • "Because business leaders invest so much time, energy and money on legacy systems, leadership teams are reluctant to invest in the latest and best systems. It has come to a point, however, where it is more expensive to ignore the technology than to invest in new systems, perhaps even abandoning the legacy technology.", P. 39<br>• "Still, the industry struggles to find the most effective way to employ the new technology. In eagerly accepting mainframe systems when they first hit the market, insurance businesses were burned. Now, these same businesses need to re-evaluate IT budget spending to avoid being burned again.", P. 39<br>• "Essentially, the insurance industry started jumping aboard a ship that was not fully prepared to set sail. Leaders at most insurance companies were eager to buy the biggest and best mainframes, now called legacy systems.", P. 40<br>• "The insurance industry, in many ways, is paying the price for being a technological pioneer. Companies starting up today have the opportunity to do things right. Older insurance companies are carrying around baggage that they need to get rid of, and get rid of fast. And it is starting with the standardisation of data across the industry.", P. 40<br>• "Simply investing in a technology strategy or web-enabling tool, however, is not enough. Businesses need to be results-oriented and data-driven. If the data is not there, the strategy suffers – there is no execution. The critical question insurers must ask is how their spending priorities and level of investment are impacting their business. The entire insurance industry is about data. Insurers must be timely, precise and strategic in this fundamental industry niche of data analysis. Can insurers afford not to provide their knowledge workers with the right tools?", P. 42 |
| **Risk management measures** | • "Recently one of six nominees for an e-Fusion Award, REGAL is an online system that allows ERC to generate life and health reinsurance quotes for customers 24 hours a day, seven days a week. Customers download the ERC software and then access the quotation system online. ERC launched the program to ten strategic customers in the Middle East during the summer of 2001. The long-term goal is to process 75 per cent of policies online, which are currently manually processed by fax and mail. This will eliminate 75 per cent of the opportunities for manual touch-point errors! The REGAL technology improves process efficiency by using web-based technology, improving quotation cycle time from days to seconds. The marketing tagline for REGAL is '48 hours to 48 seconds'. REGAL also improves productivity by allowing ERC to reach customers in different time zones at their convenience. Essentially, this project changed the way GE ERC transacts business in the Middle Eastern market. Customers have been impressed with the dramatic process improvement. ERC customers report that REGAL gives them nimbleness and versatility, enabling them to offer alternatives easily to their customers.", P. 46<br>• "ERC is also realising success with its Global Claims Induction project. A historically manual, paper-intensive process, claims processing is now completely digitised at ERC. The web-based solution leverages digital imaging technology and automated tools to convert claims documents into images and instigate workflow tasks, without human intervention. Claims are received electronically, reviewed and automatically linked to ERC's customers' system to automatically triage and dispatch claims documents to the appropriate claims adjudicators around the world. Once claims adjusters review the digital document, the information is automatically fed to ERC's payment systems and a check is issued (assuming it was a claim requiring payment). More opportunities for manual errors are eliminated. Everything from the date and time the claim data was received to the time the check was printed, is captured in ERC's global data warehouse. Within the global data warehouse, the data is electronically sorted and analysed. Results provided in the form of digital "cockpits" or gauges display the collected data in the form of usable statistics and metrics. Through digital cockpits, ERC employees graphically illustrate how the business is performing against the claims processing goals. Digital cockpits enable employees to access data real-time and drill-down capabilities to help ERC control processes and ensure that customers' expectations are met, consistently and accurately. Global Claims Induction has enabled ERC to provide the global claims team with digital information anywhere, anytime. The project has also been beneficial for ERC customers, who have the advantage of quicker decisions, consistent and on-time payments, and greater access to ERC's global expertise.", P. 46 |
| **Open scientific questions** | "Among the challenges facing the industry, key will be the ability to deploy technology at the right levels and against the right initiatives. Businesses must use technology to quickly build the platforms that will support strategies around customer retention and profitability. Time is of the essence.,", P. 47<br>How sophisticated are today's solutions? How easy are insurers to do business with? Technology holds nearly limitless possibilities to drive our industry toward an era of consistent growth.", P. 47 |

| | |
|---|---|
| **Article** | **Climate Change, Extreme Events and the Canadian Insurance Industry** |
| **Author** | Rodney White and David Etkin |
| **Journal / Publication** | Natural Hazards 16: 135 – 163, 1997 |
| **Publication date** | August 1997 |
| **Examined questions** | • "At the same time that a scientific consensus has arisen that the world will most likely experience a changing climate in the near future, with more frequent extreme events of some weather hazards, the insurance industry, worldwide, has been hit with rapidly escalating costs form weather–related disasters. This conjunction of scientific belief and economic impact has raised the questions as to (1) whether more frequent extreme events have contributed to the rising insurance costs and (2) how will future climate change affect the industry?", P. 135<br>• "The purpose of this paper is to explore the implications of climate change for the insurance industry (with particular reference to Canada) by reviewing industry losses to extreme weather within the context of how these weather extremes may vary in the future.", P. 136 |
| **Emergence of increasingly complex and bigger corporate structures** | |
| **Development of risk potential in positive and negative direction** | • "Though it is unclear whether or not the recent insurance losses are related to a statistically significant increase in extreme weather events, they do point out the sensitivity of the industry to weather. If, indeed, climate change will result in a greater number of weather disasters, then the insurance industry cannot afford to take a 'wait-and-see' position with regard to climate change.", P. 136<br>• "In one sense, coping with natural hazards is like a game (the Natural Hazards Game). Once you know the rules, you can devise a winning strategy. If the chances of good or bad events occurring are fairly well known, then the tradeoffs can be calculated with some level of comfort. But what if after playing the Natural Hazards Game for some time, it turned out that the rules were about to change? Not only that, exactly when and how they were going to change, or precisely what the new rules would be was not know? Even worse, the new set of rules would not be constant, but would evolve over time, and not planning for them could result in 'losing' the game. That is what climate change does to the Natural Hazards Game.", P. 137<br>• "Though a change in mean, such as average precipitation, can be hazardous in the sense that it represents a change from what society has adapted itself to, it is possible that the greatest impact of climate change will be due to increases or decreases in the frequency of extreme events. A discussion of the effect of a changing climate on extreme events can be read in 'Climate Models-Projects of Future Climate' (IPCC, 1995), the conclusions of which are in agreement with this discussion.", P. 139<br>• "The relevance of climate change to natural hazards is that the frequency of extreme events may increase, and thus current adaptation measures may prove to be less adequate than at present.", P. 139<br>• "Trends are most likely to occur in the frequency of heat and cold waves, followed by more frequent convective storms and floods. Drought is also expected to become more frequent, though confidence is not as high for this hazard.", P. 148<br>• "With climate change is expected to come more frequent flooding, more droughts and quite possibly more hailstorms and tornadoes, and it is likely that losses will increase in the future.", P. 152<br>• "One last trend – which we will call 'coastalisation' – is further concentrating people in high risk areas as they move to the coast in search of economic opportunity, recreation or retirement. […]. The coastal movement began in the United States at the early part of this century and the same trend is now gathering momentum in China. Thus, it is a phenomenon which is prevalent for natural hazards because of their vulnerability to storms, tsunamis and flooding (as well as earthquakes). If sea-level rise continues (as is predicted by the models of the enhanced greenhouse effect) this will further increase the risk.", P. 156<br>• "As the implications of global warming become clearer, the victims of climate change and variability will find it difficult to put claims to their insurer on the assumption that the storms are both sudden and unpredictable.", P. 158 |
| **Problems of P/C Insurance market** | • "Any assessment of risk, such as done by the insurance industry for natural hazards, that is based upon the assumption that the climate is constant is likely to be in error, perhaps seriously so. For this reason the insurance industry should not simply use past experiences as a guide to the future.", P. 140<br>• "The seriousness of this predicament has not convinced the insurance industry as a whole to advocate mitigation of greenhouse gas emissions. As in other economic sectors, opinion is divided.", P. 153<br>• "…, yet the only companies to call publicly for a reduction in greenhouse gas emissions are the major reinsurers based in Europe (Munich Re, 1996; Swiss Re, 1994).", P. 153<br>• "Right now, neither the insurance industry nor governments are prepared for climate change.", P. 155<br>• "The highly competitive nature of the [insurance] industry drives 'cycles' of underwriting which force premiums down to the point where companies exit the industry as losses mount, and then premiums rise again to cover the losses.", P. 158 |
| **Risk management measures** | • "One option for the industry would be to assist in educating the public and the politicians to understand the need to reduce greenhouse gas emissions as speedily as possible. Other efforts should go into monitoring and research activities that can enable us to adapt to the climate changes to which our actions have already committed us. The first issue for all players in the industry (and its regulators) to face is that climate change will increase the level of uncertainty. Accepting this proposition will require traditional responses such as reserve accumulation, loss reduction and so on. ", P. 159 |
| **Open scientific questions** | |

| | |
|---|---|
| **Article** | **On the Implications of the Internet for Insurance Markets and Institutions** |
| **Author** | James R. Garven |
| **Journal / Publication** | Risk Management and Insurance Review, 2002, Vol. 5, No. 2, 105 – 116 |
| **Publication date** | 2002 |
| **Examined questions** | • "This article focuses specifically on the implications of the Internet for insurance markets and institutions.", P. 105 |
| **Emergence of increasingly complex and bigger corporate structures** | |
| **Development of risk potential in positive and negative direction** | |
| **Problems of P/C Insurance market** | • "In insurance, firms are beginning to offer a wide array of online services, including online sales, needs analysis, and customer service (e.g. online policyholder account information, claims management and processing, and group insurance certificates). Coupled with other important trends such as globalisation and regulatory reform, these developments are forcing far-reaching changes upon the insurance industry and making it more competitive.", P. 105f<br>• "When Charles Schwab, Inc., first came on the scene in the early 1980s, many predicted the demise of full-commission stockbroker firms. The discount broker concept introduced competition into an industry that didn't have much of it, and the brokers who have survived have repositioned themselves in terms of the products, services, and pricing that they offer to their clients. There is every reason to believe that the Internet will have a similar impact on agents and brokers in the insurance industry. If anything, the Internet will create an added competitive pressure that, in combination with other market forces, will ultimately improve the quality of the services provided by the agents and brokers who survive.", P. 111<br>• "Network effects are also an important feature in the convergence of financial services. Since banks and brokerages naturally tend to have higher transactions volumes than insurers, it is not surprising that bank and brokerage Web sites tend to be much more highly utilised than Web sites offered by insurance companies. […]. Consequently, banks and brokerages have an easier time getting their marketing messages in front of Internet users than do insurance companies. This makes it very attractive for banks and brokerages to add insurance to their online product portfolios and, conversely, this makes it very attractive for insurers to ally themselves with highly trafficked financial Web sites operated by banks and brokerages that are interested in outsourcing insurance services.", P. 112<br>• "The professional literature is virtually unanimous about the cost advantages for insurers selling over the Internet.", P. 112f<br>• "As e-commerce becomes more fully integrated into insurers' business practices, it will provide researchers with opportunities to empirically measure the extent to which e-commerce affects insurance costs and insurer profitability. With the higher degree of competition brought about by e-commerce, we would expect to see any revenue, cost, and profit differentials between the various forms of insurance distribution become further minimised.", P. 114<br>• "Furthermore, by reducing transaction costs, e-commerce will cause insurance products and services to become even more highly intermediated than they are currently; thus new intermediaries will come into being. E-commerce will also have important implications for product design, thus giving consumers more flexibility in managing their risks.", P. 114<br>• "E-commerce also presents opportunities and challenges for regulators. By making it easier for consumers to compare prices and product attributes across insurers, e-commerce should enhance the private market's ability to resolve informational asymmetry problems that exist between policyholders and insurance companies. To the extent that e-commerce enhances the informational efficiency of insurance markets, this will likely weaken the case for price and policy form regulation. The good news for insurance regulators is that this will likely free resources that can instead be focused on addressing market conduct and solvency issues.", P. 114f<br>• "If the regulatory system cooperates by allowing the private market to pass these cost savings on to consumers, insurance will be better able to live up to its potential as a mechanism for not only funding the costs of accidents but also providing society with better incentives for loss prevention and mitigation.", P. 115 |
| **Risk management measures** | |
| **Open scientific questions** | |

| | |
|---|---|
| **Article** | **Mapping the New Political Risk** |
| **Author** | John Minor |
| **Journal / Publication** | Risk Management, March 2003, P. 16 – 21 |
| **Publication date** | March 2003 |
| **Examined questions** | • "This framework definition [of political risk] – the specifics of which are debated – covers political actions that have varied depending on the location and the era.", P. 18 |
| **Emergence of increasingly complex and bigger corporate structures** | • "Political risk is the threat that social, political or economic factors in a foreign country may affect the feasibility and profitability of an organisation's global operations. Sources of political risk can include frequent or unexpected government changes, shifts in government policies, economic instability, nationalisation, privatisation, civil unrest, endemic corruption or a lack of infrastructure.", P. 18<br>• "Prior to 1985, political risks centred largely on post-colonial declarations of independence, civil wars and left-wing takeovers. The newly formed nations would confiscate or nationalise any foreign investors' properties, declaring an end to exploitation and the start of national sovereignty.", P. 18<br>• "But despite the drama of the terrorist threat that any global company – but particularly U.S. interests – must contend with, it would be a mistake to overlook the insidious political risks that may gradually chip away at an organisation's international operations.", P. 21 |
| **Development of risk potential in positive and negative direction** | • "Although the losses remain, the sources of loss have changed. The risks are gradual – subtle developments in a foreign country that could go unnoticed (and a company go unprotected against them) until they surmount into a crisis situation. Political risk today rarely arises from the direct action of a host government to drive investors from the country. Expropriation is now a risk from local or regional politicians rather than the new head of state, as governments decentralise their power structure", P. 19<br>• "Change of government – whether voluntary or not – is another potential source of political risk. A change of government in the emerging markets could result in bad monetary policy, a deterioration of the country's balance of payments or the politicisation of contracts with foreign investors. In several of the emerging markets, new governments today are more likely to negate an agreement than confiscate assets.", P. 19<br>• "Governments also engage in selective protectionism – the unfair use of political influence (most often in court rooms or local legislatures) against foreign investors. In India, for example, an investor was forced to pull out after incurring $26 million in losses, largely from politically motivated lawsuits. Developing-country legal and regulatory systems tend to exhibit corruption, political influence and antiforeign bias. In countries where local authorities are both the owners of key corporations and the regulators of market competition, problems of this kind can be severe.", P. 20<br>• "The most drastic and far-reaching political risk has been the devastating economic downturn around the globe – and the potential of a world-wide recession. In fact, a series of economic and currency crises that hit a number of the emerging markets during the past decade were responsible for some of the largest political risk insurance claims in history.", P. 20<br>• "September 11 and the United States-led war on terrorism have brought a new dimension to the political risk concerns of the future. The potential and past threats are tragic and dramatic. […]. This intense environment, combined with worldwide economic crises, may very well bring political risk management back to its past – dictable attacks and total losses.", P. 21 |
| **Problems of P/C Insurance market** | |
| **Risk management m easures** | • "A few basic techniques to mitigate political risk include:<br>○ Contractual undertakings with the host governments. Although contracts cannot prevent a government from exercising its sovereign rights to change laws and policies, they can establish a right to compensation if the government makes such changes to the detriment of investors. Enforcement may be assisted by an agreement to refer disputes to international arbitration. Governments may also waive sovereign immunity to the enforcement of such awards in national courts.<br>○ Involving local private interest. Local joint venture partners can help to navigate the local political scene and may be in a position to exercise more influence over government policy making. More importantly, governments are less likely to act to the detriment of enterprises if doing so would harm significant local interests. Joint ventures with the government are less desirable. Historical analysis suggests that public/private joint ventures are more, not less, likely to be subject to expropriation and that such joint ventures may perform less efficiently than even wholly government-owned enterprises. The government's roles as owner, operator and regulator are easily blurred.<br>○ Community relations. Common measures include educating the public on the benefits of foreign investment and the role of the private sector in providing previously public services. Schemes to promote social welfare (schools, hospitals, etc.) and rural development can be helpful.", P. 20f |
| **Open scientific questions** | |

| | |
|---|---|
| **Article** | **Multinational Insurance Groups: The Main Problems for Supervisors** |
| **Author** | Giovanni Manghetti |
| **Journal / Publication** | The Geneva Papers on Risk and Insurance – Issues and Practice Vol. 27 No. 3, P. 310 – 319 |
| **Publication date** | July 2002 |
| **Examined questions** | • "This contribution examines the problems posed by a multinational insurance undertaking exclusively from the perspective of supervision.", P. 310 |
| **Emergence of increasingly complex and bigger corporate structures** | • "The presence of non-homogeneous financial activities within groups poses even weightier challenges for supervisors. The monitoring of financial conglomerates' soundness shows further complex problems of a technical and organisational type, the former due to the different banking/financial and insurance risk profiles, the latter due to the presence of different supervisory authorities not only from a territorial, but also from a sectoral viewpoint. In particular, from a technical viewpoint the following problems are worth mentioning:<br>○ The definition and application of the methods for assessing the conglomerate's solvency. This operation is more difficult, due to the different regulations on own-funds elements and capital requirements in the various sectors;<br>○ The verification of intra-group transactions in order to limit the risks of:<br>▪ Conflict of interests;<br>▪ Contagion;<br>▪ Regulatory arbitrage;<br>▪ Lack of transparency in the conglomerate's financial structure.<br>All these risks play a major role within conglomerates rather than in homogeneous groups.", P. 316<br>• "To sum up we can say that multinational group structures are one of the major challenges for supervisors and increase the need to work on aspects that go beyond the use of technical supervisory tools.", P. 317 |
| **Development of risk potential in positive and negative direction** | |
| **Problems of P/C Insurance market** | • "The ways in which an insurance undertaking can pursue its multinational activity are:<br>○ (a) directly from its head office by way of free provision of services;<br>○ (b) by way of establishment (through a branch);<br>○ (c) through subsidiaries or joint ventures (group structures).", P. 310<br>• "The harmonised supervisory framework of the Member States has introduced the principle of the single licence: an undertaking can pursue insurance business in another E.U. country both under the right of establishment and of free provision of services exclusively on the basis of the authorisation granted by the home country supervisor and subject to the conditions required in the same country. As to the multinational activity pursued through group structures, it must be said that each company is subject to the supervisory system of the country in which it is registered. The supervisory authorities of the Member States have, concerning the single entities of the group and, in particular, of the instruments of supplementary supervision especially devised to take account of the effect of group structures on the undertaking's situation.", P. 310<br>• "Multinational insurance groups: the main problems for supervisors<br>○ Transparency in the group's structure and activity<br>Having decided that the institutional aim of supervision over insurance undertakings is the protection of the interests of policyholders and third parties, we cannot leave out the potential risks arising out of the fact that the company is part of a larger group of undertakings with different positions on the market. [...]<br>○ Adequacy of management and internal control<br>Groups of undertakings are aggregations of entities that are legally autonomous yet placed under the unified management of the parent company. That is why in economic terms we often refer to groups as a particular structural organisation of the undertaking. Therefore the decision-making bodies and the control systems go beyond the borders of the single undertaking and country. [...]<br>○ Intra-group transaction and concentration risks<br>Another supervisory problem of paramount importance in case of insurance undertakings belonging to a group is the control over intra-group transactions concluded by the supervised undertaking with other subsidiaries of the same parent company. These transactions entail a number of risks which must be kept in due consideration by the supervisory authority.<br>○ Capital adequacy<br>Finally we move on to what is perhaps the most important problem within the framework of prudential supervision over an undertaking belonging to a group: the assessment of its solvency. In this case it can be a rather limited, if not misleading, approach to break up the focus of supervision with the legal boundaries of each entity of the group. In fact, the stability of the insurance parent company as the ultimate economic unit can be threatened despite satisfactory solvency conditions at the individual level.", P. 312 |

| **Article** | **Multinational Insurance Groups: The Main Problems for Supervisors** |
|---|---|
| **Risk management measures** | • "In the case of multinational groups, the application of these measures always calls for the contribution of all the authorities responsible for the supervision of each undertaking in the group. In the absence of close co-operation between authorities, even the theoretically more incisive interventions, both administrative and based on moral suasion, end up losing their effectiveness or may even lead to undesired effects. This co-operation between authorities should be based on the following pillars.<br>o Mutual understanding of the supervisory approaches and methods and sharing of supervisors' needs [...]<br>o Utmost collaboration [...]<br>o An efficient co-ordination of the supervisory action [...]", P. 314f<br>• "A mutual recognition of the different approaches is necessary in order to try and reconcile the applications of regulations, which vary from country to country, to very well integrated and unitarily managed groups. In this field harmonisation that can be realised through the issuing and adoption of IAIS principles, standards and guidelines represents the way forward.", P. 317<br>• "To tackle the risks connected with intra-group transactions in Italy there is a provision according to which undertakings must inform ISVAP of their intention to effect significant transactions with other undertakings of the same group. ISVAP has the power to prohibit the transaction if it may undermine the interests of policyholders. In all cases in which the counterpart in the transaction is an insurance company situated in another state or an undertaking in any way connected to it, co-operation with the authority responsible for the said company is indispensable to ISVAP's preliminary investigation.", P. 318 |
| **Open scientific questions** | |

| Article | Cyberattacks Prompt Response to Security Threat | Combating International Corruption and Fraud |
|---|---|---|
| Author | Morgan O'Rourke | W. Michael Kramer |
| Journal / Publication | Risk Management, January 2003, P. 8 | Risk Management, March 2003, P. 40 |
| Publication date | January 2003 | March 2003 |
| Examined questions | | • "Recent studies by the World Bank and other groups have found that corruption and fraud in many parts of the developing world is 'endemic', 'systematic' and 'pervasive', the norm rather than the exception.", P. 8 |
| Emergence of increasingly complex and bigger corporate structures | "Also, public companies tend to experience more attacks than private, nonprofit or government entities.", P. 8 | • "Corruption and fraud far outstrips the resources marshalled against it. In many parts of the third world, it is expected and dealt with on every project. Billions of dollars and thousands of projects are at risk. Unless more is done, corruption will threaten the reputation of and continued funding from international investors, the development and stability of the poorer countries, and even the security of the West, as corruption contributes to the poverty an despair that helps fuel international terrorism.", P. 8 |
| Development of risk potential in positive and negative direction | • "On October 21, 2002 hackers launched an unprecedented assault on the Internet's thirteen core servers. Using a method called distributed denial of service, the assailants inundated the servers with traffic, intending to overwhelm and disable the networks. Had it worked, this would have created a traffic jam capable of stopping all Internet activity from e-mail to e-commerce to simple Web surfing. While the attack was largely unsuccessful, cyberattacks, in general, have never been more prevalent.", P. 8<br>• "The assertion has been supported by the Riptech Internet Security Threat Report conducted by Riptech, Inc. of Alexandria, Virginia. It found that attack activity in a six month period ending June 2002 was 28 percent higher than activity recorded in the previous six-month period.", P. 8<br>• "Part of the problem may stem from the fear of reputation damage for companies that address the issue, implying that they have a problem. Of course, damages to reputation would likely pale in comparison to the damage of an actual security breach.", P. 8 | |
| Problems of P/C Insurance market | | |
| Risk management measures | • "The education effort may be the most important factor of the legislation. According to study by The St. Paul Companies of St. Paul, Minnesota, U.S. companies continue to underestimate risks involved with e-commerce and do not adequately train employees to deal with them. Risk managers at many companies have insufficient knowledge of technology-related risks, generally leaving that concern to information technology managers. As a result, only about half of risk managers surveyed have reviewed their existing insurance policies to determine their level of coverage for Internet liability exposure.", P. 8<br>• "Education and the use of best practices are likely the best steps towards addressing Internet security risks. This includes sitting down with IT managers as well as educating what Rodhe calls 'the weakest link' in company's cybersecurity spectrum – the employees. 'One of the first risk management focuses they need to take is educating the employees on the do's and don'ts and the possible implications to the company.'", P. 8 | "Projects at risk for corruption are difficult to investigate because of the lack of public records, shortage of competent professionals, multitude of jurisdictions involved and other barriers. However, investigations are possible.<br>o Exercise audit clause rights. [...]<br>o Investigate and analyse the net worth of suspect employees. [...]<br>o Obtain relevant financial records from the suspect employee. [...]<br>o Use international investigative consultants. [...]", P. 8 |
| Open scientific questions | | |

| | |
|---|---|
| **Article** | **Haftpflicht 2003 – Europa: Welche Deckungssummen wurden abgeschlossen?** |
| **Author** | |
| **Journal / Publication** | Marsh Studie |
| **Publication date** | 2003 |
| **Examined questions** | • „Die im Folgenden präsentierten Ergebnisse unserer Haftpflicht-Studie liefern nützliche Benchmark-Informationen über die von vergleichbaren Unternehmen abgeschlossenen Haftpflicht-Deckungssummen. Angesprochen werden einige der wichtigsten Themen, mit denen sich Versicherungseinkäufer bei der Einschätzung des Risikos von schuldhaft verursachtem Tod oder Körperverletzung Dritter auseinandersetzen sollten. Im Vordergrund steht dabei die Frage: welche Deckungssumme ist ausreichend?“, P. 1 |
| **Emergence of increasingly complex and bigger corporate structures** | • „Die Bestimmung geeigneter Deckungssummen ist nicht einfach, vor allem wenn es um die Absicherung von Verlusten geht, die für Unternehmen [...] langfristige finanzielle oder sogar existenzbedrohende Auswirkungen auf die Bilanz des Unternehmens haben könnten. Dabei spielt die Höhe der verlangten Prämien bei Kaufentscheidungen eine größere Rolle als die verfügbare Kapazität [...]“, P. 1<br>• „Geschworenenurteile bei Zivilprozessen, Gruppenklagen, Erfolgshonorare, punitive damages (Schadenersatzansprüche mit Strafcharakter), Klagen in Höhe von mehreren Millionen Euro und von Geschworenen festgelegte Urteilssummen – all dies sind typische Merkmale der US-amerikanischen Haftpflichtszene. Angesichts der Tatsache, dass fast 25% aller EU-Waren in die USA exportiert werden, müssen sich betroffene europäische Firmen der Auswirkungen dieser Faktoren auf ihre eigenen Versicherungsprogramme bewusst sein.“, P. 19 |
| **Development of risk potential in positive and negative direction** | • “[...] generell gilt, dass größere Unternehmen oder Betriebe mit hohem Risikopotential (wie z.B. Chemie oder Pharma) höhere Deckungssummen abschließen. Dennoch sind auch viele kleine und mittelständische Betriebe Risiken ausgesetzt, die zu beträchtlichen Haftpflichtansprüchen führen können. Weil einige Branchen offensichtlich gefahrenträchtiger sind als andere, besteht die Herausforderung darin, sämtliche Risiken zu analysieren, die potenziell mit hohen Schäden verbunden sind. Nicht nur große Unternehmen erleben große Schadenfälle – ein teurer Schaden kann für einen kleinen oder mittelständischen Betrieb im Verhältnis weitaus katastrophalere Folgen haben.“, P. 1<br>• „Terrorismusschäden können in Haftpflicht- (auch Exzedenten-Haftpflicht-)Versicherungen ausgeschlossen werden, und weltweit sind 43,3 Prozent der untersuchten Unternehmen davon betroffen. [...]. Viele Risikomanager beschäftigen sich bewusst mit der Frage, ob Versicherungsschutz gekauft werden sollte oder nicht, und lassen sich dabei von diversen Faktoren leiten, darunter z.B. zu hohe Prämien, knappe Kapazität oder auch ein relativ geringes Terrorismusrisiko.“, P. 4<br>• „Haftpflichtansprüche für finanzielle Verluste aufgrund von Produktmängeln sind häufiger geworden, wie auch reine Vermögensschadenansprüche einschließlich derjenigen aus der Berufs-Haftpflichtversicherung (E&O). Besonders drastisch ist der Anstieg bei Fällen medizinischer Fehlbehandlung. Im Januar 2003 wurde nach dem Rückzug zweier großer Versicherungen aus diesem Segment ein Pool gegründet, der insbesondere Gynäkologen, Chirurgen, Anästhesisten und vielen Krankenhäusern Versicherungsschutz anbietet, der auf keinen anderen Märkten erhältlich war.“, P. 6<br>• „Die Umtriebigkeit des amerikanischen ‚Plaintiff's Bar' in den USA (US-Kläger Anwaltschaft) sowie Erfolgshonorare und Gruppenklagen haben dazu geführt, dass Haftpflichtforderungen in den USA mit viel Nachdruck geltend gemacht werden. Zu den jüngsten Zielen gehören dabei Lebensmittelkonzerne und Fast-Food Ketten, die angeblich an den Gewichtsproblemen der Bürger mitschuldig sind. Bisher haben Gerichte derartige Klagen abgewiesen. Aber alle Unternehmen, die in den USA tätig sind, sollten wissen, dass ihnen ungeachtet des letztendlichen Urteils beträchtliche Verteidigungskosten entstehen können, die nur selten den erfolglosen Klägern auferlegt werden.“, P. 19 |
| **Problems of P/C Insurance market** | |
| **Risk management measures** | |
| **Open scientific questions** | |

| | |
|---|---|
| **Article** | **The Reactions guide to terror risk insurance** |
| **Author** | |
| **Journal / Publication** | Reactions.net.com (Internet report → No page references) |
| **Publication date** | 2003 |
| **Examined questions** | • "In this guide, we hope to highlight the benefits and potential difficulties TRIA [US Terrorism Risk Insurance Act] can present to the insurance industry. We also hope to clear up some of the confusion about what the Act does and which companies it affects" |
| **Emergence of increasingly complex and bigger corporate structures** | |
| **Development of risk potential in positive and negative direction** | |
| **Problems of P/C Insurance market** | • "The first big headache the industry encountered was that the moment President Bush signed the bill, insurers were suddenly exposed to billions of dollars of terrorism risk that they had excluded in the months after the September 11 terrorist attacks on the US. The Act immediately nullified any terrorism exclusions that had been put in place."<br>• "Under the terms of the Act, insurers have 90 days to notify policyholders that they are eligible for terrorism coverage and quote them a price. The policyholders then have 30 days to accept or reject the insurers' offers. But until they have received notice back from their policyholders, insurers are effectively providing terrorism coverage for free."<br>• "Not only is this placing a big administrative burden on insurance companies. It also means they now face the challenge of pricing terrorism risk - a task that has been deemed impossible by some. And if that were not enough, they need to do it quickly."<br>• "Some argue that even though the bill would protect insurers from financial ruin, it still means the industry must carry a large portion of the losses."<br>• "Rating agencies have been particularly critical of the new Act. They argue that because insurers are now exposed to risks they had excluded before, the risk profile of the industry has increased. Not only that, but it is a risk that no one has yet been able to quantify." |
| **Risk management measures** | |
| **Open scientific questions** | |

| | |
|---|---|
| **Article** | **Risk Analysis and Risk Management in an Uncertain World** |
| **Author** | Howard Kunreuther |
| **Journal / Publication** | Risk Analysis, Vol. 22, No. 4, 2002, p. 655 - 664 |
| **Publication date** | 2002 |
| **Examined questions** | • "How can we link the tools of risk assessment and our knowledge of risk perception to develop risk management options that are likely to be successfully implemented?<br>• What are the changing roles of the public and private sectors in dealing with these risks?<br>• How can we utilise lessons from dealing with past extreme events in helping to plan for the future?", P. 655 |
| **Emergence of increasingly complex and bigger corporate structures** | |
| **Development of risk potential in positive and negative direction** | • "The tragic attacks of September 11 and the ensuing bioterrorist threats associated with anthrax have raised a set of issues regarding how we deal with events where there is considerable ambiguity and uncertainty about the likelihood of their occurrence and their potential consequences.", P. 655 |
| **Problems of P/C Insurance market** | |
| **Risk management measures** | • "The field of risk assessment encompasses studies that estimate the chances of a specific set of events occurring and/or their potential consequences. For those like myself who are users rather than creators of risk assessments and vulnerability studies, we need to appreciate that most of these published papers represent the tip of icebergs – a 10-page article in Risk Analysis characterizing the likelihood of a nuclear power accident often represents the culmination of person-months or years of collecting and analyzing volumes of data.", P. 656<br>• "Scientists and engineers need to provide the users of these data with a picture of what is known regarding the nature of a particular risk and the degree of uncertainty surrounding these estimates, while at the same time being sensitive to their role as assessors of these estimates. Experts in the field need to take special care not to provide these estimates through the filter of their values.", P. 656<br>• "One way to capture what experts know and do not know about a particular risk is to construct an exceedance probability (EP) curve. An EP curve specifies the probabilities that a certain level of losses will be exceeded. The losses can be measured in terms of dollars of damage, fatalities, illness, or some other unit of analysis.", P. 656<br>• "A key question that needs to be addressed in constructing an EP curve for extreme events is the degree of uncertainty regarding both probability and outcomes. It is a lot easier to construct an EP curve for natural disasters and chemical accidents than for terrorist activities. But even for these more predictable accidents or disasters, there may be considerable uncertainty regarding both the likelihood of the occurrence of certain risks and the resulting damage.", P. 656<br>• "Risk management: In developing risk management strategies for reducing losses and providing protection against extreme events there is a need to incorporate the data from risk assessment studies and the factors that have been shown to influence risk perception. Since a number of studies indicate that people have difficulty processing data regarding low-probability events, this poses challenges for effectively communicating information on the risk to the public.", P. 659<br>• "Risk management approaches must recognize the difficulties that individuals have in collecting and analyzing data form experts.", P. 660<br>• "If the private sector feels it cannot provide insurance protection against losses from catastrophic events, then one may need some type of government pooling arrangement to cover theses losses. The Florida Hurricane Catastrophe Fund was established by Florida following Hurricane Andrew when a number of insurers claimed that they could not in the future include windstorm coverage as part of the standard homeowner coverage (Lecomte & Gahagan, 1998). After the 1994 California Northridge earthquake, insurers had similar reaction to providing earthquake coverage in California. In 1996, the state formed the California Earthquake Authority, which offers homeowners earthquake coverage as a separate polity (Roth, 1998). At the national level, a successful example of the use of an insurance pool is the one that provides coverage against losses from nuclear power plant accidents in the United States. Under the Price-Anderson Act, a group of private insurers agreed to provide coverage to utility companies for losses that can total up to $8.2 billion (U.S. Congress, 1995).", P. 661<br>• "To mitigate against the consequences of natural disasters one can build safer structures or move out of harm's way. In the case of chemical accidents, one can reduce the inventory level and/or production of specific toxins to lower the risk of another mishap occurring. When it comes to developing a strategy to reduce the risks of future terrorist activities, however we do not know who the perpetrators are, what their motivations are, the nature of their next attack, or where it will be delivered. Hence it is extraordinarily difficult to know what protective actions to take.", P. 662<br>• "There is an additional challenge associated with allocating resources for dealing with terrorism. Due to our deeply rooted fear, we may not adequately take into account the extraordinarily small likelihood that we will be impacted by a future attack. Hence the government invests huge sums of money in protection to provide reassurance. This may not be the most cost-effective way to utilize our resources. In this sense, Mayor Giuliani's constant reassurances to New Yorkers following the September 11 attacks on the World Trade Center may have done more to reduce the social amplifications of risk than millions of dollars of expenditures on pseudo-protective measures such as stationing the National Guard at airports and train stations.", P. 662<br>• "The same logic applies to the incentive of divisions of firms to invest in protection against a catastrophic accident that could bankrupt the entire organization. The actions of Nick Leeson and the trader he hired at the Barings Futures Singapore office were primarily responsible for bringing down Barings Bank. Arthur Anderson was sent into bankruptcy by the actions of its Houston branch. Both these examples illustrate this type of contamination. If a division knows that other divisions in the firm are not investing in protection, it has less incentive to incur these costs than if the other units were investing in safety measures. There may thus be a need for centralized organizational controls or third-party inspections from outside the firm to deal with this situation.", P. 663-664 |
| **Open scientific questions** | "In the light of the United States' recent responses to terrorism it is natural to ask the following:<br>• How much should we be willing to pay for small reductions in probabilities that are already extremely low?<br>• How much should we be willing to pay for actions that are primarily reassuring, but do little to change the actual risk?<br>• How can certain measures, such as strengthening the public health system, which provide much broader protection than terrorism, get the attention they deserve?", P. 662-663 |

| | |
|---|---|
| **Article** | **Ethics, Governance, Trust, Transparency, and Customer Relations** |
| **Author** | Henri de Castries |
| **Journal / Publication** | The Geneva Papers on Risk and Insurance – Issues and Practice Vol. 29 No. 1, P. 36 – 39 |
| **Publication date** | 2004 |
| **Examined questions** | • "This is what insurance is about. It is about paying for a protection against risk, that you are not sure you will be confronted with, but are fairly convinced that the protection that you have purchased is appropriate and will be operational if need be. The insurance industry is faced intrinsically with confidence and ethics issues: the only way for the insurance industry to play its role in society effectively is to prove that an insurance contract is not buying wind but creating energy.", P. 36 |
| **Emergence of increasingly complex and bigger corporate structures** | "As previously stated, insurance is very often an enabler of the economy (think of the protection of large risks for companies), yet one should not extrapolate to the insurer – payer paradigm. Otherwise, you run the risk of entering the deep pockets syndrome by which insurers should cover all risks (even foreseeable and not mutualisable) and this would be made at the detriment of trust: would you lend money to a casino gambler? Two specific areas, terrorism and medical insurance, have recently illustrated the difficulties in having governments play their roles while reaching consistent and sound solutions across the industry.", P. 38 |
| **Development of risk potential in positive and negative direction** | "As previously stated, insurance is very often an enabler of the economy (think of the protection of large risks for companies), yet one should not extrapolate to the insurer – payer paradigm. Otherwise, you run the risk of entering the deep pockets syndrome by which insurers should cover all risks (even foreseeable and not mutualisable) and this would be made at the detriment of trust: would you lend money to a casino gambler? Two specific areas, terrorism and medical insurance, have recently illustrated the difficulties in having governments play their roles while reaching consistent and sound solutions across the industry.", P. 38 |
| **Problems of P/C Insurance market** | • "The last three years have shown that winds can be capricious and have reinforced that need for solid windpumps. Whatever the circumstances, the client, when underwriting a policy, needs to be confident that:<br>o money will still be there if and when the risk arises (solvency issues);<br>o money will allow the risk to be covered adequately (profitability issues);<br>o claims will be paid (governance issues).", P. 36<br>• "Insurance needs regulation in order to work effectively: to set the rules of the game and to put all the players at the same level, in order to best protect clients' interests. Yet regulation might be at the price of ethics as illustrated by the vicious circle in Figure 2 (Regulation → Pressure on profitability → Fight for survival by all means → Less ethics → Loop)", P. 37<br>• "Over regulation brings more pressure and less accountability, hence more borderline decisions and less ethics, which in turn demands more regulation. Striking the right balance between regulation and accountability of the players is key to maintaining a steady equilibrium.", P. 38<br>• "Comparability of the players is one of the direct consequences of globalisation and the investors' quest for the best player. Yet insurance local regulations very often create local specificities, as illustrated recently by accounting of the equity assets following the sharp drop of the equity financial markets.", P. 38<br>• "The industry is also facing longer-term issues that do not require immediate action, but rather immediate action in order to build up sound and durable solutions:<br>o regulation consistency at the European / worldwide level versus over-regulation;<br>o regulation versus flexibility and reactivity;<br>o local regulation versus distortion of competition", P. 39 |
| **Risk management measures** | "The resolution of these issues lies in the hands of all the players, be it the regulators, the rating agencies or the insurers, in order to meet the stakeholders' (client, shareholder, employee) expectations. In order to work effectively, the insurance industry requires a clear, stable and agreed definition of rules, from the regulators (solvency, distribution issues) and from the accounting bodies and rating agencies. Internally, insurers need to gain full control of the value chain: from product pricing and reserving, to distribution through adequate risks, asset liability, solvency, capital management, and human capital management. This requires an appropriate combination of profitability mindset and ethics and a constant desire to protect the stakeholders' interests.", P. 38-39 |
| **Open scientific questions** | "Further questions that need to be addressed include:<br>• Are rating agencies an appropriate answer to customers' needs for better transparency?<br>• What should be the division of responsibilities in terms of prevention between governments and insurers? How can this be improved further?<br>• What kind of governance should be put in place at a group level to:<br>o optimise capital management?<br>o monitor risks better?", P. 39 |

| | |
|---|---|
| **Article** | **Insurance Economics and Legal Systems: The Treacherous Intersection of Insurance Economics and Today's Liability Systems** |
| **Author** | Walter B. Kielholz & Richard H. Murray |
| **Journal / Publication** | The Geneva Papers on Risk and Insurance – Issues and Practice Vol. 29, No. 1, 2004 |
| **Publication date** | January 2004 |
| **Examined questions** | • "Unfortunately, there is no such consensus when it comes to opinions about legal systems or insurance economics. Some people believe that traditional theories still drive the reality of events. It is like believing in the tooth fairy. The intersection where misperceptions about insurance meet false assumptions about legal regimes is, indeed, treacherous territory. It is treacherous for those seeking safe transit through the intersection, and treacherous as well for all who rely on the systemic integrity with which the intersection operates.", P. 1 |
| **Emergence of increasingly complex and bigger corporate structures** | |
| **Development of risk potential in positive and negative direction** | |
| **Problems of P/C Insurance market** | • "Consider asbestos liability claims, which have already rendered over 70 companies insolvent and threaten to ultimately generate damage awards and settlements of more then U.S.$ 250 billion. The original low-hanging fruit of asbestosis claims, on which the predators within the claimants' lawyers community has been feasting, is now dwindling. That is, the number of people made ill by asbestos is declining, and a few producers of the product are still solvent of the product are still solvent and around to pay claims. So the predators have, with the largesse of the American judiciary, found ways to establish liability without fault by successfully suing those who merely purchased properties containing asbestos products and to establish damages without harm by successfully recovering compensation for those who may have been exposed to asbestos but are not ill from it and are unlikely ever to become so.", P. 1<br>• "The insurance industry itself creates some obstacles to operate in accordance with these [insurance economics] principles. For example, cyclical pricing theory gets distorted by those who have learned how easy it is to capitalise a new underwriting entity, commit that capital to long-term volatile risks at uneconomic rates, reward themselves handsomely for the revenues generated, and let the entity collapse when claims mature.", P. 3<br>• "Today's liability regimes do not understand insurance. This is a more advanced condition in the U.S. than in Europe, but the disease is spreading. Judges and juries assume one of three things about insurance:<br>o It is a theoretically perfect system for spreading the cost of whatever damages they award throughout the economy, in a way that hurts no one.<br>o Juries sometimes take a slightly more sophisticated view. If insurance companies cannot recover all their losses through higher premiums, then it is only fair because insurance companies are fundamentally mean and evil and should be punished. A recent U.S. survey found that a total of one-third of the adult population thought insurance fraud to be quite acceptable – a view they bring with them to the jury box.<br>o Insurance funds come from another economic plane, somehow disconnected from the world of the injured parties to be compensated. This 'bottomless well of resource' school of thought is popular among judges who tolerate excessive compensatory and punitive damage awards.", P. 3<br>• "There is a similar problem running the other way: the insurance industry does not understand today's legal environment:<br>o An increasing portion of the output of the 'tort system' involves matters with no objective value. Is asbestosis worth U.S.$ 250 billion? What is the 'value' of claims against the directors of Enron, or of the auditors of Worldcom' Where is the 'objectivity' in a decision (by a judge in this case) that Phillip Morris should pay over U.S.$ 10 billion in punitive damages for attempting to convince smokers that mild cigarettes are less harmful than others?<br>o The rising costs of the tort system show now sign of being cyclical. At the rate of 14 per cent per annum, how long will it be before more money passes through the U.S. tort system than through its tax system? Leaders of European juridical systems and insurance companies need to be studying these trends closely. Otherwise the direction of the future is clear, even if the speed and size of the problem is not.", P. 4 |
| **Risk management measures** | |
| **Open scientific questions** | "The insurance cycle may be replaced by the final spiral, in which the responsibilities and opportunities of insurance and justice alike are consumed in the collision of misunderstanding and tooth fairy complacency. Surely, by focusing attention on the realities of life at the intersection, the public and private sectors together can make it once again safe for travel.", P. 4 |

# Appendix 4: State of the field research matrix for corporate knowledge management

| | |
|---|---|
| **Article** | **Knowledge management in organizations: examining the interaction between technologies, techniques, and people** |
| **Author** | Ganesh D. Bhatt |
| **Journal / Publication** | Journal of Knowledge Management; Kempston |
| **Publication date** | 2001 |
| **Examined questions** | "That the knowledge management process can be categorized into knowledge creation, knowledge validation, knowledge presentation, knowledge distribution, and knowledge application activities is argued.", P. 68-75 |
| **Corporate Knowledge Management – State of the field** | • "Both business and academic communities believe that by leveraging knowledge, an organization can sustain its long-term competitive advantages", P. 68-75<br>• "Researchers and academics have taken different perspectives on knowledge management, ranging from technological solutions to the communities of practices, and the use of the best practices", P. 68-75<br>• "For example, a majority of business managers believe in the power of computers and communication technologies in knowledge management, as they argue that information technology (IT) can provide an edge in harvesting knowledge from piles of old buried data repositories", P. 68-75<br>• "Some others, however, contend that knowledge resides in human minds and, therefore, employee training and motivation are the key factors to knowledge management.", P. 68-75<br>• "…,technologies and social systems are equally important in knowledge management.", P. 68-75<br>• "Defining data, information, and knowledge is difficult. Only through external means or from a user's perspectives, can one distinguish between data, information, and knowledge. In general, data are considered as raw facts, information is regarded as an organized set of data, and knowledge is perceived as meaningful information.", P. 68-75<br>• "The point is that the doctor moves back and forth, recursively, between data, information, and knowledge.", P. 68-75<br>• "because "data" for the doctor, in fact, become a critical part of the "information" for the specialist, which in part assists him (her) finding a useful pattern of the medical diagnosis (knowledge)", P. 68-75<br>• "However, organizational knowledge is distributed and scattered in different locations, embedded into different artifacts and procedures, and stored into different mediums such as print, disks, and optical media.", P. 68-75<br>• "In brief, knowledge management refers to changing corporate culture and business procedures to make sharing of information possible. It becomes as much a feat of developing technological solutions as working through the social and culture subsystems.", P. 68-75 → **Question: How can this be achieved?**<br>• "…, technical artifacts are enablers to organize data into information, and people are endowed with interpretative capabilities.", P. 68-75<br>• "an organization is […] a system of personal experience, social relations, and technologies.", P. 68-75<br>• "…the essence of offering a "meaning" depends on individuals.", P. 68-75 |
| **Knowledge-based risk management for complex corporations** | • "By focusing on knowledge management, we hope to strengthen the knowledge-based view of the firms.", P. 68-75<br>• "Organizational knowledge is formed through unique patterns of interactions between technologies, techniques, and people, which cannot be easily imitated by other organizations, because these interactions are shaped by the organization's unique history and culture.", P. 68-75<br>• "…the pattern of interaction between technologies, techniques, and people is unique to an organization that it cannot be easily traded in the marketplace and imitated by other organizations", P. 68-75<br>• "However, we do not recommend that, in every situation, an organization should create new knowledge from scratch. […]. For example, a firm may reconfigure and recombine existing pieces of knowledge, along with the strategy of imitation, replication, and substitution. In some cases, an organization may develop its competence by focusing on its capabilities and limiting its shortcomings.", P. 68-75 |
| **Suggestions for practical implementation of knowledge-based risk management** | • "Knowledge needs to be distributed and shared throughout the organization, before it can be exploited at the organizational level.", P. 68-75<br>• "…an organization should develop and nurture an environment of knowledge sharing, transformation, and integration between its members (Nonaka and Takeuchi, 1995)", P. 68-75<br>• "Certainly, as an organization becomes efficient in data processing, it can generate more information. […]. …, IT, at best, can be used as an enabler to turn data into information. It is only through people, that information is interpreted and turned into knowledge.", P. 68-75 → **Going a step further, the necessary consequences need to be drawn; This is where the role of the Risk Manager comes into play**<br>• "…,once a piece of knowledge no longer fits to the existing context, the organization should be swift to discard it from its knowledge base.", P. 68-75<br>• "…, IT can capture, store, and distribute information quickly, but it has its limit on information interpretation. Organizations which have been successful in obtaining long-term benefits from knowledge management, are found to carefully coordinate their social relations and technologies (Bhatt, 1998).", P. 68-75<br>• "In general, implementing knowledge management programs requires a change in organizational philosophy. For example, traditionally a number of companies collaborated on the basis of transaction cost economics; however, a knowledge management philosophy emphasizes learning collaboratively so that they can add more value to their products and services for the customers.", P. 68-75 |
| **Knowledge Management for Insurance companies** | |

| | |
|---|---|
| **Article** | **Managing organizational knowledge as a strategic asset** |
| **Author** | Audrey S. Bollinger; Robert D. Smith |
| **Journal / Publication** | Journal of Knowledge Management; Kempston |
| **Publication date** | 2001 |
| **Examined questions** | "According to the resource-based view of the firm (RBV), strategic assets are the critical determinants of an organization's ability to maintain a sustainable competitive advantage. This paper will combine RBV theory with characteristics of knowledge to show that organizational knowledge is a strategic asset", P. 8-18 |
| **Corporate Knowledge Management – State of the field** | • "Knowledge is a critical factor affecting an organization's ability to remain competitive in the new global marketplace. Organizations therefore need to recognize it as a valuable resource and develop a mechanism for tapping into the collective intelligence and skills of employees in order to create a greater organizational knowledge base. Knowledge management accomplishes this goal.", P. 8-18<br>• "There are two types of knowledge, explicit and tacit. Explicit knowledge is clearly formulated or defined, easily expressed without ambiguity or vagueness, and codified and stored in a database. Tacit knowledge is the unarticulated knowledge that is in a person's head that is often difficult to describe and transfer. It includes lessons learned, know-how, judgment, rules of thumb, and intuition (Grayson and O'Dell, 1998). There are so many nuances involved that it can be difficult, if not impossible, for individuals to describe what it is that they know. However, the sharing of tacit knowledge is a key characteristic of team-based, learning organizations.", P. 8-18<br>• "However, knowledge is not tangible, but it is measurable. An individual's knowledge is a part of who he or she is. Organizational knowledge is also intangible. It defines the organization, and is a reflection of the organizational culture.", P. 8-18 → **Measurability**<br>• "…,the goal of knowledge management for an organization should be to create a learning organization that is capable of measuring, storing, and capitalizing on the expertise of employees to create an organization that is more than the sum of its parts.", P. 8-18<br>• "…currently three major schools of thought on what knowledge management is<br>o an information technology issue, with networks of computers and GroupWare being the keys.<br>o more of a human resource issue with emphases on organizational culture and teamwork.<br>o the development of processes to measure and capture the organization's know-how.", P. 8-18<br>• "There are many techniques and technologies currently being used to manage knowledge. Some organizations are concerned mainly with capturing explicit knowledge and others are attempting to collect tacit knowledge through the use of expert systems and artificial intelligence. Knowledge-based systems (KBS) perform knowledge processing based on expert systems or deductive databases to help users find acceptable solutions to problems (Hayes-Roth and Jacobstein, 1994; Wielinga et al., 1997; Basu, 1998). This approach allows firms to capture knowledge by culling it from experts. Limitations to implementation include the need to overcome cultural barriers related to giving up information and relatively high expenses.", P. 8-18<br>• "It is difficult to codify tacit knowledge. In addition, knowledge is constantly changing both at the individual and organizational levels. The gap between what people actually do to perform their jobs and how it is documented is difficult to bridge due to the spontaneous actions people take in response to unexpected challenges and problems (Brown and Duguid, 2000). Knowledge bases that require a great deal of upkeep may tend to fall into disuse and decay due to obsolete information. Also, information taken out of context can be misleading and misinterpreted (Shum, 1997). Sometimes, too much information is available, and people are unable to assimilate it due to sheer volume and lack of appropriate tools. This results in information overload, frustration and demoralization.", P. 8-18<br>• "At the individual level, people are often reluctant to share information. Professional knowledge is perceived as a source of power (Quinn et al., 1996). There is a sense of worth and status to be gained because of expertise. People tend to have feelings of "ownership" and hoard knowledge (Cole-Gomolski, 1997). There can also be fear that there will be a diminished personal value after giving up know-how (Hibbard and Carrillo, 1998). In addition, competition among professionals can be intense. Many professionals have little respect for others outside their field. People are very mobile. Thus knowledge is volatile and vulnerable to loss (Jordan and Jones, 1997).", P. 8-18<br>• "Wiig (1997) has identified five strategies that are used by organizations to implement knowledge management systems:<br>o Some pursue knowledge as a business strategy, where the focus is on knowledge creation, capture, organization, renewal, sharing, and use at each point of action<br>o the focus on intellectual asset management such as patents, technologies, structural knowledge assets, customer relations, operations, and management practices<br>o focus on a personal knowledge asset accountability strategy. Here, each employee is responsible for his/her own knowledge-related investments, renewal of knowledge, and sharing of knowledge assets within the employee's area of accountability<br>o the knowledge creation strategy, with a focus on organizational learning, research and development, and employee motivation to innovate and learn<br>o the knowledge transfer strategy. Here the emphasis is on systemic approaches to transferring knowledge, such as acquisition, organization, restructuring, warehousing, and repackaging for distribution to the point of use. The specific method selected by an organization differs based on the individual business and its unique needs.", P. 8-18 → **All are important for Risk Management, with the last one being the most important for insurance companies**<br>• "… instead of being a management focus (e.g. chief knowledge officer), perhaps the coordination of a knowledge management implementation effort should be a human resources (HR) function.", P. 8-18 → In the industrial company, besides the HR function, this should be done by the Risk Manager<br>• "Conceptualization refers to the process of identifying, representing, and classifying knowledge with respect to organizational processes and employees. […]. However before conceptualization can occur, an organization must have experience. We suggest that the knowledge management process cycle is actually a reflection of the cycle of organizational learning.", P. 8-18<br>• Knowledge management should be directed at two goals: (1) effectively managing explicit knowledge in the form of know-what, know-how, and know-why with easily accessible databases and systems; and (2) ensuring that a supportive culture will encourage and facilitate the sharing of tacit knowledge (care-why).", P. 8-18<br>• "Every organization needs to begin analyzing their organizational knowledge. As a strategic asset, it is the key to competitive viability and growth of the learning organization. The culture of the organization is a critical element in determining the success or failure of any knowledge management program.", P. 8-18 |

| Article | Managing organizational knowledge as a strategic asset |
|---|---|
| **Knowledge-based risk management for complex corporations** | • "..., it is important that organizations find a way to tap into this knowledge base in order to preserve and expand their core competencies. Some believe that knowledge is the driving force in today's economy. If this is true, then it becomes critical for an organization to find ways of accessing existing knowledge and creating new knowledge. Certainly, effective management of knowledge will enable an organization to provide better customer service.", P. 8-18 → Industry companies: Risk Management knowledge necessary for survival<br>• "There are several benefits of knowledge management that can be anticipated (Lank, 1997). Employees will spend less time looking for information and expertise. This will enable highly paid professionals to concentrate on their areas of expertise. A knowledge management process will help employees to improve their performance and employability, by expanding resources immediately available to them and enabling them to make more intelligent decisions. An effective knowledge management process will also generate less stress for employees trying to do more with fewer resources. Knowledge management will help organizations become more competitive by using new knowledge to reduce costs, increase speed, and meet customer needs (Grayson and O'Dell, 1998).", P. 8-18<br>• "To be a strategic asset, the resource must possess four characteristics[1]. It must be: (1) valuable; (2) rare; (3) inimitable; and (4) nonsubstitutable.", P. 8-18 |
| **Suggestions for practical implementation of knowledge-based risk management** | • "Most knowledge management systems involve some aspect of computer information technology. However this is not a prerequisite. Organizational knowledge can be effectively managed by employing traditional mechanisms such as cross-functional project teams. Formal mentoring programs will allow senior employees to share their expertise with junior employees. Some mechanisms, such as project management systems or customer management systems, employ a mix of technology and non-technology. [...]. ..., there is no "one-size-fits-all" solution for knowledge management although some software products are represented in that manner.", P. 8-18<br>• "Most of the barriers to effective knowledge management involve people. Humans are complex with diverse psychological needs. Most knowledge management systems require that data and documents be stored in knowledge bases. From an organizational perspective, the process of building these knowledge repositories can be very time-consuming, labor intensive, and costly. People are already busy, and sharing knowledge may mean changing the way they work or adding extra steps to the process to extract the data and enter it into a repository (Cole-Gomolski, 1999). There has been a proliferation of jargon concerning knowledge management, which adds to the confusion. In addition, there have been significant limitations to the achievement of knowledge processing and knowledge-based systems (KBS) to date.", P. 8-18<br>• "...,organizational culture plays a primary role in the likelihood that employees will be willing to work together and share their knowledge. If the culture is not supportive, or the reward system favors only individual effort, it may be difficult to get people to work together.", P. 8-18<br>• "The following process is offered as a guide for actions that should be considered when implementing a knowledge management system:<br>o (1) Assess the organizational culture to ascertain the values, mind sets, behaviors, and outputs. Determine whether some areas may need reengineering. Areas to consider are organizational structure, reward system, networks available, and performance appraisals (Miller, 1999).<br>o (2) Identify stakeholders. Determine who needs to know. When do they need it? How do they get the knowledge they need now? What can be done from a human resource perspective to facilitate the acquisition and transfer of the knowledge needed? Establish buy-in from those involved ensuring cooperation and contribution.<br>o (3) Determine what knowledge or types of knowledge are critical to the organization. For example, is the interest primarily in knowledge assets (intellectual capital) such as patents, trademarks, etc., or is it in capturing idea-generating processes? Is the concern with product-related knowledge, or strategy?<br>o (4) Determine where the knowledge currently resides, i.e. databases, people, documents, and external sources. Is it available internally now, or will an investment in people or equipment be necessary? Does it come from communities of practice? If so, how can other such groups be encouraged?<br>o (5) Determine how the knowledge is created. What processes are currently in place for generating new knowledge? Are they formalized, or haphazard and incidental?<br>o (6) Select a business area or process to initiate knowledge management. Keeping the project small will help to keep it focused, and will enable management to better assess the success/failure of the program. Scheraga (1998) suggests breaking the value chain into discrete pieces from raw materials through distribution and examining the knowledge involved in each piece in order to determine which aspect to focus on first. The Dow Chemical Company chose to start with an area within the corporation that was familiar to many, had a high probability of success, would be an obvious value contributor, and could be implemented quickly (Petrash, 1996).<br>• The process is evolutionary. Sustainable change cannot be expected to happen immediately (Petrash, 1996). It must be supported by top management to ensure that interest is not lost, and that the effort is not pushed on to a back burner to fade away. It also needs to have user support, which can be accomplished by involving users in the development process (Cole-Gomolski, 1997). There is danger in making the knowledge management process too complicated. It needs to be natural and easily engage participants, not difficult to implement or maintain, or bogged down in rules and process, or it will be abandoned.<br>• To facilitate the capture of tacit knowledge, teams made up of people with the expertise to get the current project done should be selected. Ideally, employees should not be mandated to be on project teams. Volunteers are preferable, because they will have more enthusiasm for the project. Tacit knowledge cannot be captured explicitly, but its sharing can be encouraged and facilitated. Promotion of communities of practice within the organization, with tools for collaboration accessible to users, will facilitate benchmarking and sharing of best practices, and promote organizational learning. Incentive structures should reward the team, and encourage the "care-why".", P. 8-18<br>• "Another step managers can take is to create an environment, systems, and internal processes that facilitate the creation and transfer of knowledge. One concept that is widely discussed in the literature is that of communities of practice. Communities of practice are informal groups of people who share their ideas and expertise, similar to professional organizations (Manville and Foote, 1996; Hibbard and Carrillo, 1998; Stewart, 1997).", P. 8-18 |
| **Knowledge Management for Insurance companies** | |

| | |
|---|---|
| **Article** | **Managerial concerns in knowledge management** |
| **Author** | Josephine Chinying Lang |
| **Journal / Publication** | Journal of Knowledge Management; Kempston; 2001 |
| **Publication date** | 2001 |
| **Examined questions** | • "Knowledge differs markedly from information and data - knowledge is socially constructed in discourse communities. The task of knowledge management is to identify the barriers that exist between it and information technology and try to overcome them." |
| **Corporate Knowledge Management – State of the field** | • "It has been assumed that knowledge management tools will unproblematically enable managers to manage knowledge with reasonable ease (e.g. Anand et al., 1998).", P. 43-57<br>• "Sharing knowledge, however, will require a different set of concepts and tools. Knowledge management systems that are presently just large electronic libraries of best practices need to be rebuilt around a more accurate understanding of what knowledge is.", P. 43-57<br>• "There must be a shift towards supporting competencies for communication building, people networks, and on-the-job learning.", P. 43-57<br>• "In contrast to information stored in a library of books or the hard-drive memory in a PC, the person who knows has information about something and is able to use that information to solve problems by reflecting on that information and experience, drawing insights in creative ways to solve problems such as using back streets to avoid traffic jams when driving downtown during rush hours. Reflecting and thinking about that information and experience - turning over in our minds the present problem in relationship to facts and theories within a field - comprise the process that generates insights.", P. 43-57<br>• "For it has long been argued that an organization is indeed a network of inter-subjectively shared meanings sustained by a common language and interpretive schemas. We know that individuals bring to the situation their skills, tacit knowledge, and shared prior understandings of how things are supposed to be. Yet during interaction, such shared prior knowledge becomes a resource to construct shared understandings of a particular situation.", P. 43-57<br>• "In fact, what firms do is to organize and cultivate knowledge - often in implicit and unreflective ways - to develop a core competency or know-how, that ability to put know-what into practice. It is knowledge that holds a firm together. While know-what is explicit knowledge that can circulate freely, know-how is embedded in (collective) work practices and is therefore hard to coordinate or spread (Brown and Duguid, 1998). Know-how is know-what brought out in practice…", P. 43-57<br>• "While much knowledge exchanged may be embedded in documents (hard copy or electronic), many discussions and debates about the merits, assumptions and evaluation criteria for competing proposals, as well as decisions and their rationale are not recorded. These are not recoverable because collaboration tools currently available widely do not enable the encoding and documentation of workflows that involve deliberative discussion, argumentation and negotiation. Their representation schemes do not yet allow us to visualize perfectly such processes and products, opportunistic ideas and insights, as well as interrelationships between informal knowledge types that are hard to formalize. This problem is magnified when discussions are asynchronous and occurring between geographically dispersed participants.", P. 34-57<br>• "Much of what now passes for knowledge management is too info-centric. A key mistake many firms make is akin to the eighteenth century French encyclopedists' error in thinking that all human knowledge could be put into one book. But knowledge may be explicit or it may be tacit. Explicit knowledge is easily captured artificially through, say, manuals and standard operating procedures, and then shared with others through books or taught courses. On the other hand, tacit knowledge comprises those skills and know-how we have inside our heads that cannot be easily expressed but which get augmented and shared via interpersonal interaction and social relationships.", P. 43-57<br>• "To recapitulate, knowledge is not information and knowledge sharing is not information sharing. Therefore, knowledge management cannot be reduced to information management. Because knowledge, at rock bottom, resides with the knower and not some hardware or software, knowledge must flow among knowers. This means that human relationships within an organization are crucial considerations with regard to knowledge creation and utilization within that organization. To succeed, knowledge management must emphasize the management of these human relationships.", P. 43-57<br>• "Knowledge management effort in firms tends to be fragmented. It is still rare for a large company to have a common enterprise-wide knowledge base because daily business pressures act against initiatives for enterprise collaboration.", P. 43-57<br>• "Most firms have knowledge management projects that involve building electronic repositories of knowledge, either structured document-based knowledge or informal discussion-type knowledge. Such firms think that all their corporate knowledge can be stored on one huge server like some giant hyperlinked encyclopaedia.", P. 43-57 |
| **Knowledge-based risk management for complex corporations** | • "Knowledge management systems striving to enable the construction of computer-manipulable representations of knowledge must ensure that sufficient context is captured to accompany entries in the information base.", P. 43-57<br>• "By articulating its strategic intent, and identifying the knowledge required to execute the intended strategy, a firm can compare that to its actual knowledge, thus exposing its knowledge gaps. That is, a strategic evaluation of its knowledge based resources and capabilities will enable the firm to determine what knowledge it must acquire or develop. Knowledge management initiatives must be directed towards closing a firm's knowledge gap so identified. And they do not currently do so because of the following reasons.", P. 43-57 |
| **Suggestions for practical implementation of knowledge-based risk management** | • "…,in order for knowledge to yield business transformation, it is essential to establish a broad consensus that it is important, and to spend a lot of time on cultural and organizational issues", P. 43-57<br>• "Since the heart of knowledge resides within a community in discourse, to leverage knowledge, knowledge management must begin with identifying the natural community that owns/cares about a topic and the people who use it, not the knowledge itself.", P. 43-57<br>• "The shift from information to knowledge means that the awareness of the value of knowledge in most firms is exceeding their ability to extract it from the goods and services in which it is embedded, and to create new knowledge. The real task of knowledge management is to connect people to people to enable them to share what expertise and knowledge they have at the moment, given that cutting edge knowledge is always changing. The solution is not to try to warehouse everything one's workers ever knew.", P. 43-57<br>• "If employees are evaluated and compensated based on what they know, it may be difficult to get them to share their knowledge for the common good. Thus, it is important to reward individuals for sharing knowledge and using collective knowledge.", P. 43-57 |
| **Knowledge Management for Insurance companies** | |

| **Article** | **Overcoming cultural barriers to sharing knowledge** | **Tacit to explicit knowledge conversion: knowledge exchange protocols** |
|---|---|---|
| **Author** | Richard McDermott; Carla O'Dell; | Richard T. Herschel; Hamid Nemati; David Steiger; |
| **Journal / Publication** | Journal of Knowledge Management; Kempston | Journal of Knowledge Management; Kempston; |
| **Publication date** | 2001 | 2001 |
| **Examined questions** | • "Culture is often seen as the key inhibitor of effective knowledge sharing. A study of companies where sharing knowledge is built into the culture found that they did not change their culture to match their knowledge management initiatives.", P. 76-85 | "In the knowledge management domain, the conversion of tacit knowledge to explicit knowledge is critical because it is a prerequisite to the knowledge amplification process wherein knowledge becomes part of an organizations knowledge network. In this article, knowledge exchange protocols are examined as a vehicle for improving the tacit to explicit knowledge conversion process.", P. 107-116 |
| **Corporate Knowledge Management – State of the field** | • "Companies that successfully implement knowledge management do not try to change their culture to fit their knowledge management approach. They build their knowledge management approach to fit their culture. As a result, there is not one right way to get people to share, but many different ways depending on the values and style of the organization.", P. 76-85<br>• "...,we defined culture as the shared values, beliefs and practices of the people in the organization. Culture is reflected in the visible aspects of the organization, like its mission and espoused values.", P. 76-85<br>• "We found that overcoming "cultural barriers" to sharing knowledge has more to do with how you design and implement your knowledge management effort than with changing your culture.", P 76-85 | • "Many practitioners and researchers in the knowledge management arena are aware that there are two forms of knowledge: explicit knowledge and tacit (implicit) knowledge.", P. 107-116<br>• "Converting tacit knowledge to explicit knowledge is often time consuming and problematic (Earl and Scott, 1998; Davenport and Prusak, 1998)" , P. 107-116<br>• "A knowledge exchange protocol is a process that structures information exchange in such a way that the provider of the information and/or the recipient of the information can systematically present/recall information in a focused manner.", P. 107-116<br>• "While there is no standard way of measuring understanding, evidence of understanding is said to exist if the listener is able to effectively recall (make explicit) what he/she has learned from the teacher (Burns et al., 1990).", P. 107-116<br>• "...rich narratives may facilitate tacit to explicit knowledge conversion, but their effectiveness may critically depend on whether the recall process is structured.", P. 107-116<br>• "That is, when structure is employed in the tacit knowledge sharing process, employing it in a narrative recall procedure seems to be the most critical factor for enabling effective knowledge transfer.", P. 107-116<br>• "- How tacit knowledge is shared may not matter relative to structure - that is, it may be more important to worry most about the adequacy and richness of the narrative content than how it is structured! ", P. 107-116 |
| **Knowledge-based risk management for complex corporations** | | |
| **Suggestions for practical implementation of knowledge-based risk management** | • "There are three different ways they tie sharing knowledge to the business:<br>    o - (1) Make sharing knowledge directly part of the business strategy. [...]<br>    o - (2) Piggyback sharing knowledge on to another key business initiative. [...]<br>    o - (3) Share knowledge routinely as the "way we work".", P. 76-85<br>• "But reward and recognition is another way to make the importance of sharing knowledge visible. It highlights the things the company feels are important and demonstrates that the time and energy people spend sharing knowledge "counts" in their performance and career.", P. 76-85<br>• "...five summary lessons about aligning knowledge sharing with the organization culture:<br>    o (1) To create a knowledge sharing culture, make a visible connection between sharing knowledge and practical business goals, problems or results<br>    o (2) It is far more important to match the overall style of your organization than to directly copy the practices developed by other organizations. [...]<br>    o (3) Link sharing knowledge to widely held core values. [...]<br>    o (4) Human networks are one of the key vehicles for sharing knowledge. [...]<br>    o (5) Recruit the support of people in your organization who already share ideas and insights.", P. 76-85 | |
| **Knowledge Management for Insurance companies** | | |

| **Article** | **The knowledge management spectrum - understanding the KM landscape** |
|---|---|
| **Author** | Derek Binney |
| **Journal / Publication** | Journal of Knowledge Management; Kempston |
| **Publication date** | 2001 |
| **Examined questions** | • "The knowledge management spectrum as a synthesis of current knowledge management theories, applications, tools and technologies described in the literature is introduced in this article", P. 33-43 |
| **Corporate Knowledge Management – State of the field** | • "The KM applications described in the literature, whilst often using differing terminology, can be observed to cluster around common ideas or business problems, e.g. creation of new knowledge, process consistency or improvement, understanding patterns in vast amount of data, tapping expertise in organizations or developing employee capabilities and competencies.", P. 33-43<br>• "The KM applications described in the literature, whilst often using differing terminology, can be observed to cluster around common ideas or business problems, e.g. creation of new knowledge, process consistency or improvement, understanding patterns in vast amount of data, tapping expertise in organizations or developing employee capabilities and competencies. Individually these groupings have been called "elements" and labelled:<br>o transactional<br>o analytical<br>o asset management<br>o process based<br>o developmental; and<br>o innovation/creation knowledge management.<br>• Collectively these elements are referred to as the KM spectrum.", P. 33-43<br>• "An example of transactional KM is provided by Davenport (Davenport and Klahr, 1998), as he describes case-based reasoning in a customer service application. "Case-based reasoning provides a method for representing past situations (cases) and retrieving similar cases when a new problem is input. Given a description of a problem, the system searches for similar known cases. The system asks the user questions (proactively) about the problem to narrow the search for similar problems." ", P. 33-43<br>• "Examples of transactional KM include help desk, customer service, order entry and field support applications.", P. 33-43 → but a Risk Management Help Desk does not exist yet!<br>• "A number of the authors observed that KM is not new. What is new is the phenomenal growth of technologies that make it easier to implement KM systems.", P. 33-43<br>• "The degree of codification of knowledge decreases, moving left to right across the spectrum. Transactional systems are dealing with codified or explicit knowledge embedded in the transactional systems; they also generate new data or information, which can be used by analytical KM systems.", P. 33-43 |
| **Knowledge-based risk management for complex corporations** | |
| **Suggestions for practical implementation of knowledge-based risk management** | |
| **Knowledge Management for Insurance companies** | |

| **Article** | **From Knowledge to Action: the Impact of Benchmarking on Organisational Performance** |
|---|---|
| **Author** | Stephen A. W. Drew |
| **Journal / Publication** | Long Range Planning Vol. 30 |
| **Publication date** | June 1997 |
| **Examined questions** | • "Benchmarking seeks out, internalises, and improves upon competitors' best-practice capabilities. This article presents results of a research study into benchmarking and its links to improvements in organisational performance", P. 427 |
| **Corporate Knowledge Management – State of the field** | • "Benchmarking has been defined as 'the art of finding out, in a perfectly legal and aboveboard way, how others do something better than you do – so you can imitate – and perhaps improve upon – their techniques' (J. Main, How to steal the best ideas around, Fortune 126, (8), 102-106 (1992)", P. 427 |
| **Knowledge-based risk management for complex corporations** | • "Impetus [for benchmarking] has come from increased global competition, development of information technology, databases and networks.", P. 427-428<br>• "Benchmarking is closely associated with the success of business process redesign, total quality management, new product development and other important change initiatives." (S.A. W. Drew, BPR in financial services: factors for success, Long Range Planning 27 (5), 25-41 (1994)", P. 428<br>• "Benchmarking practice varies according to 1. the nature of the object being benchmarked and 2. the partners with whom comparisons are being made.<br>o Process benchmarking is used to compare operations, work practices and business processes.<br>o Product/service benchmarking is used to compare product and/or service offerings<br>o Strategic benchmarking is used to compare organisational structures, management practices and business strategies. (C.E. Bogan and M.J. English, Benchmarking for Best Practices, McGraw Hill, New York (1994).", P. 428 |
| **Suggestions for practical implementation of knowledge-based risk management** | • "For example, in reengineering its retail operations, Chemical Bank chose as benchmark partners competing banks, USAA insurance, American Express and Ritz Carlton Hotels. Some potential advantages and drawbacks of benchmarking with different types of partners are summarised in Table 3. In each case an added benefit is the professional development and learning of the individuals involved.", P. 429.<br>• "Benchmarking is not, in itself, a strategy for achieving competitive advantage in product or resource markets. However, it is a related set of activities which support and enhance strategies of imitation and/or collaboration leading to such advantage.<br>• Although the maxim 'adopt, adapt and improve' is often advocated, benchmarking is not, per se, a technique of organisational creativity. Where breakthrough innovations occur, usually benchmarking is but one tool used by management. For example, although Xerox has benchmarked widely, the company's advances in photocopying and digital imaging have also been underpinned by large resources committed to research and development. Benchmarking is primarily an instrument for developing and implanting strategies which are either imitative or incremental innovations, although it can also be a very useful adjunct to the process of discovering more radical innovations.<br>• Advocates of benchmarking clearly regard it as more than a means of gathering competitive intelligence. Most authors discuss benchmarking as a process of change management. Without some form of implementation – transfer and integration of best practices elsewhere – a benchmarking project would only be viewed as a partial success.", P. 429<br>• "Each of the stages of a benchmarking project shown may encounter difficulties or barriers to success.", P. 437<br>• "The results support our hypothesis that a range of barriers are important. Time is view as a very significant barrier, as well as difficulties of resourcing and finding partner. The importance of resources was confirmed by the finding that the average cost of conducting a benchmarking study was over $100,000, with a range between $3000 and $3 million. The average project length was 24 weeks, involving 30 person weeks of effort These figures indicate that few people are involved in a typical benchmarking team, or that team members usually only contribute a fraction of their time to the project.", P. 437<br>• "This investigation also raised a number of questions for further research:<br>o What is the relationship between improvements in profitability and the benchmarking process?<br>o In which industries and markets is benchmarking a significant source of sustainable competitive advantage? [...]<br>o Benchmarking can be both expensive and time-consuming. Ways must be found for doing it faster, more effectively and economically, without sacrificing rigour or integrity of approach. New sources of information and methods for analysis must be investigated. This challenge can only grow as the 'information overload' experienced by many executives and knowledge-workers increases.<br>o Knowledge, skills and the management of benchmarking projects through teams are important to find ways of accelerating the process of acquiring, deepening and renewing team-based competencies for benchmarking in many diverse areas of business activity.", P. 439 |
| **Knowledge Management for Insurance companies** | • "Benchmarking can be most effective when it is integrated with other systems such as strategic planning, budgeting and human resource management<br>• It is dangerous to rely on general impressions or anecdotes about competitor: there is usually more objective information available than is made use of<br>• Careful attention should be paid to the composition, structuring and development of benchmarking teams<br>• Benchmarking requires commitment and support form the top of the organisation<br>• The greatest benefits accrue to firms which have thought through their strategic position, competencies and market objectives and aligned their approach to these", P. 439 |

| | |
|---|---|
| **Article** | **Building Knowledge-creating Value Networks** |
| **Author** | Büchel, Bettina and Raub, Steffen |
| **Journal / Publication** | European Management Journal |
| **Publication date** | December 2002 |
| **Examined questions** | • "Our research has shown that the most valuable activities in knowledge management focus on creating knowledge networks that extend beyond the traditional concept of communities of practice. 'Business Opportunity' and 'Best Practice Transfer' networks have been shown to directly contribute to the creation of value within firms. In order to foster these value within firms. In order to foster these value creating networks, we propose a four stage process illustrated by examples of the companies that we have investigated in detail.", P. 587 |
| **Corporate Knowledge Management – State of the field** | |
| **Knowledge-based risk management for complex corporations** | • "…knowledge networks have the potential to support knowledge-intensive organisations in increasing efficiency, boosting innovation and maintaining employee morale. The success of knowledge networks is encouraging. Why is it, then, that so many executives still have difficult coming to grips with the concept? The perceived need to control a network's activities from A to Z may be one reason, However, by creating a productive environment and relinquishing some control, managers seriously committed to knowledge networks can provide a fertile context for these groupings of organisational members to help an organisation respond to market pressures. The willingness to take some risks and embrace this paradox sill e key to success.", P. 587 |
| **Suggestions for practical implementation of knowledge-based risk management** | • "Siemens Information and Communication Networks (ICN) was prompted to experiment with networks when it had the daunting task of providing highly integrated solutions with an increasingly significant service component to a diverse customer base in more then 160 countries. In the old 'product business' – one that Siemens ICN had mastered to perfection – innovation used to be a centralised process and learning hapenend in a 'broadcasting' mode from headquarters to the company's periphery. Faced with the challenges of the new 'solution business', Siemens ICN recognised that the old procedures were leading nowhere. Learning had to happen in a dynamic network and successful solutions needed to be transferred in real time. Today, ICN's state-of-the-art ShareNet solutation does just that. It forms the backbone of a worldwide network of salespeople who regularly share their experiences and insights. As a result, Siemens ICN generated cost savings and revenue increases through joint business development enabled by ShareNet amounting to nearly DM 50 million (€25 million). This figure is forecast to increase to €250 million in the near future. An interesting feature of the ShareNet story is that what had initially been developed as an internal solution became a product sold to other companies. This illustrates that networks can directly contribute to the growth of an organisation.", P. 589.<br>• "Best-practcie and Business Opportunity Networks: These are the types of networks that we see directly contributing to the bottom line. Networks focusing on the transfer focusing on the transfer of best practices work towards organisational benfits and are more often than not supported or even mandated by management. Best-practice networks are essentially institutionalised forms of knowledge sharing in organisation. They do, however, differ from the more traditional model of best-practice transfer. Wherease best-practice transfer has traditionally been regarded as a unidirectional process from a (superior) source unit to a recipient unit supervised by a high-level 'transfer coalition' (Szulanski, 1996), best-practice networks are characterised by multi-directionality: each member and each unit can, in pricnciple, learn from all the others. Responsibility for a successful process lies with each and every network member involved in the transfer.", P. 589<br>• "Again, being focused on a burning issue clearly facilitates the initial establishment of network links. Consider the experience of Siemens' chief knowledge officer Günther Klementz. He set up the first face-to-face meeting for all business unit managers to discuss the use of consultants at Siemens. With more than €250 million spent annually on consultant fees, many executives at Siemens had independently been seeking ways to reduce costs, increase the quality of service and improve the contracting process. This shared interest in an important issue formed the basis for membership and involvement of key players in the network. As the best-practice network started establishing guidelines fro contracts and specifying quality standards for the use of consultants, the interest of other managers increased.", P. 591-592 |
| **Knowledge Management for Insurance companies** | |